LIBRARY OF NEW TESTAMENT STUDIES

644

formerly the journal for the study of the New Testament Supplement series

Editor
Chris Keith

Editorial Board
Dale C. Allison, Lynn H. Cohick, R. Alan Culpepper, Craig A. Evans,
Jennifer Eyl, Robert Fowler, Juan Hernández Jr., John
S. Kloppenborg, Michael Labahn, Matthew V. Novenson, Love L. Sechrest,
Robert Wall, Catrin H. Williams, Brittany E. Wilson

Inspired by the work of the renowned Matthean scholar Richard France, this volume brings together a number of leading experts to highlight the intended and distinctive portrait of Jesus as teacher in the Gospel of Matthew. The studies illustrate in depth the background of this portrait in the Hebrew Bible and in the cultural milieu of its time as well as its uniqueness and particular influence among the early Christians. The evidence from all the canonical Gospels suggests that Jesus did appear as a teacher, and this volume gives us a balanced and well-informed account of how these didactic characteristics of the historical Jesus lived on in the memories of his disciples and were embellished to become an integral element in one of the most influential stories about him.

Samuel Byrskog
Professor of New Testament Studies
Lund University
Sweden

Although the first Christians venerated Jesus of Nazareth as Messiah and Son of God, they never forgot that he acted as a Jewish teacher. In a very comprehensive way this volume treats the Matthean representation of Jesus as teacher. It also shows the continuity of tradition from him as the historic teacher to the remaining writings of the New Testament. This volume is an important contribution to Matthean studies.

Rainer Riesner
Professor Emeritus for the New Testament
Institute for Protestant Theology at the TU Dortmund
Germany

From Craig Keener's incisive opening argument for historicity to Mariam Kovalishyn's reading of James to understand Jesus, this volume fascinates. It is rich: here is a wide variety of lenses and perspectives, seasoned scholars and new voices offering historical, source critical, comparative, and narrative readings. It is provocative: John Nolland offers a new translation of a classic Gospel verse. It is always insightful, not least in the connections it draws between Jesus as teacher in Matthew and the Hebrew Bible, Second Temple literature, Paul, the Petrine correspondence, and, especially, James. And at times, as in Charles Quarles's reading of the Sermon on the Mount, it is beautiful. The result is a multifaceted portrait of Jesus as teacher that illuminates Matthew's Gospel and has reverberations throughout the biblical corpus. It is a book for every bookshelf: accessible to the student, important to the scholarly conversation, and richly rewarding.

Catherine Sider Hamilton
Professorial Fellow for Teaching and Research
Wycliffe College
Canada

Here is a book that is truly needed. Everyone recognizes Matthew's emphasis on Jesus as teacher, but only here do we find in one volume a chorus of voices speaking into the most salient features of the teaching role of the Matthean Jesus. By dealing with the background of Jesus's teaching, the distinctive teaching of Jesus in Matthew, and the influence of Jesus's teachings in Matthew for the earliest Church, this volume covers the bases admirably and fills a glaring gap in Matthean studies.

David R. Bauer
Ralph Waldo Beeson Professor of Inductive Biblical Studies
Dean of the School of Biblical Interpretation
Asbury Theological Seminary
United States

In the first Gospel, the writer claims, "You have one master-teacher, the Messiah" (Matt 23:10). Yet this Christological affirmation, along with its narrative presentation across that Gospel, has not yet received the attention it deserves. Enter Jesus as teacher in the Gospel of Matthew. Quarles and Ridlehoover have gathered a diverse set of voices and of expertise for a fascinating conversation on Jesus as teacher in Matthew's Gospel. The contributors thoughtfully explore Jesus's influences, his distinctive teachings in Matthew, and the impact of the Matthean Jesus's teachings on other NT writings. This is a needed volume and a significant offering to an important conversation.

Jeannine Brown
The David Price Professor of Biblical and Theological Foundations
Director of Online Programs
Bethel Seminary of Bethel University
United States

Jesus as Teacher in the Gospel of Matthew

Edited by
Charles L. Quarles and
Charles Nathan Ridlehoover

t&tclark
LONDON • NEW YORK • OXFORD • NEW DELHI • SYDNEY

T&T CLARK
Bloomsbury Publishing Plc
50 Bedford Square, London, WC1B 3DP, UK
1385 Broadway, New York, NY 10018, USA
29 Earlsfort Terrace, Dublin 2, Ireland

BLOOMSBURY, T&T CLARK and the T&T Clark logo are trademarks
of Bloomsbury Publishing Plc

First published in Great Britain 2023
Paperback edition published in 2025

Copyright © Charles L. Quarles, Charles Nathan Ridlehoover and contributors, 2023

Charles L. Quarles and Charles Nathan Ridlehoover have asserted their right under the Copyright,
Designs and Patents Act, 1988, to be identified as Editors of this work.

For legal purposes the Acknowledgments on p. xii constitute an extension of this copyright page.

All rights reserved. No part of this publication may be reproduced or transmitted in
any form or by any means, electronic or mechanical, including photocopying,
recording, or any information storage or retrieval system, without prior
permission in writing from the publishers.

Bloomsbury Publishing Plc does not have any control over, or responsibility for,
any third-party websites referred to or in this book. All internet addresses given in this book were
correct at the time of going to press. The author and publisher regret any inconvenience caused if
addresses have changed or sites have ceased to exist,
but can accept no responsibility for any such changes.

A catalogue record for this book is available from the British Library.

Library of Congress Cataloging-in-Publication Data
Names: Quarles, Charles L. (Charles Leland), editor. | Ridlehoover, Charles Nathan, editor.
Title: Jesus as teacher in the gospel of Matthew / edited by Charles L.
Quarles and Charles Nathan Ridlehoover.
Description: London, UK ; New York, NY, USA : T&T CLARK/Bloomsbury
Publishing Plc, 2023. | Series: Library of New Testament studies, 2513-8790 ; 644 | Includes
bibliographical references and index. | Summary: "This volume explores the means which by
Matthew's Gospel provides distinctive elements of Jesus as teacher not featured in the other
Gospels"– Provided by publisher.
Identifiers: LCCN 2022059465 (print) | LCCN 2022059466 (ebook) |
ISBN 9780567697844 (HB) | ISBN 9780567697882 (PB) | ISBN 9780567697851 (ePDF) |
ISBN 9780567697875 (ePUB)
Subjects: LCSH: Jesus Christ–Teaching methods. |
Bible. Matthew–Criticism, interpretation, etc.
Classification: LCC BT590.T5 J47 2023 (print) | LCC BT590.T5 (ebook) |
DDC 232.9/04–dc23/eng/20230224
LC record available at https://lccn.loc.gov/2022059465
LC ebook record available at https://lccn.loc.gov/2022059466

ISBN: HB: 978-0-5676-9784-4
PB: 978-0-5676-9788-2
ePDF: 978-0-5676-9785-1
ePUB: 978-0-5676-9787-5

Series: Library of New Testament Studies, volume 644
ISSN 2513-8790

Typeset by Newgen KnowledgeWorks Pvt. Ltd., Chennai, India

To find out more about our authors and books visit www.bloomsbury.com
and sign up for our newsletters.

To the memory of R. T. France, scholar, churchman, and faithful disciple of the great kingdom scribe.
And to all the other faithful teachers who have mimicked Jesus for us.
—Matthew 13:52

Contents

List of Tables		xi
Acknowledgments		xii
Introduction: Matthew: Evangelist and Teacher, Jesus: Teacher and Evangelist *Charles L. Quarles and Charles Nathan Ridlehoover*		1
1	The Implications of Jesus as Teacher for the Historical Memory of His Teachings *Craig Keener*	3

Part 1 Jesus's Teachers

2	Jesus's Teachings and Hebrew Bible Influences *Katherine Davis*	17
3	Matthew as Teacher of Israel's Scriptures in His Judaic Context *Daniel M. Gurtner*	32
4	John the Baptist as Jesus's Teacher in the Gospel of Matthew *John Y. H. Yieh*	49

Part 2 Jesus's Teachings

5	Jesus as a Teacher of New Covenant Torah: An Examination of the Sermon on the Mount *Charles L. Quarles*	65
6	Jesus as Teacher Who Practices What He Teaches *Lena Lütticke*	83
7	What Does the *Bildungsroman* Have to Do with the Lord's Prayer? *Charles Nathan Ridlehoover*	94
8	Discipled to Be a Scribe for the Kingdom of Heaven *John Nolland*	109

| 9 | Jesus as a Teacher of Forgiveness
Jon Coutts | 123 |

Part 3 Jesus's Students

10	Jesus and Matthew: Matthew as a Discipled Scribe Patrick Schreiner	141
11	The Influence of Matthew's Gospel on the Petrine Letters Dennis R. Edwards	155
12	The Matthean Jesus Teaches John Bruce Henning	167
13	The Teaching of Jesus in Matthew, Galatians, and Paul's Letters David Wenham	180
14	Reading James to Understand Jesus Mariam Kovalishyn	195

List of Contributors	209
Hebrew Bible	213
Ancient Jewish Writers	232
Name Index	240

Tables

3.1	Old Testament Citations in Matthew	33
5.1	Extended Verbal Parallels	78
5.2	Isolated Verbal and Thematic Parallels	79
7.1	The Disciples Who Follow Their Master	102
11.1	First Peter and the Sermon on the Mount	159
11.2	Second Peter and the Sermon on the Mount	164

Acknowledgments

I (Chuck) wish to thank the students of my recent doctoral seminars who have recognized the treasures old and new in the Gospel of Matthew and are working to advance scholarship in this important field of study: Robbie Booth, Scott Brazil, Jarrod Bruton, Tyler Chesson, Alysha Clark, Tyler Craft, Joshua Engen, David Flannery, Yeongwhi Jo, Wes McKay, Lucas Moncada, and Ben Nistor. Your devotion to the study of this great Gospel inspires me.

I (Nathan) would like to personally thank my greatest teachers—Erin, for teaching me how to care about the things in life that truly matter; Jonah, Millie, and Nora for teaching me that nothing is better than fatherhood; Cathy, my mother, for teaching me faith and grit; Joe, my father, for teaching me that work is a virtue and love language; Bobby, for teaching me how to be faithful in all things; Mr. Watkins, for modeling passion for a subject for forty years; Alan, Rich, Andy, and Josh, for teaching me the art of pedagogy; Mrs. Cameron, for teaching me how to care for students; Dr. Black, for teaching me to think outside the box; Dale Allison, Ulrich Luz, and John Nolland, for teaching me to think deeply and creatively about Matthew's Gospel; Anne, Missy, Matt, Cindy, Mitch, Joe, Theresa, Kristi, and Amy, for teaching me how to care for other teachers; and last but certainly not least, David Wenham. You taught me that it is possible to live your entire life, knowing that you would do it all over again, and nothing compares to the intellectual pursuit of finding the historical Jesus in the sacred texts of Scripture. Dr. Bruce Henning reads everything I write and hates it, and I am thankful for that. Ed, Mike, Angie, and Devin, the family that I have and need. To my fellow coeditor, Chuck. Thank you for talking to me at ETS long ago about the structure of the Sermon on the Mount. I do not think we have stopped discussing things since.

The editors wish to express gratitude to Faith Haberer who produced the Index of Ancient Sources and Seth Ellington who produced the Index of Modern Authors.

Introduction

Matthew: Evangelist and Teacher, Jesus: Teacher and Evangelist

Charles L. Quarles and Charles Nathan Ridlehoover

...for you have One Teacher...

—Matthew 23:8

...for you have One Instructor, the Messiah.

—Matthew 23:10

The idea for this book was born out of two great loves. First, we (editors) are teachers, Matthean scholars, and students of Jesus and love the intersection of those three *topoi*. Second, we have long admired the work of Richard France.[1] In 1985, France published his highly influential *Matthew: Evangelist and Teacher*. France examined various aspects of Matthew's Gospel with a particular emphasis on historical questions related to the first gospel, its literary prowess, and theological implications. The final section of the book notes some portraits of Jesus but interestingly omits any exploration of Jesus as a teacher. His conclusions (and slight omission) have inspired the following question: What can we learn about Jesus as a teacher in Matthew's Gospel? Others in the scholarly world have explored this very question. Rainer Riesner,[2] Samuel Byrskog,[3] and John Yieh[4] undertook projects to explain Jesus's role as a teacher and in the case

---

[1] As Quarles wrote in the dedication of his *Theology of Matthew: Jesus Revealed as Deliverer, King, and Incarnate Creator*, Explorations in Biblical Theology 11 (Phillipsburg: P&R, 2013), xvi,

> Although I have never had the opportunity to meet him personally, perhaps no one has contributed more to my understanding of the Gospel of Matthew in particular than R.T. France. I am particularly indebted to France for his keen insights into the Old Testament background of many Matthean themes. France wrote with the mind of a scholar, the heart of a pastor, and the devotion of a faithful disciple.

[2] Rainer Riesner, *Jesus als Lehrer: Eine Untersuchung zum Ursprung der Evangelien-Überlieferung*, WUZNT 2.7 (Lieden: Mohr Siebeck, 1988).

[3] Samuel Byrskog, *Jesus as the Only Teacher: Didactic Authority and Transmission in Ancient Israel, Ancient Judaism and the Matthean Community*, ConBNT 24 (Stockholm: Almquist & Wiksell International, 1994).

[4] John Yieh, *One Teacher: Jesus' Teaching Role in Matthew's Gospel Report*, BZNT 124 (Berlin: de Gruyter, 2004).

of the latter two volumes, specifically Jesus as a teacher in Matthew's Gospel. In the following volume, we (editors) believe there is more to be said about this important topic. The attempt of each essay will be to fill some of the lacunae in this intriguing portrait of Jesus by specifically focusing on the Matthean portrait of Jesus. In his Gospel, Matthew is perhaps the most intentional about recording those teachings that show Jesus's own teachers, arranging Jesus's teachings in a comprehensive and thematic fashion, and bearing witness to Jesus's teachings that would be featured prominently in the writings of Jesus's student disciples.

We will examine each of these topics through the work of our esteemed contributors. In the spirit of Matthew's Gospel and the history of this research, we have purposedly chosen a diverse and inclusive set of contributors. The timing for this project dates back to 2019. As we were planning contributions and putting the final touches on our proposal, the world began to turn upside down—Matthew 24 comes to mind. As we can all attest, much has changed in the last couple of years—that is no less true of the initial ideas for the volume, the deadlines, and expectations for the final product. Readers will probably note something we could have added or someone who may have been an excellent contributor. There is an even chance that they signed on and something just happened. I mention this caveat because we are very proud of what is contained in these pages. We ask the reader to focus on what is here as opposed to what could have been.

In what follows, we have divided the volume into three parts with an introductory essay setting the stage for the discussion of Jesus as a teacher (Craig Keener). Part 1 explores the influences and subtle differences of Jesus's teachers. This section does not insinuate that Jesus did not have original content, but that his work is highly conversant with the Old Testament (OT) and ideas present within his cultural milieu. By examining the worlds of the Hebrew Bible (Katy Davis), Second Temple Judaism (Daniel M. Gurtner), and John the Baptist (John Y. H. Yieh), one is more prepared to understand the content of Jesus's teachings. Part 1 naturally leads to Part 2. What are some of Jesus's distinctive teachings?

In this next part, we will explore some of Jesus's distinctive teachings in Matthew's Gospel. Matthew has helpfully shaped his Gospel to highlight discourses containing Jesus's teaching and provides windows into teaching not contained in the other Gospels. This part will explore the topics of new covenant Torah in the Sermon on the Mount (Charles L. Quarles), the importance of doing what one says (Lena Lütticke), the Lord's Prayer as a coming-of-age prayer (Charles Nathan Ridlehoover), rabbi, scribes, and disciples (John Nolland), and forgiveness (Jon Coutts).

Part 3 will explore the role Jesus's teachings played in the lives and writings of his disciples. Within the New Testament (NT) and besides Matthew himself, Peter, John, Paul, and James are the first witnesses in reception history that evidence why Matthew has been considered the church's Gospel. Featured prominently in each of these writers is the Sermon on the Mount and much of Jesus's eschatological teachings. In noting the presence of these teachings in the writings of Jesus's disciples, we have grounds to assert that Jesus was a master teacher who trained and inspired his disciples to mimic his life and teachings.

1

The Implications of Jesus as Teacher for the Historical Memory of His Teachings

Craig Keener

1.1 Introduction

Nearly everyone agrees that Jesus was a teacher with disciples. This consensus has significant implications not only for Matthew's Gospel but also for the historical question of how much Jesus's teachings in this and other first-century Gospels may have in common with those of the historical Jesus. Various considerations support the probability that the disciples and those who heard them would have preserved and transmitted more than sufficient reliable memories about Jesus to fill early sources (initially such as Mark and Q), most likely with plenty left over.[1]

1.2 Reformatting Jesus's Teachings

Repeating Jesus's teachings over and over again would eventually produce patterns in recitation. When recounting their master's message and saving activity, the disciples would presumably omit elements less relevant to their audience, focus on more useful ones, and interpret them in preaching contexts.

Even though echoes of Jesus's original figures of speech show up in the Gospels, no one expected retellings to preserve wording verbatim. Variation appears in our Gospels, but paraphrase was a standard practice even in elite rhetorical training.[2] What is significant in the Jesus tradition, however, is the preservation of much of its original substance, including persistent themes, stories, the substance of climactic key sayings, and the like.[3]

---

[1] I condense and adapt material here, esp. from my *Christobiography: Memories, History, and the Reliability of the Gospels* (Grand Rapids, MI: Eerdmans, 2019), 369–448.

[2] See, e.g., Theon *Progymn.* 1.93–171.

[3] See the varied discussions in Dale C. Allison, Jr. *Constructing Jesus: Memory, Imagination, and History* (Grand Rapids, MI: Baker Academic, 2010); Richard Bauckham, *Jesus and the Eyewitnesses: The Gospels as Eyewitness Testimony*, 2nd ed. (Grand Rapids, MI: Eerdmans, 2017), 325–41 (esp. on gist in 333–4).

1.3 Collective Memory

Some have compared communal memory to a "telephone game," but this analogy is problematic for the gospel tradition, which involved net (group) rather than chain (a single line of) transmission.[4] Communities, including groups of disciples, more often practice "net" transmission, because their memories belonged to the entire group to start with.[5] Indeed, oral tradition is specifically designed to *counter* the frailties of memory such as those suggested in laboratory studies.[6]

Moreover, Jesus's disciples presumably taught *publicly*, to *many* people, rather than entrusting their message only to isolated individuals or (like later gnostics) passing on alleged "secret" teachings. Those hearers who misunderstood the message would surely correct it if they subsequently heard differently from Jesus's disciples who doubled as the community's leaders or from those whom they in turn commissioned or recognized.[7] When groups share important memories, these memories quickly assume a standardized, story form.[8]

Communal memory is common in older Middle Eastern culture,[9] and would have been relevant for Jesus's movement: Jesus did not normally instruct disciples one-on-one, but as a group (cf. e.g., Mark 3:14; 4:10), and he also taught large crowds (e.g., Mark 2:13; 3:9; 4:1; 6:34; 8:34; 11:18).[10] The Twelve (1 Cor 15:5), of course, were among those closest to Jesus during his ministry and functioned as the most authoritative witnesses (Mark 3:14–16; Acts 1:21–22).[11] Further, if Jesus ever sent disciples to extend his mission during his ministry, the disciples must have agreed on his prior message.[12]

---

[4] See Barry Schwartz, "Where There's Smoke, There's Fire: Memory and History," in *Memory and Identity in Ancient Judaism and Early Christianity: A Conversation with Barry Schwartz*, ed. Tom Thatcher; Semeia Studies 78 (Atlanta, GA: SBL, 2014), 7–37; 12; Alan Kirk, "Memory Theory and Jesus Research," in *How to Study the Historical Jesus* (vol. 1 in *Handbook for the Study of the Historical Jesus*; 4 vols.), ed. Tom Holmén and Stanley E. Porter (Leiden: Brill, 2011), 809–42; 822–4.

[5] James D. G. Dunn, *A New Perspective on Jesus: What the Quest for the Historical Jesus Missed* (Grand Rapids, MI: Baker, 2005), 43, 114–15.

[6] David Rubin, *Memory in Oral Traditions: The Cognitive Psychology of Epic, Ballads, and Counting-Out Rhymes* (New York: Oxford University Press, 1995), 144.

[7] For at least some delegation in the early Christian community, see, e.g., Acts 6:6; 14:23; 2 Tim 2:2; Tit 1:5; James 5:14; cf. Gal 6:6; 1 Thess 5:12–13; 1 Pet 5:5; 3 John 9.

[8] Alan Kirk, "The Memory-Tradition Nexus in the Synoptic Tradition: Memory, Media, and Symbolic Representation," 131–59 in *Memory and Identity*, 148, and idem, "Memory Theory," 835.

[9] Dunn, *Perspective*, 45–6.

[10] Those skeptical of more specific textual evidence should consider that a teacher without popular influence would probably have posed little threat to the elite.

[11] On the reliability of the tradition about the Twelve, see, e.g., E. P. Sanders, *Jesus and Judaism* (Philadelphia, PA: Fortress, 1985), 11, 98–101; John P. Meier, "The Circle of the Twelve: Did It Exist during Jesus' Public Ministry?" *JBL* 116.3 (1997): 635–72.

[12] James D. G. Dunn, *The Oral Gospel Tradition* (Grand Rapids, MI: Eerdmans, 2013), 242; cf. Bauckham, *Eyewitnesses*, 284–5. On the likelihood of such missions (albeit condensed in the Gospels to one or two), see Jonathan Bernier, *The Quest for the Historical Jesus after the Demise of Authenticity: Toward a Critical Realist Philosophy of History in Jesus Studies*, LNTS 540 (New York: Bloomsbury, 2016), 62. Teachers typically gave students practice (e.g., Pliny *Ep.* 2.3.5–6); wonder-working prophets also trained prophet disciples (1 Sam 3:1; 19:20–24; cf. 2 Kings 2:3–18; y. Taan. 3:8, §2; Pesiq. Rab. Kah. 24:18).

Preserving a teacher's message is not simply a modern interest. Disciples of an ancient teacher sometimes would gather after the teacher's death and weave together their memories of his teachings.[13] Jesus's disciples discussed Jesus's words among themselves during Jesus's ministry (Mark 8:16; 9:10) and surely discussed even more afterward.

1.4 Expectations for Disciples

Although collective memory merely encourages us to expect the preservation of events and the general tenor or themes of a figure's views, in Jesus's case there is also important reason to consider the preservation of more specific teachings.[14] Almost all scholars agree that whatever else Jesus was, he was a teacher with disciples.[15] Yet Jesus's role as a teacher implies that he communicated some *content*.

And that generally agreed datum adds a particularly relevant though usually neglected dimension to this discussion. Ancient audiences would recognize that Jesus's disciples, *as* disciples, would be *expected* to learn and pass on his teaching. Not only do virtually all scholars agree that Jesus was a teacher with disciples; virtually all scholars also agree that Paul wrote 1 Corinthians and Galatians. These undisputed letters in turn attest that some of Jesus's closest disciples remained in the most respected leadership roles in Jesus's continuing movement, along with Jesus's brothers. They still held these positions within just a few years of when Mark (and possibly others—Luke 1:1) wrote their Gospels (Gal 1:17–19; 2:1–2, 7–10; cf. 1 Cor 1:12; 3:22; 9:5; 15:5–7).

Disciples were normally adherents of a school[16] or, at the beginning, its founder; they passed on teachings. By definition, teachers passed on their teachings to others. At elementary levels, learning might be simply from the standard curriculum, but a sage expected his disciples to learn his teachings. One familiar term for this practice, παραδίδωμι (*paradidômi*),[17] was also applicable to passing down a founder's teachings[18] or practices.[19] In the disciples' setting, the cognate noun applies explicitly to Pharisaic traditions that were believed to be passed on meticulously,[20] and ultimately the noun

---

[13] Philostratus, *Vit. soph.* 1.22.524.
[14] Robert K. McIver, *Memory, Jesus, and the Synoptic Gospels*, SBL Resources for Biblical Study 59 (Atlanta, GA: Society of Biblical Literature, 2011), 163–82.
[15] See e.g., Samuel Byrskog, *Jesus the Only Teacher*, CBNT 24 (Stockholm: Almqvist & Wiksell International, 1994), 221–8. Even Celsus did not deny this (Origen *Cels.* 1.63, 65).
[16] Cf. Michael J. Wilkins, *Discipleship in the Ancient World and Matthew's Gospel*, 2nd ed. (Grand Rapids, MI: Baker, 1995).
[17] E.g., in Socratics, *Ep.* 20; Philostratus, *Vit. soph.* 2.29.621; Iamblichus, *Vit. Pyth.* 28.148–49; 32.226. See further Eric Eve, *Behind the Gospels: Understanding the Oral Tradition* (London: SPCK, 2013), 179; Loveday C. A. Alexander, "IPSE DIXIT: Citation of Authority in Paul and in the Jewish Hellenistic Schools," in *Paul beyond the Judaism/Hellenism Divide*, ed. Troels Engberg-Pedersen (Louisville, KY: Westminster John Knox, 2001), 103–27; 120.
[18] Lucian, *Alex.* 61; Iamblichus, *Vit. Pyth.* 28.148. Sometimes Jewish teachers cited only what they believed to be the tradition's original source (m. Eduy. 8:7; Abot 1:1; cf. 1 Cor 11:23).
[19] Iamblichus, *Vit. Pyth.* 28.149.
[20] See Matt 15:2; Mark 7:3, 5; Gal 1:14; Josephus *Ant.* 13.297, 408.

and verb applies also to the gospel tradition, beginning already in first-century sources.[21]

Indeed, in all schools "teaching was passed down from master to pupils, who in turn passed it on to their own pupils";[22] the founder's teachings often functioned as canonical for their communities.[23] Greek schools transmitted sayings attributed to their founders from one generation to the next.[24] Often the founders themselves encouraged this practice of transmission.[25] Teachers also often left it to their students to publish their teachings;[26] if followers were illiterate, of course, they could entrust this dimension of the activity to others. Yet the question of the disciples' literacy is a red herring, since dictation was the dominant practice for both the well-to-do and the illiterate in any case.[27]

One older approach, generally rejected today,[28] promoted suspicion of any alleged teachings of Jesus with which his followers agreed. Yet ancient (and modern) followers usually *did* agree with their teachers. And even if Jesus's disciples did disagree with him, would they have chosen to misrepresent his views? Even when a minority of ancient pupils did abandon their teachers' views, they were normally clear about their (respectful) disagreements, rather than claiming that the teacher instead would have agreed with them.[29]

Like most disciples of other teachers, whether Jewish[30] or gentile,[31] most of Jesus's disciples were probably in their teens, with a few possibly (like perhaps Peter, who

---

[21] Luke 1:2; 1 Cor 11:23; 15:3; 2 Thess 2:15; cf. Acts 16:4; Papias frg. 3.7, 8, 11, 14; 20.1; 21.1; perhaps Ep. Diogn. 11.1, 6; 1 Clem. 7.2.

[22] Alexander, "IPSE DIXIT," 112; cf. Rainer Riesner, *Jesus als Lehrer: Eine Untersuchung zum Ursprung der Evangelien-Überlieferung*, 2nd ed.; WUNT 2.7 (Tübingen: Mohr, 1984), 441–2; R. Alan Culpepper, *The Johannine School: An Evaluation of the Johannine-School Hypothesis Based on an Investigation of the Nature of Ancient Schools*, SBLDS 26 (Missoula, MT: Scholars, 1975), 109.

[23] Alexander, "IPSE DIXIT," 112–13; David Sedley, "The Stoic-Platonist Debate on *kathêkonta*," in *Topics in Stoic Philosophy*, ed. Katerina Ierodiakonou (Oxford: Oxford University Press, 1999), 128–52; 149.

[24] Culpepper, *School*, 193; Loveday Alexander, "Memory and Tradition in the Hellenistic Schools," in *Jesus in Memory: Traditions in Oral and Scribal Perspectives*, ed. Werner H. Kelber and Samuel Byrskog (Waco, TX: Baylor University Press, 2009), 113–53; 141; Aulus Gellius 7.10.1; Socrates *Ep.* 20.

[25] See Diogenes Laertius 10.1.12; Culpepper, *School*, 50.

[26] George A. Kennedy, "Classical and Christian Source Criticism," in *The Relationships among the Gospels: An Interdisciplinary Dialogue*, ed. William O. Walker Jr. (San Antonio, TX: Trinity University Press, 1978), 125–55; 129.

[27] See, e.g., Cicero, *Att.* 14.21; Dio Chrysostom, *Or.* 18.18; Suetonius *Vergil* 22; Galen *Grief* 83; P. Tebt. 104.40; P. Lond. 1164h.30; P. Oxy. 269.17–18; 1636.45–46; cf. further E. Randolph Richards, *Paul and First-Century Letter Writing: Secretaries, Composition, and Collection* (Downers Grove, IL: InterVarsity, 2004), 64–80, 143.

[28] The now widely criticized negative use of the criterion of dissimilarity.

[29] See, e.g., Valerius Maximus 8.15.ext. 1; Seneca *Ep. Lucil.* 108.17, 20, 22; 110.14, 20; Musonius Rufus 1, 36.6–7; Philostratus, *Vit. Apoll.* 7.22. For respect for teachers, see e.g., Abot R. Nathan 1A; 25A; Sipra Shemini Mekhilta deMiluim 99.5.6; Fronto *Ad Verum Imp.* 2.3. One pupil reportedly did *omit some* of his teacher's sayings, but because they were rhetorically inappropriate (Philostratus, *Vit. soph.* 2.29.621).

[30] See, e.g., Josephus *Life* 10; m. Abot 5:21; S. Safrai, "Education and the Study of the Torah," JPFC 945–70 (953); discussion in Craig S. Keener, *Acts: An Exegetical Commentary*, 4 vols. (Grand Rapids, MI: Baker Academic, 2012–15), 3:3210–12; cf. 2:1387, 1447–9.

[31] Quintilian, *Inst.* 2.2.3; Lucian, *Career* 1; Philostratus, *Vit. Apoll.* 1.7; Eunapius 493; Robert A. Kaster, "Grammaticus," OCD[3] 646.

was married; Mark 1:30) in their early twenties. At least in modern Western studies, subsequent recollections are most complete concerning exactly this impressionable age range.[32] Barry Schwartz even applies this information directly to Jesus's disciples, noting "that individuals are most likely to remember important events that occur in their late adolescence and early adulthood."[33]

Studies of personal memory demonstrate that personally significant events and emotional experiences reinforce memory.[34] These factors are obviously relevant for Jesus's disciples.[35]

1.5 Memory Practices in Antiquity

Ancient mnemonic skills often astonish readers in our less memory-centered modern Western culture.[36] Ancient mnemonic practices make even some of the more astonishing feats plausible.[37] While Jesus's disciples surely lacked formal training in mnemotechnics, such examples are helpful to illustrate the extent to which the ancient Mediterranean world valued memory proficiency. Such memory skills sometimes surface also in other cultures that value memory. Thus in nineteenth-century India, young Pandita Ramabai, before becoming a Christian, could recite 18,000 verses of Hindu texts.[38] Skeptics might dismiss all such stories, were not mnemonic feats of this magnitude recorded today.[39]

Ancient pedagogy without a focus on memory did not exist.[40] Many people in classical Greece learned much or even all of Homer by heart.[41] Greeks deemed memorizing some of Homer quintessential to Greek culture.[42] An emphasis on rote

---

[32] David C. Rubin, "Introduction," in *Remembering Our Past: Studies in Autobiographical Memory*, ed. David C. Rubin (Cambridge: Cambridge University Press, 1996), 1–15; 13; Joseph M. Fitzgerald, "Intersecting Meanings of Reminiscence in Adult Development and Aging," 360–83 in *Remembering Our Past*, 372–4; also McIver, *Memory*, 85–6.

[33] Schwartz, "Smoke," 17.

[34] With e.g., Rubin, "Introduction," 3; Sven-Åke Christianson and Martin A. Safer, "Emotional Events and Emotions in Autobiographical Memories," 218–43 in *Remembering Our Past*, 219, 237–8.

[35] Bauckham, *Eyewitnesses*, 341–6.

[36] See examples in Seneca *Controv.* 1.pref.2, 19; Suetonius *Gramm.* 23; Philostratus, *Vit. soph.* 1.11.495; Jocelyn Penny Small, *Wax Tablets of the Mind: Cognitive Studies of Memory and Literacy in Classical Antiquity* (London: Routledge, 1997), 126–31.

[37] Cicero, *De or.* 2.351–54; Rhet. Her. 3.16.28–40; 3.22.35; Quintilian, *Inst.* 11.2.27, 33–35; Kennedy, "Source Criticism," 98, 143; George A. Kennedy, *The Art of Rhetoric in the Roman World: 300 B.C.–A.D. 300* (Princeton, NJ: Princeton University Press, 1972), 123–5; Jocelyn Penny Small, "Memory and the Roman Orator," in *A Companion to Roman Rhetoric*, ed. William Dominik and Jon Hall (Oxford: Blackwell, 2007), 195–206; 82–6, 202–4; more extensively, Herwig Blum, *Die Antike Mnemoteknik* (Hildesheim: Olms, 1969).

[38] Mark A. Noll and Carolyn Nystrom, *Clouds of Witnesses: Christian Voices from Africa and Asia* (Downers Grove, IL: InterVarsity, 2011), 127, 129.

[39] Small, *Wax Tablets*, 110–12, 128–9.

[40] For memory in ancient education, see Riesner, *Lehrer*, 442–3.

[41] Xenophon, *Symp.* 3.5–6; Raffaella Cribiore, *Gymnastics of the Mind: Greek Education in Hellenistic and Roman Egypt* (Princeton, NJ: Princeton University Press, 2001), 197, 248.

[42] Cribiore, *Gymnastics*, 248.

memory pervaded the most basic educational level,[43] often tested with drilling.[44] The most valued learning skills in children were memory and imitating what was taught.[45]

Memory remained important in higher education, beginning in the mid-teens, for example, for memorizing model speeches.[46] Students had to remain attentive not only with texts but also during lectures.[47] Those trained in rhetoric could adjust the accounts they remembered, but such adjustments rarely added to or changed content in any substantive manner.[48]

Maxims were memorized and passed on for centuries even in elementary educational settings.[49] Students memorized and copied these maxims "letter by letter."[50] Besides providing grist for writing, reading, and memory, such maxims also offered moral principles believed to remain with students for life.[51] Like the broader Greco-Roman circulation of maxims, Judean oral training circulated various sorts of wise sayings (proverbs, parables, and the like), rhetorical forms also plainly used by Jesus.[52] One widely known pre-Christian sage speaks of those who study the law as preserving wise parables and searching out obscure proverbs or maxims.[53]

Such aphorisms, or concise and often witty statements, were normally memorable and remembered accurately.[54] Like most sages, Jesus probably reused some of his sayings in various settings;[55] nevertheless, this practice does not easily explain all the variations in context that we find. Teachers' sayings circulated both in collections and independently and could be combined with stories about the teacher.[56] Sayings could circulate independently,[57] but sayings for which context was necessary, such as in brief narratives climaxing in the protagonist's quip,[58] were often transmitted with

---

[43] See e.g., Quintilian, *Inst.* 2.4.15; Plutarch, *Educ.* 13, *Mor.* 9E; Musonius Rufus frg. 51, p. 144.3–7; Diogenes Laertius 6.2.31; Eunapius 481; Cribiore, *Gymnastics*, 49, 138, 144, 191, 194.

[44] Mark Joyal, Iain McDougall, and J. C. Yardley, *Greek and Roman Education: A Sourcebook* (New York: Routledge, 2009), 198.

[45] Quintilian, *Inst.* 1.1.36; 1.3.1.

[46] Quintilian, *Inst.* 11.2.1–51; Dio Chrysostom, *Or.* 18.19; cf. Cribiore, *Gymnastics*, 200, 231; Teresa Morgan, *Literate Education in the Hellenistic and Roman World* (Cambridge: Cambridge University Press, 1998), 90.

[47] E.g., Aulus Gellius 8.3; Philostratus, *Vit. soph.* 2.8.578.

[48] See Theon *Progymn.* 3.224–40; cf. 2.115–23; also Longinus *Subl.* 11.1; Hermogenes *Inv.* 2.7.120–21; Hermogenes *Progymn.* 3.On Chreia, 7; on fables, cf. Theon *Progymn.* 4.37–42, 80–82 Butts.

[49] Cf. Musonius Rufus frg. 51, p. 144.3–7; Hermogenes *Progymn.* 4.On Maxim, 8–10; Marion C. Moeser, *The Anecdote in Mark, the Classical World and the Rabbis*, JSNTSup 227 (Sheffield: Sheffield Academic Press, 2002), 54–5.

[50] Cribiore, *Gymnastics*, 167; on learning the maxims, cf. also Morgan, *Literate Education*, 71; Moeser, *Anecdote*, 54; Joyal, McDougall, and Yardley, *Education*, 167, 170.

[51] Quintilian, *Inst.* 1.1.35–36 in Joyal, McDougall and Yardley, *Education*, 172.

[52] Cf. Pirke Aboth; Geza Vermes, *Jesus the Jew: A Historian's Reading of the Gospels* (Philadelphia, PA: Fortress, 1973), 27.

[53] Sir. 38:34; 39:2–3, 9.

[54] McIver, *Memory*, 176 and sources noted there.

[55] Roland Mushat Frye, "The Synoptic Problems and Analogies in Other Literatures," 261–302 in *The Relationships among the Gospels*, 291; Dunn, *Tradition*, 281. Speakers such as Dio Chrysostom and Lucian also reused their material in multiple locations.

[56] See, e.g., Theon *Progymn.* 4.73–79; cf. 5.388–441.

[57] E.g., Seneca *Ep. Lucil.* 94.27–28.

[58] E.g., Diogenes Laertius 2.72, 6.2.51; Plutarch *Ages.* 21.4–5.

the gist of the basic story or context that fueled their sense;[59] biographers sometimes expressed confidence regarding the incidents in their subject's life in which a particular saying was given.[60] Thus we probably have some sayings of Jesus in the Gospels in their original essential contexts, though others (e.g., Matt 7:13–14//Luke 13:24; Matt 8:11// Luke 13:29) clearly appear in distinct contexts.

Some memories of sayings could be quite significant. Verbatim memory requires rehearsal of the material, but in nearly universal ancient pedagogical practice students did regularly rehearse such sayings, so Jesus as a teacher presumably expected his disciples to do likewise.[61] This is not to imply that all of Jesus's aphorisms would be remembered, but rather to imply that those that were remembered were probably remembered quite accurately. Noting psychological studies, Robert McIver emphasizes, "Once in long-term memory, aphorisms would usually be remembered accurately or— and this is the important point—*not at all.*"[62] Jesus's reported aphorisms tend to be memorable: concise and vivid.[63] Not surprisingly, then, the Evangelists tend to report aphorisms with something closer to verbatim agreement than found in parables.[64]

Jesus's teachings in the tradition are predesigned "for easy remembering," as James D. G. Dunn notes. "Prominent features are various kinds of parallelism, alliteration, assonance and paronomasia," as catalogued by a host of modern scholars.[65] Dunn notes the difference between this and random long-term recall of facts: "What is envisaged is not a casual recall across several decades of something once heard and little thought about since. ... What is in view is a deliberate instruction intended to be retained for its value in discipleship."[66]

Teachers expected disciples to develop their memories to learn teachings. All schools of philosophy emphasized memory, though not all to an equal degree.[67] This practice would have implications for a disciple's memoirs about a former teacher.[68] Some schools emphasized memorizing texts; others, the teacher's words.[69] Among Jesus's disciples, the teacher's words would necessarily be the focus (all the more if the disciples were illiterate, as some scholars contend).

All our sources indicate that Jewish families, of whatever social class, brought up their children with knowledge of the law and customs.[70] Some scholars have underlined subsequent rabbis' emphasis on the careful transmission of tradition.[71] Indeed, in the

---

[59] Cf. Hermogenes *Progymn.* 3.On Chreia, 6–7; Aphthonius *Progymn.* 3. On Chreia, 23S, 4R; Nicolaus *Progymn.* 4. On Chreia 19–20; 5. On Maxim, 26.
[60] Plutarch *Them.* 11.2.
[61] McIver, *Memory*, 167, 176, 180, 184.
[62] McIver, *Memory*, 176.
[63] McIver, *Memory*, 176.
[64] McIver, *Memory*, 177.
[65] Dunn, *Tradition*, 238, citing esp. C. F. Burney, T. W. Manson, Matthew Black, and Joachim Jeremias; also see Riesner, *Lehrer*, 392–404.
[66] Dunn, *Tradition*, 238.
[67] Alexander, "Memory," 133, 138.
[68] Moeser, *Anecdote*, 92.
[69] Culpepper, *School*, 177. The textual focus dominates primarily in later times.
[70] Philo *Embassy* 210.
[71] E.g., t. Yeb. 3:1; Mekilta Pisha 1.135–36, 150–53; Sipre Deut. 48.2.6. See further Riesner, *Lehrer*; Alfred F. Zimmermann, *Die urchristlichen Lehrer: Studien zum Tradentenkreis der διδάσκαλοι im frühen Urchristentum*, WUNT 2.12; 2nd ed. (Tübingen: Mohr Siebeck, 1988). Against earlier

second century outsiders often compare churches, like synagogues, with schools.[72] Moreover, well before 70, Pharisees were known for passing on their oral traditions.[73] More generally, Judeans and Galileans were known for instructing boys meticulously in the law,[74] probably especially orally and presumably therefore requiring the boys to develop skills in oral memory.[75] Even Diaspora Jews cultivated Jewish memory.[76] Teachers retained a central role in various pre-Christian Jewish circles.[77]

If one chooses to dismiss all such reports about Jewish memory as mere propaganda, one should be clear about what one is doing. One is discarding virtually all extant evidence and then complaining that no evidence supports the only position for which we have any substantial evidence at all—namely, that disciples in this period did normally seek to remember their teacher's message. Those who became teachers themselves and remained within the same school of thought were expected to pass on their school's collective memory. This was true whether the sages were philosophers or Jewish teachers of wisdom.

Even advanced students often rehearsed what they had learned, both among gentiles[78] and, at least in all sources that have survived among Jews.[79] Studies show that spaced practice and repetition establish the main points both in personal memory[80] and in oral tradition,[81] while also condensing them and conforming them more to an overarching schema. This pervasive pedagogic pattern presumably would hold for Jesus's disciples as well since, again, they were *disciples*.[82]

---

critiques, see Werner H. Kelber, "The Work of Birger Gerhardsson in Perspective," in *Jesus in Memory: Traditions in Oral and Scribal Perspectives*, ed. Werner H. Kelber and Samuel Byrskog (Waco, TX: Baylor University Press, 2009), 173–206; 191–4.

[72] Edwin A. Judge, "The Early Christians as a Scholastic Community," *JRH* 1.1 (1960): 4–15; Robert Wilken, "Toward a Social Interpretation of Early Christian Apologetics," *CH* 39.4 (1970): 437–58 (444–8); Stanley K. Stowers, "Does Pauline Christianity Resemble a Hellenistic Philosophy?" in *Paul beyond the Judaism/Hellenism Divide*, ed. Troels Engberg-Pedersen (Louisville, KY: Westminster John Knox, 2001), 81–102; Alexander, "IPSE DIXIT," 107.

[73] Mark 7:3, 8–9; Josephus *Ant.* 13.297, 408.

[74] Josephus *Ant.* 4.211; *Ag. Ap.* 1.60; 2.204; cf. *Life* 8; *Ag. Ap.* 2.171–73; m. Abot 6:6. Later, perhaps most relevant to the intelligentsia, cf. m. Abot 5:21.

[75] Everyone could learn orally in synagogue contexts (e.g., *Ag. Ap.* 2.173, 175; Philo *Hypoth.* 7.12–13); boys were also taught to recite Torah (cf. Josephus *Ant.* 20.264–65; *Life* 9–12; m. Ab. 5:21; Rainer Riesner, "Education élémentaire juive et tradition évangélique," *Hokhma* 21 [1982]: 51–64; Riesner, *Lehrer*).

[76] 2 Macc 2:25; Let. Aris. 154; Philo *Spec. Laws* 4.107.

[77] See Sir 6:34–38; 8:8–9; 51:23.

[78] See Diodorus Siculus 10.5.1; Quintilian, *Inst.* 11.2.27; Lucian, *Hermot.* 1; Iamblichus, *Vit. Pyth.* 20.94; 29.164–65; 31.188; 35.256; Philostratus, *Vit. Apoll.* 1.14; 2.30; 3.16; Small, *Wax Tablets*, 118.

[79] See m. Abot 2:8; Sipre Deut. 48.1.1–4; 48.2.6; Byrskog, *Teacher*, 136–96, esp. 158–60 (esp. m. Abot 2:8; Eduy. 1:3; Yad. 4:3; Neg. 9:3; t. Yeb. 3:4.

[80] E.g., Small, *Wax Tablets*, 117–22; Rubin, *Memory*, 125–9, 144, 154; Ann-Kathrin Stock, Hannah Gajsar, and Onur Güntürkün, "The Neuroscience of Memory," in *Memory in Ancient Rome and Early Christianity*, ed. Karl Galinsky (Oxford: Oxford University Press, 2016), 369–91; 375, 385.

[81] See e.g., Jan Assmann, *Cultural Memory and Early Civilization: Writing, Remembrance, and Political Imagination* (Cambridge: Cambridge University Press, 2011), 3–4, 81; Jan Assmann, "Memory and Culture," in *Memory: A History*, ed. Dmitri V. Nikulin (New York: Oxford University Press, 2015), 325–49; 341; Kirk, "Memory Theory," 823; Eve, *Behind Gospels*, 92; Rubin, *Memory*, 72–5, 124–9, 144, 155, 170, 228; Byrskog, *Teacher*, 397; Schwartz, "Smoke," 14.

[82] McIver, *Memory*, 184; Bauckham, *Eyewitnesses*, 341–6; cf. Allison, *Constructing Jesus*, 9n46.

If Jesus was a sage with disciples, we might expect this to mean that his disciples paid attention to his teachings. If Jesus's disciples were not learning his teaching, why would we even envision them as disciples in the first place? Indeed, given the pervasive practice of memory in learning everywhere else, Jesus might have had to explicitly warn his disciples *against* memorization if he expected his disciples *not* to learn his teachings! And if they inherited his role as leaders in his movement, what would they have been teaching his movement more than his teaching? This would be all the more true if they were, as some argue, uneducated apart from what they learned from Jesus.

Memory was crucial to every form of education we know in antiquity, including purely oral instruction. To suppose that Jesus would not have instructed disciples to remember his teachings, contrary to the basic role expected for disciples, is to make Jesus's pedagogy completely idiosyncratic in antiquity. It is also to reject virtually all the hard evidence available and to construct the opposite picture based on the silence that remains[83]—unfortunately a time-honored approach in some circles of NT scholarship.[84]

While Jesus's disciples were like other disciples in many respects, however, the tradition does highlight a key feature that differentiates them from many kinds of disciples. Their adherence to Jesus was not to one teacher among many, as in the rabbinic movement or among popular philosophers.[85] It is closer to that of disciples of a teacher founding a new school or movement, thus to disciples of Pythagoras or to followers of Qumran's teacher of righteousness. And whereas some of the teaching of the Qumran community's founder may have passed into community doctrine anonymously, the gospel tradition regularly credits Jesus and Jesus alone as the source of all authoritative teaching.[86]

1.6 What about the Witnesses' Illiteracy?

Although the evidence is virtually unanimous, some critics dismiss its relevance by contending that it derives mostly from the ranks of the elite. Since barely any nonelite textual evidence survives, however, this argument appears designed to allow a dismissal of all textual evidence, so that critics can then offer arguments from the silence that remains.

Modern Western scholars sometimes assume an elitist posture toward those who lack the opportunities for the literary education available to us. But while illiterate bards may fail in precise verbatim recall, in many societies they can recite large selections of tradition.[87] Ancients valued this skill; for example, one work depicts a widowed grandmother as illiterate, yet "at least able to recite speeches from tragedy."[88]

---

[83] McIver, *Memory*, 165.
[84] E.g., in a response to Craig S. Keener, "Assumptions in Historical Jesus Research: Using Ancient Biographies and Disciples' Traditioning as a Control," *JSHJ* 9.1 (2011): 26–58.
[85] See Byrskog, *Teacher, passim* and esp. 307–8.
[86] Byrskog, *Teacher*, 310. Against this providing incentive to invent teachings for Jesus, see our discussion of 1 Cor 7:10–12 in *Christobiography*, 486–7.
[87] Eve, *Behind Gospels*, 5; in antiquity, e.g., Xenophon, *Symp.* 3.6.
[88] Cribiore, *Gymnastics*, 163.

It is far from certain that any of Jesus's disciples took notes during his ministry, but ancient practice at least allows the possibility. Disciples of advanced Greek teachers often took notes during their teachers' lectures.[89] As early as five centuries before the era of Jesus's disciples, such notes were sometimes published,[90] a practice that continued in the period in which the Gospels were published.[91] At least one of Jesus's followers, a tax-collector (Matt 10:3; Mark 2:14; Luke 5:27; cf. also Luke 19:2), should have had the skills to take such notes—at least if we may infer anything from ancient tax records.[92]

However literate Jesus's disciples were, some in the rapidly growing Jerusalem church probably took notes even in the earliest years. Literacy was more common in urban areas; even in impoverished Egypt, most metropolites (citizens of Greek-speaking nome capitals), in contrast to typical rural agriculturalists, could read and write.[93] Even an average literacy as low as 3 percent would yield some literate persons, even if the Jesus movement included only several hundred persons (cf. 1 Cor 15:6). If Jesus's immediate disciples could not write, some of *their* followers surely could.[94] Paul converted probably within at the most just a few years after Jesus's death (1 Cor 15:8), and it is most improbable that he alone was literate.[95]

But the disciples' literacy is a moot point in any case. Apart from what rhetoricians called artificial memory, which uses elaborate mnemonic devices, memory practices noted among ancient disciples apply to disciples in general, not exclusively to the literate. Not all disciples of sages came from the ranks of the educated.[96] Lucian complains that not only many disciples but even their teachers were uneducated members of the working class.[97] Greek schools varied among themselves whether to emphasize oral memory or learning texts.[98] Literacy is not necessary to pass on the substance of what one learns orally.

Whether literate or illiterate, disciples by definition were supposed to learn their teachers' teachings. Even later rabbis emphasized oral more than written transmission of their legal traditions.[99] If Jesus's disciples learned orally, their literacy is strictly irrelevant.

---

[89] Cf. Quintilian, *Inst.* 11.2.2, 25; Seneca, *Ep. Lucil.* 108.6; Epictetus pref. 2; Arius Didymus 2.7.11k, p. 80.36–82.1; Lucian, *Hermot.* 2; see also Kennedy, "Source Criticism," 131.
[90] George Kennedy, *Classical Rhetoric and Its Christian and Secular Tradition from Ancient to Modern Times* (Chapel Hill: University of North Carolina Press, 1980), 19.
[91] Quintilian, *Inst.* 1.pref. 7–8; Epictetus, *Diatr.* 1.pref. For the nature of ancient publication, cf. discussion in Keener, *Acts*, 1:43–50.
[92] See e.g., Roger S. Bagnall, *Reading Papyri, Writing Ancient History* (New York: Routledge, 2003), 16, 32–3; Hélène Cuvigny, "The Finds of Papyri: The Archaeology of Papyri," in *The Oxford Handbook of Papyrology*, ed. Roger S. Bagnall (Oxford: Oxford University Press, 2011), 30–58; 43, 48.
[93] Naphtali Lewis, *Life in Egypt under Roman Rule* (Oxford: Clarendon, 1983), 61–2.
[94] See Bernier, *Quest*, 136–7.
[95] Cf. Acts 4:36–37; 6:7, 9–10; 15:22–29; 16:37; 18:24 (with Keener, *Acts*, 2799–808); Rom 16:7, 22–23; 2 Cor 1:19; 1 Thess 1:1; Titus 3:13; 1 Pet 5:12.
[96] Cf. e.g., Alciphron *Farm.* 11.3.14; 38 (Euthydicus to Philiscus), 3.40.
[97] Lucian, *Runaways* 12, 14.
[98] Culpepper, *School*, 177.
[99] See e.g., the purportedly late first-century traditions regarding oral law in Sipra Behuq. pq. 8.269.2.14; Sipre Deut. 306.25.1; 351.1.2, 3; probably early material in Sipra Behuq. par. 2.264.1.1; Sipre Deut. 115.1.1–2; 161.1.3.

Verbatim memory is stronger in societies where literacy exists, but gist memory, more relevant to most of the Jesus tradition, can flourish with or without literacy.[100] Even if all Jesus's disciples, even the tax collector, were illiterate, they would need to rely all the more on what they had learned from Jesus. Of course, as already noted, since most authors of all social classes dictated their work orally, objections to the disciples' ability to write is a red herring anyway.[101]

1.7 Memory among Nonelites: General Considerations

Not only elites but a significant proportion of people in some other oral societies can recall extensive amounts of shared tradition. Variation is standard fare in oral performance; just as a good preacher or professor today may take account of implicit audience feedback while preaching or teaching, oral performers adapted their presentations for their audiences.

This usual practice of variation suggests that even the eyewitnesses of Jesus's ministry would have retold the same stories in varying ways; the Evangelists, therefore, had little reason to strive for verbatim reproduction. Not surprisingly, then, some scholars suggest that this practice in most renditions of oral tradition helps explain some of the range of differences in the Gospels, a variation that nevertheless leaves intact the essential gist.[102] Such variations may also reflect the ancient rhetorical practice of paraphrase[103] and literary use of gist memory in adapting sources.[104]

Even so, most Synoptic accounts actually diverge from one another far less than one encounters in many oral traditions and in many cases of ancient literary dependence.[105] Their conspicuous similarity may reflect their respect for the authoritative status of their material, their lesser rhetorical interest in paraphrase, and, most relevantly here, their brief chronological distance from their material. Again, the period of exclusively oral transmission between Jesus's execution and the first of the circulated Gospels cannot be more than about four decades, that is, well within living memory. (Living memory is usually estimated at 60–80 years.)

Many bards could recite from memory the entire *Iliad* and *Odyssey*, even though the educated often looked down on them as lacking critical skills.[106] That some persons

---

[100] See John S. Kloppenborg, "Memory, Performance, and the Sayings of Jesus," in *Memory in Ancient Rome and Early Christianity*, 286–323; 293–4.
[101] See e.g., Cicero, *Att.* 14.21; Richards, *Letter Writing*, 64–80, 143.
[102] Dunn, *Perspective*, 110, 112, 118, 122; Dunn, *Tradition*, 301. For oral history in NT scholarship, see Byrskog, *Story*, 33–40; Paul Rhodes Eddy and Gregory A. Boyd, *The Jesus Legend: A Case for the Historical Reliability of the Synoptic Jesus Tradition* (Grand Rapids, MI: Baker Academic, 2007), 239–68 (esp. 252–9).
[103] See, e.g., Theon *Progymn.* 1.93–171.
[104] Small, *Wax Tablets*, 192.
[105] For the latter, see R. A. Derrenbacker Jr. *Ancient Compositional Practices and the Synoptic Problem*, BETS 186 (Leuven: Leuven University Press, 2005), 95–6; John S. Kloppenborg, "Variation in the Reproduction of the Double Tradition and an Oral Q?" *ETL* 83 (2007): 53–80; Michael R. Licona, *Why Are There Differences in the Gospels? What We Can Learn from Ancient Biography* (New York: Oxford University Press, 2017), 199.
[106] Xenophon, *Symp.* 3.6.

today who are illiterate in Arabic memorize the Qur'an makes plausible even the ancient claim that one ancient people knew the *Iliad* from memory even though they no longer spoke good Greek.[107]

Ancient researchers trusted local oral traditions sufficiently that they often depended on them even when they were centuries old.[108] This illustrates the expectation that those interested in memories (such as localities to whom they mattered) preserved them. All the canonical Gospels, by contrast, were likely composed within a maximum of six and a half decades after the events they narrate.

Most relevantly, Jewish boys necessarily developed memory skills; whether or not they could read and (still more rarely) write, Jewish boys learned to recite Torah. Those who were not literate therefore learned Torah orally.[109] Ordinary Galileans who passed on stories with family or neighbors probably had memory skills more developed than those of their highly literate modern Western critics. Like Jesus's disciples, ordinary Judean and Galilean boys lacked any "professional" training, but they were brought up to know and obey their ancestral laws, which they would also teach to their own children.[110]

1.8 Conclusion

After a thorough survey of the results of memory studies, Robert McIver offers some basic predictions of what form the gospel traditions should take if they depend on eyewitness material. He concludes that they look surprisingly like the memories we have recorded in the Gospels.[111]

No one would have expected Jesus's disciples to remember everything that Jesus said, or to repeat his words in a verbatim form (although many of his aphorisms would be recalled closer to this form). But they would expect memory of his key teachings—such as the Gospels provide. Ancient Mediterranean culture valued and thus trained memory more than modern Western culture does. In light of the foregoing discussion, the most appropriate starting assumption should be that Jesus's disciples would have learned and transmitted his teachings no less carefully than most other ancient disciples transmitted the wisdom of their mentors.[112]

To assume that Jesus's disciples acted completely unlike other disciples with regard to transmitting their teachers' ideas—despite the comparatively early publication of sources about Jesus—is to value one's skepticism about Jesus more highly than the concrete comparative evidence.

---

[107] Dio Chrysostom, *Or.* 36.9. External sources confirm at least some of Dio's report.
[108] E.g., Pausanias 1.23.2.
[109] Alan Kirk, "Memory," 155–72 in *Jesus in Memory*, 157–8.
[110] Cf. Josephus *Ant.* 4.211; *Apion* 1.60; 2.178, 204, even allowing for some likely hyperbole; see Deut 6:7; 11:19; Ps 78:4–8 (LXX 77:4–8).
[111] McIver, *Memory*, passim.
[112] Cf. similarly Eddy and Boyd, *Legend*, 269–306.

Part 1

Jesus's Teachers

2

Jesus's Teachings and Hebrew Bible Influences

Katherine Davis

2.1 Introduction

Jesus's ministry, as portrayed by Matthew's Gospel, is shaped by the Law, the Prophets, and the Writings. This is evidenced most clearly by Jesus's appropriation of the Hebrew Bible from his testing in the wilderness (Matt 4:1–11) to crying out Psalm 22:1 on the cross (Matt 27:46).[1] This chapter explores the extent to which Matthew's portrayal of Jesus's teachings is influenced by, or conversant with, Israel's Scriptures.

To attend to this question, this chapter focuses on the echoes, allusions, and quotes from the Hebrew Bible in Jesus's teaching since these are explicit evidence of influence and of Jesus's familiarity with the Hebrew Bible in the Matthean portrayal. However, since there are over seventy-four echoes, allusions, and quotes, it is impossible in the scope of this chapter to examine the breadth of this evidence. Consequently, this chapter has chosen a selection of these across the three parts of the Hebrew Scriptures, from the Law, the Prophets, and the Writings.

Furthermore, while Matthew's depiction of Jesus's teaching is shaped into five discourse sections within the Gospel (5:1–7:29, 9:35–11:1, 13:1–53, 18:1–35, 23:1–25:46), he is also portrayed teaching through his relational interactions with crowds, with those he heals, with his disciples, and with the Pharisees. For this reason, this chapter explores the influences of the Hebrew Bible in every dimension of Jesus's teaching and not solely in the discourse sections of Matthew's Gospel. In doing so, this chapter demonstrates that Jesus's teaching is not *merely* influenced by the Hebrew Bible, nor is he *just* conversant with Israel's Scriptures; the Matthean depiction of Jesus's teaching embodies the instruction and ideology of the Hebrew Bible with an unparalleled mastery of Israel's Scriptures.

---

[1] For definitions of an "echo," "allusion," and "quote," and how each term differs to the other, see Richard B. Hays, *Echoes of Scripture in the Gospels* (Waco, TX: Baylor University Press, 2016), 10–11.

2.2 The Influence of the Law in Jesus's Teaching

Jesus's teaching in the Matthean portrayal is imbued with echoes, allusions, and quotes from the Law.[2] For example, in 5:17–48, Jesus exemplifies how his identity and ministry fulfils the Law by drawing on Israel's legal texts. Moreover, Jesus's teaching during the healing sequence in 8:1–9:26 also echoes Levitical cultic instruction about forgiveness, impurity, and purity. These examples are examined below, as well as an allusion to the creation narratives of Genesis in 19:1–6.

2.2.1 The Influence of Legal Instruction in the Sermon on the Mount

In Matt 5:17–20, Jesus focuses his teaching on the relationship of his person and ministry to the Hebrew Bible, particularly the Law and the Prophets. He clarifies that this relationship is not one of abolition where the instructions of the Law disappear but rather of fulfillment where the teaching of the Law and the Prophets endure (5:17–18). In 5:21–48, Jesus demonstrates this relationship by giving examples from Exodus, Leviticus, and Deuteronomy.

The first example in 5:21 is drawn from the Decalogue in Exod 20:13. Jesus quotes Jewish tradition where the prohibition against murder from Exod 20:13 is stated first, but then two clauses are added: ὃς δ' ἂν φονεύσῃ and ἔνοχος ἔσται τῇ κρίσει. In v. 22, Jesus points to the internal attitude of anger and repeats the clause, ἔνοχος ἔσται τῇ κρίσει. By repeating what tradition has added to Exod 20:13, Jesus identifies the root cause of murder—anger—and highlights that the internal attitude of anger, not only the outworking of this emotion in the act of murder, invites justice. Jesus demonstrates in Matt 5:21–22 that he is conversant with tradition that itself appropriates the Decalogue, and by doing so, he realigns tradition to the spirit of the Decalogue's prohibition.

Furthermore, Jesus uses this first example in vv. 21–22 to highlight a practical application in vv. 23–24 that echoes the ideology of the reparation offering from Lev 5:20–26. The protasis in v. 23 raises the situation where one from Jesus's audience may present a gift – and this gift could be any from Lev 1–5 – but then remember that he or she is not at peace with another, that is, they know they have wronged another and this brother or sister still holds this offence against them.[3] The apodosis in v. 24 then instructs the audience to leave their gift, be reconciled first, and then return to offer the gift. There are three points worth observing. First, it is the one who has caused offence that is to seek reconciliation, and this too is the beginning of the reparation offering in Lev 5:20–26. The offeror is motivated to bring their gift to YHWH having realized that they are guilty of an offence against their neighbor. Second, in Matt 5:24, the one who has wronged his or her brother or sister should then seek reconciliation

---

[2] For example, Matt 4:4–10//Deut 6–8; 5:21//Exod 20:13; 5:23–24//Lev 1–5; 5:27//Exod 20:14; 5:31//Deut 24:1; 5:38//Exod 21:24, Lev 24:20, Deut 19:21; 5:43//Lev 19:18; 9:1–2//Lev 4–5; 10:5//Gen 18:1–19:25; 11:24//Gen 18:1–19:25; 12:5//Lev 2; 24:1–9; 15:4//Exod 20:12, 21:17, Lev 20:9, Deut 5:16; 15:11//Lev 11; 18:5–16//Deut 19:15; 19:4–6//Gen 1:1–2:25; 19:18–19//Exod 20:1–17, Deut 5:16–20, Lev 19:18; 22:29–31//Exod 3:6; 22:37//Deut 6:5; 22:39//Lev 19:18; 24:36–41//Gen 6–9; 26:9–11//Deut 15:11; 26:28//Lev 17.

[3] Contrary to John Nolland, *The Gospel of Matthew*, NIGTC (Grand Rapids, MI: Eerdmans, 2005), 232.

before offering their gift to God. In Lev 5:20-26, the one who committed the offence must restore the situation with his or her neighbor before bringing his or her reparation gift to YHWH. The reason for this order is that breaking faith with a neighbor is also an offence against God; for reconciliation with God to occur, the offender must first make redress with their neighbor. Third, while Matt 5:23-24 is not specifically about the reparation offering, Jesus's teaching reflects the priority that his disciples must first repair the situation with their neighbor and so be in a condition of relational order before seeking to approach God in good relationship or to restore relationship. These resonances between Matt 5:23-24 and the ideology of Lev 5:20-26 suggests that Jesus's teaching about being reconciled with a brother or sister is shaped by the pattern established in the reparation offering.

The second example is also a quote from the Decalogue and is the prohibition against adultery in Exod 20:14. In Matt 5:27, Jesus introduces Exod 20:14 by acknowledging the audience's familiarity with the prohibition but then reinterprets the prohibition in 5:28 by pointing to the internal attitude of lust as committing adultery. That is, Jesus highlights that the offence of adultery is not just the act of sexual intercourse that transgresses a marriage relationship, but that anyone who even looks at another with sexual intent is already guilty.[4] That is, as Nolland observes, "the concern is with the secret violation of another's marriage."[5] By emphasizing the root cause that might lead to adultery, Jesus is not contradicting the Decalogue; rather, he points to the internal issue at the crux of the prohibition.[6]

The third example in 5:31 is Deuteronomy's instruction to give a divorce certificate when a man divorces his wife. Curiously, Jesus's reference to Deut 24:1 summarizes the protasis from Deut 24:1 and omits the intent of the divorce. He then alludes to the apodosis by choosing the second verbal idea, δίδωμι, in the sequence, …וְכָתַב …וְנָתַן וְשִׁלְּחָהּ, with the object being the certificate of divorce (ἀποστάσιον). In Matt 5:32, Jesus reinterprets the protasis of Deut 24:1 to allow sexual immorality (πορνεία) to be the only ground for which divorce may occur. He clearly evinces that any other motivation is then causing the wife to commit adultery. Worth noting is that Deut 24:1 is not giving permission for divorce. Rather, the protasis acknowledges the brokenness that might motivate divorce, so, considering this reality, the apodosis contains instruction to protect the wife. Thus, Jesus's instruction in Matt 5:32 is not contrary to the case law of Deut 24:1. He restricts the situation addressed by the protasis and highlights the offence of divorce for any other reason.[7] Significantly, for the subject of this chapter, Jesus introduces this restriction by the quotative frame, ἐγὼ δὲ λέγω ὑμῖν,

---

[4] Also, Craig S. Keener, *A Commentary on the Gospel of Matthew* (Grand Rapids, MI: Eerdmans, 1999), 190; Blomberg, "Matthew," in *CNTUOT*, ed. G. K Beale and D. A. Carson (Grand Rapids, MI: Baker, 2007), 22, correctly notes that in ANE context, adultery would have been understood as a married man or woman having sexual relations with someone not their spouse. However, the basic point that the two offenders are not married does not preclude two unmarried people from the definition of adultery.

[5] Nolland, *Matthew*, 236.

[6] Also, Donald A. Hagner, *Matthew 1-13*, WBC 33A (Grand Rapids, MI: Zondervan, 2000), 121.

[7] Also, Jeannine K. Brown and Kyle Roberts, *Matthew*, THNTC (Grand Rapids, MI: Eerdmans, 2018), 64.

which conveys authority. Jesus demonstrates that he is not merely conversant with Deuteronomy 24 but has the authority to restrict its application.

The fourth example in 5:38 centers on Jesus's quote of the *lex talionis* that is repeated in Exod 21:24, Lev 24:20, and Deut 19:21. Introduced by the quotative frame, ἐγὼ δὲ λέγω ὑμῖν, Jesus's explanation in v. 39 seems to be the opposite of what he quoted; instead of seeking retribution or attempting to stop the evil being done, the disciple should resist being complicit.[8] However, the *lex talionis* is one specific part of a wider retributive justice framework encompassing Israel's Law. For instance, in Gen 12:4, YHWH promises Abram that he will bless those who bless him and curse those who curse him. Then YHWH instructs his covenant nation in Lev 19:18 not to take revenge; instead, they are to love their neighbor as themselves. In Deut 32:35, Moses extols how it is YHWH's prerogative to seek vengeance and to repay. It is because of this conviction that responsibility for vengeance lies with their covenant God that the psalmists in the Writings then seek to surrender retribution to YHWH in the Psalms.[9] I would suggest that Jesus's teaching is entrenched within this retributive justice framework when he instructs his audience not to be implicated in the harm by reciprocating in kind.

A possible objection to this understanding is that Jesus does not teach in 5:38–42 that, having restrained the desire for retaliation, his disciples are then to ask God for vengeance. However, Jesus's explanation in vv. 39–42 segues into the final example where Jesus quotes Lev 19:18c, ἀγαπήσεις τὸν πλησίον σου, in Matt 5:43 and then adds to this a second clause, καὶ μισήσεις τὸν ἐχθρόν σου, which is not found in Israel's Scriptures. By quoting Lev 19:18c, Jesus evokes the context of the whole verse where YHWH exhorts his nation not to take vengeance. Furthermore, in Matt 5:44, Jesus declares to his disciples the opposite of the added second clause; instead of hating their enemies, they are to love their enemies and pray for those who persecute them. This latter action of praying for those who persecute follows the model of how the psalmists surrender retribution to God. For these reasons, it is appropriate to understand Jesus's teaching in Matt 5:38–47 as returning to the heart of the Law's retributive theology by accentuating that the responsibility of the faithful is not to return evil with evil but to return evil with good and then to surrender vengeance to God in petition to him.

As Jesus demonstrates how the Law is fulfilled in his own person and ministry, he uses each of the five examples in such a way that suggests these instructions and prohibitions have been misappropriated in Jesus's context. The indicators of misappropriation are the way that the commands have been added to by tradition or, in the case concerning divorce, by how he restricts the situation where divorce is permissible. In each instance, Jesus realigns his audience's understanding to what faithfulness looks like under the covenantal framework of the Law. By doing so, Jesus demonstrates that he is not merely conversant with the world of the Hebrew

---

[8] Please note that the use of ἀνθίστημι in 5:39 could suggest restraint in a court setting. For example, Blomberg, *Matthew*, 113; Don Carson, "Matthew," ed. T. Longman III and D. E. Garland (Grand Rapids, MI: Zondervan, 2010), 189. However, the understanding represented above is that Jesus's teaching is for a broader situation than solely a judicial process. For this view, see Brown and Roberts, *Matthew*, 64–5; Hagner, *Matthew 1–13*, 131; Nolland, *Matthew*, 257–8.

[9] David G. Firth, *Surrendering Retribution in the Psalms: Responses to Violence in Individual Complaints* (Eugene, OR: Wipf & Stock, 2005), 14n43, 36–42, 102–109, 125–137. For example, Pss 5, 6, 12, 40, 59, 69, 109, 137, 143.

Bible but rather has a mastery of the Law's instructions so that he is able to correct misinterpretation and misapplication of the Law's teaching.

However, the echo of the Law in the Sermon on the Mount is not limited to the above five examples. As Jesus concludes his exhortation to love their enemies in 5:43–47, he then adds two clauses in v. 48, ἔσεσθε οὖν ὑμεῖς τέλειοι and ὡς ὁ πατὴρ ὑμῶν ὁ οὐράνιος τέλειός ἐστιν. These two clauses echo the mimetic pattern of Lev 11:44c, 11:45b, 19:2, and 20:26 where YHWH instructs Israel to be holy as he is holy. However, while he echoes the mimesis, Jesus uses the adjective τέλειος rather than Leviticus's קָדוֹשׁ (LXX ἅγιος). This could suggest that Jesus borrowed the mimetic technique without the intent of echoing Leviticus and its context. However, τέλειος shares a semantic domain with ἅγιος, and this is especially true within Lev 11. Leviticus 11 teaches the Israelites about the distinction between impurity and purity through applying this distinction to what can and cannot be eaten, as well as what can and cannot be touched. YHWH defines impure animals or fish as those that do not represent all characteristics that the pure animals or fish exemplify (11:1–12). For example, impure animals are those that chew the cud *or* have cloven hoofs (11:4), whereas a pure animal exemplifies *both* characteristics (11:2–3). That is, they represent the complete picture of what is pure.[10] As Lev 11 progresses, YHWH also teaches that impurity is associated with death and rebellion (11:29–42).[11] The way in which Israel is to be holy is to be set apart in their condition of purity to YHWH, and thus they are to be set apart in a condition that represents completeness, as well as life and faithfulness (as opposed to death and rebellion). Wenham states, "We can conclude that holiness is exemplified by completeness. Holiness requires that individuals shall conform to the class to which they belong."[12] The Israelites by virtue of the covenant relationship, which was a goal of the exodus event, belong to YHWH and thus must "conform" to the one to whom they belong. The adjective τέλειος conveys the idea of being complete, as well as of being whole and blameless, which is part of the ideological basis of purity as instructed in Lev 11. Thus, Jesus's use of mimesis in Matt 5:48 echoes the mimesis of Lev 11:44–45 by substituting language of holiness with language associated with purity.

Therefore, while Jesus does not use the exact language of holiness as found in the mimesis of Lev 11:44–45, the use of τέλειος is an interpretation of Leviticus's understanding of purity and holiness. By doing so, Jesus has appropriated the mimetic pattern and substituted terminology that expresses the crux of Leviticus's ideology of purity and holiness. Again, this shows Jesus's knowledge of the Law as surpassing familiarity; rather his teaching embodies the teaching of the Law. In turn, the rhetorical function of Jesus's teaching embodying the Law is to shape disciples into a "community that embodies radical obedience to the Torah."[13]

---

[10] See Mary Douglas, *Purity and Danger: An Analysis of Concepts of Pollution and Taboo* (London: Routledge, 1966), 64–5.
[11] Leigh M. Trevaskis, *Holiness, Ethics, and Ritual in Leviticus*, HBM (Sheffield: Sheffield Phoenix, 2011), 89.
[12] Gordon J. Wenham, *The Book of Leviticus*, NICOT (Grand Rapids, MI: Eerdmans, 2009), 24.
[13] Hays, *Echoes of Scripture in the Gospels*, 121.

2.2.2 The Influence of Israel's Cultic Instruction in Jesus's Teaching

During the healing sequence in 8:1–9:38, Jesus's teaching in his relational interactions echoes cultic instruction from Lev 1–16, particularly in 8:1–4 and 9:1–8. The discussion below explores these two examples, as well as echoes of Leviticus's cultic instruction in 15:1–20.

After Jesus finished teaching in 5:1–7:29, 8:1 depicts Jesus coming down the mountain with the large crowds following him. In this context, a man with leprosy knelt before him and declared that Jesus could purify him (δύνασαί με καθαρίσαι), if he is willing (8:2). According to Lev 13:1–44, leprosy is a skin disease that would cause the sufferer to be in a condition of impurity, and for as long as they are in this condition, they are to remain isolated from the community (Lev 13:46). Leviticus 14 is equally clear that the only means by which they can be restored to the community is by a priest having witnessed that the sufferer has been healed (v. 3) and then by submitting to a two-stage sacrificial process (vv. 4–31). The first stage of this sacrificial process is the purification process where a bird is killed (v. 5), after which a living bird is dipped into the dead bird's blood (v. 6) and then used to sprinkle the healed person (v. 7a). The living bird is then released after the priest declares the person to be in a pure condition (v. 7b-c). The second stage of the sacrificial process is the bringing of a guilt offering (vv. 12–18), a sin offering (v. 19a-b), a burnt offering (v. 19c), and a cereal offering (v. 20).

The leper's request in Matt 8:2 for healing is so that he can be restored to his community. Curiously, after Jesus chose to heal him and so turn his condition of impurity into one of purity, he then instructed the healed man to go to the priest and "bring *the gift* that was commanded by Moses." However, τὸ δῶρον is singular, whereas the instructions in Lev 14:4–31 note the presenting of at least two birds in the initial stage and then four gifts during the second stage.[14] Due to the singular use of τὸ δῶρον and the purpose of presenting "the gift" to the priest, I am inclined to think that Jesus is referring to the first stage of the sacrificial process. The healed man would then be deemed ritually pure and be able to enter his community. The purpose stated in Matt 8:4c is, εἰς μαρτύριον αὐτοῖς. While there is contention as to whether εἰς is be understood as an indicator of purpose (i.e., "to") or as "against," the former makes sense both of the Matthean context and of Lev 14. When the skin diseased person has been healed, he or she is brought to the priest, and this happens by the priest coming to the place where they have been excluded from their community (Lev 14:1–2). The priest is then to examine the person to verify that the person is healed. Once witnessed, the priest can then mediate, by the sacrifice of the bird, the process by which the healed person is able to move from being excluded by their community to being restored inside the community (vv. 4–7). In Matt 8:3–4, Jesus has healed the man, but for restoration into community, this healing needs to be verified, or witnessed, by the priesthood.[15] The resonance between Lev 14:1–7 and Matt 8:1–4 suggests that Jesus is

---

[14] It is curious that these discrepancies are not noted by Matthean scholars, instead there is a general thought that there is coherence between Jesus's instruction here and Lev 13–14 without stating how and why. For example, see Brown and Roberts, *Matthew*, 84; Hagner, *Matthew 1–13*, 199; Keener, *Matthew*, 263; Nolland, *Matthew*, 349–50.

[15] Also, Hagner, *Matthew 1–13*, 199–200.

instructing the healed man to act in accordance with Lev 14:1–7. On this basis, it is appropriate to suggest that Jesus's instruction in Matt 8:4 is shaped by Lev 14:1–7.

A second example from the healing sequence is Jesus's declaration to the paralyzed man that his sins are forgiven in 9:2. According to the Law, being paralyzed does not make a person impure; this is only true for an Aaronic priest (see Lev 21:17–23). However, sin is a form of impurity (Lev 4–5, 16, 19–20). For a person who realizes that he or she is guilty of unintentional sin, Lev 4:1–5:13 provides different scenarios where that person can offer a purification offering (חַטָּאת) that atones for the impurity caused by their sin and through this means is able to be declared forgiven (סָלַח; LXX ἀφίημι). The purification offering is the only means by which an individual can seek forgiveness after realizing his or her guilt, and the means is solely through atonement made through sacrifice. While the priest might declare the offeror "forgiven," the priest does so on behalf of YHWH whom the offeror has ultimately offended. When Jesus declares in Matt 9:2, ἀφίενταί σου αἱ ἁμαρτίαι, he is making a declaration that can only be made once a purification offering has been accepted. Moreover, the authority to declare forgiveness belongs to YHWH and is mediated solely by his priesthood. These observations, along with the use of purification offering terminology, suggests that Jesus's declaration in 9:2 echoes the goal of the purification offering from Lev 4:1–5:13. By appropriating the language of forgiveness from Lev 4:1–5:13, Jesus is teaching about his identity and the origin of his authority to declare the forgiveness of sin.

The third example occurs in the context of 15:1–20 where Jesus enters a brief dialogue about what is pure and impure with the Pharisees. The Pharisees confront Jesus about his disciples not conforming to the Jewish tradition of washing before eating (v. 2). Jesus responds in vv. 5–11 by highlighting the Pharisees' propensity to elevate tradition over God's commands, such as the command to honor their mother and father (Exod 20:12; Deut 5:16) and the death penalty when a parent is cursed by their children (Lev 20:9). Jesus is appropriating a command that is repeated in the Law and where the breaking of the command is a form of ethical impurity (see Lev 20). Jesus states in v. 11 that it is not what goes into a person that makes them impure but rather what comes out of a person. At a glance, Jesus's statement in v. 11 seems to reverse Israel's food laws from Lev 11. However, the incongruence does not stop there. By stating v. 11, Jesus seems to reverse his own teaching from vv. 5–11 too. In these verses, he accentuates the importance of embodying faithful obedience to God's commands in the Law as he addresses the Pharisees' contempt of the Law. This perception of incongruence suggests that there might be more afoot in Matt 15:11 than Jesus having "a casual stance" on the food laws from Lev 11.[16] To understand what Jesus is doing in Matt 15:11, it is helpful to explore Lev 11 in its context.

In Lev 10:10, YHWH instructs the priesthood that part of their responsibility is to teach the Israelites the distinction between the two conditions of impurity and purity, as well as between the states of being holy and common.[17] Leviticus 11–15 then

---

[16] Hays, *Echoes of Scripture in the Gospels*, 122.

[17] For the language of "impurity" and "purity" being two conditions, while "common" and "holy" refer to two states, Richard. E. Averbeck, "Clean and Unclean," *NIDOTTE*, ed. W. A. VanGemeren, vol. 4 (Grand Rapids, MI: Zondervan, 1997), 481.

instructs about how to make this distinction between what is impure and what is pure. Leviticus 11 teaches this distinction in the domain of food. The strategy of the food laws is to help the Israelites learn to avoid what is associated with impurity and to consume that which is associated with the condition of purity. Through this means, the Israelites learn that they are to be set apart to belong to YHWH in a condition of purity (11:44–45).

However, the purpose of these instructions within the ritual domain is so that the Israelites could apply this distinction in the ethical domain. That is, by learning that they should avoid what is associated with incompleteness, disorder, rebellion, and death, they learn to avoid behavior that represents these characteristics in every domain of life (Lev 18–22). Conversely, by learning that they should consume what is associated with completeness, order, obedience, and life, the Israelites learn to embody behavior exemplifying these attributes (Lev 19). This is the reason Lev 20 alludes to the distinctions taught by the food laws of Lev 11 as a means of learning that they are to avoid the impure practices associated with the other nations and to embody YHWH's commands. As Jesus declares in Matt 15:11 that it is what comes out of a person that makes a person impure, he is pointing to the ideology being taught by the food laws. The food laws were put in place to learn the distinction through a tangible means in everyday life. That is, the food laws were intended to point to a deeper reality—attitudes and actions cause a person to be in a condition of purity or impurity. Thus, as Jesus rebukes the Pharisees in Matt 15:11, he is pointing to the reality that the food laws from Lev 11 are intended by God to symbolize and teach.[18] In this instance, the echo of Lev 11 in Matt 15:11 demonstrates Jesus's intimate understanding of the Law in contrast to the Pharisees' hypocrisy.

2.2.3 The Influence of Genesis' Narratives in Jesus's Teaching

At intermittent points throughout Matthew's Gospel, Jesus's teaching echoes and alludes to narratives from the Book of Genesis.[19] For instance, in 19:1–6, in response to a test from the Pharisees, Jesus alludes to Gen 1–2. This test occurred in the context of Jesus entering Judea and healing those in a large crowd who followed him out of Galilee (v. 1). In v. 3, Pharisees seek to test Jesus by asking whether it is lawful for a man to divorce his wife without cause. Jesus begins his response by a rhetorical question in vv. 4–5 that has three parts. The first part, οὐκ ἀνέγνωτε, sets up the rhetorical question to have the expected answer, "Yes, of course!" The rhetorical impact is to cast doubt on the veracity of the test being offered by the Pharisees and so their character. In the second part, Jesus connects two ideas from Gen 1:1–2:4. The first idea is shaped by Gen 1:1 by alluding to the Creator (ὁ κτίσας) who created "from the beginning"

---

[18] Contrary to Hays, *Echoes of Scripture in the Gospels*, 122, who views Matthew's concern in 15:11 to "not advocate a program of rejecting Jewish food laws but rather to shift the emphasis to purity of heart as the Torah's chief concerns." The issue with Hays's view of Matt 5:11 is that Jesus is not "shift[ing] the emphasis" but is pointing to the core ideology that Lev 11 teaches so that Israel would embody the distinction.

[19] For example, Matt 10:15; 11:24//Gen 18:1–19:25; 12:39–41//Jonah 2:1–11.

(ἀπ' ἀρχῆς).[20] The second idea from Gen 1:27 is that this same Creator made humanity male and female. The third part in v. 5 is a quote from Gen 2:23, which begins with the connecting phrase ἕνεκα τούτου. This connecting phrase retains its causal function within the context of Jesus's rhetorical question, so the demonstrative τούτου is anaphoric referring to the connection made in v. 4. Because the same Creator, who created from the beginning, made humanity male and female, then the consequence is that a man leaves his father and mother, cleaves to his wife, and so becomes one flesh with her. The reason this is the consequence is that the Creator, who made them with this distinction of being male and female, also purposed them to become one flesh after they are united as man and wife.[21] After posing the rhetorical question that assumes an affirmation from the Pharisees that they have indeed read Gen 1–2, Jesus then answers the test in v. 5 by referring to the permanency of the one flesh formed by the husband and wife. As Jesus teaches by his response to the Pharisees, his answer is informed and shaped by texts from Gen 1–2. He demonstrates that his teaching is aligned and in unity with Israel's Law. Brown and Roberts conclude, "Matthew continues to portray Jesus as faithful interpreter of the Scriptures and, beyond this, the one who knows God's deepest intentions revealed with them."[22]

2.3 The Influence of the Prophets in Jesus's Teaching

Just as Jesus's teaching in Matthew's Gospel exemplifies an intimate knowledge of the Law to the extent that his teaching embodies it, so too the Prophets. To demonstrate this argument, this section considers examples from Isaiah and Hosea.

2.3.1 The Influence of Isaiah in Jesus's Teaching

Echoes of Isaiah's themes occur at significant points in Jesus's teaching.[23] The discussion below examines four examples where Jesus appropriates texts from Isa 1–39.

The first occurs in Matt 11:4–6 where Jesus sends his response to John the Baptist through John's disciples. The message that John's disciples are to report is a sequence of healings and miracles where there is a reversal in the plights of the blind, the lame, those with leprosy, the deaf, and the dead. In each instance, order is restored from disorder, and life is brought from death (v. 5a-e). These reversals echo new exodus language from Isa 35:5–6, which arises in the context of the wilderness flowering (vv. 1–2), God coming with vengeance to save (vv. 3–4), and a way being prepared for the redeemed to enter Zion with singing (vv. 7–10). The two reversals that are not present in Isa 35:5–6, such as those with leprosy being purified and the dead being

---

[20] Also, Nolland, *Matthew*, 771. Generally, scholars tend to highlight Gen 1:27 assuming an implied connection to Gen 1:1.
[21] Carson, "Matthew," 466.
[22] Brown and Roberts, *Matthew*, 177.
[23] For example, Matt 4:14–15//Isa 9:1–2, 42:7; 5:3//Isa 61:1, 66:2; 5:4//61:2–3; 8:16–17//Isa 53:4; 11:4–6//Isa 35:5–6; 12:16–16//Isa 42:1–4; 13:13–15//Isa 6:9–10; 15:7–9//Isa 29:13; 24:29–30//Isa 13:10, 34:4.

raised, are Jesus's additions where he might have the ministries of Elijah and Elisha in mind (see 1 Kings 17:17–24; 2 Kings 5:1–19). The cluster of miracles in Elijah and Elisha's prophetic ministries are characteristic of an era of covenant enforcement in a rebellious era of Israel's past (see 1 Kgs 17–2 Kgs 9), and, considering Jesus's quote from Mal 3:1 about an Elijah-like figure in Matt 11:10, this might be a possibility. However, the final clause of Jesus's message to John the Baptist in 11:5f, πτωχοὶ εὐαγγελίζονται, echoes the declaration of the servant in Isa 61:1 who describes being anointed "to proclaim good news to the poor" (εὐαγγελίσασθαι πτωχοῖς). Jesus's message to John the Baptist is that the era of the new exodus and the Isaianic servant is here; he is the Messiah. Thus, Jesus describes his mission by appropriating new exodus language and the message of the anointed servant from Isaiah.

The second example is Jesus's quote of Isa 6:9–10 (LXX) in Matt 13:13–15. In Isa 1–5, YHWH declares that he will bring a refining justice to Jerusalem because of the rebelliousness of his covenant people, yet through this justice, there is a future hope for Zion. Then, Isa 6:1–3 contrasts the death of Jerusalem's king, Uzziah, with the living and reigning YHWH of armies who is declared as holy. As Isaiah witnesses the holiness of YHWH, he declares his condition of being impure. In response, YHWH provides a means for Isaiah to stand in his presence and live (6:5–7). YHWH commissions Isaiah to proclaim his message to Jerusalem, with the effect that the people may listen but not understand, until YHWH's justice culminates with the city's destruction (6:9–13). YHWH had purposed that this Israelite generation, Isaiah's audience, should not perceive Isaiah's message because of the extent of their rebelliousness; there was a need for the purification of YHWH's covenant people. Thus, in YHWH's commissioning speech from Isa 6:9–10, he reveals to Isaiah the effect of being YHWH's messenger: hearing but not understanding, seeing but not perceiving, *lest* they should hear, see, understand, turn, and be healed (Isa 6:9–10). Jesus appropriates Isa 6:9–10 in two stages. In Matt 13:13, he alludes to Isa 6:9 when explaining, "Although they might see, they do not see and although they hear, they do not hear or understand." Although using similar language (e.g., ἀκούω, βλέπω), 13:13 is not a quote of Isa 6:9;[24] yet 13:13 and Isa 6:9 convey the same idea. Then Jesus quotes Isa 6:9–10 in 13:14–15. The impact is an emphasis on Isa 6:9 which accentuates the reason for speaking in parables: so his audience would hear but not understand *lest* (μήποτε) they too turn and be healed.[25] By appropriating this text, Jesus is declaring that his audience within the world of Matthew's Gospel is in an equivalent situation to preexilic Jerusalem; their rebelliousness has reached a point where there is a need for purification through justice. As Jesus warns about God's purifying justice, he teaches through the agency of Israel's Scripture in Isaiah. Moreover, he teaches through the agency of Scripture in this instance to demonstrate the fulfilment of Isa 6:9–10 in his audience.[26]

---

[24] Also, Blomberg, *CNTUOT*, 46.
[25] Contrary to Hays, *Echoes of Scripture in the Gospels*, 130–1, who views the future indicative of ἰάσομαι to suggest a certainty that "God will bring deliverance and healing." Yet this reading misses the impact of μήποτε at the beginning of the verbal sequence beginning in 13:15d.
[26] See also Blomberg, *CNTUOT*, 47–8.

The third example concerns an aspect of Isaiah's critique of Jerusalem, which is that his people were presenting their offerings and speaking the right words, while their hearts were far from him and their conduct in community was full of injustice (Isa 1:11–13; 29:13). As Jesus interacts with the Pharisees and scribes in 15:1–6, who have asked why his disciples break tradition by not washing before they eat, we have noted above that Jesus uses a command from the Decalogue to unveil the Pharisees' hypocrisy; they preferred obedience to human tradition over God's commands and so have made the word of God void. To press this point further in vv. 8–9, he quotes Isaiah's critique of the emptiness of Jerusalem's worship from Isa 29:13. The effect of Jesus's appropriation of Isaiah's message is a rebuke of the Pharisees' and scribes' concern for human tradition when their hearts are also far from God. Jesus admonishes the Pharisees and scribes through the agency of Scripture. It is not that Jesus is influenced by Isaiah per se nor that he is merely conversant with the Prophets; he has an intimate knowledge of the prophet's message with an authority to apply its teaching to his audience. Furthermore, he applies Isa 29:13 to this particular generation of Pharisees by suggesting in v. 7 that Isaiah was prophesying about them directly (i.e., περὶ ὑμῶν; "about you").[27] Thus, Jesus applies Isa 29:13 to this generation of Pharisees as the recipients of Isaiah's message.

The fourth example, in Matt 24:29–30, arises in the context where Jesus is teaching about justice for Jerusalem, both in the near future and at an unknown point. To describe what this justice will be like, Jesus alludes to the cosmic language of Isa 13:10 and 34:4. Curiously, Isa 13 is the beginning of YHWH's oracles to the nations where he announces future justice, and similarly Isa 34 calls the nations to hear how YHWH will destroy them as a recompense for Zion's destruction. In Isa 13:1–22, YHWH's message concerns his retributive justice against Babylon where he is mustering his army for battle to avenge for the evil done. After 13:9 describes the fierce nature of that day, v. 10 depicts how the justice done in Babylon has cosmic consequences where the stars and their constellations no longer give light, the sun is dark as it rises, and the moon no longer sheds light. This description conveys two ideas. The first is that the stars, sun, and moon will no longer fulfill their created function, which is to give light. The second idea is that the stars, sun, and moon were often associated with particular Babylonian gods (e.g. Samas was the Babylonian sun god), so 13:10 is also highlighting that with the defeat of Babylon, their gods will be rendered powerless.[28] Similarly, as Isa 34:4 depicts the hosts (i.e. stars) of the heavens falling like leaves from a vine or fig tree, Isaiah is portraying the cosmic consequences after the nations have been defeated with mountains being soaked with the blood of the slain (34:3). With the fall of the nations, their gods, who are represented by the starry hosts, will too fall. As Jesus describes the future justice that will precede the coming of the Son of Man by appropriating this cosmic language from Isa 13–34, he is applying a description of God's justice to both Jerusalem and all tribes that in its Isaianic context is about God's justice against Babylon and Edom. The implication is that the cause of justice against Jerusalem is akin

---

[27] Blomberg, *CNTUOT*, 54. This is different to Hays, *Echoes of Scripture in the Gospel*, 131, who views Isaiah's message as being "reinterpreted as an indictment of Israel's *leaders*."

[28] Similarly, John N. Oswalt, *The Book of Isaiah Chapters 1–39*, NICOT (Grand Rapids, MI: Eerdmans, 1986), 306.

to that of Babylon and Edom. At the very least, Jesus appropriates the cosmic imagery from Isa 13–23 to shape his message about future justice against Jerusalem. But if the observations above are sound, then once again Jesus's use of the Prophets extends beyond influence or familiarity; his teaching is instilled with an intimate knowledge of the prophets to the point that he interprets and applies the Isaianic cosmic imagery within the situation that he is teaching.

2.3.2 The Influence of Hosea in Jesus's Teaching

In Matt 9:13 and 12:7, Jesus uses Hos 6:6 as he responds to the Pharisees. In 9:9–13, Jesus has been reclining with Matthew, other tax collectors, and sinners, when the Pharisees challenge Jesus's disciples about his choice of company around the table (vv. 9–11). Jesus then responds in v. 12 with a saying that highlights that his ministry is for the sick. He then identifies "the sick" as those who are sinners (ἁμαρτωλούς) in v. 13d. However, before he makes this identification in v. 13d, he rebukes the Pharisees by commanding them to "go and learn" (πορευθέντες δὲ μάθετε) the meaning of ἔλεος θέλω καὶ οὐ θυσίαν, which is Hos 6:6a.[29] In Hos 6, YHWH is rebuking the thought of the northern kingdom that YHWH's healing and restoration will be quick (6:1–2), while their covenant faithfulness (חֶסֶד; LXX ἔλεος) is transient (6:4). The consequence is that YHWH has executed his justice through his words (6:5). Hosea 6:6 is then the reason for YHWH speaking his justice against the northern kingdom, which is that he desires חֶסֶד ("covenant faithfulness") rather than sacrifice and knowledge of God rather than burnt offerings.[30] God desires genuine relationship rather than the right outward actions alone. Jesus's appropriation of Hos 6:6a is a rebuke of the Pharisees' obeying the external actions of the Law rather than embodying what God desires of his people. Similarly, in Matt 12:1–2, the Pharisees rebuked Jesus for his disciples gathering grain on the Sabbath, stating that it is "not lawful" (οὐκ ἔξεστιν). Jesus concludes his dialogue with the Pharisees by stating in v. 7 that if the Pharisees had known the meaning of ἔλεος θέλω καὶ οὐ θυσίαν (Hos 6:6a), then they would not have "condemned the guiltless." Once more, Jesus appropriates the message of Hos 6:6a to highlight the Pharisees' problem, which is that they have more concern about outward obedience than covenant faithfulness and knowing God. In both 9:13 and 12:7, if the Pharisees had embodied covenant faithfulness, then they too would have understood God's concerns in his world.[31] In these examples from Hosea, Jesus rebukes by the agency of Scripture with an authority that surpasses the Pharisees.

---

[29] See also Keener, *Matthew*, 298, "But when Jesus introduces his quote from Hosea with 'Go and learn' in the context of a response to a challenge, he is insultingly suggesting his interlocutors' ignorance of the point of Scripture."

[30] Also, Carson, "Matthew," 264.

[31] Contrary to Blomberg, *CNTUOT*, 34. W. D. Davies and Dale C. Allison Jr, *Matthew 8–18*, ICC (London: T&T Clark, 1991), 104. Jesus is not using Scripture to justify a "creative" innovation but rather is accentuating just how far the Pharisees are from God's purposes as revealed by Israel's Scriptures. Blomberg, *CNTUOT*, 35, is closer to this view when he states, "This is not a text about the fulfillment of Scripture so much as the application of a fundamental moral principle of the OT that continues through the new age that Jesus is inaugurating."

2.4 The Influence of the Writings in Jesus's Teaching

Jesus's use of echoes and allusions to the Writings in his teaching is consistent with how he appropriates echoes and allusions to the Law and to the Prophets. He teaches through the agency of Israel's Scriptures. This section explores examples from the Psalms. While there are echoes, allusions, quotes from the Psalms throughout Jesus's teaching,[32] there are three instances in Matt 21–22 that are helpful to explore and which share the common context of Jesus interacting with the Pharisees.

The first instance occurs after Jesus cleanses the temple and the Pharisees hear children proclaiming, "Hosanna to the Son of David," in 21:12–17. In this context, there is already a confluence of echoes, allusions, and quotes from the Hebrew Bible. As Jesus cleanses the temple in 21:13, he rebukes those undertaking commercial trading within the temple by quoting Isa 56:7d to describe what the temple should be in contrast with the allusion to Jer 7:11, which indicts the condition of the temple. Then the narrator portrays the blind and the lame coming to the temple to be healed by Jesus in 21:14, which is the familiar echo of new exodus language (e.g., Isa 35:5–6). While this is occurring, the Pharisees heard the children, and they ask Jesus in 21:16 whether he too has heard what the children are saying. Jesus affirms with the pithy particle ναί that he did indeed hear. Then he reciprocates with a rhetorical question that also expects the answer "yes" but begins with the negative to highlight just how discordant the Pharisees' character is with Israel's Scriptures, οὐδέποτε ἀνέγνωτε. This introduction to Jesus's rhetorical question is then followed by a quote of the first clause in Ps 8:3, minus the causal phrase, ἕνεκα τῶν ἐχθρῶν σου.[33] Jesus's use of Ps 8:3 suggests that it is God who has appointed this praise from the mouths of children and so rebukes the Pharisees' complaint. However, by missing the final phrase of Ps 8:3, Jesus avoids the open provocation of suggesting that the purpose is to cause his enemies to cease (לְהַשְׁבִּית; i.e., the Pharisees). While this use of Ps 8:3 functions as a rebuke to the Pharisees, the significance of the context of Ps 8:3 would not have been lost either; the voice of the Davidic king extolling how YHWH is Creator yet who is mindful of humanity and cares for the "son of man" (υἱὸς ἀνθρώπου). It is not that the Psalms have influenced or shaped Jesus's teaching in this instance; rather, he uses the words of Ps 8:3 and the implied context of the Psalm to rebuke. He is teaching through the agency of the Psalms.[34]

After Jesus's brief altercation with the Pharisees in 21:15–16, he then withdrew to Bethany and in the morning returned to Jerusalem (21:17–18). In 21:23, the narrator notes that after reentering the temple, the chief priests and elders approached him while he was teaching. The purpose of their approach is to ask Jesus on whose

---

[32] For example, Matt 5:5//Ps 37:11; 5:6//Ps 42:2, 55:1; 13:34–35//Ps 78:2; 21:16//Ps 8:3; 21:42//Ps 118:22, 23; 22:44–45//Ps 110:1; 23:39//Ps 118:26.

[33] Please note that Matthew depicts Jesus using the LXX translation of Ps 8:3 that renders עֹז ("strength") as αἶνος ("praise").

[34] Contrary to R. T. France, *Jesus and the Old Testament* (Downers Grove, IL: IVP, 1971), 151–2, who states "Jesus' use of the verse depends on its applicability to the children's praise *of him*, and to *his* adversaries. Unless he is here setting himself in the place of Yahweh, the argument is a *non sequitur.*"

authority he is doing "these things," that is, teaching. After Jesus refuses to answer their question in 21:24-27, he then begins teaching in parables in 21:28-43, of which the last parable in the sequence is the parable of the tenants where the tenants plot to kill the son and take his inheritance (21:33-41). Jesus teaches in 21:40-41 that the master of the vineyard would put those tenants to death in response and find new tenants who would fulfill their responsibilities. Jesus then asks a rhetorical question in v. 42 where the expected answer is, "Of course!"—yet it is phrased negatively, οὐδέποτε ἀνέγνωτε ἐν ταῖς γραφαῖς. This quotative frame then introduces Ps 118:22-23.

Psalm 118 is placed after the *hallel* psalms (Pss 111-117) and before the great *torah* psalm, Ps 119. In this context, Ps 118 is a thanksgiving for YHWH's help in battle. Yet, it is also an antiphonal psalm that envisions the "king leading the people in a public celebration of YAHWEH's faithfulness toward himself specifically ... and also towards the people in general."[35] Furthermore, the king is singing Ps 118 at the entrance of the temple as he asks for the gates of righteousness to be opened, so that he can enter and give thanks (vv. 19-20).[36] After the king's voice in vv. 5-21, the voice of the assembly then declares a proverb in v. 22, λίθον, ὃν ἀπεδοκίμασαν οἱ οἰκοδομοῦντες, οὗτος ἐγενήθη εἰς κεφαλὴν γωνίας.[37] There is some contention as to whether the phrase κεφαλὴν γωνίας ("head of the corner") refers to the capstone, which is the final stone placed at the top of the building that marks completion, or the cornerstone, which is the stone laid first from which the whole is built.[38] Either way, a stone that was not deemed worthy to be part of the building was then used at an essential point. The psalmist attributes this reversal from rejection to elevation to none other than YHWH in v. 23. By using this quote after the parable where the son is killed by the tenants, the intimation is that while Jesus might be rejected by the Jewish leadership, it is God's doing that he has a pivotal purpose in the kingdom of heaven. Also, by quoting Ps 118:22-23, Jesus evokes the context of the whole psalm. It is not insignificant that Jesus is inside the temple as he quotes a psalm where the Davidic king is asking to enter and affirms that only the righteous may enter (Ps 118:20b). By applying Ps 118:22-23 to himself, Jesus is essentially making the claim that he is the Davidic king. Again, Jesus teaches through the agency of Scripture, which is to rebuke yet also to reveal his self-understanding about the significance of his identity.

The final example is Jesus's use of Ps 110:1 in 22:44-45. With the Pharisees huddled together, Jesus asks them about their view of the Messiah and whose son he is (22:41-42). While the Pharisees affirmed the Messiah will be the son of David, Jesus then asks in 22:43 how David can call the Messiah "lord" in Ps 110:1b-d (LXX), which he then quotes (22:44). The issue here is not the initial "Lord" (ὁ κύριος) in the LXX translation

---

[35] Jamie A. Grant, *King as Exemplar: The Function of Deuteronomy's Kingship Law in the Shaping of the Book of Psalms* (Atlanta, GA: SBL, 2010), 127.
[36] Also, Grant, *The King as Exemplar*, 128-9.
[37] The voice of the assembly continues to 118:27 and this is observed by the use of the plural in these verses. See Hans-Joachim Kraus, *Psalms 60-150*, CC (Minneapolis, MN: Fortress, 1993), 394-5; W. Dennis Tucker and Jamie A. Grant, *Psalms Volume 2*, NIVAC (Grand Rapids, MI: Zondervan, 2018), 676.
[38] For the understanding of capstone, see Tucker and Grant, *Psalms Volume 2*, 684; Hagner, *Matthew 14-28*, 622. See Blomberg, *CNTUOT*, 73, as an example of the view that the cornerstone is a foundation stone.

of Ps 110:1, as this is יְהֹוָה in Hebrew, but rather the "lord" referred to in the phrase Τῷ κυρίῳ μου. Jesus posits a second rhetorical question in v. 45 following his quote of Ps 110:1b-d, which focuses on how the Messiah can be David's son when David calls him Lord. The purpose of Jesus's rhetorical questions in 22:43–45 is to highlight the Pharisees' lack of understanding about their own Scriptures when they fail to articulate that the Messiah is both divine and the son of David. Sandwiched between these two questions, Jesus appropriates Ps 110:1b-d to exemplify his point. While Jesus is not using Scripture as an agent of teaching in this instance, his use of Ps 110:1b-d shows an intimate understanding of Israel's Scriptures that once more surpasses that of the Pharisees.

2.5 Conclusion

By examining examples of how Jesus uses the Law, the Prophets, and the Writings, in his teaching as portrayed by Matthew's Gospel, this chapter has observed that Jesus is not *merely* influenced by, or conversant with, Israel's Scriptures in the Hebrew Bible. Jesus's teaching is shaped by the Hebrew Bible and embodies the Law, the Prophets, and the Writings. Jesus teaches through the agency of Israel's Scriptures when correcting and rebuking misappropriated applications and understandings. Matthew depicts Jesus's teaching as being characterized by an intimate understanding of Israel's Scriptures where his ability to interpret Scripture is unparalleled by his contemporaries within his setting. Concerning the Law specifically, Jesus's teaching is far from being contrary to its commands and instructions or even being "reinterpreted" for a new era in salvation history. Jesus's teaching, as portrayed by Matthew, realigns the present understandings of the Law within the narrative world of the Gospel to the ideological basis of Israel's Law and, specifically, to the nature of covenant faithfulness.

3

Matthew as Teacher of Israel's Scriptures in His Judaic Context

Daniel M. Gurtner

3.1 Introduction

R. T. France's *Matthew: Evangelist and Teacher* has been a primer for serious scholarly inquiry into the first gospel since its publication in 1989.[1] Few single volumes have covered such a wide range of issues with such mastery of the primary and secondary material. Even where one disagrees with France's assessments and conclusions, in *Matthew: Evangelist and Teacher*, his commentary,[2] or other works on the Gospels,[3] he serves as a profitable dialogue partner for critical research in the First Gospel. And he has gone to considerable lengths to analyze Matthew's use of the Old Testament (OT) throughout his important works. In particular, he demonstrates the centrality of "fulfillment" of the Hebrew Bible among the themes of Matthew's Gospel.[4] In his most recent commentary France notes at least fifty-four direct citations of the OT, in addition to 262 allusions and parallels, many of which are concerned with the theme of fulfillment.[5] Table 3.1 attempts to document some of the more widely recognized citations of the OT in Matthew.[6]

This data illustrates the evangelist's well-known preoccupation with the sacred texts of the Hebrew Bible in his narration of the story of Jesus, and is well covered

---

[1] R. T. France, *Matthew: Evangelist and Teacher* (Downers Grove, IL: InterVarsity Press, 1989).
[2] R. T. France, *The Gospel of Matthew*, NICNT (Grand Rapids, MI Eerdmans, 2007).
[3] E.g., R. T. France, *Jesus and the Old Testament* (London: Tyndale, 1971).
[4] See, e.g., France, *Matthew: Evangelist and Teacher*, 166–205.
[5] France, *The Gospel of Matthew*, 10–11.
[6] For the sake of consistency, we will take our cue from France's observation and focus on texts noted as citations by the United Bible Society's 5th edition. Derived from Barbara Aland, Kurt Aland, Johannes Karavidopoulos, Carlo Martini, and Bruce Metzger, eds, *The Greek New Testament*, 5th revised ed. (Stuttgart: Deutsche Bibelgesellschaft, 2014), 860. No effort is made here to identify the veracity or precise textual affinity with these citations, as they are largely agreed upon in other reference works as well as the NA28. Barbara and Kurt Aland, Johannes Karavidopoulos, Carlo Martini, Bruce Metzger, eds. *Novum Testamentum Graece*, 28th revised ed. (Stuttgart: Deutsche Bibelgesellschaft, 2012), 836–78. These and others are fully explored in the dated, but still instructive, work of Robert H. Gundry, *The Use of the Old Testament in St. Matthew's Gospel, with Special Reference to the Messianic Hope*, NovTSup18 (Leiden: Brill, 1967).

Table 3.1 Old Testament Citations in Matthew

Matt 1:23a	Isa 7:14
Matt 1:23b	Isa 8:8, 10
Matt 2:6	Mic 5:2
Matt 2:15	Hos 11:1
Matt 2:18	Jer 31:15
Matt 3:3	Isa 40:3
Matt 4:4	Deut 8:3
Matt 4:6	Ps 91:11–12
Matt 4:7	Deut 6:16
Matt 4:10	Deut 6:13
Matt 4:15–16	Isa 9:1–2
Matt 5:21	Exod 20:13
	Deut 5:17
Matt 5:27	Exod 20:14
	Deut 5:18
Matt 5:31	Deut 24:1
Matt 5:33	Lev 19:12
	Num 30:2
Matt 5:38	Exod 21:24
	Lev 24:20
	Deut 19:21
Matt 5:43	Lev 19:18
Matt 8:17	Isa 53:4
Matt 9:13	Hos 6:6
Matt 10:35–36	Mic 7:6
Matt 11:10	Mal 3:1
Matt 12:7	Hos 6:6
Matt 12:18–20	Isa 42:1–3
Matt 12:21	Isa 42:4
Matt 12:40	Jon 1:17
Matt 13:14–15	Isa 6:9–10
Matt 13:35	Ps 78:2
Matt 15:4a	Exod 20:12
	Deut 5:16
Matt 15:4b	Exod 21:17
Matt 15:8–9	Isa 29:13
Matt 18:16	Deut 19:15
Matt 19:4	Gen 1:27, 5:2
Matt 19:5	Gen 2:24
Matt 19:7	Deut 24:1
Matt 19:18–19	Exod 20:12–16

(continued)

Table 3.1 (continued)

	Deut 5:16–20
Matt 19:19	Lev 19:18
Matt 21:5	Isa 62:11
	Zech 9:9
Matt 21:9	Ps 118:25–26
Matt 21:13	Isa 56:7
Matt 21:16	Ps 8:3
Matt 21:42	Ps 118:22–23
Matt 22:24	Deut 25:5
Matt 22:32	Exod 3:6, 15
Matt 22:37	Deut 6:5
Matt 22:39	Lev 19:18
Matt 22:44	Ps 110:1
Matt 23:39	Ps 118:26
Matt 24:30	Dan 7:13
Matt 26:31	Zech 13:7
Matt 26:64a	Ps 110:1
Matt 26:64b	Dan 7:13
Matt 27:9–10	Zech 11:12–13
Matt 27:46	Ps 22:1

by France and many others. But there is also room to build upon France's important book in relation to his interface with Second Temple Judaism in general and, in particular, instances where Matthew cites OT passages that are also cited by roughly contemporary Jewish sources. Though such considerations are outside the scope of *Matthew: Evangelist and Teacher,* France does engage some of the material, such as in his discussion of the Matthew's literary character (cf. 2 Macc 2:23; Philo, *Moses*; Josephus' *Vita*)[7] and its proposed "school" analogous to the Qumran sectarians (1QS),[8] or its function as a community document similar to that of Qumran (1QS).[9] France naturally turns to the important historical events surrounding the destruction of the temple for the date and setting of the gospel (Josephus, *B.J.* 6.300–9; 353–5, 363–4, 406–8; 7.218; *A.J.* 8.45–9).[10] He utilizes Second Temple literature in his study of Matthew's "fulfillment" language (4QTest; 4QFlor)[11] and typology (cf. Josephus, *A.J.* 2.205ff),[12] in addition to Matthew's affinities with various aspects of wisdom traditions (Wis 6:12–11:1; Sir 6:23–30; 24:8–12; 51:23–27; cf. 1 En 42; Bar 3:37).[13] France's rich discussion of

---

[7] France, *Matthew: Evangelist and Teacher*, 124, 126, 143n.27.
[8] France, *Matthew: Evangelist and Teacher*, 113.
[9] France, *Matthew: Evangelist and Teacher*, 252.
[10] France, *Matthew: Evangelist and Teacher*, 84, 88, 214.
[11] France, *Matthew: Evangelist and Teacher*, 177.
[12] France, *Matthew: Evangelist and Teacher*, 188.
[13] France, *Matthew: Evangelist and Teacher*, 272, 302, 304.

Matthean Christology is augmented by his utilization of Second Temple material in his consideration of the "Son of Man" (e.g., 1 En 37–71)[14] and "Son of God" (e.g., Wis 2:10–20; 5:5; Sir 4:10; Ps Sol 13:9; 1QSa 2.11–12; 4QpsDanA^a; 4QFlor)[15] traditions they contain. What seldom receives attention by France or others, however, is the manner in which Jewish authors roughly contemporary with Matthew utilize those same texts.

The purpose of the present chapter is to reflect upon these texts largely in a comparative manner, determining in what ways Matthew may have interpreted authoritative texts from Israel's past for his own purposes in a manner that is distinct or similar to other Jews of antiquity. The Jewish sources considered here are deliberately broad: the various texts from Qumran (Dead Sea Scrolls) and the Judean Desert (Masada, Wadi Muraba'at, Naḥal Ḥever, etc.), the Apocrypha from the LXX, a selection of Jewish Pseudepigrapha from the Second Temple period,[16] as well as the writings of Flavius Josephus and Philo of Alexandria.

3.2 Common Citations

Of the numerous OT texts cited in Matthew, some are not attested at all in Second Temple Jewish texts.[17] Others appear but not as citations but rather as manuscripts of the OT texts themselves.[18] Still others are cited in Matthew and Second Temple texts, but the latter are of disputed provenance.[19] Finally, there are some OT texts which seem to be quite important in Second Temple material but seem much less important to Matthew. For our purposes it is sufficient to survey in broad brush strokes OT texts that are cited in both Matthew and Second Temple Jewish texts.

---

[14] France, *Matthew: Evangelist and Teacher*, 288–92.
[15] France, *Matthew: Evangelist and Teacher*, 292–8.
[16] For a definition and articulation of this scope, see Daniel M. Gurtner, *Introducing the Pseudepigrapha of Second Temple Judaism: Message, Context, and Significance* (Grand Rapids, MI: Baker, 2021), 1–18.
[17] Gen 5:2 (Matt 19:4); Deut 6:16 (Matt 4:7); Job 16:19 (Matt 21:9); Ps 6:9 (ET 8) (Matt 7:23); Ps 8:3 (ET 2) (Matt 21:16); Ps 22:2 (ET 1) (Matt 27:46); Ps 22:19 (ET 18) (Matt 27:35); Ps 62:13 (ET 12) (Matt 16:27); Ps 78:2 (Matt 13:35); Ps 110:1 (Matt 22:44; 26:64a); Isa 8:23–9:1 (ET 9:1–2) (Matt 4:15–16); Isa 29:13 (Matt 15:8–9); Isa 29:18 (Matt 11:5); Jer 6:16 (Matt 11:29); Jer 7:11 (Matt 21:13); Dan 3:6 (Matt 13:42, 50); Hos 11:1 (Matt 2:15); Zech 11:12–13 (Matt 27:9–10); Mal 3:1 (Matt 11:10).
[18] Lev 24:20 (Matt 5:38; 4QRP^d [4Q366]); Num 30:2 (Matt 5:33; 4QNum^b [4Q27]); Deut 10:20 (Matt 4:10; 4Qmez^c [4Q151]); Deut 19:15 (Matt 18:16; 4QDeut^{k2} [4Q38a]); Deut 19:21 (Matt 5:38; 4QDeut^f [4Q33]; 4QRP^c [4Q365]; 4QDeut^h [4Q35?]); Deut 24:1 (Matt 5:31; 4QDeut^a [4Q28]; Matt 19:7; 4QDeut^a [4Q28]); Ps 42:6, 12 (ET 5, 11) (Matt 26:38; 4QPs^c [4Q85]; 4QPs^u [4Q98^d]); Ps 91:11–12 (Matt 4:6; 11QApocryphalPss VI [11Q11]; 4QPs^b [4Q84]); Ps 104:12 (Matt 13:32; 4QPs^j [4Q93]); Ps 118:22–23 (Matt 21:42; 4QPs^b [4Q84]); Ps 118:25–26 (Matt 21:9; 4QPs^b [4Q84]; 11QPs^a [11Q5]); Ps 118:26 (Matt 23:39; 4QPs^b [4Q84]; 11QPs^a [11Q5]; 4QPs^b [4Q84]); Ps 148:1 (Matt 21:9; 11QPs^a [11Q5]); Isa 6:9–10 (Matt 13:14–15; 4QpIsa^b [4Q162]?; 4QIsa^f [4Q60]); Isa 7:14 (Matt 1:23a; 4QIsa^l [4Q65]); Isa 8:10 (Matt 1:23b; 4QIsa^e [4Q59]; 4QIsa^f [4Q60]); Isa 13:10 (Matt 11:5; 4QIsa^b [4Q56]); Isa 35:5 (Matt 11:5; 1QIsa^b [1Q8]); Isa 42:4 (Matt 12:21; 4QIsa^b [4Q56]; 4QIsa^h [4Q62]); Isa 42:18 (Matt 11:5; 4QIsa^g [4Q61]); Isa 53:4 (Matt 8:17; 1QIsa^a [1Q8]); Isa 56:7 (Matt 21:13; 1QIsa^a [1Q8]; 4QIsa^i [4Q62a]); Isa 62:11 (Matt 21:5; 1QIsa^b [1Q8]); Mic 5:1, 3 (ET 5:2, 4) (Matt 2:6; 8ḤevXII gr [8Ḥev1]).
[19] There are too many to account for here. However, some are found in the Testament of Solomon (e.g., Ps 22:1 [Matt 27:46]; T. Sol. 6:8]; Ps 118:22–23 [Matt 21:42; T. Sol. 22:7; 23:4]; Isa 7:14 [Matt 1:23; T. Sol. 6:8; 11:6; 15:12] see Gurtner, *Pseudepigrapha*, 208) and others in the Testament of Abraham (Deut 19:15 in T. Abr 13:8 [Rec A]; see D. C. Allison Jr., *Testament of Abraham*, CEJL [Berlin: de Gruyter, 2003], 28–32, 38–9).

3.2.1 Common Citations from the Pentateuch

The Gospel of Matthew gives surprisingly little explicit (citation) attention to the book of Genesis, and does so only in connection with the subject of marriage in a single pericope (Matt 19:4 [Gen 1:27]; Matt 19:5 [Gen 2:24]). In the context Jesus arrives in the region of Judea beyond the Jordan (Matt 19:1), where he is followed by large crowds, whom he cures (19:2). There he is confronted by some Pharisees who come "testing him" (πειράζοντες αὐτὸν, 19:3a), asking him whether it is lawful for a man to divorce his wife "for any cause" (κατὰ πᾶσαν αἰτίαν, 19:3b). Jesus responds with an appeal that at the beginning God "made them male and female" (Matt 19:4), which clearly draws from Gen 1:27 (cf. Gen 5:2), and goes on to argue (Matt 19:5) that the statement "the two shall become one flesh," quoting Gen 2:24, implies a unity joined by God which should not be broken (Matt 19:6). The passage goes on to discuss Moses's concession of divorce (Matt 19:7–8a), God's intention for marriage (Matt 19:8b), and Jesus's teaching on the subject (Matt 19:9). The question surely centers around debated interpretations of Deut 24:1, which pertains to a marriage in which a wife does not please her husband and so he writes her a certificate of divorce. The position of the school of Hillel, who likely held the dominant view (cf. Philo, *Spec. Laws.* 3.30; Josephus, *A.J.* 4.253), held that many things constituted grounds for divorce (cf. Tg. Onq. Deut. 24:1; Pal. Tg. Deut. 24:1).[20] Jesus seems to align more with the school of Shammai, which understood the text of Deut. 24:1 to refer to the wife's unchastity in particular (*m. Giṭ.* 9.10; *b. Giṭ.* 90a-b; *Sipre* on Deut. 24.1).[21]

Both texts from Genesis are cited in Second Temple material, but with differing emphases. Most allusions to Gen 1:27 focus on the creation of humanity in the image of God (Wis 2:23; Sir 17:3; Philo, *Heir* 48 §231; 4Q504 frag 8 (recto).4; cf. T. Naph. 8:6), a notion not raised in the Matthean citation. Others use it as the basis for expounding aspects of the nature of humanity's original creation, whether it is dominion over creatures (Wis 9:2), the power of free choice (Sir 15:14), emotions and inclinations (4 Macc 2:21). Only twice it is used in the context of marriage. In Tobit it is alluded to in a prayer by Tobias as the grounds for taking Sarah as his wife (Tob 8:4–7). At Qumran it seems to be used as grounds for monogamy (6Q15 1.3; par CD-A 4.21).

The passage from Gen 2:24 relates to a man leaving his parents and clinging to his wife as one flesh. Matthew uses this not simply as a statement about the nature of marriage but its permanent state ("what God has joined together, let no one separate" (NRSV), Matt 19:5–6). In Second Temple Judaism the text is only found in manuscripts of 4QInstruction (4Q416 [=4QInstruction[b]] frg 2 iii 21–iv 1; par 4Q418

---

[20] See W. D. Davies and Dale C. Allison, *A Critical and Exegetical Commentary on the Gospel According to Saint Matthew*, 3 vols. (Edinburgh: T&T Clark, 1988, 1991, 1997), 3.9.

[21] Davies and Allison, *Matthew*, 1.530.

[=4QInstructionᵈ] 10.4–5),²² which is a Jewish wisdom text preserved in fragmentary copies from Qumran caves 1 and 4 (1Q26, 4Q415, 4Q416, 4Q417, 4Q418, 4Q418a, 4Q418c [?], and 4Q423).²³ This text urges the addressee to pursue truth, receive instruction, and gain understanding (e.g., 4Q417 1 i 25, 2 i 1–7; 4Q418 81.17), with the explicit goal for the reader to be able to distinguish between good and bad (e.g., 4Q416 1.15, 4Q417 2 i 8, 4Q418 2.7).²⁴ The present citation occurs in a pragmatic section advising the addressee about social relations to one's spouse (e.g., 4Q416 2 ii 21 [?], 2 iii 20–21).²⁵ Among other things, it gives instructions on marriage heavily dependent on Gen 1–3.²⁶ It pertains to instructions on taking one's wife, and being "joined together" (in marriage; בהתחברכה; 4Q416 2.iii.21), and describes walking together "with the help of your flesh" (יחד התהלך עם עזר בשרכה), an allusion to Eve being made of the flesh of Adam (cf. Gen 2:23). Elsewhere 4QInstruction affirms that the husband and wife are "one flesh" (4Q416 2.iv.4; cf. Gen 2:24). The end of 4Q416 2.iii.21 is fragmentary, but surely cites Gen 2:24: "therefore a man leaves," as is seen by the next line (4Q416 2.iv.1):²⁷ " 'his father [and] his mother,' and thus you will clea[ve to his wife, and become one flesh (with her)]" (4Q416 2.iv.1). The text goes on to describe the nature of their marriage; that the husband has dominion over the wife (ll. 2–3) and that they shall be one flesh (ותהיה [לך לבשׂר אחד, ll. 3–4). The overriding burden of this portion of 4Q416, especially column iv of fragment 2, is that of marriage and the authority of the husband over the wife. In this regard one sees the appeal to the oneness of the married couple found in Gen 2:24 and referenced by Jesus, but there is nothing in this text regarding the permanence of marriage or the question of divorce, as in Matthew's text.

There are several common citations from the book of Exodus, most of which pertain to the Decalogue. The setting is Moses atop Mount Sinai (Exod 19:16–25) and recounts the words spoken by God himself (Exod 20:1), and is repeated elsewhere with variations (Exod 34:17–26; Deut 5:6–21; 27:15–26; cf. Ps 15:2–5; Lev 19:1–4, 11–19a, 26–37; Ezek 18:5–9; etc.).²⁸ In the Exodus account, first the Lord identifies himself as the one who delivered Israel from slavery in Egypt (Exod 20:2) and exhorts Israel to have no other gods (20:3), make no idols as rivals to God (20:4–6), and to honor his name (20:7). It is the following section (Exod 20:8–17) where the familiar list of regulations is found, and from which Matthew and other Jewish literary contemporaries draw.

---

[22] Elisa Uusimäki, "Instruction (4QInstruction)," in *The T&T Clark Encyclopedia of Second Temple Judaism*, 2 vols., ed. Daniel M. Gurtner and Loren T. Stuckenbruck (London: T&T Clark, 2020), 1.247–9. (= *ESTJ*)

[23] E. J. C. Tigchelaar, *To Increase Learning for the Understanding Ones: Reading and Reconstructing the Fragmentary Early Jewish Sapiential Text 4QInstruction*, STDJ 44 (Leiden: Brill, 2001), Matthew J. Goff, *4QInstruction*, WLAW 2 (Atlanta, GA: Society of Biblical Literature, 2013), 1–7.

[24] Uusimäki, "Instruction (4QInstruction)," 1.247.

[25] It is noted for promoting "social hierarchy between sexes" and giving "a subordinate position to women" (e.g., 4Q415 9.8–9; 4Q416 2 iv 1–7). Uusimäki, "Instruction (4QInstruction)," 1.249.

[26] See detailed discussion and further secondary literature in Goff, *4Q Instruction*, 116.

[27] Goff, *4QInstruction*, 117; also Jean-Sébastien Rey, *4QInstruction: Sagesse et eschatology*, STDJ 81 (Leiden: Brill, 2009), 168; John Strugnell and Daniel J. Harrington, *Qumran Cave 4.XXIV: Sapiential Texts, Part 2. 4QInstruction (Mûsār Lĕ Mēbîn): 4Q415ff. With a Re-edition of 1Q26*, DJD 34 (Oxford: Clarendon, 1999), 113.

[28] See John I. Durham, *Exodus*, WBC 3 (Waco, TX: Word, 1987), 280–1.

Matthew records the instruction to *honor one's father and mother* twice (Matt 15:4a; 19:19a), and it is found in two OT sources (Exod 20:12; Deut 5:16). In the first citation Pharisees and scribes come to Jesus in Jerusalem (Matt 15), where they confront Jesus about his disciples' handwashing practices (Matt 15:2). In response Jesus accuses his opponents of breaking the "commandment of God" (τὴν ἐντολὴν τοῦ θεοῦ) for the sake of their traditions (Matt 15:3). Specifically, he accuses them of breaking two commandments: First, "honor your father and mother" (Matt 15:4a) and, second, "Whoever speaks evil of father or mother must surely die" (Matt 15:4b). The first of these comes from Exod 20:12 and Deut 5:16. Both of these in their original contexts come with promises of a result ("so that"; ἵνα; לְמַעַן) for long life in the Promised Land (Exod 20:12b; Deut 5:16b). Both texts are found in manuscript form at Qumran but primarily in, for the Deuteronomy text, phylacteries[29] and once, for Exod 20:12b, in mezuzot (4Qmez^a [=4Q149]). These are segments of texts from the Torah written on animal skin and placed within leather containers.[30] Phylacteries were attached by leather thongs on the forehead and the hand. Mezuzot were attached to the gates and doorposts of homes. This practice was based on the instructions from the Pentateuch itself (Exod 13:9, 16; Deut 6:8; 11:18).[31] Fragments from twenty-six phylacteries were found at Qumran,[32] in which citations from Exodus (12:43–13:16) and Deuteronomy (5:1–6:9; 10:12–11:21; 32) are most common.[33] Only once is either of our texts preserved at Qumran in a manuscript form (4QDeutⁿ [4Q141]).

Matthew uses the citation as an example of legal regulations that he presumes are still valid yet which Jesus's opponents neglect in favor of their traditions (παράδοσις, Matt 15:4). The same holds true in the second instance where Matthew cites Exod 20:12/ Deut 5:16 (Matt 19:19a) in relation to a command that Jesus instructs a would-be disciple to keep (Matt 19:17), and that he does indeed keep (Matt 19:20). Given its popularity in phylacteries and mezuzot it comes as no surprise that it was widely cited and alluded to in Jewish texts of the second temple period. By far the earliest of these occurs in the Ahiqar Proverbs, an Aramaic wisdom text dating originally no later than the fifth century BCE.[34] It pronounces as evil one who takes no pride in his father and mother's name, and wishes that "Shama[sh] not shine [on him]" (*Ahiq*. 138). This is a reference to the Mesopotamian sun-god, who functions as the administrator of justice in some ancient Near Eastern contexts.[35] Literary dependence is anything but clear,

---

[29] E.g., 1Qphyl (1Q13); 4Qphyl^b (4Q129); 4Qphyl^g (4Q134); 4Qphyl^j (4Q137); 4Qphyl^l (4Q139); 4Qphyl^o (4Q142).

[30] Stephen Alan Reed, "Phylacteries and Mezuzot," *ESTJ* 2.610–611. See also S. Reed, "Physical Features of Excerpted Torah Texts," in *Jewish and Christian Scripture as Artifact and Canon*, ed. Craig Evans and Daniel Zacharias (London: T&T Clark, 2009), 82–104.

[31] It is attested in Second Temple literature (*Arist*. 159; Philo, *Spec. Leg*. 26.137–139; cf. Matt 23:5; Josephus, *A.J*. 4.213).

[32] See E. Tov, "Appendix: Phylacteries (Tefillin) and Mezuzot," *Revised Lists of the Texts from the Judaean Desert* (Oxford: Clarendon, 2010), 131–2.

[33] Reed, "Phylacteries and Mezuzot," *ESTJ* 2.610.

[34] Seth A. Bledsoe, "Ahiqar Proverbs," *ESTJ* 1.100–3. See I. Kottsieper, *Die Sprache der Ahiqarsprüche*, BZAW 194 (Berlin: De Gruyter, 1990).

[35] J. M. Lindenberger, "Ahiqar (Seventh to Sixth Century B.C.): A New Introduction and Translation," in *The Old Testament Pseudepigrapha*, 2 vols., ed. J. H. Charlesworth (New York: Doubleday, 1983, 1985), 2.485.

and it may be more likely that Ahiqar shares a common milieu with the OT texts than that it is at this point dependent on it. But the biblical text's appearance is found elsewhere in Second Temple wisdom traditions, such as the Sentences of Pseudo-Phocylides. This is a Greek didactic wisdom poem of 230 verses that expounds on a combination of ethical commands from the Greek translation (Septuagint) of the Law alongside non-Jewish Hellenistic writers of moral treatises completed by the middle of the first century CE.[36] It exhorts the virtues of honoring God first "and afterward your parents" (*Ps. Phoc.* 8; cf. vv. 179–180; 4Q416 2 iii.15–19 [=4QInstruction^b]; 4Q418 9–10). The same notion is reflected in the Sibylline Oracles, where the author lauds those who "honor only the Immortal who always rules, and then their parents" (*Sib. Or.* 3.594; OTP). Nearly an entire chapter of Sirach (ch. 3, mss A and C) is devoted to expounding the commandment about honoring one's father and mother, claiming that "those who honor their father atone for sins, and those who respect their mother are like those who lay up treasure" (Sir 3:3–4 NRSV; cf. Sir 7:27). The chapter continues (vv. 5–16) to extol the virtues and blessings of honoring one's father and mother, and corresponding curses for those who forsakes a father and angers a mother. The *Letter of Aristeas* too insists that the ones to whom a person must show honor are, first, "To his parents, always, for God's very great commandment concerns the honor due to parents" (*Arist.* 228; OTP). In Jubilees the instruction to honor one's father and mother was given by Noah to his progeny in the twenty-eighth jubilee (Jub 7:20), and Isaac claims that his son, Jacob, honored his parents (Jub 35:12–13).[37] The same command is issued in *Biblical Antiquities*, where the promise of God's blessings to the obedient is embellished from the Exodus text (*LAB* 11:9; cf. *LAB* 4:5; 13:7; 21:2; 60:2).[38] Later in a series of indictments against Israel for breaking his commands (cf. Judges 17), God says, "whereas I have told them to love father and mother, they have dishonored me, their Creator" (*LAB* 44:7; OTP).[39] On his deathbed Tobit exhorts his son, Tobias: "Honor your mother and do not abandon her all the days of her life. Do whatever pleases her, and do not grieve her in anything" (Tob 4:3 NRSV). In these and other instances (e.g., Philo, *Spec. Leg.* 2.235, 261; 4Q158 [4QRP^a] *frags.* 7–8 l. 1) the instruction is well known, cited, and utilized as an ethical mandate for Israelites.

The second citation in Jesus's rebuke of his opponents comes from Exod 21:17, in a series of case laws (Exod 21:1–23:9), this one pertaining to one who speaks evil of one's father or mother, who is to be put to death (τελευτήσει θανάτῳ; מוֹת יוּמָת).[40] This is cited only in Philo of Alexandria (*Spec. Leg.* 2.248), in an expanded discussion of those who ill-treat parents and its consequences.

Other commands from the Decalogue are also cited in Matthew and Second Temple texts. Notably the prohibition of *murder* (Exod 20:13 // Deut 5:17) is cited as an ethical mandate in both Judaism (*LAB* 11:11; 44:6; Philo, *Dec.* 1.36; *Spec. Leg.* 4.1; Ps. Phoc. 4; cf. 4Q158 [4QRP^a] *frags.* 7–8 l.1) and Matthew (Matt 19:18b), but it is

---

[36] Gurtner, *Pseudepigrapha*, 353.
[37] See James C. VanderKam, *Jubilees 22–50*, Hermeneia (Minneapolis, MN: Fortress, 2018), 945–6.
[38] Frederick J. Murphy, *Pseudo-Philo: Rewriting the Bible* (Oxford: Oxford University Press, 1993), 67.
[39] In this context, the nature of their dishonoring God is idolatry. See Murphy, *Pseudo-Philo*, 173–7.
[40] See William H. C. Propp, *Exodus 19–40*, ABC 2a (New York: Doubleday, 2006), 213.

also accounted for in Matthew among the items requiring a righteousness exceeding that of the scribes and Pharisees (Matt 5:20), where Jesus explains that violation of this command (Matt 5:21) also includes anger (Matt 5:22). The same can be said for prohibition of *adultery* (Exod 20:14 // Deut 5:18), which is a Jewish ethical mandate (*LAB* 11:10; Ps Phoc 3; Philo, *Spec. Leg.* 4.1; *Dec.* 1.36) found in Matthew (Matt 19:18c) and a regulation violated by lust (ἐπιθυμέω, Matt 5:27–29). However, the Deuteronomy form of the command is mostly found in phylacteries[41] and once in manuscript form (4QDeut^n [4Q141]). For Matthew, then, these ethical mandates require attention to what occurs "in [one's] heart" (ἐν τῇ καρδίᾳ αὐτοῦ, Matt 5:28) in order to enter the kingdom of heaven (εἰσέλθητε εἰς τὴν βασιλείαν τῶν οὐρανῶν, Matt 5:20).

Other laws common to Matthew and Judaism are used slightly differently in Matthew, where they do not occur in the context of advocating a superior righteousness, as in the antitheses (Matt 5:20–48). Instead, they are cited in the expected regulations repeated by Jesus to the rich young ruler (Matt 19:18). These include, first, the prohibition of *stealing* (Exod 20:15; Matt 19:18d), which is attested at Qumran (4Q158 [4QRP^a] *frags.* 7–8 l. 1) and simply recited as ethical instruction by Philo (*Spec. Leg.* 4.1; *Dec.* 1.36). The regulation against *bearing false witness* (Exod 20:16) is also cited as an ethical regulation both in Matthew (19:18e) and Judaism (*LAB* 11:12; 44:6–7; Ps. Phoc. 7, 12–14; cf. 4Q158 [4QRP^a] *frags.* 7–8 l. 2). A final law from Exodus regarding *retributive justice* (Exod 21:24), found once in textual form at Qumran (4QpaleoExod^m [4Q22]), is cited in Matt 5:38, where again the greater righteousness application of it is espoused (Matt 5:39). Its single appearance in Second Temple material describes how Cain was killed when the stones of his house fell upon him, because he killed Abel with a stone. And so, the author asserts, "with a stone he was killed by righteous judgment" (Jub 4:31, OTP).[42]

One more citation of Exodus is found in Matt 11 in an extended teaching by Jesus on John the Baptist (Matt 11:7–15). Here Jesus declares that John is the messenger sent before Jesus to prepare his way (Matt 11:10). But the citation properly comes from Mal 3:23–24, as most scholars recognize, in relation to the coming of an eschatological Elijah at the day of the Lord (Mal 4:5).[43] The Malachi text is only vaguely referenced in Judaism (4Q558 *frag.* 1 ii.3–4). But the Exodus passage itself is an expansion upon the role of God's angel in the deliverance of Israel from Egypt (Exod 23:20; cf. Philo, *Agr.* 1.51; *Mirg.* 1.174). But in Matthew the connection with Exodus is less explicit and developed than it is in Mark, where it is conflated with Mal 3:1 and Isa 40:3 (Mark 1:2–3).[44]

Similar to laws from Exodus, a law from Leviticus is also found in Matt 5 and contemporary Jewish texts. The instruction to Israel, given by God himself, prohibits the Israelite from swearing falsely "by my name" (בִשְׁמִי לַשָּׁקֶר, τῷ ὀνόματί μου; Lev 19:12a), suggesting that such would constitute "profaning the name of your God" (וְחִלַּלְתָּ אֶת־שֵׁם אֱלֹהֶיךָ, βεβηλώσετε τὸ ὄνομα τοῦ θεοῦ ὑμῶν; Lev 19:12b).[45] Matthew

---

[41] 1Qphyl (1Q13); 4Qphyl^b (4Q129); 4Qphyl^g (4Q134); 4Qphyl^j (4Q137); 4Qphyl^l (4Q139).
[42] See James C. VanderKam, *Jubilees 1–21*, Hermeneia (Minneapolis, MN: Fortress, 2018), 266–7.
[43] See, e.g., Ulrich Luz, *Matthew 8–10*, Hermeneia (Minneapolis, MN: Fortress, 2001), 138.
[44] See Daniel M. Gurtner, "'Old Exodus' and 'New Exodus' in the Gospel of Mark," in *Exodus in the New Testament*, LNTS, ed. Seth M. Ehorn (London: T&T Clark, 2022), 57–72.
[45] See John E. Hartley, *Leviticus*, WBC 4 (Dallas, TX: Word, 1992), 314–15.

raises this text when addressing traditions of the "ancients" (τοῖς ἀρχαίοις, Matt 5:33) that prohibit swearing falsely (οὐκ ἐπιορκήσεις) but require keeping vows made to the Lord (ἀποδώσεις δὲ τῷ κυρίῳ τοὺς ὅρκους σου, Matt 5:33). Matthew's Jesus responds by insisting that one not swear at all (μὴ ὀμόσαι ὅλως, Matt 5:34) and simply keep one's word (ναὶ ναί, οὒ οὔ, Matt 5:37). Pseudo-Phocylides applies the concept by forbidding perjury (*Ps. Phoc.* 16–17). The Damascus Document (CD-A) affirms that if one swears and transgresses, he profanes God's name (15.3). The remainder of the usages pertain to swearing the "oath of the covenant" (בשבועת הברית, CD 1.6) that Moses established with Israel (CD 15.8–9) and an elaborate system of oath-taking among the Qumran sectarians.[46] Matthew is distinct in his absolute prohibition of vows, though explicit citation of the Levitical text is wanting.

A Levitical regulation of a very different kind is cited explicitly no less than three times in Matthew alone. In the context of prohibition of personal vengeance (Lev 19:18a), the law affirms that the Israelite "shall love your neighbor as yourself" (וְאָהַבְתָּ לְרֵעֲךָ כָּמוֹךָ, καὶ ἀγαπήσεις τὸν πλησίον σου ὡς σεαυτόν; Lev 19:18b). The three locations in Matthew in which the text is cited are, first, in the "antitheses" of the Sermon on the Mount, where the evangelist conflates the command with a surprising alternative: "You shall love your neighbor" (Lev 19:18b; Matt 5:43a) and "hate your enemy" (Matt 5:43b). In response ("but I say to you..."; ἐγὼ δὲ λέγω ὑμῖν, Matt 5:44) Jesus commands his disciples to, among other things, love their enemies (ἀγαπᾶτε τοὺς ἐχθροὺς ὑμῶν, 5:44b). The instruction is seemingly in response to a mistaken alternative to the positive aspect of the command. Of course there is no such command to one's enemies, though Davies and Allison characteristically muster a host of texts—Jewish and otherwise—that may be taken to infer a similar sentiment.[47] The closest parallels they find are from Qumran, where the sectarians are exhorted "to detest all the sons of darkness" (ולשנוא כול בני חושך, 1QS 1.10). Similarly, Matthew's Jesus lists this command among others in response to the young man's inquiry about inheriting eternal life (Matt 19:19). Finally, a lawyer among the Pharisees asks Jesus which commandment in the law is greatest (Matt 22:34–36). After first citing the command to love God (Matt 22:37; cf. Deut 6:5; 10:12; Josh 22:5), he quotes Lev 19:18: "You shall love your neighbor as yourself" (Matt 22:39). Jesus claims this command is "like" the first (ὁμοία, 22:39), and insists all the law and the prophets "hang" (κρέμαται) hang on these two commands (ἐν ταύταις ταῖς δυσὶν ἐντολαῖς, Matt 22:40).

This love command is echoed in the instructions of Noah in Jubilees (Jub 7:20) and a hallmark of the Jewish faith recited to the king in the *Letter of Aristeas* (§228). In Sirach it is not commanded but observed as a commonality: "Every creature loves its like, and every person the neighbor" (Sir 13:15 NRSV). Elsewhere citation of the love command is found only in the Damascus Document, where it is listed as among the charitable characteristics of the sectarian community for "each to love his brother like

---

[46] See Yonder Moynihan Gillihan, "Oaths and Vows," *ESTJ* 2.549–50. J.-A. Martens, "A Second Best Voyage: Judaism and Jesus on Oaths and Vows" (PhD diss., MacMaster University, Canada, 1991).
[47] Davies and Allison, *Matthew*, 1.549, citing Deut 7:20; 20:16; 23:4, 7; 30:7; Pss 26:5; 137:7–9; 139:19–22; cf. Polybius 18.37.7; Hesiod, *Op.* 342–3; Plato, *Tim.* 17d–18a; *Rep.* 375c; *Meno* 71e; Tacitus, *Hist.* 5.5–6.

himself" (לאהוב איש את אחיהו כמהו, CD A 6.20–21). While the allusion is undoubtedly to the Leviticus love command, it seems that the language of "his brother" (אחיהו) rather than "neighbor" (עֵר, Lev 19:18) applies the command more immediately to fellow Qumran sectarians (cf. CD-A 8.5–6).

From the book of Numbers Matthew and contemporary Jewish texts cite only a single source, Num 27:17. Here Moses speaks to the Lord, asking him to appoint someone to succeed him in leading Israel when he is gone "so that the congregation of the Lord may not be like sheep without a shepherd" (LXX ὡσεὶ πρόβατα οἷς οὐκ ἔστιν ποιμήν, Num 27:17). Then the Lord appoints Joshua for the task (Num 27:18). The statement appears verbatim in Hebrew in 2 Chron 18:16, where the prophet Micaiah utters it against the king of Israel. In Matthew the designation of people as sheep without a shepherd is applied to the crowds to whom Jesus ministered, who were harassed and helpless, "like sheep without a shepherd" (ὡσεὶ πρόβατα μὴ ἔχοντα ποιμένα, Matt 9:36). This is sometimes inferred to be a polemic against Jewish leadership (cf. Zech 11:16–17), but Luz is correct that there is no indication of such polemic here.[48] The "shepherd" becomes a metaphor for messianic figures (cf. Jer 3:15; Ezek 34:23–23; 47:24; Ps. Sol. 17:40), and has been discussed extensively by Wayne Baxter.[49] While the metaphor is widely used in contemporary Jewish writings,[50] citations of Num 27:17 are sparse. It is cited in Judith 11:19, where Israel will be left like a "sheep without a shepherd"[51] in reference not to a wayward leader of Israel but God's benevolent protection, which will be withdrawn from Jerusalem and Judea to allow Assyrian conquest when the inhabitants violate God's dietary laws (Jdt 11:13).[52] Philo of Alexandria likens the mind's rejection of pleasure and attachment to virtue as analogues to a shepherd of sheep (ποιμὴν προβάτων), a charioteer and pilot, not permitting it to be without "superintendent or guide" (ἐπιστάτου καὶ ἡγεμόνος; Philo, Sacr. 1.45). These analogies may connote the LXX concept of ὡσεὶ πρόβατα οἷς οὐκ ἔστιν ποιμήν (Num 27:17). Though not explicitly citing Numbers, 5Q504 regards King David as "like a shepherd, a prince over [God's] people" (4Q504 1-2 iv 17.6–7). Regardless, in the Hebrew Bible/LXX and elsewhere the motif of shepherd connotes leadership, and the evocation of Num 27:17 in at least one instance (Jdt 11:19) suggests a protective role of that leadership. In Matthew, as we have seen, this role is attributed to Jesus as protector and caregiver.

Some common citations from Deuteronomy mirror identical texts in Exodus (e.g., Deut 5:17 // Exod 20:13 [Matt 5:21] and Deut 5:18 // Exod 20:14 [Matt 5:27]), discussed above. Here we begin with two passages from Deut 6 (Deut 6:5 [Matt 22:37]; Deut 6:13 [Matt 4:10]), a chapter that begins with a statement by Moses that what follows constitutes the "commandment" (singular, הַמִּצְוָה; Deut 6:1) the Lord charged him to teach Israel, that they are to observe in the land they are about to occupy, and to pass it along to their progeny (Deut 6:1–3). Christiansen remarks that these verses serve as a

---

[48] Luz, *Matthew 8–20*, 64.
[49] Wayne Baxter, *Israel's Only Shepherd: Matthew's Shepherd Motif and His Social Setting*, LNTS 457 (London: T&T Clark, 2012).
[50] See Baxter, *Israel's Only Shepherd*, 60–86.
[51] *Pace* Carey A. Moore, *Judith*, ABC 40 (New York: Doubleday, 1985), 211.
[52] See Baxter, *Israel's Only Shepherd*, 73–4.

"bridge" from the Decalogue proper (Deut 4:44–5:33) to what he regards as a "sermonic elaboration of the first commandments" (Deut 6:4–25).[53] This begins with the familiar command: "you shall love the Lord your God with all your heart, and with all your soul, and with all your might" (Deut 6:5). In Matthew this is cited in the pericope discussed above (Matt 22:34–39), where Jesus is asked "which commandment in the law is the greatest?" (ποία ἐντολὴ μεγάλη ἐν τῷ νόμῳ, Matt 22:37). Jesus's response cites Deut 6:5, as follows: "You shall love the Lord your God with all your heart, and with all your soul, and with all your mind" (Matt 22:37).[54] In Second Temple Judaism this passage is widely attested in textual form primarily in phylacteries[55] and mezuzot[56] from Qumran, a phylactery from Wadi Murabba'at (MurPhyl [Mur 4]) and a manuscript from Qumran (4QDeut^p [4Q43]). Elsewhere it is alluded to in the wisdom teachings of Sirach (Sir 7:30 MS A) and in an exhortation statement from Tobit to his progeny (Tob 14:9), but otherwise without explicit quotation.

Similarly, in the same context from Deut 6, Moses exhorts Israel to fear the Lord, serve him, and swear by his name alone (Deut 6:13) in a context intended as an affront to following other gods (Deut 6:14–15).[57] In Matthew Jesus cites the verse explicitly in rebuttal to Satan's request for worship (Matt 4:10). The response is grounded in the scriptural claim that what Satan requests of Jesus is the exclusive prerogative of Israel's God. Unlike the text from Deut 6:5, Deut 6:13 is nowhere attested in manuscript form, though it is once alluded to in Tob 14, where "those who sincerely love God will rejoice" (14:7), in contrast to "those who commit sin and injustice" who will "vanish from all the earth" (Tob 14:7). Importantly, the notion of loving God is contrasted with sin and injustice, suggesting a moral component to loving God. Otherwise, this text is nowhere directly cited or clearly alluded to in extant Second Temple materials.

Two other common passages from Deuteronomy require some attention (Deut 8:3 [Matt 4:4]; Deut 25:5 [Matt 22:24]). Deut 8:3 occurs in the broader context of perils of disobedience to the Lord (Deut 8:1–20),[58] beginning with an exhortation to do all the law (8:1) and recall (וְזָכַרְתָּ) how God tested them, to determine whether or not they would keep his commandments (vv. 2–6).[59] He humbled them by letting them hunger and then feeding them with manna for the stated purpose to help them understand that "one does not live by bread alone, but by every word that comes from the mouth of the LORD" (8:3, NRSV).[60] This is cited by Jesus in Matt 4 as an affirmation of

---

[53] Duane L. Christiansen, *Deuteronomy 1–21:9*, 2nd ed., WBC 6a (Nashville, TN: Thomas Nelson, 2001), 135–6. So also Jeffrey H. Tigay, *Deuteronomy*, JPS (Philadelphia, PA: JPS, 1996), 75.
[54] Matthew's wording is distinct from the LXX as follows: ἀγαπήσεις κύριον τὸν θεόν σου ἐν ὅλῃ τῇ καρδίᾳ (LXX ἐξ ὅλης τῆς καρδίας) σου καὶ ἐν ὅλῃ τῇ ψυχῇ (LXX: ἐξ ὅλης τῆς ψυχῆς) σου καὶ ἐν ὅλῃ τῇ διανοίᾳ (LXX: ἐξ ὅλης τῆς δυνάμεώς) σου (Deut 6:5 LXX). On the Matthean text form, see Gundry, *The Use of the Old Testament in St. Matthew's Gospel*, 22–5.
[55] 4Qphyl^b (4Q129); 4Qphyl^c (4Q130); 4Qphyl^h (4Q135); 4Qphyl^m (4Q140).
[56] 4Qmez^b (4Q150); 4Qmez^c (4Q151); 4Qmez^d (4Q152).
[57] See Christiansen, *Deuteronomy 1–21:9*, 147.
[58] See Christiansen, *Deuteronomy 1–11*, 69.
[59] Christiansen, *Deuteronomy 1–11*, 173.
[60] The only notable differences are the inclusion of the τῷ in LXX Deut 8:3b, omitted by Matthew, and the inclusion of the final phrase ζήσεται ὁ ἄνθρωπος (MT יִחְיֶה הָאָדָם), which Matthew omits, perhaps from redundancy.

unconditional obedience to the will of God, regardless of the paucity of sustaining resources (cf. Wis 16:26).[61] In this respect the temptation serves to underscore the unconditional obedience to God's purposes, which becomes a fundamental and even defining characteristic of the "son of God" designation in Matthew. In Judaism the passage is found in two manuscripts from Qumran (4QDeut[c] [4Q30]; 4QDeut[f] [4Q33]) and in Philo of Alexandria in a characteristically protracted discourse on "hungering" for virtue as opposed to passion and vice (*Alleg. Interp.* 3.174–5).

A final citation from Deuteronomy appears in a set of laws pertaining to a brother who dies and leaves no son, in which case the husband's brother shall father children on the dead brother's behalf (Deut 25:5). In Matthew, the Sadducees, who deny resurrection (Matt 22:23) cite this verse (Deut 25:5) as evidence for the potential for seven brothers to be married to the same woman in life, and so precludes the possibility of a resurrection (Matt 22:24–28). Jesus responds that their error lies in their ignorance of the scriptures and the power of God (Matt 22:29), claiming that at the resurrection there is no marriage (Matt 22:30–32). In Judaism this passage from Deuteronomy is found in two manuscripts from Qumran (4QDeut[f] [4Q33]; 4QDeut[g] [4Q34]) and in the writings of Josephus, who simply recounts the regulation and its practice among Jews (*A.J.* 4.254).

3.2.2 Common Citations from the Prophets

Two texts from the Prophet Isaiah are found in Matthew and contemporary Jewish writings. The first is taken from Isa 40:3 (Matt 3:3). In the context of Isaiah the prophet speaks a series of commissions issued by the Lord to a people in exile (40:1–11) anticipating the coming of God's reign.[62] It issues an exhortation of "comfort" (נחם) (cf. Isa 49:13; 51:3; 52:9)[63] to "my people" (עַמִּי, Isa 40:1), Jerusalem (40:2). Matthew's citation comes from v. 3, which constitutes commission to prepare the way for the coming of the Lord (Isa 40:3–5; פַּנּוּ דֶּרֶךְ יְהוָה; cf. Pss 24:7–10; 68).[64] In Matthew's context the "voice" is identified as John the Baptist (Matt 3:1–2), with the clear implication that the "Lord" to come is none other than Jesus.[65]

The text is attested in several instances at Qumran[66] and in two clear uses in Qumran *Serek* texts.[67] A citation of Isaiah 40:3 is found in 1QS 8, which is part of a larger, pragmatic

---

[61] Similarly Peter C. Craigie, *The Book of Deuteronomy*, NICOT (Grand Rapids, MI: Eerdmans, 1976), 185.

[62] John Goldingay and David Payne, *Isaiah 40–55*, vol. 1, ICC (London: T&T Clark, 2014), 61.

[63] Goldingay and Payne, *Isaiah 40–55*, 63.

[64] See N. L. Tidwell, "No Highway!" *VT* 45 (1995): 251–69; N. L. Tidwell, "A Road and a Way," *Semitics* 7 (1980): 50–80. Goldingay and Payne, *Isaiah 40–55*, 74; citing F. M. Cross, *Canaanite Myth and Hebrew Epic* (Cambridge, MA: Harvard University Press, 1973), 108, 173–4.

[65] See Davies and Allison, *Matthew*, 1.92–94.

[66] 1QIsa[a]; 1QIsa[b] (1Q8); 4QIsa[b] (4Q56); 4QTanḥ (4Q176 1–2 i.6–7). On 4Q176, see Jesper Høgenhaven, "4Q176 (4QTanhumim)," *ESTJ* 1.521–3; H. Lichtenberger, "Consolations (4Q176 = 4QTanh)," *PTSDSS* 6B (2002), 329–49; C. D. Stanley, "The Importance of 4QTanhumim (4Q176)," *RevQ* 15/60 (1991–2): 569–82.

[67] The context of 4Q176 does not make clear the use of Isa 40:3, so it is not discussed here in terms of its exegesis but rather its textual witness.

segment describing the holiness of the community (8.1–9.11),⁶⁸ more particularly espousing the "council of the community" (עצת היחד, 8.1) to separate themselves from the men of injustice, and "go into the wilderness to prepare there *the way of him, as it is written: "In the wilderness prepare the way of* ••••; *make level in the desert a highway for our God*" (כאשר כתוב במדבר פנו דרך **** ישרו בערבה מסלה לאלוהינו, 1QS 8.13–14).⁶⁹ The citation here is from Isa 40:3, but its importance lies in the explanation that follows:

> This (way) is the study of the law t[hat] he commanded through Moses, that they should act in accordance with all that has been revealed from time to time and in accordance with what the prophets revealed by his holy spirit." (1QS 8.15–16a)

It then goes on (lines 16b–19) to explain that anyone who leaves such commands unfulfilled shall not "touch the purity of the men of holiness or know any of their counsel until his deeds have been cleansed from all injustice by walking in perfection of way" (lines 17–19).⁷⁰ And so it is widely recognized that the Qumran group separated themselves from the Jerusalem establishment, the sacrifices of which are defiled by impurities of its administration, to settle in the Judean desert.⁷¹ In this way the group fulfills the Isaianic exhortation *in themselves*. The manner in which they do this is to study the Law, and in so doing prepare the way for the Lord's coming.⁷²

Isaiah 40:3 is also found in 1QS 9.19–20, a section (9.12–25) that contains "rules for the wise leader" or *maskil* (החוקים למשכיל, 1QS 9.12), which reiterates the group formation statement in viii.13–14 above. This section contains a series of ten "he shall" statements, the ninth of which reads: "He shall guide them with knowledge and likewise instruct them in the mysteries of wonder and truth in the midst of the men of the community that they may walk perfectly with one another in all that has been revealed to them" (9.18–19). For the Qumran sect, "this is the time to prepare the way to the wilderness" (למדבר היאה עת פנות הדרך, 9.19–20 // par 4Q258 13.4).

The prophetic voice claimed by the unnamed Isaianic figure and taken by the Qumran sectarians belongs, for Matthew, to John the Baptist. The Lord whose preparation is made is not the Isaianic YHWH or the Qumran ****, but Jesus. But unlike at Qumran, the manner in which John prepares the way is not stated here in Matt 3:3, but is deduced from other factors. This includes bearing witness to him (Matt 3:11–12, 14)⁷³ and calling people to repentance (Matt 3:8, 10; 11:16–19) in accord with his role as the new Elijah (Matt 11:14; 17:11–13; Mal 4:6; cf. 48:10).

---

⁶⁸ Arjen Bakker, "Rule of the Community," *ESTJ* 1.476.
⁶⁹ Translation is from Sarianna Metso, *The Community Rule: A Critical Edition with Translation*, EJL 51 (Atlanta, GA: SBL, 2019), 43, 45. Parallel accounts in other *Serek* manuscripts (4Q258 6 6; 4Q259 3 4–5) are less complete than the 1QS, and not examined closely here. (The italics indicate direct quotation of the OT. The dots and asterisks are substitutions for the divine name.)
⁷⁰ On the function of this section (1QS 8.1–16a pars) in the document as a whole, see Charlotte Hempel, *The Community Rules from Qumran*, TSAJ 183 (Tübingen: Mohr Siebeck, 2020), 217–18.
⁷¹ See James C. VanderKam, *The Dead Sea Scrolls Today*, 2nd ed. (Grand Rapids, MI: Eerdmans, 2010), 134–5.
⁷² Importantly, this likely refers to events around the end of the second or early first century BCE. See VanderKam, *Dead Sea Scrolls Today*, 135.
⁷³ Davies and Allison, *Matthew*, 1.294.

Two final common citations are taken from the prophet Zechariah. The first is taken from his utterance to "strike the shepherd" and scatter the sheep (Zech 13:7). This is appropriated by Matthew as fulfilled in the abuse of Jesus and abandonment of his disciples (Matt 26:31). At Qumran the citation is found in the Damascus Document (CD-B col. 19), where the sword that strikes Zechariah's "shepherd" will be wielded against those who do not revere God[74] and escape in the "age of visitation" (בקץ הפקדה, l. 10), which will occur "when there comes the messiah of Aaron and Israel" (בבוא משיח אהרן וישראל, ll. 10–11).[75] The shepherd here is the Qumran teacher, whose slaying inaugurates a time of eschatological intervention by God's messiah.[76]

Finally, a prophetic utterance of Zechariah exhorts the daughter of Zion to rejoice, for her triumphant and victorious king is coming (Zech 9:9). This is utilized in Matthew in reference to Jesus's entry into Jerusalem (Matt 21:5), including the notion of "humility" and riding on a colt (Zech 9:9; Matt 21:5). A similar exhortation for Zion to rejoice is found in the War Scroll (1Q33 [1QM] 19.5 par 4Q494 [4QM^b] 1.5). But the exhortation occurs in the context where the *Yaḥad* goes out into battle with the "mighty one" and the "king of glory" on their side (19.1) and a battle cry of subjugation of the enemy ensues (19.2–4a). This is followed by an exhortation to what seems to be taking plunder of the enemies (19.4b), concluding:

> Rejoice, Zion, passionately! Exult, all the cities of Ju[dah! Open] 6 [your gates continuously so that] the wealth of the nations [can be brought to you!] Their kings shall wait on you, [al]l your [oppressors] lie prone before you, 7 [the dust of your feet they shall lick.] Daughters of my people, shout with jubilant voice! Adorn yourselves with splendid finery! R[u]le over the kingdom of 8 [… to] your [camp]s, and Israel to reign for ever. *Blank* (1QM 19.5–8)[77]

The allusion to opening gates and rejoicing evokes a similar notion to what one finds in Zechariah, but there is nothing of the humility of the coming king and the gentleness gives way to violence. Instead, there is the plundering of enemies and destruction of oppressors.

3.3 Conclusion

To these citations may be added a host of citations in Matthew that find clear allusions in the Second Temple material, of which a few of the more prominent may

---

[74] Or, more specifically, those who reject the commandments.

[75] Cf. CD 12.23–13.1; 14.19 par; Charlotte Hempel, *The Damascus Document*, CQS 1 (Sheffield: Academic Press, 2000), 76; Charlotte Hempel, *The Laws of the Damascus Document: Sources, Traditions, & Redaction*, STDJ 29 (Leiden: Brill, 1998), 108–10.

[76] On the complicated and debated meaning of משיח אהרן וישראל, see Philip R. Davies, *The Damascus Covenant: An Interpretation of the "Damascus Document,"* JSOTSup 2 (Sheffield: Sheffield Academic Press, 1983), 143–72; M. A. Knibb, *The Qumran Community* (Cambridge: Cambridge University Press, 1987), 56–63.

[77] Translation from Florentino García Martínez, *The Dead Sea Scrolls Translated*, Second Edition (Leiden and Grand Rapids: E.J. Brill and W.B. Eerdmans, 1996), 115.

be mentioned. The discussion of the Isaianic servant (Isa 42:1–3) is clearly identified with Jesus in Matthew (Matt 12:18–20) but referenced either in textual form (4QIsaᵇ [4Q56]) or ambiguous "servant" language in other texts (1QHᵃ 12.25; Pss Sol 17:21; 1 En 49:1–4). Daniel's vision of the "Son of Man" (Dan 7:13) becomes an important Christological designation in the first gospel (Matt 9:6; 12:8; 26:64; etc.) but again finds only vague allusion in the Jewish literature (*Sib. Or.* 5.256; *4 Ezra* 13:3–4). Daniel's mention of an "abomination that desolates" (Dan 9:27; 11:31; 12:11) is assigned to an ambiguous eschatological event in Matthew (Matt 24:14) but clearly to historical events surrounding Antiochus IV Epiphanes at the outset of the Maccabean revolt in the contemporary literature (e.g., Josephus, *A.J.* 12.253; 1 Macc 4:43; 2 Macc 6:5; cf. *Pr. Man.* 10). The broad brush strokes taken in the present study are by no means exhaustive but they are nonetheless broadly complete and allow us to draw a number of conclusions regarding the way Matthew and roughly contemporary Jewish sources utilized shared sacred texts of Israel. For despite the important role the Hebrew Bible plays in Matthew and his contemporaries, they exhibit both similarities and differences in the ways in which identical texts are appropriated.

Similarities are found in several instances in common citations from the Decalogue (Exod 20 // Deut 5). The command to honor one's father and mother (Exod 20:12; Deut 5:16) is clearly regarded as an expectation and requirement for the first evangelist (Matt 15:4a; 19:19a), and its attestation manuscript form, including phylacteries and mezuzot from Qumran, indicates the same expectations were in view among the *Yaḥad* and more broadly regarded as an expectation among other Jewish contemporaries (e.g., *Ps. Phoc.* 8; Sir 3; *Arist.* 228; Jub 7:20; 35:12–13; etc.). Similarly, the prohibition of murder (Exod 20:13 // Deut 5:17) is continued by Matthew (Matt 5:22; 19:18) and his contemporaries (e.g., *LAB* 11:11; 44:6; Philo *Dec.* 1.36; etc.). The same could be said for the prohibition of adultery (Exod 20:14 // Deut 5:18; Matt 5:27–29; 19:18), stealing (Exod 20:15; Matt 19:18), and bearing false witness (Exod 20:16; Matt 19:18). The so-called "love command" (Lev 19:18) is both affirmed and illustrated in Matthew (Matt 5:43–44), who also regards it as the greatest commandment in the law (Matt 22:34–36). This is regarded as a hallmark of Jewish faith (*Arist.* 228; cf. Jub 7:20; Sir 13:15).

Among the differences are the citations of Gen 1:27, which Matthew uses as grounds for the permanence of marriage (Matt 19:4), whereas Jewish contemporaries seem to evoke it for the institution of marriage itself (Tob 8:4–7) and perhaps grounds for monogamy (6Q15 1.3; par CD-A 4.21). Otherwise other portions of the Gen 1:27 are cited that have nothing to do with marriage but rather the nature of humanity and its role in the created order. Genesis 2:24 is also used by Matthew for the permanence of marriage (Matt 19:5–6), whereas in Qumran wisdom literature (e.g., 4Q416 pars) it is cited among pragmatic instructions for marriage and the unity of the joined couple, but as above without mention of the divorce. A law regarding retributive justice (Exod 21:24) is prohibited on a personal level in Matthew (Matt 5:38) though presumed to be enacted in the death of Cain (Jub 4:31). The prohibition against swearing falsely by God's name (Lev 19:12) is applied in Matthew in terms of not swearing at all (Matt 5:33–34), whereas other texts seem to apply it rather to perjury (*Ps. Phoc.* 16–17; CD-A 15.3). The law regarding a brother who dies and leaves no son, in which case the husband's brother shall father children on the dead brother's behalf (Deut 25:5) is used in Matthew as a foil for Jesus's teaching on the resurrection (Matt 22:24–30), whereas elsewhere it is simply cited as a practice among Jews (*A.J.* 4.254). The Isaianic figure who prepares the way of the Lord (Isa 40:3) is regarded by Matthew as John the Baptist, who prepares the way for Jesus by preaching repentance (Matt 3:3). At Qumran it is instead the *Yaḥad* itself, which prepares the way for the coming of Israel's God by their study of the Law (1QS 8; etc.). Similarly Zechariah's utterance regarding striking the shepherd and the scattering sheep (Zech 13:7) is applied by the evangelist to the sufferings of Jesus (Matt 26:31) while at Qumran it is their (sectarian) teacher whose slaying inaugurates the coming of God's messiah (CD-B 19). Zechariah's exhortation for the daughters of Zion to rejoice at the coming of their king (Zech 9:9) is clearly attributed to the arrival of Jesus into Jerusalem (Matt 21:5). In the Qumran War Scroll such rejoicing occurs at the destruction of the *Yaḥad*'s enemies in the eschatological battle (e.g., 1QM 19.5–8).

In common with some of his contemporaries, Matthew regards a number of ethical regulations as still in force for his readers. Others he recognizes but applies in a manner distinct to his own particular teachings, such as the nature of marriage or the doctrine of resurrection. Despite his preoccupation with the fulfillment of Israel's scriptures, none of these common citations in any way indicate that OT texts are "fulfilled" in the sense that they are no longer valid for the Matthean reader. Rather the ethical mandates are in force, but always through the mediation of Jesus's teaching. But probably what distinguishes Matthean uses of common citations from those of his contemporaries is the obvious and manifold roles of Jesus. It is his interpretation of the cited OT text that is regarded as authoritative for the reader. The eschatological figures and events cited from OT texts are all defined in terms of their relation to Jesus. For Matthew, his framing of citations of OT texts regards the person of Jesus—in some respect—as the lens through which the text is to be read.

4

John the Baptist as Jesus's Teacher in the Gospel of Matthew

John Y. H. Yieh

4.1 Introduction

Jesus's role and function as a supreme teacher of God's will in the Gospel of Matthew has been well researched in recent scholarship.[1] Jesus came to fulfill the law and prophets as the new Moses (5:17). He summoned the crowd to take his yoke and learn from him as the personified Wisdom (11:28). He denounced the hypocritic Pharisees and scribes as the one Teacher (23:8–10). And he commissioned his disciples to make disciples of all nations by teaching the baptized to obey his commandments as the Lord of the heavens and earth (28:19–20). One next question might be: How does Matthew's Jesus become a supreme teacher of God's will? Or: Who could Jesus's teacher be and how might he influence Jesus? If we learn more about Jesus's teachers, we will gain a deeper appreciation of Jesus's characteristics as teacher in Matthew.

Who could Jesus's teacher or teachers be? It may be helpful to begin by defining what teacher (*didaskalos*) meant for Jesus and Matthew. As a social role, a teacher is someone who possesses a specialized body of knowledge, experience, and skills and who is in a position or relationship to instruct, guide, and train his hearers, followers, and disciples, to inform, reform, and transform their viewpoints, values, and behaviors. *Didaskalos* is not a title reserved only for the philosopher in school, the rabbi in yeshivah, or a founder in sectarian group. Primary-education tutors, trade masters, and wandering prophets also belonged to the broader category of teacher. Growing up in the Jewish village of Nazareth in the culturally mixed region of Galilee in the first

---

[1] M. Jack Saggs, *Wisdom, Christology, and Law in Matthew's Gospel* (Cambridge, MA: Harvard University Press, 1970), 31–61; John Meier, *The Vision of Matthew: Christ, Church, and Morality in the First Gospel* (New York: Paulist, 1979), 45–51; Rainer Riesner, *Jesus als Lehrer. Eine Untersuchung zum Ursprung der Evangelien-Überlieferung*, 3rd ed. (Tübingen: Mohr Siebeck, 1988), 259–64; Dale Allison, *The New Moses: A Matthean Typology* (Minneapolis: Fortress, 1993); Samuel Byrskog, *Jesus the Only Teacher: Didactic Authority and Transmission in Ancient Israel, Ancient Judaism and the Matthean Community* (Stockholm: Almqvist & Wiksell, 1994); Celia Deutsch, *Lady Wisdom, Jesus, and the Sages: Metaphor and Social Context in Matthew's Gospel* (Valley Forge, PA: Trinity, 1996); R. T. France, *Matthew: Evangelist & Teacher* (Downers Grove, IL: IVP, 1998); John Yieh, *One Teacher: Jesus' Teaching Role in Matthew's Gospel Report* (Berlin: de Gruyter, 2004); Ian Boxall, *Discovering Matthew: Context, Interpretation, Reception* (London: SPCK, 2014), 91–105.

century CE, Jesus was exposed to several types of teachers.[2] Among them, Pharisees were learned instructors of the Jewish law. Scribes were educated elites ministering official business. Sadducees in Capernaum and Tiberius were savvy dealers in politics and commerce. Local priests taught villagers how to observe holy days and Sabbath in the synagogue. Working in Sepphoris, Herod Antipas's capital city, Jesus might also know some Greek philosophers or Latin teachers who served as advisors to officials and tutors to the children of wealthy families. It is safe to assume that Jesus would have primary-education tutors teaching him to read and count and have scribes in the *beth ha-midrash* teaching him Bible stories and Jewish customs.[3] It is probable that he would have his father Joseph and other artisans as his trade masters under whom he apprenticed. Based on the Gospel of Matthew, it is likely that some well-known figures in Jewish scripture and Hellenistic culture, such as Moses, Isaiah, Hosea, Jeremiah, Teacher of Righteousness, Socrates, and Epictetus could also be regarded as teachers of wisdom known to him. All these teachers in life and in culture would have played a part in making Jesus the impressive teacher of God's will who taught the Sermon on the Mount, explained the mystery of the kingdom of heaven, debated the Pharisees, and astounded the chief priests in Jerusalem as well as the crowds in Galilee (7:28; 21:23; 22:46).

Among many types of teachers in Jesus's life and culture, John the Baptist stood out as the most prominent one who had a strong connection with Jesus and a huge impact on his formation to become a teacher. John was a respected prophet of the kingdom of heaven. All Evangelists refer to him as the voice in the wilderness (per Isa 40:3) who preached the baptism of repentance and commanded respect from all walks of life. They believe John was Elijah who would come to restore all things before the day of the Lord (per Mal 3:1) even though John himself denied such an association (per John 1:21). All four report Jesus's baptism by John in the Jordan River, and one Q source records Jesus's defense of John against the evil generation (Luke 7:31–35; Matt 11:16–19). The debate about John's baptism versus Jesus's baptism did continue in the early church (Acts 1:5; 18:25), but the competition between the followers of John and of Jesus seems amicable. Such positive portraits of John are remarkable in view of the early Christian effort to prove Jesus's superiority in the history of salvation. Evangelists faced a delicate task of proving Jesus to be the Messiah who ushered in the kingdom of heaven while honoring John as the herald who prepared Israel for the way of the Lord. So, who was the historical John? There have been major studies in recent years to answer this question, and they all take note of the intriguing relationship between John and Jesus with noticeable similarities and dissimilarities.[4] Different from those studies,

---

[2] Pheme Perkins, *Jesus as Teacher* (Cambridge: Cambridge University Press, 1990), 1–22.
[3] Paul Foster, "Educating Jesus: The Search for a Plausible Context," *JSHJ* 4.1 (2006): 7–33; Chris Keith, "Teachers in the Time of Jesus: Scribal Literacy and Social Roles" in *Jesus Against the Scribal Elite: The Origins of the Conflict* (London: T & T Clark, 2020), 15–38.
[4] John Reumann, "The Quest for the Historical Baptist," in *Understanding Sacred Text: Essays in Honor of Morton S. Enslin on the Hebrew Bible and Christian Beginnings*, ed. John Reumann (Valley Forge, PA: Judson, 1972), 181–99; Jürgen Becker, *Johannes der Täufer und Jesus von Nazareth* (Neukirchen-Vluyn: Neukirchener Verlag, 1972); Josef Ernst, *Johannes der Täufer: Interpretation, Geschichte*, Wirkungsgeschichte (Berlin: de Gruyter, 1989), 268–348; Robert Webb, *John the Baptizer and Prophet: A Socio-Historical Study* (Sheffield: JSOT, 1991), 349–789; John Meier, *A Marginal*

however, this chapter is focused not on the historical John but Matthew's John, just as it is not on the historical Jesus but Matthew's Jesus.

Among recent studies of John the Baptist in the Gospel of Matthew, Wolfgang Trilling's seminal article, "Die Täufertradition bei Mattäus" (1959), calls attention to John's violent fate as a prophet who suffered in the hands of king and leaders. Recalling the motif of Israel's disobedience in the Deuteronomistic tradition, Trilling argues, Matthew uses John's tragic fate to explain why Jesus, even with his miracles, was rejected by Jewish leaders who constituted "Die gottfeindliche Front" (the anti-God front).[5] Based on Trilling's analysis, Walter Wink further argues that Matthew develops John's role in relation to the kingdom of heaven and underscores his identity as Elijah to explain how John functioned in the redemptive history. John's suffering illustrates "the hostility of 'pseudo-Israel' to every overture from God."[6] Reviewing all references to John in Matthew's Gospel, John Meier further contends the reason why Matthew presents John as both parallel and subordinate to Jesus was to make John standing with Jesus in the middle of salvation history, completing the time of the law and prophets and welcoming the arrival of the time of the church.[7] These studies use historical-critical and redaction critical methods to determine how the stories of John reflect or amplify Matthew's theological views of salvation history, Christology, and ecclesiology. In a recent article, "John the Baptist and Jesus the Baptist: A Narrative Critical Approach" (2012), Joan Taylor and Federico Adinolfi adopt a narrative-critical approach to study John and Jesus as immersers in the Gospel of Mark and ask why Mark regards Jesus's baptism of Holy Spirit as a continuation of John's baptism of water. They point out that whereas John's water baptism was a ritual of purity symbolizing remission of sin, Jesus's Spirit baptism was his miracles of healing and exorcism that expelled illness and demons caused by sin. Both baptisms can therefore be understood in the same purity framework, within which Jesus's baptism continued John's baptism and granted inner purity. Their study shows that "narrative patterns can be indicative of history masked by overt rhetoric."[8] In this chapter, I will take the same narrative critical approach to analyze the stories of John in the Gospel of Matthew to see how Matthew's telling of those stories reveals John's personal relationship with Jesus. Specifically, does Matthew present John the Baptist as Jesus's teacher? If so, how does John influence Jesus as teacher? To answer these questions, I raise four further questions: How does Matthew as narrator characterize John at the narrative level? How does Jesus as protagonist remark on John's significance at the story level? How compatible are their

---

Jew: Rethinking the Historical Jesus, Vol. II: Mentor, Message, and Miracles (New York: Yale University Press, 1994), 19–233, esp. 116–30; Joan Taylor, The Immerser: John the Baptist within Second Temple Judaism (Grand Rapids, MI: Eerdmans, 1997), 261–316; Joel Marcus, John the Baptist in History and Theology (Columbia: University of South Carolina Press, 2018), 81–97. For major points of current debate on the historical John, see Joel Marcus, "Response to the Respondents: Competition, Qumran and Supersessionism," JSHJ 19 (2021): 99–133.

[5] Wolfgang Trilling, "Die Täufertradition bei Mattäus," BZ 3 (1959): 271–89, esp. 274.
[6] Walter Wink, John the Baptist in the Gospel Tradition (Cambridge: Cambridge University Press, 1968), 27–41, esp. 41.
[7] John Meier, "John the Baptist in Matthew's Gospel," JBL 99.3 (1980): 383–405.
[8] Joan Taylor and Federico Adinolfi, "John the Baptist and Jesus the Baptist: A Narrative Critical Approach," JSHJ 10 (2012): 247–84, esp. 247.

main teachings? How comparable are their featured actions? Matthew's portrait of John unveils his perception of John as Jesus's teacher, and it may point to their personal relationship in social reality.

4.2 Matthew the Narrator

John the Baptist appears in nine settings in the Gospel of Matthew: Judean wilderness (3:1–12), Jordan River (3:13–17), Matthew's house (9:14–17), Antipas's prison (11:2–6), Galilean cities (11:7–19), the royal court (14:1–12), Caesarea Philippi (16:13–15), down the mount of Transfiguration (17:9–13), and the Temple (21:23–27). With significant details and explicit comments, Matthew tells several stories—anecdotes, *chreiai*, dialogues, *and* interactions—to characterize John the Baptist as a popular and revered prophet of the imminent kingdom of heaven by the Jordan in the Judean wilderness. John, in interaction with Jesus, then serves as a foil for Matthew's characterization of Jesus the hero.[9] I will discuss how Matthew as narrator depicts John in six ways as a mentor to Jesus who then flourished into an amazing teacher of God's will in Galilee and Jerusalem.

First, Matthew introduces John as a prophet extraordinaire for the imminent kingdom of heaven (3:1–10). In John's first appearance in the Gospel, Matthew cites Isa 40:3 to introduce him as the "voice crying out in the wilderness" to preach the imminence of the kingdom of heaven and urge repentance to avert divine judgment (3:1–4). He wore a simple attire and lived an ascetic lifestyle like a prophet (3:5; 11:7–9) and admonished Pharisees and Sadducees to bear fruit worthy of repentance (3:7–10). Later in the narrative, Matthew tactfully mentions John's imprisonment twice to create a suspension for readers (4:12; 11:2), before he explains in shocking details why John was thrown in prison and how he was brutally beheaded, plotted by the cold-blooded Herodias and her dancing daughter (14:1–12). John was persecuted because he had the courage to condemn King Herod Antipas for his illicit relationship with his brother Philip's wife, and consequently, he paid the grand price of a true prophet. By highlighting John's eschatological message and prophetic martyrdom, Matthew affectively explains why John was popular and revered by the crowds, the priests, and the elders (3:5; 21:23–27).

Second, Matthew records John's prediction about a person who was "coming after" him (ὁ δὲ ὀπίσω μου ἐρχόμενος) but "more powerful" than he was (ἰσχυρότερός μού) (3:11–12). That more powerful person would baptize people with the Holy Spirit and fire. The Holy Spirit refers to the miracles of healing and exorcism, and the fire implies the purifying force of the final judgment. This powerful person would judge the world in justice by sorting out wheat and chaff with a winnowing fork at the harvest time. "Then (*tote*)," the narrator adds, "Jesus came from Galilee to John at the Jordan, to be baptized by him" (3:13). This temporal adverb connects the two episodes and makes it clear that Jesus was the more powerful person with authority to save the righteous and

---

[9] F. P. Viljoen, "The Matthean Characterisation of Jesus by John the Baptist," *In Die Skriflit* 54 (2020): 1–11.

judge the wicked. Indeed, John recognized Jesus as that "more powerful" one whose sandals he was not worthy to carry, so he declined Jesus's request of baptism and said he himself needed to be baptized by Jesus (3:14). These narratorial details have Christological implications to support the claim that Jesus was the Messiah while John was the prophet who came earlier to testify to Jesus. To say Jesus came "after" John (ὀπίσω μου) indicates that John was Jesus's predecessor in the ministry of the kingdom of heaven, but it also suggests that Jesus came to follow "after" John as a disciple. Jesus used the same expression to call his disciples, "Come, follow me (Δεῦτε ὀπίσω μου, 'come after me'), and I will make you fishers of men" (4:19) and "If any want to become my followers (ὀπίσω μου ἐλθεῖν, 'come after me'), let them deny themselves and take up their cross and follow me (16:24)." To say that Jesus came from Galilee to the Jordan to be baptized by John presumes that Jesus was so fascinated by John as a prophet with life-changing message that he would make a long journey to go to John to learn about his teaching and observe his character and lifestyle. In their time, it was customary for a student to take the initiative to go to a philosopher or rabbi whom they admire to ask for permission to stay and study with him. For a charismatic leader of a religious movement, would-be followers would also take the initiative to flock to the leaders' side.[10] This episode also characterizes John as a wise teacher who was insightful about his disciples as well as knowledgeable in his specialty. He recognizes which disciple has the best talent, like Samuel the prophet who recognized David the young shepherd boy, not his stronger brothers, was the one chosen by God to be anointed as the future king of Israel (1 Sam 16:1–13). John might have seen Jesus as one of his followers who had the potential to do better than he did for the kingdom of heaven.

Third, Matthew recounts a dialogue in which Jesus insisted that John baptize him (3:13). John initially declined Jesus's request by reason of his unworthiness (3:14) but rescinded his decision after Jesus said, "Let it be so now; for it is proper for us in this way to fulfill all righteousness" (3:15). Righteousness (*dikaiosune*) is a key theme in Matthew's Gospel. Here it means "a demand from Israel's covenant God that people are to fulfill."[11] "To fulfill all righteousness" implies baptism is an act of righteousness, and every demand of God should be obeyed. It is intriguing that Jesus insisted on being baptized by John, because John's baptism was a ritual of purity to confess one's sins (3:6) and commit to repentance (3:11). Three questions may arise: Did Jesus admit being a sinner in need of forgiveness? What did Jesus mean about fulfilling all righteousness? Does it not suggest Jesus had a lower status than John? As a Christian leader, Matthew must have been aware of these questions. In telling this story, therefore, Matthew has tried to remove the implication of Jesus's admission to sins by showing John's vehement attempt to prevent him from taking the baptism and by calling baptism here an act of righteousness instead of confession for forgiveness. Jesus called John's baptism an act of righteousness because he believed it was divinely sanctioned. If it is a divine demand, Jesus will submit to it with obedience. Receiving baptism from John would indeed be perceived as an indication of Jesus's lower status, but "for now" when Jesus

---

[10] Martin Hengel, *The Charismatic Leader and His Followers* (New York: Crossroad, 1981), 16–37.
[11] Ulrich Luz, *Matthew 1–7* (Minneapolis, MN: Fortress, 2007), 142. W. D. Davies and Dale Allison, *The Gospel according to Saint Matthew*, vol. 1 (Edinburgh: T & T Clark, 1988), 327.

was a student of John, it was a proper thing to do. In fact, precisely because he could be seen as inferior to John, Jesus's willingness reveals his character of humility. In the light of his final commission to make disciples of all nations by baptizing believers and teaching the baptized (28:19-20), Jesus's own baptism by John here signals that "the Jesus who is obedient to the will of God becomes the Christians' prototype and model."[12] There is no doubt that John's humble deference to Jesus concerning baptism (3:13-15) and the divine announcement of Jesus as the beloved Son of God in the ensuing theophany (3:16-17) work together to solidify Jesus's divine authority and bolster his superiority. It is just as clear that Jesus's baptism puts Jesus's character traits of obedience and humility on display and lifts him up as a model for discipleship. It also indicates Jesus was an ardent follower of John and he adopted John's baptism as a ritual of initiation for his disciples (28:19). Jesus was a disciple of John at least in a broad sense.[13]

Fourth, Matthew uses several short narratorial notes to remind readers of Jesus's close relationship with John. Readers are told that immediately after his baptism Jesus was led up by the Spirit into the wilderness, presumably near where John stayed and conducted his ministry, to fast and pray for forty days and forty nights (4:1). Wilderness is a place where one experiences solitude, loneliness, and vulnerability. It is also the place where one meets God as Moses received his mission from God in the burning bush and Elijah heard the still voice of God in a cave. Fasting in the wilderness afforded Jesus a time for meditation and prayer to process his identity as the beloved Son of God and his call to ministry. John had stayed in the wilderness for a long while; he could very well offer Jesus his spiritual experience in that setting. After his spiritual retreat in the wilderness tempted by the devil (4:1-11), Jesus spent some more time with John at the Jordan because, the narrator notes, Jesus withdrew to Galilee only after hearing John's arrest (4:12).[14] In those days Jesus might be someone like a postulant in John's movement and became acquainted with some of John's disciples who were core members of John's inner circle. This would perhaps explain why, later in the narrative, the incarcerated John would send his disciples to ask Jesus whether he was the Messiah (11:2) and his disciples would send words to Jesus when John was executed (14:12). In both cases, it is presumed that John's disciples knew Jesus personally and considered him a close associate of John.

Fifth, Matthew reports a popular belief that Jesus was John resurrected from death, which explained why Jesus had divine power to perform miracles. Herod Antipas, who beheaded John, was convinced with great fear that Jesus was John resurrected once he heard reports of Jesus's miracles (14:1-2).[15] In Caesarea Philippi, Jesus's disciples told him that many people thought he was John the Baptist, or a prophet, or Elijah (16:14). Why would Herod Antipas and the crowd identify Jesus with John the Baptist? They had heard them preaching the same messages about the imminent kingdom of heaven,

---

[12] Ulrich Luz, *Matthew 1-7*, 142.
[13] John Meier, *A Marginal Jew: Rethinking the Historical Jesus, Vol. II: Mentor, Message, and Miracles*, 116.
[14] Graham Twelftree, "Jesus the Baptist," *JSHJ* 7 (2009): 103-25.
[15] According to Josephus, the Jews believed the defeat of Herod Antipas by the Nabataeans was a divine punishment for his execution of the Baptist. Josephus, *Antiquities* 18.118-19.

and they revered both as genuine prophets of God. These outsiders' view is another clue that John was Jesus's teacher and Jesus was believed to be John's successor.

Finally, Matthew places the story of John in the beginning of his narrative to suggest John was a major influence in Jesus's formative years. Ancient biography of public figures (heroes, sages, teachers) normally has a tripartite structure: the beginning section on the hero's unusual birth and youth, the middle section on his remarkable career and contribution, and the final section on his memorable death and legacy.[16] The beginning section often provides the genealogy and special education of the young hero to explain why he grows up to make so many achievements for the public and leave the world with enduring legacy. Following the pattern of ancient biography, Matthew provides the readers with Jesus's family and educational background in Chs. 1-4. The genealogy tracking Jesus back to David and Abraham offers Jesus's credential as the Messiah who comes to fulfill God's covenant with Israel (1:1-17). The story of the virgin birth, the visit of the wise men, and the escape to and return from Egypt all point to Jesus's identity as the Son of God (1:18-2:23). With the stories of John's preaching in the wilderness and Jesus's baptism by John (3:1-4:11), then, Matthew presents John as a distinguished teacher who, not to underestimate Jesus's own virtue as displayed in the temptation story, nurtured Jesus's spiritual character, taught him the imminence of the kingdom of heaven, and prepared him for his ministry in Galilee (4:12).

4.3 Jesus the Protagonist

Jesus is the protagonist of Matthew's story. He has one direct conversation with John regarding his baptism for the righteousness' sake (3:15). This dialogue is significant because it is Jesus's first word in the story. As discussed above, it showcases Jesus's obedience and humility, sets him up as a role model for discipleship, and indicates his respect of John as his teacher. In three other occasions, Jesus gives several pithy remarks on John in public, which reveal his opinion on John and their close relationship.

The first occasion happened after the departure of John's disciples who came to check out Jesus's messiahship (11:2-6) when Jesus declared to the crowds that John was Elijah who is to come (11:7-15). Up to this point, Jesus had run a successful ministry in Galilee. He had greatly astonished the crowds with his Sermon on the Mount (Chs. 5-7), his miracles of healing and exorcism (Chs. 8-9), and his disciples' missionary work in various cities (Ch. 10). Everybody wanted to know more about him, and some began to think he might be the Messiah (11:2 "what the Messiah was doing"). John, now in jail, was also anxious to ascertain whether Jesus was the one to come whom he earlier predicted. So, he sent his disciples to ask Jesus. Jesus called their attention to the many wonders he had done for the blind, the lame, the lepers, the deaf, the dead, and

---

[16] Dirk Frickenschmidt, *Evangelium als Biographie. Die vier Evangelien im Rahmen antiker Erzählkunst* (Tübingen: Francke, 1997), 184, 192-350; John Yieh, *One Teacher*, 13-15; Richard Burridge, *What Are the Gospels? A Comparison with Graeco-Roman Biography*, 2nd ed. (Grand Rapids, MI: Eerdmans, 2004), 105-23; Craig Keener, *Christobiography: Memory, History, and the Reliability of the Gospels* (Grand Rapids, MI: Eerdmans, 2019), 145-7.

the poor, which reveal God's mercy and Jesus's power, and essentially confirmed their expectation. Then, "as they went away," Jesus turned to the crowds and began to talk about John (11:7). Jesus knew that, once he admitted he was the Messiah, people would be wondering who John was because they believed John had come from God.[17] Jesus described John as "a prophet in the wilderness," indeed "more than a prophet," who was God's messenger to "prepare your way before you" (11:7-10; per Mal 3:1), echoing and reinforcing the narrator's initial introduction to John as the "voice crying out in the wilderness" who came to "prepare the way of the Lord'" (3:3; per Isa 40:3). Jesus continued to praise John as the greatest man ever born because he stood at a pivotal position in the history of salvation, between the age of the law and prophets and the new age of the kingdom of heaven (11:11-13). Indeed, Jesus stated John was "Elijah" who was expected to return to the world before the "day of the Lord" (11:14; 2 Kings 2:1, 11; Mal 4:5-6). From a redaction-critical point of view, Elijah of the end time is the most characteristic profile of John in Matthew, compared to the voice in the wilderness in Mark, the unusual birth in Luke, and the first witness to Jesus in John. Finally, Jesus invited the crowds to hear the deeper meaning of his remarks saying, "Let anyone with ears, listen!" (11:15). John was the greatest prophet whose message was too important to be ignored. His ministry was a sign that the day of the Lord had arrived. Now, people must strive hard to enter the kingdom of heaven. It was with such high respect that Jesus spoke publicly about John's eschatological role in the history of salvation.

The second occasion follows Jesus's declaration of John as more than a prophet and Elijah (11:11-15) when Jesus seemed saddened by John's imprisonment and began to lament over the evil generation's rejection of them as a pair (11:16-19). Like children in the marketplace refusing to join the game of wedding or funeral, many people rejected their call for repentance. Worse than apathy, they mocked them as "the fasting John and the feasting Jesus."[18] John led an ascetic life to prepare for divine wrath, and Jesus befriended sinners, tax collectors, and prostitutes to enact divine mercy, but they received snub and distain especially from the leaders. Though suppressed, Jesus was confident of their mission and found comfort in God saying, "Yet wisdom is vindicated by her deeds" (11:19). This lament shows Jesus considered John and himself a pair of faithful prophets calling people to return to God as the personified Wisdom did (Prov 8-9; Wis 7:22-8:21). Though rejected and scorned by the people, they shall be vindicated by God. They are associated with each other in their call, faithfulness, and fate as prophets of the kingdom of heaven.

Jesus's third and last remark on John was heard in the Temple where the chief priests and the elders challenged his authority to drive out merchants and overturn the tables of the money changers (21:23-27). In a diatribe, Jesus countered their question with a question, "Did the baptism of John come from heaven, or was it of human origin?" (21:25). Why would Jesus choose John's baptism as a subject to retort those leaders? Evidently Jesus considered John's authority comparable to his own; both are from God. To help the readers understand why Jesus's question could put those leaders in the

---

[17] According to the Gospel of John, some priests and Levites thought John the Baptist might be the Messiah (John 1:19-20).

[18] John Crossan, *Jesus: A Revolutionary Biography* (San Francisco, CA: HarperCollins, 1994), 47.

bind, the narrator publicizes their internal debate and political calculation on the pro and con of their answer. They did not believe John's baptism was from God, but they did not want to offend the crowds who believed John to be a prophet of God either. What they were concerned about was simply to maintain authority in the Temple. With this question, Jesus outwitted those hostile leaders. To conclude his final remark on John, Jesus then said, John came "in the way of righteousness" (ἐν ὁδῷ δικαιοσύνης, 21:32), which in the Jewish wisdom tradition (cf. Prov 8:20; 12:28; 16:31) refers to the life that corresponds to the will of God.[19] The upshot of this description of John was to chastise the leaders, who were too political to show any integrity, for not following the way of righteousness. By associating himself with John, Jesus was also saying, like John he was teaching the will of God and like John he would not be intimidated by the powers that be. To him, John was an esteemed role model in the ministry of the kingdom of heaven.

4.4 Major Teachings

John and Jesus shared several key concepts in their teachings, but they also differed from each other on fine points.[20] What can their similar but different teachings tell us about their relationship? First to be noted is that Jesus is the hero of the Gospels which seek to encourage the readers to believe and follow Jesus, and John is little more than a foil to Jesus; naturally, the Evangelists present much more teaching of Jesus than that of John. Following the Gospels' purpose to advocate Jesus's superiority over John, scholars tend to amplify their differences into antitheses, pitching, for instance, Jesus's view of divine salvation against John's divine wrath, and Jesus's lifestyle of celebration against John's asceticism.[21] This "antithetical" perspective differentiates Jesus's theology from John's with more clarity, but it also obscures the fact that their vital similarities attest that "Jesus appears to have been fundamentally indebted to John throughout his ministry."[22] For our purpose to explore Jesus's relationship with John, their similarities should not be underestimated because they reveal a deep affinity which points to continuity rather than antagonism, in comparison to Jesus's relationship with other characters such as Pharisees, Sadducees, chief priests, and elders. In view of the disparity of information and prejudgment of viewpoint, it is very significant that Matthew's Jesus agreed with all of John's teaching points featured in the Gospel and adopted them as the foundation of his core teachings.

---

[19] Ulrich Luz, *Matthew 21–28* (Minneapolis, MN: Fortress, 2005), 31.
[20] John Meier, *A Marginal Jew: Rethinking the Historical Jesus, Vol. II: Mentor, Message, and Miracles*, 19–99.
[21] See, for instance, Gerd Theissen and Annette Merz, *The Historical Jesus: A Comprehensive Guide* (Minneapolis, MN: Fortress, 1998), 208–11.
[22] Dale Allison examines three of their shared concepts unique among their contemporaries (descent from Abraham and judgment, shared images in their teachings, Jesus and John's Coming One) to reach this conclusion. Dale Allison, "The Continuity between John and Jesus," *JSHJ* 1.1 (2003): 6–27, esp. 16. See also Daniel Dapaah, *The Relationship between John the Baptist and Jesus of Nazareth: A Critical Study* (Lanham, MD: University Press of America, 2005).

John and Jesus proclaimed the same message regarding the imminence of the kingdom of heaven: "Repent, for the kingdom of heaven has come near" (3:2b; 4:17b). Both used the concept "kingdom of God" ("kingdom of heaven" in Matthew) from the *Targum*[23] to alert people to the arriving of the day of the Lord that God had ordained for final vindication of the righteous and punishment of the wicked (Isa 13:6, 9, 13; Zach 9:16; 12:4; Mal 4:1, 3, 5). They did have different opinions on what the kingdom of heaven most importantly entails. For John, the coming of the kingdom of heaven was an ominous time of judgment when sinners would face the wrath of God (3:7). The ax was already lying at the root of the trees; every tree that did not bear good fruit would be cut down and burned in fire (3:10; 3:12). "Burning in fire" was a traditional image of judgment in the Hebrew scripture (Isa 10:33–34; 32:19; Dan 7:10, 11; Mal 3:2), which Jesus also used in his parables in reference to the final judgment (5:22; 7:19; 13:40, 42, 50; 18:8, 9; 25:41). So, now was the time to seek clemency from the holy God. For Jesus, the coming of the kingdom of heaven was also good news (4:17, 23; 9:35) because God would act in strength to reveal God's glory and save God's people from evil, sin, corruption, and oppression. Hence, Jesus's return to Galilee was compared to a "great light" for the people in darkness to see (4:16; Isa 9:2). In the Beatitudes, Jesus announced now was a time of blessing, because the kingdom of heaven would be given to the poor in spirit and those persecuted for righteousness' sake. People would receive comfort, satisfaction, mercy, and the privilege as God's children. They could pray to the almighty God as their Father in heaven and worry not about their lives or future because God would take care of them. Jesus also performed many miracles of healing and exorcism to prove his identity as the Messiah and the Son of God and to embody God's power to save people from sins and suffering. It would be amiss to think of John and Jesus only in antithesis, however; because John's warning of judgment serves to steer people back to God's favor and Jesus's mighty words and deeds that show God's strength in mercy includes admonition against complacency or indifference to God's demand. Jesus ends the Sermon on the Mount with a warning to do the will of God in order to enter the kingdom of heaven "on that day" (7:21–22). Only those who act on his instructions would be the wise people who build a house on the rock to be safe from the rain, flood, and wind (7:24–27). While healing the sick and casting out demons with compassion and power, Jesus also denounced the hypocritical Pharisees (23:13–39) and the corrupted priests and elders (21:31–32, 43–44). In other words, John and Jesus shared the same eschatological outlook on the kingdom of heaven which manifests both God's mercy and God's justice.

In response to the coming of the kingdom of heaven, John and Jesus urged people to "repent" (3:2a; 4:17a). Repentance in Greek is *metanoia* (change of mind), a term used by philosophers and easy to understand for Gentile readers.[24] For John and Jesus, however, it was most probably understood in Hebrew as *shuv* meaning "a complete reversal of direction away from sin, in accordance with the biblical and post-biblical

---

[23] Bruce Chilton, "God in Strength," in *The Kingdom of God*, ed. Bruce Chilton (Philadelphia, PA: Fortress, 1984), 121–32.

[24] James, Crossley, "The Semitic Background to Repentance in the Teaching of John the Baptist and Jesus," *JSHJ* 2.2 (2004): 138–57.

Hebrew dual concept of 'turning' vis. 'turning away from' or 'returning to.'"[25] In view of the imminent judgment, John warned the Pharisees and Sadducees to bear fruit worthy of repentance (3:8) because they could not rely on their privileged status as Abraham's children to flee from God's wrath (3:9). The only way to escape was to bear good fruit (3:10), to do what God commanded. To repent, people need to recognize first where they have gone wrong. So, John encouraged his followers to fast regularly (9:14) that they might examine their lives, mourn for wrongdoings, pray for forgiveness, and seek God's guidance to lead a new life in keeping with the law and prophets. Like John, Jesus also urged people to "repent" (4:17) and used the same image of bearing fruit to define the action of repentance. He forewarned the chief priests and Pharisees in Jerusalem saying, "Therefore, I tell you, the kingdom of God will be taken away from you and given to a people that produces the fruits of the kingdom" (21:43). Unlike John, however, Jesus did not require his disciples to fast. He wanted to emphasize the kingdom of heaven was an occasion for joy like wedding. While the bridegroom was present, therefore, the guests should celebrate and rejoice rather than mourn or grieve (9:15). Fundamentally, however, divine wrath and divine mercy are two sides of the same coin. So, like John, Jesus also issued warnings to his followers that they would be shut out of the kingdom of heaven if they did not obey the will of God and act on his words (7:21–24). For John and Jesus, repentance is absolutely required for the kingdom of heaven, and it is understood as an action in obedience to the will of God.

To encourage true repentance, John and Jesus adopted baptism as a public ritual to express one's confession of sins and commitment to new life (3:6, 13, 15; 28:19). John urged people to be baptized by water as a sign of their sins being forgiven and their lives being cleansed. It was a ritual of purity in response to the coming of God's wrath. It was also a gesture of commitment to a godly life to avoid judgment. For Jesus, baptism was a ritual of purity and commitment and therefore a proper way to fulfill all righteousness, but it was also an occasion of theophany in which he experienced the Holy Spirit and God as the beloved Son. For all these good reasons, Jesus prescribed baptism as the first step to disciple-making in the great commission, "Go and make disciples of all nations, baptizing them in the name of the father and of the Son and of the Holy Spirit, and teaching them to obey everything that I have commanded you. And remember, I am with you always, to the end of the age" (28:19–20). Baptism symbolizes leaving the sin behind and entering the new relationship with God and enables the baptized to learn and obey Jesus's commandments with Jesus's eternal presence. From an "affinity" perspective, it seems Jesus inherited John's idea of baptism as a ritual for the confession of sins and commitment to obedience that was consistent with other Jewish teaching on baptism, but he did add to it the idea of reconciliation with God and assurance of divine presence. He did not object to John's view in this case but rather enriched its meaning.

To guide their followers to live a good life worthy of repentance and baptism, John and Jesus focused on the idea of doing righteousness (*dikaiosune*). It is true that John

---

[25] Geza Vermes, *The Religion of Jesus the Jew* (London: SCM, 1993), 191.

never used the word "righteousness" in his teaching, but in the Gospel of Matthew Jesus lauded John as coming "in the way of righteousness" (21:32) in his retort to the chief priests and elders in the Temple. Righteousness (or justice) in Hebrew (*tsedaqah*) is a key concept with a constellation of meanings and nuances. Used in various contexts in the Hebrew scripture, it refers to the right relationship with God and with each other, right character and conducts, and acquittal from legal judgment. For instance, Abraham believed God's promise to give him a son in old age. "And he believed the Lord; and the Lord reckoned it to him as righteousness" (Gen 15:6). God who led Israel out of Egypt gave commandments to Israel for their good, so "If we diligently observe this entire commandment before the Lord our God, as he has commanded us, we will be in the right" (Deut 6:25). The prophet Hosea appealed to Israel, "Sow for yourselves righteousness; reap steadfast love; break up your fallow ground for it is time to seek the Lord, that he may come and rain righteousness upon you" (Hos 10:12). It would not be a stretch to assume these basic ideas of righteousness and justice lay behind John's teaching of bearing good fruit and his own way of righteousness. Doing righteousness as God had commanded was also the capstone of Jesus's teaching.[26] Jesus blessed those who hungered and thirsted for righteousness that they would be filled to satisfaction (5:6). He promised the kingdom of heaven to those who were persecuted for the sake of righteousness (5:10). He urged his followers to do righteousness exceeding that of the most law-observant scribes and Pharisees so that they may enter the kingdom of heaven (5:20). He also called almsgiving, fasting, and praying the "deeds of righteousness" and taught people how to practice them rightly and properly (6:1). Finally, he commanded his hearers to strive first for the kingdom of God and his righteousness with a promise that God would provide all their needs (6:33). Leander Keck aptly summarizes Jesus's teaching in this way, "The [Jesus's] instruction did not take the form of a theory about the kingdom or God's character. Rather, Jesus simply appealed to it as the warrant for his call for moral change that is to reflect God. Right response is not just right doctrine (he assumed that) or esoteric knowledge of God (he rejected that) but rather a righteous life."[27] It is remarkable that Matthew's Jesus, who taught righteousness and lived righteously, would label John as coming in the way of righteousness. Clearly, Jesus respected John as a righteous teacher. It was probably under John's influence that Jesus decided to make doing righteousness the center of his own teaching.

All the concepts discussed above were not exclusive of John and Jesus. Many of which could be found in the writings of the Pharisees and the Essenes. But the combination and centrality of these concepts in their teachings, coupled with the fact that Jesus had stayed with John but was opposed to the Pharisees and unrelated to the Essenes, suggest that Jesus was indebted to John for many of his basic concepts about the kingdom of heaven.

---

[26] Georg Strecker, *Der Weg der Gerechtigkeit: Untersuchung zur de Matthäus* (Vandenhoeck & Ruprecht, Göttingen, 1971); Benno Przybylski, *Righteousness in Matthew and His World of Thought* (Cambridge: Cambridge University Press, 1980).

[27] Leander Keck, *Who Is Jesus?: History in Perfect Tense* (Columbia: University of South Carolina, 2000), 102.

4.5 Featured Actions

A good teacher exerts influence on his students through inspiring deeds as well as wise words. In Matthew's story, four featured actions that John and Jesus shared are noteworthy. They suggest John made a deep impact on Jesus and Jesus imitated John as a student did his teacher.

A charismatic teacher attracts followers from all over the place to gather around and listen to his teaching, and usually has a group of enthusiastic disciples staying with him as an inner circle to support his movement. In a culture where famous teachers—philosophers or rabbis—normally taught at school or home, John and Jesus acted differently from the rest by preaching in open places allowing access to people from all walks of life, including the *am ha-aretz* (people of the dirt).[28] John preached and baptized outdoors but stayed mostly in one area by the Jordan River in Judea. After his arrest, Jesus took John's eschatological message to the Galilean region in the north and followed John's example to preach in the open so that all people could hear the gospel, not only the few privileged elites who could afford a tuition or gift for their teachers. But then, Jesus expanded his ministry by making itinerant rounds to villages, towns, and cities (4:23; 9:35) and sending his disciples out to the lost sheep of Israel (10:5) and in the end to all nations (28:19). The good news of the kingdom of heaven was too important to be kept in one location; it should be broadcast to all people everywhere, city dwellers and country peasants. So, Jesus took it on the road. Like an ingenious young entrepreneur with smart strategies, Jesus modeled his ministry after John's open movement but built a wider network with broader reach to all people. Their differences in ministry tactics signal evolution rather than opposition.

An authentic teacher lives his life in accordance with his conviction or philosophy. A true Stoic is expected to conduct every affair following reason, principle, and moderation. An ideal Cynic is expected to live his life with simplicity, freedom, and contentment. A pious Pharisee is expected to keep all purity and dietary laws to command respect from his fellow Jews. In Matthew's Gospel, John was a prophet with integrity. He believed that the kingdom of heaven was coming near, so he was keen on preaching the baptism of repentance. He was contented to live in the wilderness away from the comfort of a city, wore clothes of camel fur and a belt of leather, and ate locusts and wild honey. His location, lifestyle, and attire matched his prophetic call as a voice of God from the margin of the society with an urgent message of warning. Like John, Jesus also believed the kingdom of heaven had come near, so he was eager to spread the good news of God's salvation to all the people. He traveled everywhere in Galilee to teach in the synagogues, proclaim the gospel, cure diseases, and cast out demons. He trusted God's care, so he did not carry extra coats or bags, relying simply on the generosity of the people who accepted his message and volunteered to provide. He once described his lifestyle to a would-be disciple saying, "Foxes have holes, and birds of the air have nests; but the Son of Man has nowhere to lay his head" (8:20). He

---

[28] Martin Hengel, *The Charismatic Leader and His Followers*, 16–37, esp. 34–7.

would be tired and hungry, and sometimes praying all night, but he remained totally dedicated to his ministry as John did.

A respected teacher believes in the truth he teaches and will not be intimidated, tempted, or bribed to tell lies or speak falsehood. Socrates and Elijah were honored as great sage and prophet because they were fearless truth-speakers. In the Gospel of Matthew, John spoke truth to the power with courage. He challenged Pharisees and Sadducees to obey the law of God. He condemned Herod Antipas for his illicit relationship with Herodias. He was imprisoned and beheaded because he called out sin without fear. As a result, his martyrdom won reverence from many people including Herod Antipas. Jesus did the same thing. He denounced Pharisees and scribes, the teachers of the law, calling out their incompetency and hypocrisy. He befriended sinners, tax-collectors, and prostitutes to the ire of religious leaders (9:10–13; 11:19). And he overturned the tables of money changers and animal dealers in the Temple to chastise the chief priests and the elders' corruption and greed. Both John and Jesus spoke truth to the power without fear, and they both died as martyrs.

Finally, an inspiring teacher sets a good example for students by practicing what he preaches. In the Gospel of Matthew, John followed his own preaching on doing what God commanded in the face of the kingdom of heaven to live simply, teach fervently, baptize prudently, and confront evil daringly; so, he was revered. Like John, Jesus also practiced what he preached. Following his own advice on striving first for the kingdom of God and his righteousness, he knowingly and willingly traveled to Jerusalem to suffer in the hands of the priests and the elders and to be crucified. At the night of his arrest in the Garden of Gethsemane, he prayed for the removal of his cup of suffering but only if God wishes (26:39). Both John and Jesus spoke truth and obey God's will in life and death. In so doing, they became role models for their followers. These featured actions show that, like his teacher John, Jesus was charismatic, authentic, respected, and inspiring.

4.6 Conclusion

In a Gospel in which Jesus is the main character and his superiority the priority, it is remarkable to see how some significant anecdotes and *chreiai* of John are favorably reported and how his personal relationship with Jesus is affectionately depicted. John the Baptist was the only known teacher of Jesus with whom Jesus stayed and studied for some time in his formative years. Having received John's baptism and kept associations with him, Jesus inherited John's main teachings and imitated his featured actions. John proclaimed the coming of the kingdom of God, preached the baptism of repentance, confronted hypocritic religious teachers and corrupted political leaders, and died an inspiring death as martyr of truth. Jesus shared the same eschatological message, exhibited the same spiritual character, displayed the same moral courage, and died on the cross with the same valor. Showing so many substantial affinities between John and Jesus behind their apparent differences in their teachings and actions, Matthew has robustly attested to John the Baptist as the most influential teacher of Jesus. He inspired and shaped Jesus to grow and evolve into the supreme teacher of God's will, whose commandments were to be taught and obeyed from disciples to disciples.

Part 2

Jesus's Teachings

5

Jesus as a Teacher of New Covenant Torah: An Examination of the Sermon on the Mount

Charles L. Quarles

5.1 Introduction

In 1902, Benjamin Bacon, professor of New Testament (NT) studies at Yale University, published a brief book titled *The Sermon on the Mount: Its Literary Structure and Didactic Purpose* based on a series of lectures that he had delivered at Wellesley College. Bacon argued that the Sermon on the Mount begins the story of Jesus's teaching ministry by "conspicuously placing the Mount of Beatitudes over against the Mount of the Law" so that Jesus as the "true Prophet, the second Moses" delivers a discourse "whose subject was the new Torah of the righteousness of the kingdom of God."[1] He further argued that this new Torah is what Paul calls "the Law of the Messiah" (Gal 6:2) and what James refers to as "the law of liberty" and the "royal law" (Jas 1:25; 2:8, 12).[2]

Elements of Bacon's view are affirmed by several more recent commentators on the Gospel of Matthew. Robert Gundry, for example, calls the Sermon on the Mount "the word of God as taught by the greater Moses" and adds: "Because it falls between the ascent of Jesus up the mountain and his descent, the sermon gains the connotation of law, related to the Mosaic law, which was also issued from a mountain."[3] Dale Allison goes significantly farther: "The typology is thus extensive and consistently thought through. So when Jesus goes up on the mountain to utter the sermon on the mount, he is speaking as the mosaic Messiah and delivering messianic Torah."[4] He concludes: "I am lured to believe that Matthew 1–5 presents Jesus as the new lawgiver, the eschatological revealer and interpreter of Torah, the Messiah who brought the definitive, end-time revelation for the heart, as foretold by Jeremiah's ancient oracle (cf. Just, Dial. 11)."[5]

---

[1] Benjamin W. Bacon, *The Sermon on the Mount: Its Literary Structure and Didactic Purpose* (New York: Macmillan Company, 1902), 7, 23, 46.
[2] Bacon, *The Sermon on the Mount*, 7.
[3] Robert H. Gundry, *Matthew: A Commentary on His Literary and Theological Art* (Grand Rapids, MI: Eerdmans, 1982), 65–6.
[4] W. D. Davies and D. C. Allison, *Matthew 1–7*, ICC (New York: T&T Clark, 2004), 427.
[5] Dale C. Allison Jr., *The New Moses: A Matthean Typology* (Minneapolis, MN: Fortress, 1993), 190. Readers should consult the very helpful and carefully nuanced discussion of "Jesus and the Torah (5:17–48)," in *New Moses*, 182–90 which supports in detail the conclusion quoted above.

Craig Keener insists: "But a central point of the sermon is Jesus's unique authority as the supreme expositor of the law's message, a new Moses."[6]

Recent commentaries focusing specifically on the Sermon on the Mount have come to similar conclusions. My 2011 commentary states: "Jesus' ascent of a mount to deliver His authoritative and application of God's law to His people is strongly reminiscent of Moses' ascent of Sinai to receive and deliver the law of God (Exod 19:3)."[7] Scot McKnight argued that the introduction to the Sermon on the Mount when interpreted against the background of the Mosaic typology in the four preceding chapters implied that "Jesus is teaching the new law as the new Moses for the new people of God."[8] Though he prefers to categorize the Sermon on the Mount as wisdom literature, Jonathan Pennington states that the Sermon on the Mount presents Jesus "as the new and final arbiter of God's law, thereby functioning as a new and final Moses."[9] Pennington affirmingly quotes Allison's description of the sermon as the "Messianic Torah."[10]

On the other hand, several scholars have expressed serious reservations about a prominent new Moses typology in Matthew and particularly in the Sermon on the Mount. D. A. Carson is representative of these concerns:

> A debate that is sometimes tied to one or another of the theological approaches just listed concerns possible affinities between Jesus and Moses (see discussion in Chapter 1). Some see the tightest possible affinities; others remain unconvinced, preferring a nuanced judgment like that of Garland: "While Matthew presents Jesus as Moses-like, he does not depict him as a new Moses, but as the Lord, the son of God." Though these and other interpretive grids highlight neglected themes, they overlook the thrust of the sermon as a whole and its place in Matthew.[11]

---

[6] Craig S. Keener, *A Commentary on the Gospel of Matthew* (Grand Rapids, MI: Eerdmans, 1999), 162. For similar views, see Craig Evans, *Matthew*, New Cambridge Bible Commentary (New York: Cambridge, 2012), 98; David Turner, *Matthew*, BECNT (Grand Rapids, MI: Baker, 2008), 149.

[7] Charles L. Quarles, *The Sermon on the Mount*, NAC Studies in Bible and Theology (Nashville, TN: B&H Academic, 2011), 35. I further argue that the new Moses typology is essential for understanding the Sermon on the Mount, though one must appreciate the categorical distinction between the old covenant Torah and the Torah written on the heart in fulfillment of the new covenant. See ibid., 20–38. For additional arguments, see Quarles, "The Blessings of the New Moses: An Examination of the Theological Purpose of the Matthean Beatitudes." *JSHS* 13 (2015): 305–25.

[8] Scot McKnight, *Sermon on the Mount*, The Story of God Bible Commentary (Grand Rapids, MI: Zondervan, 2013), 24. McKnight also argued that Jesus's messianic ethics include "ethics from above" which he defined as "Torah" (8–10).

[9] Jonathan Pennington, *The Sermon on the Mount and Human Flourishing: A Theological Commentary* (Grand Rapids, MI: Baker, 2017), 139. For the classification as wisdom literature, see esp. 25–38. This classification constitutes the thesis of his plenary address, "The Sermon on the Mount as Wisdom Literature," (paper presented at the Annual Meeting of the Eastern Region of the ETS, Lynchburg, VA, April 6, 2019).

[10] Pennington, *The Sermon on the Mount and Human Flourishing*, 140.

[11] D. A. Carson, "Matthew," in *Matthew & Mark*, Expositor's Bible Commentary 9, rev. ed. (Grand Rapids, MI: Zondervan, 2010), 157. See the note on 159 for Carson's clear rejection of the new Moses theme.

John Nolland acknowledges the possibility of an allusion to the giving of the law at Mount Sinai but argues that if such an allusion is intended by Matthew, "it can play only a minor role."[12] Michael Wilkins also rejects Bacon's interpretation:

> Expositors have wondered whether Matthew draws parallels with Old Testament incidents or themes, such as Moses' going up to Sinai to receive the Law (Ex 19–20). It is doubtful, however, that Jesus is to be seen as a new Moses giving a new Torah in the five discourses, as some have suggested. Jesus does not give a new law, rather he is the One whose life and teaching fulfills the law (cf. 5:17–20).[13]

This chapter will present the case that Bacon's understanding of the purpose of the Sermon on the Mount was largely correct. The case will rely on six arguments: (1) The Pentateuch foretold the coming of a prophet like Moses who would deliver new divine commandments. (2) Jews of the Second Temple era and rabbinic period expected the coming of a new Moses who would mediate a new covenant and teach a new Torah. (3) Matthew presents Jesus as the new and better Moses. (4) Matthew presents Jesus as the one who enacts the new covenant. (5) Matthew presents the Sermon on the Mount as the new covenant Torah delivered by the new Moses. (6) Other NT authors and early reception history support recognition of the Sermon on the Mount as the messianic Torah.

5.2 The Pentateuch Foretold the Coming of a Prophet like Moses Who Would Deliver New Divine Commandments

Moses's prophecy in Deut 18:15–19 taught that when the Messiah came, he would resemble Moses in important ways. The prophecy itself focuses primarily on the new Moses's authoritative teaching. It insists, "I will put my words in his mouth and he will tell them everything I command him" (Deut 18:15).[14] Moses insisted, "You must listen to him," and the verb "listen" refers to careful hearing with an obedient response.[15] Similarly YAHWEH himself says, "I will hold accountable whoever does not listen to my words that he speaks in my name." The focus of the prophecy is that the new Moses will relay divine commands to the people which they must obey. The new Moses will be a lawgiver. Some first-century Jews regarded this text as a prophecy that foretold the coming of a Messiah-like figure (John 6:14; 7:40). The apostle Peter and Stephen recognized the text as a messianic prophecy (Acts 3:11–26; 7:37) and applied it specifically to Jesus.

---

[12] John Nolland, *Matthew*, NIGTC (Grand Rapids, MI: Eerdmans, 2005), 192–3.
[13] Michael J. Wilkins, *Matthew*, NIV Application Commentary (Grand Rapids, MI: Zondervan, 2004), 191–2.
[14] John Yieh, *One Teacher: Jesus' Teaching Role in Matthew's Gospel Report*, BZNW 124 (New York: Walter de Gruyter, 2004), 250 insightfully comments that Jesus "likens his own words of instruction to God's will (Matt 7:21, 24)," thereby confirming that he is the prophet like Moses who speaks God's commands.
[15] See "שׁמע," HALOT, def. 4.

5.3 Jews of the Second Temple Era and Rabbinic Period Expected the Coming of a New Moses Who Would Mediate a New Covenant and Teach a New Torah

A later Rabbinic tradition shows that for nearly a millennium after the time of Jesus, Jews continued to expect a Messiah who would be like Moses:

> R. Berekiah said in the name of R. Isaac: As the first redeemer [Moses] was, so shall the latter Redeemer [Messiah] be.[16]

Numerous texts demonstrate that this widespread rabbinic Messianic expectation was not a late development. Evidence of it appears in Qumran documents, Josephus, and elsewhere in the NT.[17]

4Q175 quotes the prophet like Moses prophecy of Deut 18:18-19 in a series of texts thought to be a "messianic anthology." Like Moses, the Messiah would "tell them all that I command him," that is, deliver God's own commandments to his people. Damascus Document 7:18 quotes Baalam's oracle about the star that will come out of Jacob (Num 24:17), which was widely regarded as a prophecy about the Messiah[18] and states that the prophecy is fulfilled by "the interpreter of the law."

Since the Messiah was to be like Moses, he was naturally associated with a new covenant and a new law. Jewish literature of the Second Temple era very frequently describes Moses as a "lawgiver." The portrayal of Moses as a lawgiver is prominent in early Judaism as expressed by Philo, Josephus, and the Mishnah.

In the works of Philo, Moses is described as the "lawgiver" at least 80 times and sometimes with adjectives such as "Jewish lawgiver," "great lawgiver," or "holy lawgiver."[19] In *Names* 126, Philo even claims that Moses was called a "lawgiver" by God himself. He argues that the name Moses means "handling" and refers to Moses "handling divine things" by interpreting a code of laws. Philo wrote his *On the Life of Moses* to present Moses as the supreme example of four major roles: king, lawgiver, high priest, and prophet.

A similar view of Moses is evident a few decades later in the writings of Josephus. In *Jewish Antiquities* 1 §18 he writes: "Almost all our constitution depends on the wisdom of Moses, our legislator." He also describes Moses as "the legislator of the Jews" (*Ant.* 1.3.6 §95), "Moses, their legislator" (*Ant.* 1.13.4 §240), and "our lawgiver Moses" (*Ag.*

---

[16] Eccl. Rab. 1:9; Pesiq. Rab. 15:10; Ruth Rab. 2:14.

[17] Charles L. Quarles, "'Out of Egypt I Called My Son': Intertextuality and Metalepsis in Matthew 2:15," *STR* 8.1 (2017): 3–20. Evidence also appears elsewhere in the NT as will be demonstrated later.

[18] J. J. Collins, *The Scepter and the Star: The Messiahs of the Dead Sea Scrolls and Other Ancient Literature* (New York: Doubleday, 1995), esp. 24, 63–70. See also J. A. Fitzmyer, *The Dead Sea Scrolls and Christian Origins* (Grand Rapids, MI: Eerdmans, 2000), 75, 86, 98; C. G. Boyles, "The Redeeming King: Psalm 72's Contribution to the Messianic Ideal," in *Eschatology, Messianism, and the Dead Sea Scrolls*, ed. C. A. Evans and P. W. Flint (Grand Rapids, MI: Eerdmans, 1997), 23.

[19] *Leg.* 2:14; 3:145; *Cher.* 53; *Sacr.* 136; 138; *Det.* 62; 115; 135; 171; *Post.* 47; 57; 78; 128; 133; 166; *Gig.* 32; 58; 65; 66; *Deus* 21, 23, 52, 67, 125; *Agr.* 22, 27, 84, 86, 144; *Plant.* 66, 141; *Ebr.* 1, 2, 13, 47, 109; *Sobr.* 1, 46; *Conf.* 5, 23, 107, 135, 142, 191; *Migr.* 23, 113; *Her.* 163, 292; *Fug.* 120, 173, 175, 188, 194; *Mut.* 126; *Somn.* 1:39, 93, 112, 121; 2:4, 71, 192; *Abr.* 5, 28, 31; *Mos.* 1:1, 128, 162, 334; 2:3, 5, 6, 8, 9, 14, 45, 66, 187, 188, 190, 292.

Ap. 2.15 §145). Moses recorded the laws dictated by God (*Ant.* 3.5.4 §90) and "went no longer up to Mount Sinai, but went into the tabernacle, and learned of God what they were to do, and what laws should be made" (*Ant.* 3.8.10 §222). Later Josephus writes that "Moses made these laws" (*Ant.* 3.11.4 §266) and "Truly Moses gave them all these precepts" (*Ant.* 3.12.3 §280; cf. 4.8.44 §302). He repeatedly summarizes principles of the law with the words "Moses forbade" (*Ant.* 3.11.5 §269; 3.12.1 §274). He frequently refers to the "laws of Moses."[20] He claims that Moses was "powerful in making men give credit to what he delivered, not only during the time of his natural life, but even there is still no one of the Hebrews who does not act even now as if Moses were present, and ready to punish him if he should do anything that is indecent; nay, there is no one but is obedient to what laws he ordained, although they might be concealed in their transgressions" (*Ant.* 3.15.3 §317). Josephus calls the OT Law the "constitutions of Moses" (*Ant.* 4.8.44 §308), "the body of laws that Moses had given them" (*Ant.* 6.5.6 §93), "the commands of Moses" (*Ant.* 6.7.3 §133; 7.13.1 §318), "[God's] commands, and his laws, which he hath given us by Moses" (*Ant.* 7.14.2 §338; 7.15.1 §384), "the command of Moses" (*Ant.* 8.3.7 §90; 8.3.8 §94), "the ten commandments, which God spoke to Moses in Mount Sinai" (*Ant.* 8.4.1 §104), and "those precepts which God had given them by Moses, because by that means the Hebrew nation would be happy, and indeed the most blessed of all nations among all mankind" (*Ant.* 8.4.4 §120). Josephus insists that "Moses received his laws from God" (8.13.7 §349) and refers to "the laws which God gave them by Moses" (9.1.1 §2). In describing the views of the Jews in *J.W.* 2.8.9 §145, Josephus writes: "What they most of all honor, after God himself, is the name of their legislator [Moses]; whom, if anyone blaspheme, he is punished capitally."

In the Mishnah the characterization of Moses that seems most common is "lawgiver." The Mishnah stresses that the law was given to Moses on Sinai (m. Peah 2:6; m. Ed. 8:7; m. Avot 1:1; m. Yad. 4:3). Consequently, it refers to the Law as "the Torah of Moses, your servant" (m. Yoma 3:8; 4:2; 6:2) and "the law of Moses" (Ket 7:6).

Since the prophet like Moses prophecy stressed the prophet's role in delivering divine commandments and since first-century Jewish and early rabbinic texts characterized Moses primarily as a lawgiver, one should expect the new Moses to deliver new commandments, a new Torah. This new Torah would have continuity with the Torah of Moses and yet have fresh aspects as well. As Jeremias demonstrated, this prompted at least some first-century Jews to link the Deut 18 prophecy with prophecies related to the new covenant and thus to expect the new Moses to deliver the new covenant.[21] The Samaritans of the NT era held to a messianic interpretation of the Deut 18 prophecy.

---

[20] *Ant.* 3.15.3 §319; 4.6.10 §141; 4.8.22 §242; 8.7.5 §191; 8.15.2 §395; 9.7.4 §153; 9.9.1 §187; 10.4.2 §59; 10.4.3 §63; 10.4.5 §72; 11.1.3 §17; 11.4.1 §76; 11.4.7 §108; 11.5.1 §121; 11.5.5 §154; 13.3.4 §79; 13.10.6 §297; 17.6.3 §159; 18.3.5 §81; 20.2.4 §44; 20.5.4 §44; *Ag. Ap.* 1.8 §39.

[21] J. Jeremias, "Μωυσῆς," *TDNT* 4.861–2. Peter Gentry has helpfully identified "Major Texts Dealing with a New Covenant" in Peter Gentry and Stephen Wellum, *Kingdom through Covenant*, 448. He points to Jeremiah 31:31–34; 32:36–41; 50:2–5; Ezekiel 11:18–21; 16:59–63; 18:30–32; 34:20–31 (esp. v. 25); 36:24–32 (esp. v. 26) [cf. Isa 59:21]; 37:15–28 (esp. v. 26); Isa 54:1–10 (esp. vv. 9–10); 55:1–5; 61:8–9. In a later chapter, Gentry correctly expands the list to include Daniel 9:25–27. See 541–71. He implicitly connects the promise of the return from exile (which consists of two stages) in Deut 30:1–10 to the new covenant as well referencing, in particular, the circumcision of the heart in Deut 30:6 (547–50, 650).

These expectations prompted the Samaritan woman in John 4:25 to say, "When that [Messiah] comes, he will teach us all things."[22]

Later Jewish literature expresses similar views. Targum Onqelos on Gen 49:11 states that the Messiah will gather the righteous ones around him and will instruct the doers of the Torah. Similarly, the Targum on Isa 52:13–53:12 identifies the "servant" as the Messiah and states "by his teaching peace will increase upon us, and when we follow his words, our sins will be forgiven" (Tg. Isa. 53:5). It adds that in the kingdom of the Messiah, those who do "the Torah of the Lord will succeed by his favor," and he will subject both the righteous and the rebels to the Torah. Rabbinic exegetical works stated that when King Messiah comes he would "elucidate for them the words of the Torah" and "gather the exiles and give them thirty commandments" (Gen Rab. 98:9). These thirty commandments are apparently an expansion of the Decalogue. Some rabbis argued that in the messianic age, God's people would receive a new Torah.[23] This Torah could even be described specifically as the "Torah of the Messiah" (Mid. Eccl. 11:8).

5.4 Matthew Presents Jesus as the New and Better Moses

A prominent theme of Matthew's Gospel portrays Jesus as the new Moses, the prophet like Moses of Deut 18. The most thorough defense of this position to date is Dale Allison's, *The New Moses: A Matthean Typology*. Allison's extended treatment is largely persuasive, and his thesis can be reinforced by additional features of Matthew's Gospel that Allison did not treat.[24] Matthew's Jesus is like Moses in his infancy, teaching ministry, fasting, miracles, and transfiguration. For the sake of space, we will consider now just the first and last of these parallels.

To Jewish Christian readers, Herod's slaughter of the male Israelite infants of Bethlehem age two and younger in Matt 2 would have been reminiscent of Pharaoh's order to kill all male Israelite infants in Exod 1. In both accounts, an evil pagan king murdered male Israelite infants, but God providentially spared the baby who would become the future deliverer. The Matthean account reverberates with even greater similarities to popular Jewish traditions about Moses's birth that are preserved in texts such as Josephus's *Jewish Antiquities*. In Josephus's account, a "sacred scribe" in Pharaoh's court foretold that an Israelite boy would be born who would bring down the Egyptian dominion, raise the Israelites, be more righteous than any other man, and obtain a glory that would be remembered through all ages. The frightened king responded by ordering that all male Israelite infants be cast into the Nile and killed.[25]

---

[22] For a brief but helpful discussion of early Jewish sources referring to the Messiah as one who is taught by God and who teaches others, see Stephen E. Witmer, *Divine Instruction in Early Christianity*, WUNT 246 (Tübingen: Mohr Siebeck, 2008), 56–62.

[23] Lev. Rab. 13:3; Tg. Isa. 12:3; Tg. Ket. on Songs 5:10; Midr. Eccl. 2:1; Yal. on Isa. 26:2.

[24] See Charles L. Quarles, *A Theology of Matthew: Jesus Revealed as Deliverer, King, and Incarnate Creator*, Explorations in Biblical Theology (Phillipsburg, NJ: P&R, 2013). Chapters 3 and 4 summarize some of Allison's argument, reinforcing the view at certain points and showing the Christological implications of this insight.

[25] Josephus, *Ant.* 2.9.3 §§210–16.

In both Matthew's account and Josephus's account, a pagan king ordered the slaughter of male Israelite infants because he feared he would be overthrown by their coming deliverer, but God providentially rescued that deliverer.

The parallels between Jesus and Moses are even more pronounced in Matt 2:20b. The words "Those seeking the life of the child are dead" are a clear and direct quotation of the Greek version (LXX) of Exod 3:19. These words were originally spoken to Moses by God from the burning bush. But now these words about Moses are applied by the angel to Jesus. The angel of the Lord seems to quote these words in order to signal that Jesus will somehow be like Moses.

Although many other parallels exist between Jesus and Moses in Matthew, perhaps the most important occur at Jesus's transfiguration in Matt 17. All three of the Synoptic Gospels (Matt 17:1-9; Mark 9:2-10; Luke 9:28-36) describe Jesus's transfiguration in terms that are clearly reminiscent of Moses's experience on Sinai recorded in Exod 24 and 34. The following parallels exist between the Gospel accounts and the Exodus narrative:

1. The events occur after a period of six days (Exod 24:16; Matt 17:1)
2. The events occur on a high mountain (Exod 24:12,15-18; 34:3; Matt 17:1)
3. A cloud descended and covered the mountain (Exod 24:15-18; 34:5; Matt 17:5)
4. A voice spoke from the cloud (Exod 24:16; Matt 17:5)
5. The central figure reflected or radiated the divine glory (Exod 34:29-30,35; Matt 17:2)
6. Three individuals are given special mention (Exod 24:1; Matt 17:1)
7. Those who saw the radiance were struck with fear (Exod 34:29-30; Matt 17:6)[26]

Some of these parallels would likely have escaped the attention of the casual reader. On the other hand, some of them practically leapt off the page. 2 Maccabees 2:8 indicates that the glory of the Lord and the cloud were especially associated with Moses.

Although the major parallels between Jesus and Moses are present in Mark's and Luke's accounts, Matthew contains a few additional descriptions that are designed to heighten the parallel. For example, only Matthew's account mentions that Jesus's "face shone like the sun" (Matt 17:2). Although this detail was not mentioned in the Old Testament (OT) accounts of Moses's encounter with YAHWEH, it was emphasized in later Jewish traditions about Moses's experience. When Philo described the event, he mentioned that "those who saw him [Moses] wondered and were amazed, and could no longer endure to look upon him with their eyes, inasmuch as his countenance shone like the light of the sun."[27] Similarly, a passage in the Babylonian Talmud distinguishes the glory of Moses from that of Joshua by saying, "The face of Moses glows like the face of the sun, the face of Joshua like the face of the moon."[28]

Perhaps most importantly, the divine utterance at the transfiguration alludes to the prophecy about the prophet like Moses in Deut 18:15. The utterance is identical to the

---

[26] Allison, *New Moses*, 243-4.
[27] Philo, *Mos.* 2:70.
[28] b. B. Bat. 75a. See also LAB 12; Sipre Num. 140; Deut. Rab. 11 (207c).

one given at Jesus's baptism, except for the addition of the words "Listen to him" (Matt 17:5; Mark 9:7; Luke 9:35). Deuteronomy 18:15 said that when the prophet like Moses came, "it is to him you shall listen." The two phrases are identical in Greek except for the grammatical forms of the verbs. The Septuagint used the imperatival future, while the Gospels use the normal imperative rather than the more archaic form.

Many other features of Matthew's Gospel confirm his intention of demonstrating Jesus's similarity to Moses. However, those mentioned above should be sufficient to show that the portrayal of Jesus as the prophet like Moses was an important part of Matthew's theological purpose. This Moses typology is particularly prominent in the introduction to the Sermon on the Mount as well (Matt 5:1–2).[29]

5.5 Matthew Presents Jesus as the One Who Enacts the New Covenant

Matthew alluded to the new covenant at both the beginning and end of Jesus's ministry. The first allusion to the new covenant appears in Matt 1:21, which scholars generally recognize as the programmatic statement for the Gospel.[30] The angel explained to Joseph the significance of the name "Jesus" with the words "for he will save his people from their sins." Interpreters still debate the OT background for the statement. Many argue for Ps 130:8, "he will redeem Israel from all his iniquities," though a few opt for Judg 13:5, "he will begin to save Israel from the power of the Philistines."[31] Nevertheless, Matt 1:21 seems to have a tighter connection to Ezek 36–37 both semantically and thematically.[32] Ezekiel 36:29a says, "I will save you from all your uncleannesses." Although the parallels with Matt 1:21 initially seem modest, they are heightened when one observes that "you" is identified as "my people" in the previous clause. Furthermore, when the promise is repeated in Ezek 37:23b, Israel's lawless deeds are described as acts in which they "sinned." Thus the promises in Ezekiel share the three critical terms "save," "people," and "sin" with Matt 1:21.

This allusion to Ezek 37:23 appears to be an example of metalepsis.[33] In other words, the angelic announcement that Jesus will fulfill Ezek 36:23 implies that he will also make the "covenant of peace" (Ezek 36:26), the new covenant. These two promises are

---

[29] Although these features pointing to Moses may seem subtle, Pennington (*Sermon on the Mount*, 24) rightly argues that Gospel interpretation requires "an approach that is sensitive to how texts communicate and how language functions at the evocative or connotative level, not merely the denotative."

[30] Davies and Allison, *Matthew 1–7*, 1:210.

[31] For examples of scholars who see a connection with Ps 130:8, see Joachim Gnilka, *Das Matthäusevangelium*, NTKNT, 2nd ed., 2 vols. (Freiburg: Herder, 1992–3), 1:19; Nolland, *Matthew*, 99n.63. For an example of those who see a dependence on Judg 13:5, see Helen Milton, "The Structure of the Prologue to St. Matthew's Gospel," *JBL* 81 (1962): 180. For other examples of these views, see Nicholas Piotrowski, "'I Will Save My People from Their Sins': The Influence of Ezekiel 36:28b–29a; 37:23b on Matthew 1:21" *TB* 64.1 (2013): 36n.8.

[32] R. T. France, *The Gospel of Matthew*, NICNT (Grand Rapids, MI: Eerdmans, 2007), 54; Piotrowski, "'I Will Save My People from Their Sins,'" 33–54.

[33] Richard B. Hays, *Echoes of Scripture in the Gospels* (Waco, TX: Baylor University Press, 2016), 11.

spoken by the LORD on the same occasion and as part of the same oracle (Ezek 36:21–28). The reference to Ezekiel's new covenant oracle in the programmatic statement of the Gospel no less suggests that the new covenant is a significant theme of Matthew's Gospel.

Matthew also likely stirred his readers' memory of new covenant promises through metalepsis by his citation of Jer 31:15 in Matt 2:17–18. Jeremiah 31:15 precedes the promise of the new covenant by only a few verses. The citation thus strategically signals that God was on the brink of fulfilling the promise of Jer 31:31–34. The era of the new covenant had dawned with the coming of Messiah Jesus.[34]

The truth implied by the citations of Ezek 36–37 and Jer 31 is made abundantly clear by the content of John the Baptist's message to Israel. John preached, "I baptize you with water for repentance … He will baptize you with the Holy Spirit and with fire" (Matt 3:11). The reference to the Messiah baptizing with the Holy Spirit most likely alludes to prophetic references to the eschatological outpouring of the Spirit of God (Isa 32:15; 44:3; Ezek 36:26–27; 39:29; Joel 2:28–29).[35] John's coupling of references to water and the Spirit recall, on the one hand, the references to "pouring out" the Spirit in which the Spirit is compared to a liquid that is dispensed and, on the other hand, the combination of references to water and Spirit in Ezek 36. With the promise of the new covenant, God assured his people that he would "sprinkle clean water on you, and you shall be clean from all your uncleannesses" and that he would "put my Spirit within you."

Finally, Jesus directly referred to the new covenant toward the close of his ministry. During the last supper, Jesus gave thanks for the cup, then passed it to his disciples with the words, "This is my blood of the covenant, which is poured out for many for the forgiveness of sins" (Matt 26:28). The statement alludes to the fact that God's earlier covenants with Israel were generally established through an act of sacrifice (cf. Gen 15:1–20). The Mosaic covenant was initiated by the sacrifice of oxen. Moses collected the blood of the slain oxen and threw half of the blood against the altar. Then he read the Book of the Covenant to the people and threw the other half of the sacrificial blood on them, shouting, "Behold the blood of the covenant that the LORD has made with you in accordance with all these words" (Exod 24:8). The words "blood of the covenant" appear only twice in the Old Testament, in Exod 24:8 and in Zech 9:11 (which appears to allude to Exod 24:8). Consequently, Jesus's words indicate that by his death he is initiating a covenant that will replace the Mosaic covenant. This covenant is none other than the "new covenant" that was promised by Moses, Isaiah, Jeremiah, and Ezekiel, as the parallel in Luke 22:20 explicitly states.[36]

---

[34] Jack Lundbom, an OT scholar who specializes in Jeremiah studies, has argued correctly that the Gospel of Matthew is a "new covenant document." See his *Jesus' Sermon on the Mount: Mandating a Better Righteousness* (Minneapolis, MN: Fortress Press, 2015), 27–43.

[35] Carson, "Matthew," 104–5; France, *Matthew*, 114–15; John Nolland, *Matthew*, NIGNT (Grand Rapids, MI: Eerdmans, 2005), 145–7. For a more extensive treatment, see Daniel McManigal, *A Baptist of Judgment in the Fire of the Holy Spirit: John's Eschatological Proclamation in Matthew 3*, LNTS (London: T&T Clark, 2019).

[36] See Peter Gentry and Stephen Wellum, *Kingdom through Covenant: A Biblical-Theological Understanding of the Covenants* (Wheaton, IL: Crossway, 2012), 103–4;

5.6 Matthew Presents the Sermon on the Mount as the New Moses Delivering a New Covenant Torah

The Sermon on the Mount has a number of features that confirm Matthew's intention to present Jesus's teaching as the Torah of the new covenant taught by the new Moses. The specific wording of the introduction to the Sermon makes Jesus's ascent up a mountain to deliver his authoritative interpretation and application of the law of Moses to his disciples strangely reminiscent of Moses's ascent of Mount Sinai to receive and deliver the law. The words "he went up on the mountain" in Matt 5:1 are a verbatim quotation of Exod 19:3, a description of Moses ascending Sinai where he would receive the law from God. This specific phrase appears only three times in the Greek OT. All three of the occurrences are descriptions of Moses's ascent of Sinai (Exod 19:3; 24:18; 34:4). The expression "and he sat down" is probably yet another allusion to the Moses narrative. The Hebrew text of Deut 9:9 was interpreted by many Jews to mean that Moses sat on the mountain when he received the Law. This interpretation reflects later Jewish practices as described in Matt 23:2, where the teachers of the law and the Pharisees sit on the "seat of Moses."

The unusual phrase "he opened his mouth," which is not used elsewhere in Matthew apart from an OT quotation, also likely presents Jesus as the new Moses revealing the new covenant Torah. Matthew 13:34–35 claims that Jesus taught the crowds in parables in order to fulfill the prophecy contained in Ps 78:2: "I will open my mouth in parables; I will declare things kept secret from the foundation of the world." But the preceding verse of the Psalm begins the Psalm with the words: "My people, hear my instruction [literally 'Torah']." By applying the expression "he opened his mouth" from Ps 78 to Jesus, Matthew implies that Jesus is both the teacher of parables and the teacher of Torah.

The Beatitudes likely confirm Jesus's identity as the new Moses. Several scholars have argued that the blessings of Matt 5 and the woes of Matt 23 are juxtaposed in such a way as to recall the curses and blessings of the old covenant. I have argued that the Beatitudes are instead modeled on Moses's final blessing on Israel in Deut 33:29 identifying Jesus's disciples as the new Israel who will experience a new exodus and new conquest so they can inherit the land of promise.[37] But in either interpretation, Jesus's identity as the new Moses is in view. The Beatitudes are saturated with references to Isa 61 (61:1, 2, and 7), which belongs to the section of Isaiah known as "the Messiah's Jubilee." Pennington noted: "Many have rightly observed that the primary subtext of

---

> Before we leave the discussion of typology, it is important to note how closely typological structures and biblical covenants are related...One cannot properly think of them [the typological structures which include Moses and the exodus event] apart from wrestling with how the covenants relate to each other and how the covenants as a whole point forward to the coming of Christ and the new covenant age. In this way, all of biblical history is prophetic, not merely in terms of verbal predictions but in types/patterns associated with the covenants, which anticipate and predict the dawning of the end of the ages in the coming of the Lord of Glory.

[37] Quarles, "The Blessings of the New Moses: An Examination of the Theological Purpose of the Matthean Beatitudes," 305–25.

the Beatitudes is Isa 61 (also with the influence of several psalms), which does indeed greatly inform, shape, and color each of these macarisms."[38] This subtext is a key new covenant text that repeats the promise of the everlasting covenant from Isa 55.

A specific reference to the new covenant emerges with the Beatitude, "Blessed are the pure in heart." Jesus clearly teaches in Matthew that the heart is not naturally pure. An evil heart is the source of adultery (5:28), evil words (12:34), and is far from God (15:8). Matthew 19:8 describes the sinner's heart as "hard." Even more explicitly, Matt 15:19–20 says, "For from the heart come evil thoughts, murders, adulteries, sexual immoralities, thefts, false testimonies, blasphemies. These are the things that defile a man." The heart is defiled, not pure. Thus, the pure heart in the Beatitude must be a heart that God has cleansed and transformed. It is the heart described in the new covenant promise in Deut 30:6, the circumcised heart that loves God completely. It is the heart described in the new covenant promise of Ezek 36:26, the "new heart," the "heart of flesh," that replaced the "heart of stone," the heart indwelled by the Spirit. It is the heart described in the new covenant promise of Jer 31:33, the heart on which the new covenant Torah has been inscribed.

Jesus's identity as the new Moses teaching the Torah of the new covenant is implied by his denial: "Do not think that I came to abolish the Law." For who could abolish the Law but a new and greater Moses? Then Jesus claims that he "fulfills" the Law. He accomplishes all that the Law promises and fulfills all that the Law predicted. The repeated themes of Matthew's Gospel suggest that Jesus had his fulfillment of Deut 18 particularly in view.

Then Jesus insists that his disciples must have a righteousness that surpasses that of the scribes and Pharisees, those most dedicated to the laws of Moses, those who epitomized the righteousness that one could attain under the old covenant. This surpassing righteousness, which is as natural to the disciple as the good fruit produced by the good tree (Matt 7:16-17), is the righteousness promised in Isa 61, a new covenant text to which the first three beatitudes clearly allude: "They will be called righteous trees, planted by the LORD to glorify him" and "As the earth brings forth its growth, and as a garden enables what is sown to spring up, so the Lord God will cause righteousness and praise to spring up before all the nations" (Isa 61:3, 11). Matthew's readers will likely have picked up on this allusion, especially after Matt 5:16, a verse unique to Matthew, which refers to people seeing your good works and glorifying your Father in heaven.

The introductory formula used with the so-called Antitheses is designed to portray Jesus's teaching as the new covenant Torah. The full formula "You have heard that it was said to our ancestors," which appears in 5:21 and 5:33, is implied even in the more abbreviated forms that appear with the other four Antitheses. "It was said" is a divine passive that confirms that the Mosaic law was indeed the word of God. "To

---

[38] Pennington, *Sermon on the Mount and Human Flourishing*, 60. See also David Wenham, "How Do the Beatitudes Work? Some Observations on the Structure of the Beatitudes in Matthew," in *The Earliest Perceptions of Jesus in Context: Essays in Honor of John Nolland*, LNTS 566, eds. Aaron White, David Wenham, and Craig Evans (London: T&T Clark, 2018), 208–11; Quarles, *Sermon on the Mount*, 52–61.

our ancestors" identifies the original recipients of the Law. The Greek term ἀρχαίοις literally means "to the people of ancient times." It appears to be the Greek equivalent of a Hebrew term used in the Dead Sea Scrolls and Rabbinic literature to refer to the Sinai generation.[39] The description is reminiscent of Jeremiah's new covenant promise's description of the old covenant: "the covenant I made with their ancestors when I took them by the hand to bring them out of the land of Egypt." Jesus's "but I say to you" contrasts Jesus's disciples with the Sinai generation in a manner that implies that they belong to a different era, a distinct era of salvation history. They are the generation that will receive the new covenant accompanied by a new Torah.

In the teaching that follows Jesus never contradicts or nullifies the Torah. Instead, he correctly interprets it and explains the full implications of its principles. He sometimes quotes directly from the Torah and at other times merely alludes to its contents. But the connection of Jesus's teaching to the Torah is unmistakable.

Jesus's Torah relates to the Decalogue. The first two Antitheses (Matt 5:21–30) take up the fifth and sixth commandments of the Law (Exod 20:13–14). The second Antithesis (Matt 5:27–28) relates closely to the 10th commandment (Exod 20:17) since the adultery of the heart that Jesus describes is coveting the neighbor's wife.

The essence of the OT Torah was the *imitatio Dei*, the imitation of God, displaying the image of God and manifesting the very character of God. The OT Torah expressed this idea with the command: "Be holy, because I, Yahweh your God, am holy" (Lev 19:2). Jesus expressed the principle by conflating Lev 19:2 and Deut 18:13, "You must be blameless [perfect] before the LORD your God," in Matt 5:48, "Be perfect, therefore, as your heavenly Father is perfect."

Other themes of the Torah also appear in the Sermon. An important emphasis of the old covenant Torah was separateness, for being like YAHWEH meant being unlike the pagan nations that surrounded Israel. Deuteronomy 18:9 illustrates this: "When you enter the land the LORD your God is giving you, do not imitate the detestable customs of those nations." Jesus's Torah contains this element. Jesus's disciples are not to be like the Gentiles by only loving those who love them (Matt 5:47) or like the Gentiles by babbling when they pray (Matt 6:7) or like the Gentiles by obsessing over what they will eat, drink, or wear (Matt 6:31–32).

The OT Torah gave instructions for recognizing and handling a false prophet (Deut 18:20). Jesus taught his disciples how to recognize false prophets and false professors (Matt 7:15–20). Like the Torah, Jesus's Sermon expounds the "Two Ways." In Deut 30:19, Moses said, "I call heaven and earth as witnesses against you today that I have set before you life and death, blessing and curse. Choose life so that you and your descendants may live." The path of life is characterized by obedience to the Lord. The path of death is characterized by rebellion against God. Deuteronomy 11:28 and 31:29 describe the way of life that pleases God as the "path I have commanded you." "Path" (Heb.: הַדֶּרֶךְ) is translated in the LXX as ὁδός, the term used to describe the "way" or "road" that leads to life and the way or road that leads to destruction in Matt 7:13–14.[40]

---

[39] Luz, *Matthew*, 1:230n.34.
[40] Todd Penner correctly noted, "The origins of the 'two ways' tradition lies in the Hebrew Bible covenantal material reflected in Deuteronomy (cf. 30:15–20) and in other Old Testament passages

The role that Jesus expects his teachings to play in determining one's eternal fate also shows that his teaching is the new Torah. In Matt 7:21–23, entrance into the eschatological kingdom is conditioned upon the confession of Jesus as Lord and doing the will of his Father in heaven. Those who verbally confess Jesus as Lord but do not obey the Father's will are rejected as "lawbreakers" or "workers of lawlessness." But what is this law that expresses the Father's will which they break? Matthew 5:17–20 shows that it is the commands taught by Jesus. This is confirmed at the conclusion of the Sermon on the Mount in which the storm of eschatological judgment destroys the foolish person who "hears these words of mine and doesn't act on them" (Matt 7:26). An emphasis on obeying Jesus's commands not only appears at the conclusion of the Sermon on the Mount but does so at the climax of the Gospel as well. After new disciples are baptized, Jesus commands his followers to "teach them to obey all things that I [Jesus] have commanded." The basis for moral and ethical instruction in the new covenant community is the commandments, not of Moses, but of Jesus! Luz has pointed out that the Sermon on the Mount is "the only discourse of Jesus that almost exclusively contains commandments of Jesus" so that in the Great Commission "the thought is probably of the Sermon on the Mount."[41] Thus Jesus's own commandments are the basis of instruction for Jesus's followers much as the Torah given by Moses served as the basis of instruction for the community of Israel (Deut 6:1; Lev 10:11; 2 Chr 17:9; Ezra 7:10, 25) and Israelite children (Deut 6:6–8; 11:19).

5.7 Other New Testament Authors Recognized the Sermon on the Mount as the Messianic Torah

The Epistle of James appears to view the Sermon on the Mount as the new covenant Torah. There is little room for doubt that James knew the content of the Sermon on the Mount.[42] Perhaps the clearest evidence for James's knowledge of the Sermon is the extensive parallelism between James's teaching regarding oaths and Jesus's teaching on the topic. Although Jesus's teaching against using oaths in everyday life is clearly contrary to the teaching of the Pharisees, some of his Jewish contemporaries shared his aversion to oathtaking. Josephus refers to the Essenes refusal to take oaths (except for the oath to enter the community), and Philo also agreed "to swear not at all is the best course."[43] Despite this general agreement on the ethical question, no other parallels exist to several of the specific features in Jas 5:12 except for the Sermon. Table 5.1 shows the striking parallels between Jas 5:12 and Matt 5:33–37.

(cf. Ps 1; Prov 4:10–27)." See his *The Epistle of James and Eschatology: Re-reading an Ancient Christian Letter*, JSNTSS 121 (Sheffield: Sheffield Academic Press, 1996), 224–33, here 224.

[41] Ulrich Luz, *Matthew 1–7*, trans. James E. Crouch, Hermeneia (Minneapolis, MN: Fortress, 1989), 1:176–77.

[42] Hans Dieter Betz, *Sermon on the Mount*, Hermeneia (Minneapolis, MN: Fortress, 1995), 6 states that the problem of the relationship between the Sermon on the Mount and the Epistles of James is "completely unresolved." He admits that similarities and parallels between the two "exist in abundance."

[43] Jos. *J.W.* 2.8.7 §§139–42; Philo, *Decal.* 84.

Table 5.1 Extended Verbal Parallels

Matthew 5:33–37	James 5:12
μὴ ὀμόσαι	μὴ ὀμνύετε
ὅλως	μήτε ἄλλον τινὰ ὅρκον
μήτε ἐν τῷ οὐρανῷ	μήτε τὸν οὐρανὸν
μήτε ἐν τῇ γῇ	μήτε τὴν γῆν
ἔστω δὲ ὁ λόγος ὑμῶν ναὶ ναί, οὒ οὔ	ἤτω δὲ ὑμῶν τὸ ναὶ ναὶ καὶ τὸ οὒ οὔ,

These clear thematic and verbal parallels should make the interpreter attentive to other possible parallels. Table 5.2 displays some of these other parallels.

The high volume of these parallels is persuasive evidence that James knew Jesus's sermon.[44] Thus it is appropriate to consider whether Bacon's equation of the "royal law" (Jas 2:10), the "law of liberty" (Jas 2:12), with the Sermon on the Mount is correct. The royal law is thus named because it was expounded and clarified by the Messianic king. That law is Lev 19:18, "Love your neighbor as yourself," which Jesus expounded in Matt 5:43–48.[45] James characterizes it as the "law of liberty" because he views Jesus's instruction as the new covenant Torah inscribed on the disciple's heart so that he is prompted from within to obey Jesus's instructions.[46] This interpretation is supported by Jas 4:12 which says "There is one lawgiver and judge." Some interpreters assume

---

[44] Other scholars agree that James was familiar with the contents of the Sermon on the Mount in either written (Q[mt] or Matt) or oral form. See the discussion of James's dependence on the Jesus tradition in Dale C. Allison, Jr., *A Critical and Exegetical Commentary on the Epistle of James* (New York, NY: Bloomsbury, 2013), 56–62. Allison observes "James shows overlap particularly with Matthew" and suggests the hypothesis that James (which Allison dates to the early 3rd century) knew the Gospel of Matthew (59–62). See also Dean B. Deppe, *The Sayings of Jesus in the Epistle of James* (Chelsea, NY: Bookcrafters, 1989); and P. J. Hartin, *James and the Q Sayings of Jesus*, JSNTSup 47 (Sheffield: JSOT Press, 1991), 141–2; Hartin, "James and the Q Sermon on the Mount/Plain," SBLSP 28 (1989): 440–57; Ben Witherington III, *Jesus the Sage: The Pilgrimage of Wisdom*, rev. ed (Minneapolis, MN: Fortress, 2000), 240; Todd C. Penner, *The Epistle of James and Eschatology* (Sheffield: Sheffield Academic, 1996), 241–53, esp. 249. Joseph Mayor (*The Epistle of St. James: The Greek Text with Introduction, Notes and Comments* (New York: Macmillan, 1892): lxxxv–lxxxviii) lists 58 parallels in James to the Synoptic Gospels. Twenty-three of these (nearly half) are from the Sermon on the Mount. Mayor rightly concluded that "a marked feature of our Epistle is the close connexion between it and the Sermon on the Mount" (lxii). Peter H. Davids (*The Epistle of James*, NIGTC (Grand Rapids, MI: Eerdmans, 1982), 47–8) identifies 36 parallels between James and the Synoptic tradition (plus 9 more general parallels in thought). Of the 36 parallels, 25 belong to the Sermon on the Mount and 3 to the Sermon on the Plain. Davids supports Davies's claim that early Christian communities saw Jesus's words as constituting a "new law."

[45] Davids (*The Epistle of James*, 114) and Craig Blomberg and Mariam Kammel (*James*, Exegetical Commentary on the New Testament (Grand Rapids, MI: Zondervan, 2008), 116–17) are examples of the numerous scholars who see the "royal law" as the Torah as interpreted by Jesus. See especially H. Frankemölle, *Der Brief des Jakobus*, 2 vols. (Gütersloh, Gütersloher Verlagshaus and Würzburg: Echter, 1994), 2: 400–2; and Douglas J. Moo, *The Letter of James*, PNTC (Grand Rapids, MI: Eerdmans, 2000), 112.

[46] See esp. Willibald Beyschlag, *Der Brief des Jacobus*, 6th ed., KEKNT (Göttingen: Vandenhoeck & Ruprecht, 1897), 89.

Table 5.2 Isolated Verbal and Thematic Parallels

James 1:4	Matthew 5:48
So that you may be perfect (ἵνα ἦτε τέλειοι)	Therefore you must be perfect (ἔσεσθε οὖν ὑμεῖς τέλειοι)
James 1:10	Matthew 6:28–30
The flower of grass will disappear	The lily of the field that clothes the grass lasts only a day
James 1:19–20	Matthew 5:21
Be slow to anger, because human anger does not perform God's righteousness	Everyone who is angry with his brother will be liable to judgment
James 1:22	Matthew 7:26
Be doers of the word and not hearers only	Everyone who hears these words of mine and does not do them
James 2:5	Matthew 5:3, 10
"heirs of the kingdom which he promised to those who love him"	"for theirs is the kingdom of heaven"
James 2:13	Matthew 5:7
"there will be judgment without mercy to the one who does not show mercy"	"Blessed are the merciful, for they will be shown mercy"
James 2:14	Matthew 7:21
"If someone claims to have faith, but does not have works, is that faith able to save him?"	"Not everyone who says to me, 'Lord, Lord,' will enter the kingdom of heaven, but only the one who does the will of my Father in heaven."
James 3:17	Matthew 7:18
"good fruits" (καρπῶν ἀγαθῶν)	"good fruits" (καρποὺς καλοὺς)
James 4:4	Matthew 7:7
"You do not have because you do not ask"	"Ask and it will be given you"
James 4:9–10	Matthew 5:4
"Grieve, mourn, and lament … and he will exalt you"	"Blessed are those who mourn, because they will be comforted"
James 4:11	Matthew 7:1–5
"The one who judges his brother"	"Do not judge [your brother]"
James 5:2	Matthew 6:19
"Your garments have become moth-eaten"	"where moths … ruin"
James 5:3	Matthew 6:19
"You stored up treasure"	"Do not store up treasures"

that this lawgiver and judge is God the Father.[47] But the context requires that Jesus be identified as this one lawgiver and judge. James 5:8 says that "the coming of the Lord

---

[47] (ICC; 637). He gives two reasons: (1) the text recalls the Shema and (2) no one before Justin Martyr refers to Jesus as "lawgiver," and Justin qualifies the title with καίνος or a reference to the new covenant to distinguish Jesus from Moses. However, the text resembles Matt 23:10 just as closely as Deut 6:4. Justin's treatment belongs to a trajectory including the Epistle of Barnabas. James could as easily have introduced the term in this application as Justin.

is near." The next verse adds, "Behold, the judge is at the very door."[48] The Parousia of Jesus is the approach of the eschatological judge.[49] If Jesus is the judge, he is also the lawgiver since "there is one lawgiver and judge." Thus, James gives to Jesus the title "lawgiver," a title normally given by the Jews to Moses. He sees the teaching of Jesus, particularly in the Sermon on the Mount, as the new covenant Torah delivered by the new Moses.

In addition to James, Paul, to a lesser extent, seems to echo this understanding of Jesus's teaching. Bacon argued that Jesus's teaching in the Sermon on the Mount (SM) was what Paul intended to refer to by the expression "the law of Christ" in Gal 6:2.[50] Scholars who hold the view that the "law of Christ" at least includes Jesus's teaching include W. D. Davies,[51] C. H. Dodd,[52] Richard Longenecker,[53] and Douglas Moo.[54] Allison has suggested that Paul's phrase is equivalent to a Hebrew expression in Eccl. Mid. 11:8: "The Torah which a man learns in this world is vanity compared with the Torah of the Messiah."[55] McKnight defines "law of Christ" as "nothing other than (1) submission to the teachings of Jesus that fulfill the law (Matt 5:17–20) and (2) life in the Spirit, which is essentially love and which itself fulfills the law of Moses (Gal 5:6, 14, 18, 22).[56] Bruce defines it as "the whole tradition of Jesus' ethical teaching, confirmed by his character and conduct (cf. Rom. 13:14; 2 Cor. 10:1) and reproduced within his people by the power of the Spirit."[57]

---

[48] Allison hesitates to identity the "Lord" in these texts and simply states that Jews would read the text as referring to God and Christians as referring to Jesus. But the allusion to Mark 13:29//Matt 24:33 ("he [Jesus] is at the gates") strongly supports the "Christian" interpretation. Allison admits that reference to God is "a minority opinion." See his *A Critical and Exegetical Commentary on the Epistle of James*, 707. Moo identifies the Judge in 4:12 as God and the Judge in 5:8 as Jesus. See Moo, *The Letter of James*, 221.

[49] This is the "majority view" represented by Beyschlag, *Der Brief des Jacobus*, 217; J. Marty, *L' Épitre de Jacques* (Paris: Alcan, 1935), 192; S. Laws, *The Epistle of James* (San Francisco, CA: Harper & Row 1980), 208–9; Davids, *The Epistle of James*, 182; M. A. Jackson-McCabe, "The Messiah Jesus in the Mystic World of James," *JBL* 122 (2003): 727; C. Burchard, *Der Jakobusbrief* (Tübingen: Mohr Siebeck, 2000), 198.

[50] The most extensive and persuasive defense of this interpretation of Paul's phrase is Femi Adeyemi, *The New Covenant Torah in Jeremiah and the Law of Christ in Paul* (New York: Lang, 2006).

[51] W. D. Davies, *Paul and Rabbinic Judaism: Some Rabbinic Elements in Pauline Theology* (New York: Harper, 1948), 34, 136, 141–4.

[52] C. H. Dodd, "ΕΝΝΟΜΟΣ ΧΡΙΣΤΟΥ," in *Studia Paulina: In Honorem Johannis de Zwaan Septuagenarii*, ed. J. N. Sevenster and W. C. van Unnik (Haarlem: De Erven F. Bohn, 1953), 97–110.

[53] Richard Longenecker, *Paul Apostle of Liberty* (New York: Harper & Row, 1964), 192.

[54] Douglas J. Moo, "The Law of Christ as the Fulfillment of the Law of Moses," in *The Law, the Gospel, and the Modern Christian: Five Views* (Grand Rapids, MI: Zondervan, 1993), 343. Longenecker and Moo both insist that this "law" includes both Jesus's teaching and his personal example as well as the guiding influence of the Holy Spirit.

[55] See Allison, *New Moses*, 187.

[56] Scot McKnight, *Galatians*, NIVAC 9 (Grand Rapids: Zondervan, 1995), 285.

[57] F. F. Bruce, *Galatians*, NIGTC (Grand Rapids, MI: Eerdmans, 1982), 261. Graham Stanton (*Studies in Matthew and Early Christianity*, WUNT 309, ed. Markus Bockmuehl and David Lincicum (Tübingen: Mohr Siebeck, 2013), 322) rejected the view that "the law of Christ" in Gal 6:2 refers to Jesus's teaching but acknowledged "that understanding of the phrase has been dominant throughout the Christian tradition."

5.8 Early Reception History Supports Recognition of the Sermon on the Mount as the Messianic Torah

Not only does this understanding of the SM appear primarily in James and more tangentially in the writings of Paul, we find it also in the early church fathers.[58] In the middle of the second century, Justin Martyr describes the Sermon on the Mount as the essential expression of the new covenant Torah. In *Dialogue with Trypho* 24:1 Justin writes that another covenant and another Law had gone forth from Zion and he describes this as spiritual circumcision that produces a righteous people. Yet, in *Dialogue* 113.6, Justin explains that the "knives of stone" with which Christ performs this "second circumcision" are "the words of our Lord Jesus." In 114, he explains that this spiritual circumcision effected by the words of Jesus circumcises our hearts of all evil and vice.

More importantly, in *Dialogue* 18 Justin urges Trypho to receive spiritual circumcision, and he illustrates this Christian experience of spiritual circumcision by writing "even amid cruelties unutterable, death and torments, we pray for mercy to those who inflict such things upon us, and do not wish to give the least retort to anyone, even as the new Lawgiver commanded us." Justin is clearly alluding to Matt 5:44: "Love your enemies and pray for those who persecute you." He describes this as a command of the "new Lawgiver," the Torah of the new Moses. Justin describes Jesus as the new Legislator or Lawgiver repeatedly (*Dial.* 12.2; 14.3; 18.3). In *Dialogue* 12 he refers to Christian teaching that calls for abandoning a lifestyle of perjury, theft, and adultery as "the new Law."

A few decades later in the second century, Irenaeus (Against Heresies 4.34.4) argues that Jesus has enacted the new covenant and that the "law of liberty, that is, the word of God" is radically transforming lives. He states that "the precepts of an absolutely perfect life" are "the same in each Testament" (*Haer.* 4.12.3). Shortly afterward (*Haer.* 4.13.1), Irenaeus insists that the new covenant does not abrogate the "natural precepts" (by which he means the moral principles) of the law. Instead, Jesus extended them, fulfilled them, and gave them greater scope. Interestingly, every one of the quotations that Irenaeus gives except one (Matt 19:21) is drawn from the Sermon on the Mount and the Sermon on the Plain (Matt 5:27, 28; 5:21,22; 5:33; 5:20; Luke 6:29-31; Matt 5:41). He explains, "Now He did not teach us these things as being opposed to the law, but as fulfilling the law, and implanting in us the varied righteousness of the law." The "implanting" refers to the internalization of the principles of the new Torah described in Jer 31 and that James also described as the implanted word.

John Chrysostom likewise saw Jesus as a new lawgiver or legislator and the Sermon on the Mount as the new Torah. Chrysostom describes the moral and ethical principles of the SM thusly: "He wrote in their mind those wondrous laws ..." (*Hom. Matt.* 16.2). By stating that these "wondrous laws" were written on the mind, Chrysostom closely

---

[58] Femi Adeyemi provides a thorough treatment of this subject including the views of these prominent authors: Justin Martyr, Irenaeus, Tertullian, Augustine, Aquinas, and Luther (*The New Covenant Torah in Jeremiah and the Law of Christ in Paul*, 21-35).

associated the contents of the Sermon on the Mount with the new covenant promise in Jer 31:33 (LXX) in which YAHWEH says, "I will place my laws in their mind and I will write them upon their hearts." Chrysostom also speaks of Christ here "adding to the law, entire as it was, another entire code of laws." In 16.4 he again refers to the Sermon on the Mount as "that future code of laws, which He was about to deliver to them." He goes on in 16.8 to explicitly equate the Sermon on the Mount with the new covenant and refers to the commands of the sermon as examples of the high standards of the new covenant. He refers to Christ as the lawgiver and legislator and explicitly cites Jer 31:31, and again in 17.2 he refers to Jesus as the "lawgiver." He also compares the Sermon on the Mount to the preceding pericope in which Jesus performed miracles of physical healing and describes the Sermon on the Mount as an act of spiritual healing in which Christ was "amending their souls," (i.e., the disciples' souls).

5.9 Conclusion

Bacon's view of the Sermon on the Mount is supported by compelling evidence. The best paradigm for understanding the sermon is as the new covenant Torah delivered by the new Moses. Although Bacon may be credited with reintroducing this view in modern NT scholarship, this view appears to have been the view of Matthew, James, and Paul and was clearly the view of some leaders of the early church including Justin Martyr, Irenaeus, and John Chrysostom.

6

Jesus as Teacher Who Practices What He Teaches

Lena Lütticke

6.1 Introduction

Do they practice what they preach? With (or: In) their infamous song "Where is the Love?," the Black Eyed Peas boldly address (religious) leaders who preach peaceful resistance but seem to fail "turning the other cheek." They raise the question of congruence between word and action, i.e., the topic of integrity. This chapter aims at analysing the *behavior of Jesus as a teacher* in the Gospel of Matthew and specifically asks whether his *actions* correspond with his *teachings*. While it would be simple to examine examples like Jesus's silent resistance before Caiaphas and the Council (Matt 26:57–68, esp. v. 67), which is in line with his teaching on retaliation (5:38–42, esp. v. 39), this chapter will focus on an overlooked dynamic instead—Jesus's teaching on *prayer*.

The Gospel of Matthew is the only canonical gospel that specifically narrates Jesus's teaching on prayer (Matt 6:5–15). Even though Luke may be more concerned with the topic as such,[1] it is Matthew who depicts Jesus as teaching on prayer and, as I will argue in the following chapters, who also depicts him as praying in accordance with his teaching. Within the context of the Sermon on the Mount, the Matthean Jesus explicates the concept of righteousness (δικαιοσύνη) firstly with regard to fellow human beings (5:17–48), and then with regard to the heavenly Father (6:1–21). For the evangelist righteousness is a *relational* category: it describes the way in which the followers of Jesus (should) maintain their relationship with others and with God.[2]

---

[1] Cf., e.g., Oscar Cullmann, *Das Gebet im Neuen Testament, Zugleich Versuch einer vom Neuen Testament aus zu erteilenden Antwort auf heutige Fragen* (Tübingen: Mohr Siebeck, 1994), 25, who speaks of Luke as "the evangelist of prayer" ("in besonderer Weise der Evangelist des Gebets"). This is because Luke depicts several figures as praying: the λαός (1:10), Zachariah (1:13), or Hannah (2:37), and because the canticles in Luke 1:46–55 (*Magnificat*); 1:68–79 (*Benedictus*); 2:29–32 (*Nunc dimittis*) are being used in the liturgy of the hours of all Christian confessions. Jesus's advice to "pray always and not lose heart" in Luke 18:1 sums up perfectly the importance of prayer for the evangelist.

[2] Of the manifold literature on the Matthean concept of righteousness (δικαιοσύνη), I will only point to two renowned English studies: Benno Przybylski, *Righteousness in Matthew and His World of Thought*, SNTS (Cambridge: Cambridge University Press, 1980); Donald A. Hagner, "Righteousness in Matthew's Theology," in *Worship, Theology and Ministry in the Early Church, Essays in Honor of Ralph P. Martin*, LNTS 87, ed. Michael J. Wilkins and Terence Paige (Sheffield: JSOT, 1992), 101–20. In my dissertation, "God's hidden presence in Matt 6.1–6.16–18" (Diss. Regensburg, Germany,

When it comes to the relationship with the heavenly Father, Jesus lists three acts of piety to exemplify the principle of δικαιοσύνη: charity, prayer, and fasting.[3] The section on prayer is the most elaborate of the three, because it famously entails the Lord's Prayer. It is commonly known that Jesus's model prayer "is found in the center not only of the cultic teaching in 6:1–18 but of the Sermon on the Mount (SM) as a whole."[4] If, then, we assume prayer to be the most prominent means of communicating with God and fostering one's personal relationship with him, what does Jesus say about its proper performance?

6.2 The Foundation: Jesus's Teaching on Prayer in Matt 6:5–8

To answer this question, it is best to look closely at the text itself:

Matt 6:1.5–8[5]

1a		Pay attention (Προσέχετε [δὲ])
		not to do your righteousness in front of other people (τὴν δικαιοσύνην ὑμῶν μὴ ποιεῖν ἔμπροσθεν τῶν ἀνθρώπων)
	b	in order to be seen by them (πρὸς τὸ θεαθῆναι αὐτοῖς·).
	c	If not (εἰ δὲ μή γε),
	d	you do not have reward with[6] your Father in the heavens (μισθὸν οὐκ ἔχετε παρὰ τῷ πατρὶ ὑμῶν τῷ ἐν τοῖς οὐρανοῖς).
5a		And when you pray (Καὶ ὅταν προσεύχησθε),
	b	do not be like the hypocrites (οὐκ ἔσεσθε ὡς οἱ ὑποκριταί),
	c	because they love (ὅτι φιλοῦσιν)
		to pray standing in the synagogues and in the corners of the main streets (ἐν ταῖς συναγωγαῖς καὶ ἐν ταῖς γωνίαις τῶν πλατειῶν ἑστῶτες προσεύχεσθαι),
	d	in order to shine before other people (ὅπως φανῶσιν τοῖς ἀνθρώποις·).
	e	Amen, I say to you (ἀμὴν λέγω ὑμῖν),

2022), I deal with the topic in detail while discussing "Your Father who is in secret and sees in secret ..." (Matt 6:4.6.18).

[3] Craig S. Keener, *The Gospel of Matthew. A Socio-Rhetorical Commentary* (Grand Rapids, MI: Baker, 2009), 207, emphasizes that "Jesus' three examples are random; he intends secrecy to apply to all acts of righteousness."

[4] H. D. Betz, *The Sermon on the Mount. A Commentary on the Sermon on the Mount Including the Sermon on the Plain (Matthew 5:3–7:27 and Luke 6:20–49)*, Hermeneia (Minneapolis, MN: Fortress, 1995), 351.

[5] With my own working translation, I try to stay as close as possible to the Greek original while at the same time maintaining intelligibility.

[6] On the importance of reading "*with* your Father", see Nathan Eubank, "Storing Up Treasure with God in the Heavens. Celestial Investments in Matthew 6:1–21," *CBQ* 76.1 (2014): 77–92, see esp. 91.

f	they have their reward (ἀπέχουσιν τὸν μισθὸν αὐτῶν).
6a	But when you (sg.) pray (σὺ δὲ ὅταν προσεύχῃ),
b	go into your innermost room (εἴσελθε εἰς τὸ ταμεῖόν σου)
c	and when you have shut your door (καὶ κλείσας τὴν θύραν σου)
d	pray to your Father who is in secret (πρόσευξαι τῷ πατρί σου τῷ ἐν τῷ κρυπτῷ·).
e	And your Father who sees in secret (καὶ ὁ πατήρ σου ὁ βλέπων ἐν τῷ κρυπτῷ)
f	will reward you (ἀποδώσει σοι).
7a	But when you (pl.) pray (Προσευχόμενοι δὲ),
b	do not babble like the Gentiles (μὴ βατταλογήσητε ὥσπερ οἱ ἐθνικοί),
c	for they think (δοκοῦσιν γὰρ)
d	that they will be heard with their many words (ὅτι ἐν τῇ πολυλογίᾳ αὐτῶν εἰσακουσθήσονται).
8a	Therefore, do not assimilate to them (μὴ οὖν ὁμοιωθῆτε αὐτοῖς·).
b	For your Father knows (οἶδεν γὰρ ὁ πατὴρ ὑμῶν)
c	what need you have (ὧν χρείαν ἔχετε)
d	before you ask him (πρὸ τοῦ ὑμᾶς αἰτῆσαι αὐτόν).

Ever since H. D. Betz classified Matt 6:1–6.16–18 as "cultic didache,"[7] New Testament exegesis has widely taken for granted that the text really is a teaching on something like "cult" or "piety."[8] While it is true that it gives proper instructions how *not* to behave when giving to charity, praying, or fasting, and what to do instead,[9] the text seems to have little interest in quantitative measures, such as when or how often to pray (what to give, how long to fast etc.). Rather, as U. Luz and others have noted, it is concerned with *qualitative matters*,[10] that is, the inner disposition that leads to a proper conduct of charity, prayer, and fasting. What, then, is the subject of Jesus's teaching in Matt 6:1–18?

Jesus tells his followers they should not seek their own glory when they perform righteousness. This is not only true for the ritual performance depicted in 6:1–18 but

---

[7] H. D. Betz, "Eine judenchristliche Kult-Didache in Matthäus 6,1–18. Überlegungen und Fragen im Blick auf das Problem des historischen Jesus," in *Jesus Christus in Historie und Theologie*, FS H. Conzelmann, ed. Georg. Strecker (Tübingen: Mohr Siebeck, 1975), 445–57.

[8] Ernst Baasland is one recent scholar who criticizes these classifications, cf. Ernst Baasland, *Parables and Rhetoric in the Sermon on the Mount: New Approaches to a Classical Text*, WUNT 351 (Tübingen: Mohr Siebeck, 2015), 295.

[9] In terms of structure, a counterexample precedes the positive example in each of the three sections on charity, prayer, and fasting.

[10] Cf. Ulrich Luz, *Das Evangelium nach Matthäus I (Mt 1–7)*, EKK I/1 (Zürich: Benziger, 2002), 419–20, 426, 428.

also true for all forms of righteousness towards others as described by the so-called antitheses[11] in 5:17–48. Even though the followers of Jesus can be recognized by their good deeds (καλὰ ἔργα), which means that in contrast to charity, prayer, and fasting they will perform them publicly, 5:16 emphasizes that the δόξα belongs only to the Father. Within this framework, Jesus teaches his disciples (and the overhearing crowds[12]) to pray in a way that they do not shine (φαίνω) before other people. He addresses them individually in the second-person singular and uses quite concrete hyperbolic imagery: they should go into their innermost room, shut the door, and then pray to their Father. It is important to note, however, that this does *not* mean they should refrain from communal prayer (especially in the synagogue).[13] Both private and community prayer should be directed to God as though they were happening behind closed doors, in a way that they are aimed at God only.[14] It is therefore not necessary—but certainly helpful—to retreat into a separate room for private prayer. There is an ongoing debate over the architectural meaning of the word "chamber" (ταμεῖον), which is not really productive;[15] just like many of the other images used in Matt 6:1-6, 16–18, the "chamber" is explicated by its context. It designates seclusion and privacy, which is ultimately what Jesus advises over against the behaviour of the "hypocrites."[16] With their ostentatious prayer "in the synagogues and in the corners

---

[11] The term "antitheses," which has been established to describe Jesus's radical demands in Matt 5:21–48, is somewhat problematic. It is commonly argued that the particle δέ is to be translated with "but," and this is taken as a philological reason to label them "antitheses." However, it is probably better not to translate the particle at all, and to abandon the label "antitheses" (for Matt 5:21–48) altogether. For a detailed discussion of the term, cf. Peter Fiedler, *Das Matthäusevangelium*, ThKNT (Stuttgart: Kohlhammer, 2006), 130–1, summarizing ibid. 131: "Deshalb ist es nicht nur berechtigt, sondern auch notwendig, die irreführende Bezeichnung 'Antithesen' aufzugeben."

[12] Cf. W. D. Davies and D. C. Allison, *A Critical and Exegetical Commentary on the Gospel According to St. Matthew, vol. 1 (Matthew 1-7)*, ICC (London: T&T Clark, 2004), 725: "We are apparently to think of Jesus addressing his disciples in the midst of a crowd that overhears."

[13] Contra, e.g., Jerome H. Neyrey, *Honor and Shame in the Gospel of Matthew* (Louisville, KY: WJKP, 1998), 2219: "Jesus mandates that his disciples stay away from the synagogues and refrain from joining other Judean males in their customary acts of piety. Moreover, he informs them that the honorable place to practice piety is the household, not the synagogue."

[14] K. Barth has found a nice way of putting it: "Gebet ist kein Gebet, wenn man dabei einem Anderen als Gott etwas sagen will." ("Prayer is not prayer if you want to address someone other than God."), in Karl Barth, *Die kirchliche Dogmatik. Bd. 3: Die Lehre von der Schöpfung* (Zürich: Theologischer Verlag, 1951), 96.

[15] The most favourable opinion is that of Carolyn Osiek, "When You Pray, Go into Your ταμεῖον" (Matthew 6:6). But Why?," *CBQ* 71.4 (2009): 723–40, which has been specified recently by Warren Carter, "Praying the Lord's Prayer in (Some Sort of) *Tameion* (Matt 6:6)," in *Petitioners, Penitents, and Poets. On Prayer and Praying in Second Temple Judaism*, BZAW 524, ed. Ariel Feldman and Timothy J. Sandoval (Berlin: De Gruyter, 2020), 247–66. Probably misleading is the view of Luz (and others) who argue that the ταμεῖον designates some sort of "storeroom," cf. Luz, *Matt I* (cf. n. 11), 425n.61. While this might be true for Luke, Osiek is probably right that in Matthew, the ταμεῖον rather is a chamber into which one retreats "with deliberate concealment" to meet one's "most important guest," cf. Osiek, "When you pray," 740.

[16] In Matt 6:1–6,16–18, the ὑποκριταί should primarily be considered a rhetoric figure. They provide a contrasting foil that illuminates how *not* to perform righteousness. Within the bigger picture of the gospel account, especially Matt 23, it seems natural to retrospectively identify them with the Jewish elites (i.e., the scribes and Pharisees). This is, however, not implied by the text as such. Since ὑποκριταί can (also) be found in the synagogues, it is certainly true that several Jews show hypocritical behaviour. This does not generally apply to "the Jews," of course, but only to several *individuals*, and it specifically applies to their *behaviour* (ποιεῖν). Most importantly, ὑποκριταί

of the main streets," they act as a contrasting foil for the conduct which the "children of God" (5:45, 48) ought to achieve. This is true in a similar way for "the Gentiles" (οἱ ἐθνικοί) who are portrayed as uttering long prayers and, what is more crucial, as believing they will be heard *because of* the many words they make. The neologisms βατταλογέω and πολυλογία underline just how absurd this assumption is.

The picture of God as illustrated by the Sermon on the Mount, however, is different. The "heavenly Father" is not impressed by extensive or publicly displayed prayers. In fact, he does not *need* his children's prayers at all (which is not to say that he does not *want* them nevertheless![17]). He knows what they need even before they ask him, and he sees their charity, prayer, and fasting where no one else can see: in "the hidden," or "in secret" (ἐν τῷ κρυπτῷ/ κρυφαίῳ). The God of the Sermon on the Mount, therefore, is an *all-seeing, omniscient* God. It is this idea of God that is the basis of Jesus's teaching in Matt 6:1–6, 16–18. Rather than offering a "cultic didache" (Betz), Jesus teaches his followers something about their Father and how they can establish a relationship with him. This makes Matt 6:1–6, 16–18 altogether different from other texts, such as the Didache,[18] which are concerned with cultic performance and actually give practical instructions (cf., e.g., Did 8:1–3). Matthew 6, by contrast, is not so much interested in charity, prayer, and fasting *as such* but rather in the praying (almsgiving, fasting) *subject*—and their relationship to the Father. The text is certainly didactic in nature but it is not a cultic instruction (and not a doctrine of God either). It is best understood in connection with the preceding section on the righteous behaviour toward others (the so-called antitheses) and should be read as a *guideline on how to perform righteousness toward God*.

When providing this guideline, Jesus frequently refers to "your (sg.) Father who is in the hidden/in secret and sees in the hidden/in secret." Many translations overlook the structural similarity between these two statements about God and translate the preposition ἐν imprecisely.[19] For the understanding of Matt 6:4, 6, 18 it is crucial that *God is himself present and seeing* "in the hidden/in secret." He does not merely see "what is done in secret" (NIV, EÜ 2016) or look "into" the secret from the distance (Lutherbibel 2017) but is himself present in this realm. This is where he is available and where his children can in a way "approach" him. As opposed to the very tangible "synagogues and street corners," however, the "hiddenness" is not so much a concrete place but rather a *mode*: If they perform their righteousness "in secret," that is, in a way that imitates the hiddenness of the Father (by directing their righteousness to God only), he will reward his children. Jesus's teaching on prayer is thus grounded in the belief that God is present with those who beseech him properly. What implications does this have for Jesus's own prayer practice?

---

occur both within and outside of the Matthean community(ies) that partly consist(s) of Jews who came to believe in Christ.

[17] Cf. the programmatic heading of chapter II.1.2 in Cullmann, *Gebet*, (cf. n. 2), "Gott braucht nicht, aber er will das Gebet der Menschen" ("God does not need our prayer but he wants it").

[18] Comparing Matt 6 and *Did* 8, Kari Syreeni, "Separation and Identity. Aspects of the Symbolic World of Matt 6.1–18," *NTS* 40 (1994): 522–41, here: 541, argues: "*There* [sc. Did 8] it is really appropriate to speak of a cultic didache." (emphasis original).

[19] This is in fact more so a problem for German translations.

6.3 The Implementation: Jesus's Prayer Practice in Matt 26:36–46

Jesus is the only narrative figure who is explicitly *praying* (προσεύχομαι) in the Gospel of Matthew. This is different from Mark and Luke who portray other figures as praying, too (cf. Luke 1:10, 13; 2:37). Strikingly, each time he prays Jesus retreats into private space. While the motif can be found in all three Synoptic Gospels, it is *only in Matthew* that *Jesus never prays publicly* (the disciples must, e.g., be close in Luke 11:1). This has the effect that Jesus's own practice is neatly consistent with his teaching on prayer. He never literally retreats into a ταμεῖον but, for instance, prays on a mountain (Matt 14:13, 23) that is commonly regarded as a place of God's presence.[20] One scene in particular stands out where Jesus leaves his disciples behind to pray: his sorrowful prayer in Gethsemane. The verb προσεύχομαι occurs fifteen times in the Gospel of Matthew, almost all of these occurrences are found in two clusters in chapters 6 (six occurrences) and 26 (five occurrences). Matthew 26:36–46 will therefore be the focus of the remaining chapter.

All three Synoptic Gospels narrate Jesus's withdrawal for prayer (Mark 14:32–42; Matt 26:36–46; Luke 22:39–46). The Matthean account is very close to the Markan which is why these two will be compared thoroughly. First of all, Jesus takes along Peter, James, and John (Mark 14:33 par. Matt 26:37) and leaves the other disciples behind. He then moves further away from the three (προελθὼν μικρόν) before he begins his prayer. It is striking, however, that Matthew emphasizes Jesus's solitude more than Mark:

	Mt 26,36.39.42.44		Mk 14,32.34.39.41
36a	Τότε ἔρχεται μετ' αὐτῶν ὁ Ἰησοῦς	32a	Καὶ ἔρχονται εἰς χωρίον
b	εἰς χωρίον λεγόμενον Γεθσημανὶ	b	οὗ τὸ ὄνομα Γεθσημανὶ
c	καὶ λέγει τοῖς μαθηταῖς·	c	καὶ λέγει τοῖς μαθηταῖς αὐτοῦ·
d	καθίσατε αὐτοῦ ἕως [οὗ]	d	καθίσατε ὧδε
e	<u>ἀπελθὼν ἐκεῖ</u>	34a	ἕως προσεύξωμαι.
f	προσεύξωμαι.	b	(…)
39a	(…)	c	καὶ προελθὼν μικρὸν
b	Καὶ προελθὼν μικρὸν	39a	ἔπιπτεν ἐπὶ τῆς γῆς
c	ἔπεσεν ἐπὶ πρόσωπον αὐτοῦ	b	καὶ προσηύχετο
d	προσευχόμενος	c	(…)
42a	καὶ λέγων·	41a	Καὶ πάλιν ἀπελθὼν
b	(…)	b	προσηύξατο
c	Πάλιν ἐκ δευτέρου <u>ἀπελθὼν</u>		τὸν αὐτὸν λόγον εἰπών.
44a	προσηύξατο		(…)
b	λέγων·		Καὶ ἔρχεται τὸ τρίτον
c	(…)		καὶ λέγει αὐτοῖς
d	Καὶ ἀφεὶς αὐτοὺς		(…)
	πάλιν <u>ἀπελθὼν</u>		
	προσηύξατο ἐκ τρίτου		
	τὸν αὐτὸν λόγον εἰπὼν πάλιν		

---

[20] For the OT/Jewish connotations of the "mountain," c.f. Matthias Konradt, *Das Evangelium nach Matthäus*, NTD 1 (Göttingen: Vandenhoeck & Ruprecht, 2015), 65–6.

In Mark's version, Jesus just tells his disciples to "sit here" (Mark 14:32c: ὧδε) while he prays. Matthew, somewhat redundantly, adds that they should sit while he *goes over there* (Matt 26:36e: ἀπελθὼν ἐκεῖ) and prays. Jesus's solitude is already given by Mark's separation of the three disciples sitting and waiting for Jesus who moves further (προελθὼν μικρόν) to pray, but Matthew seems to find it important to add that Jesus not only goes a little *further* (προ-ἔρχομαι) but he actually goes *away* (ἀπ-ἔρχομαι). Thereby, the Matthean Jesus does not move around randomly, but he announces this move as part of his intended prayer—He says he was going to "go over there and pray," and then he does actually "go a little farther"—and prays (v. 39). Most importantly, the addition in v. 36e corresponds not only to the first but also to Jesus's second and third withdrawal for prayer which is narrated again in vv. 42a and 44b. Matthew repeats this combination of ἀπέρχομαι and προσεύχομαι three times which makes Jesus's prayer scenes appear even more symmetrical than in Mark, and which at the same time strengthens the impression that Jesus retreats for prayer each time.

It seems that Matthew specifically wants to portray Jesus's prayer practice to match with his teaching. Biblical scholars have long noted that Jesus utters the exact words of the third petition of his own model prayer in Gethsemane: γενηθήτω τὸ θέλημά σου (Matt 26:42; cf. 6:10). A synoptic comparison of the Markan and the Matthean Gethsemane account shows that it is the second prayer that Matthew rearranges most significantly (Matt 26:42 par. Mark 14:39). Mark narrates that Jesus "went away once more and prayed the same words" (τὸν αὐτὸν λόγον εἰπών), thereby referring back to vv. 35–38., which implies that Jesus again prays something like: αββα ὁ πατήρ, πάντα δυνατά σοι· παρένεγκε τὸ ποτήριον τοῦτο ἀπ' ἐμοῦ· ἀλλ' οὐ τί ἐγὼ θέλω ἀλλὰ τί σύ. Matthew, by contrast, puts new, more consoled words into Jesus's mouth, ending with "may your will be done." Even Jesus's first prayer is not quite as rebellious and demanding as in the Markan version. Matthew alleviates Jesus's cry for help by removing the statement πάντα δυνατά σοι as well as the demand παρένεγκε τὸ ποτήριον τοῦτο ἀπ' ἐμοῦ (Mark 14:36), and by introducing the prayer with direct speech: πάτερ μου, εἰ δυνατόν ἐστιν, παρελθάτω ἀπ' ἐμοῦ τὸ ποτήριον τοῦτο (Matt 26:39).[21] When Jesus addresses God as "*my* Father" (instead of the Markan "Abba, Father"), this can be considered the first of many reminiscences of the Lord's Prayer.[22]

In the Matthean account, Jesus does *not* pray "the same words" when he retreats to pray for the second time (Πάλιν ἐκ δευτέρου) in 26:42. The first prayer seems to have had an impact on him: The "cup" still poses a big challenge, but Jesus is already more willing to accept it. Other than in his first attempt (and different from Mark), Jesus's second prayer is no longer phrased as a supplication but is more like an assent to his (deadly) fate. The verbatim agreement between 26:42 and 6:10 further underlines

---

[21] According to Matt 26:39 it is the "cup" that should be taken from Jesus, not the "hour" (as in Mark 14:35). On the meaning of this "cup" (τὸ ποτήριον τοῦτο), cf., e.g., Keener, *Matthew* (cf. n. 4), 637–38: "The 'cup' refers to Jesus' sufferings and death on the cross (20:22; 26:27–28; cf. 27:48), possibly alluding, like his interpretation of the cup at dinner, to the Hallel's 'cup of salvation' (Ps 116:13; cf. Gen. Rab. 88:5). The image probably alludes as well to the frequent biblical picture of God's 'cup of wrath' against the nations. Thus, Jesus may not merely shrink from death but from dying as a sacrifice under his Father's wrath." A different view is proposed by Konradt, *Matt* (cf. n. 21), 413.

[22] Cf. Konradt, *Matt* (cf. n. 21), 412.

that Jesus subordinates his own will to the Father's. Prior to this allusion to the third petition of the Lord's Prayer is an allusion to the sixth petition when Jesus asks his disciples to "watch and pray" so they do not enter into temptation (ἵνα μὴ εἰσέλθητε εἰς πειρασμόν).[23]

These manifold reminiscences have a twofold effect. First, they authorize the Lord's Prayer as *the* model prayer that is not only taught but also used by Jesus who utters at least some of its words in a situation of agony and testing.[24] Second, they emphasize the importance of prayer (specifically the Lord's Prayer), which, according to Matthew, is *a means to win over temptation*. At the beginning of the pericope, Jesus is confronted with feelings of fear and sorrow (cf. Matt 26:37–38). His first prayer reveals that he would rather avoid his passion.[25] Even though the actual verb πειράζειν is not attributed to Jesus in this context but only to his disciples (v. 41), he is struggling with God's will and is, in a way, "tempted" to disobey.[26] At the end of the scene, he subordinates his will to the Father's and encourages his disciples to rise and join him on his way to his passion (cf. v. 45f.). The disciples' inability to "watch and pray," on the other hand, provides a contrasting foil to their teacher's (final) obedience.[27] The "weakness of their flesh" (v. 41) makes them fall asleep and betray their master. Jesus, by contrast, shows that it is possible to overcome weakness and temptation by means of *prayer*.[28]

It is true for both the Markan and the Matthean account that Jesus repeatedly "prays himself" into alignment with the Father's will. The *effect of prayer*, however, is more visible in Matthew because in his second attempt Jesus does no longer ask for the cup to be removed (this is true by implication for the third prayer as well). While Mark suggests that Jesus utters the same words (τὸν αὐτὸν λόγον) each time he prays, he seems a little more consoled and willing to accept his fate after the first prayer in

---

[23] Matthew modifies the verb from Mark: ἔρχομαι (Mark 14:38) is turned into εἰσέρχομαι (Matt 26:41), which is closer related to the verb εἰσφέρω (Matt 6:13). This kind of "doubling" of verbs with the prefix εἰσ- in combination with the preposition εἰς is typically Matthean (cf., e.g., 2:21; 5:20; 6:6.13; 7:21) and is often used to designate the entry into the βασιλεία τῶν οὐρανῶν.

[24] Contra Peter Wick, "Der historische Ort von Mt 6,1–18," *RB* 105.3 (1998): 332–58, who argues ibid. 344 that Jesus does *not* pray the Lord's Prayer in Gethsemane.

[25] Cf. Keener, *Matthew* (cf. n. 4), 639: "Jesus had lived his life in filial obedience to his Father's will; now he chooses the Father's plan over his own desire. Jesus' obedience is an example for disciples (12:50, cf. 7:21). Loving God does not always mean that they *want* to face what God calls them to face; it does mean that they choose to face it anyway." (emphasis original).

[26] On Jesus's temptation, cf. Lena Lütticke and H.-U Weidemann, " 'He himself was tempted' (Heb 2:18). The Temptation of Jesus in the New Testament," in *Impeccability and Temptation: Understanding Christ's Divine and Human Will*, Routledge Studies in Analytic and Systematic Theology, ed. J. Grössl/ K. v. Stosch (London: Routledge, 2020), 50–74. Jeffrey B. Gibson, *The Temptations of Jesus in Early Christianity*, JSNT 112 (Sheffield: Sheffield Academic, 1995), 251, points out that "obedience produces nothing but a literal dead end." He argues Jesus's request (ibid., 253) for the "cup" to be removed implies "the desire to be allowed to implement a plan of action to accomplish the Messianic task which is the very opposite of God's will in this regard, one namely, that uses violence and domination, instead of suffering and service, to achieve this end."

[27] Cf., e.g., Keener, *Matthew* (cf. n. 4), 637: "The disciples' disobedience provides a foil that illumines the contrasting obedience of Jesus." According to Walter Schmidthals, *Das Evangelium nach Markus II*, ÖTK 2.2 (Gütersloh: Echter-Verlag, 1986), 636, this is the very point of the Gethsemane scene.

[28] Cf. Gibson, *Temptations* (cf. n. 27), 247: "Jesus further says that the πειρασμός is something that is to be resisted and overcome through prayer (cf. 14:38a)." Also, Konradt, *Matt* (cf. n. 21), 413, argues that prayer is a "probates Mittel, um gegen die stets lauernden Versuchungen gewappnet zu sein."

Matthew's version. The result is effectively the same: Jesus "watches and prays," which aligns him with God's will and helps him overcome the temptation to disobey his Father. It is also important to note that—other than in Luke—God *remains silent* and does not send an angel to strengthen Jesus (cf. Luke 22:43: ὤφθη δὲ αὐτῷ ἄγγελος ἀπ' οὐρανοῦ ἐνισχύων αὐτόν). Since Matthew assumes that God is present in the hidden for those who approach him properly (see above), it does make sense that he emphasizes the *paracletic effect of God's hidden presence in prayer*. Hence, Matt 26:36–46 can be read as a *narrative counterpart* to Matt 6:5–13—not only regarding Jesus's *verbal* agreement with his own model prayer but also with respect to the *performative congruence* between his teaching (6:5–15) and prayer practice (26:36, 39, 42, 44). The fact that the Matthean Jesus cites phrases from the Our Father (Matt 26:39, 42: πάτερ μου, 26:42: γενηθήτω τὸ θέλημά σου) makes the analogy all the more striking: he prays *in the way* and *with the words* he taught his followers to pray. Matthew 6 and 26 are linked by their theology which implies that God may be addressed and approached as "Father" who is present ἐν τῷ κρυπτῷ.

When reading Matt 6 as the theoretical background of Matt 26, it is also possible to answer the question of Ps 41:4, 11 LXX, which is alluded to in Matt 26:38: "Where is your God?" (Ποῦ ἐστιν ὁ θεός σου;). God, whom Jesus addresses as πάτερ μου in Matt 26:39, 42, is *there*; he is present "in the hidden." He does not answer through a heavenly voice (as he does in 3:17; 17:5) and does not send a strengthening angel either (as he does in Luke 22:43). God is present exactly in the way as described by Jesus in Matt 6:6—he is present as a Father who "is and sees in the hidden," whose will be done (6:10), and who helps to overcome temptation (6:13). Thus, Matthew (both theoretically *and* practically) shows that prayer is the means to keep in touch with God even at times when he seems absent.[29] The idea of God's hidden presence in prayer situations (προσεύχεσθαι) is the foundation of Matthew's prayer theology (and thereby the foundation of Jesus's teaching on prayer). The Gethsemane scene showcases this as Jesus gradually prays himself into alignment with God's will. According to his own teaching, Jesus approaches his Father properly, that is, in a way that his prayer is aimed at God only because he withdraws from the outside world. This is not only true for Gethsemane but for all of Jesus's (προσεύχεσθαι-) prayers throughout the Gospel account.

With his trust in God's hidden presence in prayer situations, Jesus becomes a *role model for prayer*. He specifically turns to God when his presence is not very obvious: prior to his passion and also at the cross, that is, in moments that mark the boundary of Jesus's life. He radically shows it is necessary to subordinate one's own will to God's will and to trustfully pray: "*Your* will be done" (Matt 6:10; cf. 26:42).[30] In this way the Gospel of Matthew offers prayer instructions which are not merely theoretical (as in 6:1–18, cf. also 21:22) but *narratively realized* in a most existential manner.

---

[29] Cullmann, *Gebet* (cf. n. 2), 44, argues that this closeness is especially tangible at the cross.
[30] Cf. Cullmann, *Gebet* (cf. n. 2), 43, who claims that God's silence is alleviated by Jesus's subordination to the Father's will which means that his prayers were heard eventually: "[M]it dem Sichfügen unter Gottes Willen wird die Nichterhörung so entschärft, daß sie vom Licht dieses auf unser Heil zielenden Willens überstrahlt und auf dieser neuen Ebene zur *Erhörung* wird" (emphasis original).

Matthew's prayer teaching, thus, is oriented towards Jesus's example. This example, in turn, is contrasted with the counterexamples illustrated in 6:1–18 (the pretentious behaviour of the "hypocrites") and also in 26:36–46 (the disciples' failure to watch and pray). The readers of the Gospel of Matthew get a very precise idea of how to pray—and how *not* to pray. First, they learn (from the negative example of the ὑποκριταί) what they should *not* do when they pray or, more generally, when they practice their righteousness: they should not act for the praise of other people (6:1, 5). Then they are told their prayer should be said "behind closed doors" so it is exclusively aimed at the "Father who is and sees in the hidden" and who will reward those prayers (6:6). What that really means, however, is shown by Jesus's example who purposefully prays to "his Father" (26:39, 42: πάτερ μου). Each time he turns to God he explicitly withdraws from the outside world (26:36, 42, 44, ἀπέρχομαι + προσεύχομαι, cf. also 14:23), and he uses the words of his own model prayer (26:42). The fact that he is doing so in a moment of agony underlines just how much he trusts in God's strengthening presence in prayer—and that each "child of God" (cf. 5:45) should have the same hope and trust.

6.4 Conclusion

This chapter has looked at Jesus's teaching on prayer in the Gospel of Matthew. It has particularly considered Matt 6:5–15 and argues that the assumption of *God's hidden presence in prayer situations* serves as the foundation of Matthew's prayer theology (and thereby as the foundation of Jesus's teaching on prayer). Its leading question was how Matthew narrates Jesus's prayer practice in the light of this teaching, or more specifically, whether Jesus's prayer practice is in accord with his own teaching. The analysis of the Gethsemane scene has shown that Jesus is actually portrayed as a teacher who practices what he teaches: he turns to his Father as he experiences fear of death and is tempted to deviate from God's plan. With the words of his own model prayer, however, he prays himself into alignment with God's will and thus manages to overcome this temptation. This study has pointed out that in Gethsemane Jesus becomes a role model for prayer not just because of the *verbal* but also because of the *performative congruence* with his teaching. He prays with the words and in the way he has taught his followers to pray. His thrice repeated retreats for prayer are especially highlighted in the Matthean Gethsemane account, and the effect of God's strengthening presence in prayer is also more visible here than in Mark.

To reinforce this argument, one might want to draw attention to other moments when Jesus addresses God in prayer (with the verb προσεύχεσθαι). Matthew, for instance, transforms Jesus's recreational retreat together with his disciples (cf. Mark 6:31) into two scenes in which Jesus retreats on his own (Matt 14:13, 23). At least in Matt 14:23 he is doing so to pray in solitude, but also in his first retreat (Matt 14:13) he does not want to regain strength (as in Mark 6:31). Rather, Jesus seems to need some time on his own to process the news of John's death (cf. Matt 14:1–12). The feeding of the five thousand (Matt 14:13–21) then disrupts his solitude that is resumed in Matt 14:23. Even though Jesus also retreats onto the mountain in Mark 6:46, this prayer scene is more pronounced in Matthew. In Mark, the short sequence is tightly interwoven with Jesus's walking on the water. It is a narrative repetition of the action in Mark 1:35 and primarily serves to introduce the following epiphany. Matthew, by contrast, places a stronger narrative emphasis on Jesus's prayer retreat by mentioning his solitude twice (κατ' ἰδίαν … μόνος) and by separating the scene more distinctly from the subsequent walk on the water.

Finally, even though προσεύχομαι-terminology is missing, Jesus's outcry at the cross (Matt 27:46) is another one of his prayers to God. Like in Mark, Jesus dies after uttering some words from Ps 22, lamenting that his God has forsaken him (θεέ μου θεέ μου, ἱνατί με ἐγκατέλιπες;). The centurion and the guards eventually confess him as "the Son of God" (27:54). Other than in Mark, however, this human confession is preceded by *God's confession to his Son*: In 27:51b–53, Matthew narrates a list of cosmic phenomena which, in a way, can be considered *God's answer to Jesus's prayer*. He does not answer directly; in fact, Jesus cannot even take note of most of the phenomena (except for the darkness, cf. v. 45) because they happen after his death. Rather, the tearing of the veil of the temple, the earthquake, the opening of the tombs, and the resurrection of the "many bodies of the saints" are a *publicly visible* response to Jesus' lamentation (not merely to his death). Jesus accuses God of being *absent*, and God unmistakably shows he was and is *present*. These further examples underline the importance of the idea of God's (hidden) presence in prayer situations which the Matthean Jesus depicts both in his teaching and practice.

What Does the *Bildungsroman* Have to Do with the Lord's Prayer?

Charles Nathan Ridlehoover

7.1 Introduction

Tertullian famously quipped: "What has Athens to do with Jerusalem?" Jerome took the question one step farther and framed the question in specifically literary terms: "What has Horace to do with the Psalter? Or Virgil with the Gospel? Or Cicero with the Apostle?"[1] Tertullian's quote has the ring of one who is hesitant to bridge the gap between the sacred and the secular but is at least considering the option, while Jerome assumes that similar genres can be compared and lessons can be gleaned.[2] The questions are important in that they consider the possibility of using extracanonical sources of literature and philosophy as frameworks for understanding biblical texts.

So, what does the *Bildungsroman* have to do with the Lord's Prayer?[3] Or rather, can the genre of "coming-of-age" function as a framework and comparative tool for understanding one of the purposes of the Lord's Prayer? I will argue in the affirmative. Ancient interpreters frequently noted the ethical/catechistic/educational aspects of the Lord's Prayer and how it develops the disciple, but more modern treatments of the prayer have spent little time with this function.[4] The exception to this absence is the recent work of Clifton Black.[5] Black argues that to pray the Lord's Prayer is to enroll in a twofold curriculum: one of *educere* (Latin, "to lead out") and of *educare* ("to bring up"). Black explains that *educere* and *educare* capture the Prayer's message that "what we most profoundly need is evoked and exposed; what we most ardently desire is developed and disciplined." In what follows, I will examine this important purpose

---

[1] For a modern treatment of Virgil's *Aeneid* and a biblical comparison, see R. W. Moberly, *The Bible in a Disenchanted Age: The Enduring Possibility of Christian Faith* (Grand Rapids, MI: Baker, 2018).
[2] The means through which these texts were read together was an allegorical reading of Scripture.
[3] The *Bildungsroman* is a literary genre that focuses on the psychological and moral growth of the main protagonist from childhood to adulthood. More on this below.
[4] These three words are used interchangeably throughout the secondary literature to refer to the "development" of the petitioner.
[5] Clifton Black, *The Lord's Prayer*, Interpretation (Louisville, KY: WJK, 2018). See also, Jeffrey Gibson, *The Disciple's Prayer: The Prayer Jesus Taught in Its Historical Setting* (Minneapolis, MN: Fortress, 2015). Gibson argues that the prayer is designed to train the disciple but unnecessarily narrows the prayer's focus to the temptation petition.

of the Lord's Prayer but from a slightly different yet complementary angle to Black's research. I will implement the literary characteristics of the *Bildungsroman* genre as a heuristic framework for understanding the purpose of the Lord's Prayer as a part of Matthew's Gospel.[6] I will begin with some initial observations and presuppositions before turning to the *Bildungsroman* genre and a comparison with the Lord's Prayer in Matthew's Gospel.

7.2 Initial Observations and Presuppositions

The following comparison will be a narrative reading of the Lord's Prayer in its context. Of course, the Lord's Prayer is just a few short lines (Matt 6:7–8), and the *Bildungsroman* is a novel, but when the prayer is understood in its broader context, its length and depth are enhanced for the intended comparison. Matthew's immediate context for the Lord's Prayer is the Sermon on the Mount. As the structural, theological, and teleological center of the Sermon, the Lord's Prayer should be understood as part of the Sermon's discipleship program.[7] Another important observation is the Sermon's placement in Matthew's narrative. I will assume that this placement is not incidental. In literary analysis, it is frequently noted that the author of a text will introduce material at the beginning of his work to implicate its importance. This literary device is called the primacy effect.[8] The term suggests that material which occurs first tends to have a high impact on the reader. This observation is not intended to argue that the first narrative block is somehow more important than Matthew's other discourses or narrative sections but that this placement makes the "first impression" for the reader.

In addition to these observations concerning the placement of the Lord's Prayer in Matthew's Gospel, it is also important to consider some of the clues from the early church concerning the prayer's use. The earliest evidence for the Lord's Prayer as part of the petitioner's development comes by way of the *Didache*.[9] The *Didache* is one of the earliest church documents following the closing of the biblical canon (ca.100 AD).[10] The Lord's Prayer is discussed in chapter 8 which appears between chapter 7, on baptism, and chapter 9, on communion. The implication of this ordering is that once a believer was baptized as a sign of salvation, they followed in the recitation of the Lord's Prayer. From the *Didache*'s perspective, it was incumbent upon the new believer to know and understand the Lord's Prayer before taking communion.[11] From these incipient

---

[6] The reasoning for choosing the Matthean version of the Lord's Prayer is its preference among the early church and its familiarity to today's audience. The Lukan version of the prayer is situated in an extended section on prayer (Luke 11:1–11).

[7] I will assume the centrality of the Lord's Prayer. This conclusion has been argued in a variety of recent commentaries. For a survey of these positions and my own proposal, see *The Lord's Prayer and the Sermon on the Mount in Matthew's Gospel*, LNTS 616 (London: T&T Clark, 2019).

[8] On the primacy effect, see James L. Resseguie, *Narrative Criticism of the New Testament* (Grand Rapids, MI: Baker, 2005), 209–10.

[9] The *Didache* is also the earliest appearance of the prayer outside of the canonical Gospels.

[10] On the canon, see Michael J. Kruger, *Canon Revisited: Establishing the Origins and Authority of the New Testament Books* (Wheaton, IL: Crossway, 2012).

[11] Cf. Jeremias, 83. Also, David A. Clark, *On Earth as in Heaven: The Lord's Prayer from Jewish Prayer to Christian Ritual* (Minneapolis: Fortress, 2017).

moments, the prayer would become one of the means through which a new disciple would navigate life's circumstances. Interestingly, the believer is instructed to pray the Lord's Prayer three times a day from that point forward.[12] As Jeremias points out, new converts "prayed it daily, and it formed a token of their identification as Christians."

7.3 The *Bildungsroman* Defined

The primary emphasis of the *Bildungsroman* is to trace the formation of the character, his or her growth into maturation, and hence, "coming-of-age."[9] The form is familiar to the modern audience because of its ease in adaption to the big screen. "Coming-of-age" movies include *Ferris Bueller's Day Off*, *Stand by Me*, *The Breakfast Club*, *Dead Poet's Society*, *Little Women*, and *The Goonies*. Popular writings include *Candide*, *Jane Eyre*, *Great Expectations*, *The Adventures of Huckleberry Finn*, *Little Women*, *To Kill a Mockingbird*, and the *Harry Potter* catalogue. These books and movies (and in some cases, their novel precedents) produce a certain relatability to the audience. By generating forms that are familiar to human experience, the mediums allow the audience to become involved in the process of growth/development and participate vicariously through the main characters.

Studies of the *Bildungsroman* genre usually fall into three categories. The first category is concerned with the term's origin. By isolating its original usage, the first category limits itself to the original intentions of the pioneers of the genre. The second category seeks to establish an agreed-upon set of criteria that marks all examples of the genre. In other words, the genre is made up of works that share tropes or meta-themes. These themes typically include growth of the character, education, whole-person development, and conquering an obstacle. The third category is more concerned with how the genre has evolved throughout history. In this latter case, a *Bildungsroman* is subject to change as the characters are marked by differing cultures and development. The present study will work generally from these categories with primary attention to the development of the main character being described.

Historically, the *Bildungsroman* was used in secular ideologies to describe purely physical growth. But, as Kelsey L. Bennett has argued, "The idea of *Bild* appears at the source of identity in its metaphysical dimensions. The King James version of Gen 1:26–27 reads: 'And God said, Let us make man in our image, after our likeness … So God created man in his own image, in the image of God created he him; male and female created he them.'[13] Luther's German translation reads: 'Und Gott sprach: Lasset

---

[12] These conclusions are also corroborated by several ancient texts that relate the Lord's Prayer to baptism. For a list of texts and engagement with these sources, see Justo L. González, *Teach Us to Pray: The Lord's Prayer in the Early Church and Today* (Grand Rapids, MI: Eerdmans, 2020), 14–16. González associates the Lord's Prayer as a pre-baptismal ritual despite the ordering of the *Didache*, which places the Lord's Prayer after baptism. Cyril of Jerusalem also prefers the Lord's Prayer after baptism. The ordering is not as significant to my argument, only the association. The version of the Lord's Prayer in the *Didache* is the version presented in Matthew's Gospel. It is very likely that both authors had access to the same source material or that Matthew was the direct source for the *Didache*.

[13] The KJV is preferred here because of its redundancy of "image."

uns Menschen machen, ein Bild, das uns gleich sei ... Und Gott schuf den Menschen ihm zum Bilde, zum Bilde Gottes schuf er ihn; und er schuf sie ein Männlein und Fräulein.'"[14] Bennett notes here that Luther collapses the meanings of image (i.e., physical) and likeness (i.e., spiritual) into one term, "*Bild.*" Within the individual, the spiritual is fused with the physical and, in both cases, in need of development. As I will argue below, this is exactly how Matthew's context envisions whole-person development through the Lord's Prayer. The *telos* of Jesus's teachings is the transformation of the individual into the *imago Christi*, both internally and externally.

Wilhelm Dilthey, who popularized the critical distinctives of the *Bildungsroman*, identifies four aspects of the genre that set it apart from other genres and are helpful for the current study.[15] First, the genre is set in a political culture of sorts. Second, the emphasis is biographical thus giving it a universal quality. Third, the genre is concerned with the commensurability of world-experience with inner aptitude. Fourth, the genre is philosophical because it aims for the ideal human by charting the development of a modulating character. This picture is therefore defined by general growth, education, development of the artist, and shows development of the inside and outside of the individual—the genre will often depict outward challenges to illuminate internal changes. This dualism presents a world of conflict in which the individual is developing *through*.

In a more updated exploration of the genre, Petru Golban traces the development of the genre from Dilthey to the Romantic era. His definition is as follows:

> We would define the *Bildungsroman* in short as the novel of identity formation. With certain caveats, of course; namely, that the formation of identity is textualized as a process, diachronic and large-scale, from birth or early childhood through adolescence and youth to entering upon adulthood; this process is rendered in a biographical or autobiographical manner as development—spiritual, psychological, and moral, rather than physical—leading to the formation of personality.[16]

Golban's observations are important because they note the characteristics of textualization and process. As a character works through time, they are being formed into the ideal. In what follows, I will use the basic outline set forth by Dilthey and modified by Golban with one slight alteration, which will become more apparent below.

7.4 The Politics of the Prayer

Dilthey's first distinctive is the political setting of the protagonist. In Matthew's cultural milieu, politics was not a static category that referred to a singular government. For

---

[14] Kelsey L. Bennett, *Principle and Prosperity: Experience and Religion in the Nineteenth-Century British and American Bildungsroman* (Columbia: University of South Carolina Press, 2014), 3–4.
[15] See *Das Erlebnis und die Dichtung: Lessing, Goethe, Novalis, Hölderlin* (Poetry and Experience 1906).
[16] *The History of the Bildungsroman: From Ancient Beginnings to Romanticism* (Cambridge: Cambridge Scholars Publishing, 2018), 18.

first-century Jews (including Matthew), formal politics and religion were almost inseparable. Therefore, foreign oppression and the relationship between the realms of heaven and earth were pivotal categories for understanding one's identity. For the ease of explanation, I have narrowed Matthew's world to (1) its historical and theological layer and (2) its cosmological and eschatological layer.[17]

First, there is the historical and theological layer.[18] The events in the Gospel of Matthew take place within Judea, which is a Roman province. Matthew's most probable audience is a group in Syria of Antioch. The scholarly guild is divided on the timing of Matthew's Gospel. Is Matthew written before or after the fall of Jerusalem (AD 70)? Following the fall of Jerusalem is a council convened at Jamnia. It is speculated that during this meeting, Jews begin to define their brand of exclusivism. The growing Christian community began to create an identity apart from formative Judaism. This parting of ways is highly debated but is mainly occupied by two separate camps. The first group is those who see the Matthean church within established Judaism, or what is considered *intra muros*.[19] In *The Setting of the Sermon on the Mount*, W. D. Davies argues that because of the events of Jamnia, it is reasonable to see the contents of the Sermon on the Mount as a response to the decrees of this Pharisaic meeting.[20] The contents are a counter-Jamnia designed to promote the flourishing of the Matthean church and critique Judaism. Davies posits that the contents of the Gospel are dealing with interfamily issues.

While Davies's ideas have been influential in the years since his initial proposal, there is a handful of scholars that are not as convinced as to the details of Jamnia's influence.[21] The second group is those that assert that the Matthean church has officially split from the established religion of Judaism, existing *extra muros*. The argument is as follows: there is tension (some attribute this to Jamnia and the *Birkat ha-Minim* ["Blessing on the heretics"]; others to the increasing number of Jesus followers who employ liberty in regard to certain Judaist laws prior to Jamnia) within the established religion and Jewish Christians, or rather Christian Jews, are starting to define their existence exclusively by Jesus's teaching.[22] Graham Stanton gives four arguments for this

---

[17] For the most up-to-date treatment, see David Wenham, *Jesus in Context: Making Sense of the Historical Figure* (Cambridge: Cambridge University Press, 2021).

[18] R. T. France, *Matthew: Evangelist and Teacher* (Downers Grove, IL: IVP, 1989), 81, states, "Whichever aspect you begin with must be discussed in light of the other, and that will mean taking on trust conclusions which cannot be justified until a later stage of the argument."

[19] The three most notable proponents for Matthew's church remaining well within Judaism are Anthony J. Saldarini, *Matthew's Christian-Jewish Community* (Chicago: University of Chicago Press, 1994); J. A. Overman, *Matthew's Gospel and Formative Judaism* (Minneapolis, MN: Fortress Press, 1990); and D. C. Sim, "The Gospel of Matthew and the Gentiles," *JSNT* 57 (1996): 19–48. Set against these arguments, cf. D. R. A. Hare, "How Jewish Is Matthew's Gospel," *Catholic Biblical Quarterly* 62 (2000): 264–77.

[20] W. D. Davies, *The Setting of the Sermon on the Mount* (Cambridge: University Press, 1964), 256–315.

[21] For an explanation of this thought, cf. Donald A. Hagner, *Matthew 1–13*, WBC (Nashville, TN: Thomas Nelson, 1993), lxviii–lxxi; Donald Senior, *What Are They Saying About Matthew?* (New York: Paulist, 1996), 8–15. Most recently, Anders Runesson and Daniel M. Gurtner, eds., *Matthew within Judaism: Israel and the Nations in the First Gospel*, Early Christianity and Its Literature, vol. 27 (Atlanta, GA: SBL, 2020).

[22] Cf. Anthony J. Saldarini for explanations of this terminology. *Matthew's Christian-Jewish Community* (Chicago: University of Chicago Press, 1994), 11–26. Saldarini argues that the Matthean church is still well within the bounds of Judaism. In his opinion, the sectarian nature of Judaism following the fall of Jerusalem allows this sort of reading.

proposal. (1) The disciples in Matthew are sent to all nations and should expect rejection from Jews and gentiles. Therefore, the Matthean church is not necessarily a group of gentile Christians set apart or against Jewish sectarianism.[23] (2) There are derogatory references in Matthew to not only contemporary Judaism but also the gentile world.[24] Stanton sees this Matthean group as committed to a mission that includes gentiles but nonetheless views this group as foreign and threatening.[25] (3) Matthew has increased apocalyptic language (chs. 24–25). In contemporary literature, the employment of this language was always in the context of struggle among groups vying for corporate solidarity.[26] Stanton argues that this would be in keeping with a Matthean group trying to reconcile its existence with the status quo. (4) Matthew's narration is like other Christian writings which evidence a strained relationship to Judaism (1 Thess, John, the *Didache*, 4 Ezra, and 5 Ezra).[27] In Stanton's estimation, this backdrop helps the reader to understand the content of Matthew, especially the anti-Jewish polemic in chapter 23.[28] Christians are distinct from their counterparts but struggling with their identities in Jesus.

France has rightly noted that most of the discussions regarding these points are guilty of an either/or fallacy.[29] The tensions among the church and synagogue are much more complex. He states, "It is more probable that the separation of Jewish Christians from the synagogue was a gradual process, prompted as much by Christian hostility toward non-Christian Judaism as by any official action on behalf of the synagogue to exclude them, and that the process developed at different rates in different communities."[30] It seems safe to assert this general idea based on the evidence from first-century history and the already present tensions of Christians and Jews evidenced in Paul's writings (i.e., Galatians).[31]

Second, there is the cosmological and eschatological layer. Matthew's writing constructs a world in which there is a dualism between heaven and earth. When heaven and earth are not being used as a merism to refer to the totality of creation, Matthew has the spheres in an antithetical relationship. It is probable that Matthew is drawing on the political influence of the book of Daniel and its vision of the kingdom of heaven against the kingdoms of earth.[32] As Jonathan Pennington notes, this comparison is to emphasize that the kingdom of heaven is unlike all earthly

---

[23] Graham N. Stanton, *A Gospel for a New People: Studies in Matthew* (Louisville, KY: Westminster/John Knox, 1992), 158.
[24] Stanton, *Gospel*, 160.
[25] Senior, *Saying about Matthew*, 12.
[26] Stanton, *Gospel*, 161–3.
[27] Stanton, *Gospel*, 165.
[28] Stanton, *Gospel*, 166.
[29] Also cf. Richard Bauckham, ed. *The Gospel for All Christians: Rethinking the Gospel Audiences* (Grand Rapids, MI: Eerdmans, 1998). Bauckham argues that the Gospels display a general nature that would have been intended to reach a broad audience and that inference from the Gospel itself as to an intended audience is a fallacious endeavor.
[30] R. T. France, *The Gospel of Matthew*, NICNT (Grand Rapids, MI: Eerdmans, 2007), 16.
[31] Cf. Robert Gundry, *Matthew: A Commentary on His Handbook for a Mixed Church under Persecution*, 2nd ed. (Grand Rapids, MI: Eerdmans, 1994), 599–602.
[32] Jonathan T. Pennington, *Heaven and Earth in the Gospel of Matthew* (Grand Rapids, MI: Baker, 2007), 291–2.

kingdoms. The heavenly kingdom is marked by its radical reorientation of the earthly social order. God's blessings are extended to the poor in spirit, the mourners, the meek, the persecuted (5:3–12). First in the new kingdom (19:30) will be those who care for the poor and those who are considered the "least"—the lowly ones (18:1–4), the strangers, the hungry, the thirsty, the naked, the sick, and the imprisoned ones (25:31).[33] The application of this comparison is that God's new kingdom will usher in a sense of hope to those in Matthew's church who are seeking to define themselves and attempting to cope with Roman occupation. Contrary to the current Jewish expectation of a violent overthrow of Roman oppression, Matthew's church is primed to endure with the promise that their current plight will be reversed when the kingdom of heaven is finally here. This longing for the final kingdom to come is the hallmark of Matthew's eschatology. Matthew's narrative presents a tension between what Jesus has accomplished in his coming (3:2; 4:17) and the promise of a future kingdom. Jesus is now the God who is "with us,"[34] but the kingdom is not fully present. Jesus's teaching in the latter half of Matthew looks forward to the final consummation of the kingdom (Matt 24–25) with the arrival of the Son of Man (another reference to Daniel).

Against this backdrop, the Lord's Prayer is given to a group that is seeking to establish their identity in a tumultuous political, religious, and eschatological time. Within these layers, the Lord's Prayer gives the petitioner an identity and vision for the future. The petitioner prays to their Father as a son and daughter and acknowledges that the Father is the king ("your kingdom come") of heaven.[35] The petitioner also longs for a kingdom that is from heaven to *finally* come ("your will be done on earth as in heaven") and the final world order to become manifest on earth over and against the current earthly powers. The Father's kingdom is further defined by its complete dependence on his will and radical forgiveness.

7.5 The Life and Lifestyle of the Petitioner

Dilthey's second distinctive is the biographical nature of the writing. The Gospels are biographies, and their primary character is Jesus.[36] But, the careful reader will note that a story about Jesus does not fit the definition of "coming-of-age." Jesus is not depicted throughout the Gospels as learning from his mistakes or having a grand epiphany about his purpose and mission. He also does not necessarily evolve toward some sort of ideal. In Matthew's story, Jesus functions as an ideal for the disciples. Matthew does give a complex picture of the disciples as secondary characters with a particular emphasis on Peter. The disciples are the recipients of the Lord's Prayer and Sermon and are depicted throughout Matthew's Gospel as growing. For this reason, I want to combine Dilthey's second and fourth distinctive. Dilthey's fourth distinctive

---

[33] Pennington, 323.
[34] On the significance of this designation, see Richard Bauckham, *Who Is God?: Key Moments of Biblical Revelation* (Grand Rapids, MI: Baker, 2020), 19–23.
[35] Unless otherwise noted, all translations are mine.
[36] See the references below concerning Burridge and Keener.

is the development of an evolving character aiming for the ideal. The biography of the disciples is told through the story of Jesus, and as these disciples are following Jesus, they are evolving into the *imago Christi*.

In this section, I will demonstrate that Jesus had an effective ministry among his disciples. By effective, I am referring to Jesus impacting his disciples in such a way that they would follow his teachings. The primary evidence for this claim is (1) the feature of *mimesis* in the Gospel's genre and (2) Matthew's development of a discipleship motif that unites Jesus's teachings and his disciples.

In recent years, there has been a renewed interest in understanding the genre of the Gospels. Since the groundbreaking work of Richard Burridge, the Gospels have been seen as close parallels to the Greco-Roman *bios*.[37] More recently, Craig Keener has given an extensive investigation into every extant *bios* for the most up-to-date and in-depth account of the Gospel's genre.[38] Keener argues persuasively that *mimesis* is a key feature of the Gospels genre.[39] *Mimesis*, in this context, refers to the copying of a master. Verses throughout Matthew's narrative reflect Matthew's interests in Jesus's disciples being followers of their master:

Matthew 5:44–45: "But I tell you, love your enemies and pray for those who persecute you, so that you may be children of your Father in heaven."

Matthew 10:24–25: "A disciple is not above the teacher, nor a slave above the master; it is enough for the disciple to be like the teacher, and the slave like the master."

Matthew 12:49b–50: "Here are ... my brothers! For whoever does the will of my Father in heaven is my brother."

Matthew 28:20a: "Observe all that I have commanded you."

In these verses, discipleship is defined first by adherence to the will of God. Second, discipleship in Matthew is pledging one's allegiances to Jesus's words and deed (I will address this point in more detail below). Third, discipleship is described in terms of familial language, most frequently as devotion to the Father in heaven. Fourth, allegiance to the Father in heaven subverts biological relationships.

Closely related to these key verses is Matthew's inclusion of the disciples' commissioning as followers of Jesus. Allison notes the ways in which the disciples copy their master (Table 7.1).[40]

---

[37] Richard A. Burridge, *What Are the Gospels?: A Comparison with Graeco-Roman Biography*, 2nd ed. (Grand Rapids, MI: Eerdmans, 2004).

[38] Craig S. Keener, *Christobiography: Memory, History, and the Reliability of the Gospels* (Grand Rapids, MI: Eerdmans, 2019).

[39] This statement is not intended to be of theological significance. Opponents of *mimesis* will often point out that human efforts of discipleship negate the word of the Holy Spirit. The following argument does not intend to weigh in on the ongoing discussion of the Spirit's role versus human effort. I am assuming that Jesus was a genuine human that was worthy of emulation.

[40] Dale C. Allison, "Structure, Biographical Impulse, and the *Imitatio Christi*," in *Studies in Matthew: Interpretation Past and Present* (Grand Rapids, MI: Baker, 2005), 151. See also the insightful work of Brown, *Gospels as Stories*, 85–104.

Table 7.1 The Disciples Who Follow Their Master

The Disciples	Jesus
They are to heal every disease and every infirmity (10:1)	He heals every disease and every infirmity (4:23)
They are to preach that "the kingdom of heaven is at hand" (10:7)	He preaches that "the kingdom of heaven is at hand" (4:17)
They are to cast out demons (10:8)	He cast out demons (9:32–33, etc.)
They are to heal lepers (10:8)	He heals lepers (11:5)
They are to raise the dead (10:8)	He raises the dead (11:5)
They are not to go to the Samaritans but to the lost sheep of Israel (10:6)	He does not go to the Samaritans but to the lost sheep of Israel (15:24)
They will be handed over to sanhedrins/persecution (10:17)	Jesus is handed over to the Sanhedrin/persecution (26:57–68)
They will be dragged before governors (10:18)	Jesus is taken before the governor (27:1–26)
They will be called Beelzebul (10:25)	Jesus is called Beelzebul (9:34; 10:25)
The disciples will carry a cross (10:38)	Jesus is crucified (20:19; etc.)

Jeannine Brown and Kyle Roberts have noted that throughout his Gospel, Matthew uses generic characters to challenge the reader to follow Jesus. These characters serve as examples of "what to do" and "what not to do." The disciples learn faith from those who seek Jesus in faith (9:2, 22, 29), gentiles who show "greater" faith (8:10; 15:28), tax collectors and prostitutes who believe John's message (21:32), the woman who anoints Jesus before burial (26:6–13), Pilate's wife (27:19), the women who stay with Jesus after the disciples desert him (27:55–56), and the two faithful Josephs (1:18–25; 27:57–60).[41] Negative examples of discipleship include Jesus's hometown (13:54–58), Jewish leaders throughout Matthew's Gospel, as well as the "hypocrite."[42]

In summary, one can discern a pattern of describing and prescribing the ideal throughout Matthew's Gospel. Throughout, discipleship is defined by obedience to Jesus's teachings. When it comes to the Lord's Prayer, Jesus instructs his disciples to "pray then in this way." Although I will address Matthew's recording of prayer in more detail below, it is important to note the insinuation that the disciples hear the prayer and commit to its teaching. Incidentally, the Lord's Prayer is the only prayer throughout the Gospels that Jesus specifically teaches. The immediate context of the prayer also juxtaposes sons and daughters of the Father to hypocrites and gentiles (Matt 6:5–8). While Jesus functions as the ideal petitioner with the ideal prayer, the hypocrites and gentiles function as ones who love attention and pray in empty prose.[43]

---

[41] Jeannine K. Brown and Kyle Roberts, *Matthew*, THNTC (Grand Rapids, MI: Eerdmans, 2018), 335.

[42] Brown and Roberts, *Matthew*, 335–6. The two groups who are present for the Sermon are the disciples and the "crowds." The disciples will ultimately heed Jesus's teachings, while the "crowds" will be the ones chanting "Crucify him!" (26:47). On a more detailed look at the progression of the crowds as characters, see Warren Carter, "The Crowds in Matthew's Gospel," *CBQ* 55.1 (1993): 54–67.

[43] It is also important to note that Jesus makes clear that he will come alongside those who chose to follow him. Twice, Jesus makes this clear in Matthew's Gospel. Matthew 18:20 states, "For where

7.6 Shaping the Heart through Circumstances

Dilthey's third distinctive concerns the shaping of the heart through outward circumstances. Golban highlights the spiritual, psychological, and moral development that expresses itself through the personality as it is working through external circumstances. Matthew's Gospel frequently correlates the inward and outward aspects of life. This theme is expressed throughout Matthew's Gospel in the form of hearing and doing, or word and deed. This theme is expressed in two differing but complimentary ways. First, Matthew insists on unity within one's person. What one says is expected in one's actions with hypocrisy denounced at every turn. Also, the heart is shaped through obedience to Jesus's teachings in the face of temptation and persecution. This aspect centers in the individual, and Jesus is the example *par excellence* of practicing what he preaches. Second, Jesus gives his disciples a series of teachings and expects them to be performed. In this section, I will point out three pieces of evidence that reflect the above aspects and show the close connection between word and deed/hearing and doing in Matthew's Gospel.

First, Matthew has structured his Gospel to reflect the close connection between Jesus's words and deeds. Although this argument extends to the end of the Gospel with Matthew's discourse/narrative structure, I will focus on the structural and thematic progression between chapters 5 through 10. Matthew 4 closes with a summation of Jesus's ministry in Galilee. The verses state,

> Jesus went throughout Galilee, teaching in their synagogues and proclaiming the good news of the kingdom and curing every disease and every sickness among the people. So his fame spread throughout all Syria, and they brought to him all the sick, those who were afflicted with various diseases and pains, demoniacs, epileptics, and paralytics, and he cured them. And great crowds followed him from Galilee, the Decapolis, Jerusalem, Judea, and from beyond the Jordan. (Matt 4:23–25)

The closing of chapter 4 repeats at the end of chapter 9 in an abbreviated form. Verses 35–36 state,

> Then Jesus went about all the cities and villages, teaching in their synagogues, and proclaiming the good news of the kingdom, and curing every disease and every sickness. When he saw the crowds, he had compassion for them, because they were harassed and helpless, like sheep without a shepherd.

The repetition of these summaries signals an *inclusio* around chapters 5–9. Chapters 5–7 are Jesus's teachings on discipleship (i.e., the Sermon on the Mount). Chapters 8–9 depict Jesus living his Sermon teachings. The parallels of Jesus's words in chapters 5–7

---

two or three are gathered in my name, I am there among them," along with the word in Matt 28:20b: "And remember, I am with you always, to the end of the age."

and deeds in chapters 8–9 include the proclaiming of the kingdom of heaven, forgiving of sins, loving your neighbor, and attending to the "least." This combination alone serves as evidence for the "word and deed" motif, but chapter 10 takes the parallel one step further (see the previous section for examples).

In the closing verses of Matt 9, Jesus instructs the disciples to pray that they may be prepared to go out (vv. 37-8).[44] The verses state, "The harvest is plentiful, but the laborers are few; therefore ask the Lord of the harvest to send out laborers into his harvest." In chapter 10, Jesus's disciples are pictured as the harvesters who embody their teacher's example. In their mission, the disciples proclaim the kingdom of heaven, heal the sick, and forsake all.[45] By extension then, the disciples also embody the words of the Sermon on the Mount. Worth noting also is the words of prayer at the transitional seam of chapter 9 and the commission of the disciples in chapter 10.[46] The disciples are instructed to "ask" (δεήθητε) the Lord for more workers in the field. More on this type of connection below.

Second, Jesus explicitly addresses the importance of hearing and doing. In Jesus's final instruction to his disciples, he states: "Observe all that I have commanded you" (Matt 28:20c). Jesus uses the word "observe" to encourage obedience on the part of those who would follow him. The passage forms an *inclusio* with Matt 4:9–10, in which Jesus dismisses the devil and his temptations. Jesus proclaims in 4:10, "Worship the Lord your God, and serve only him." The dual references to "worship" enclose Jesus's instructions throughout chapters 5–28. Jesus is also back on the "mountain" in which he inaugurated his teaching ministry (chapters 5–7). Discipleship is featured prominently here in Jesus's instruction to baptize in the name of the Father, Son, and Holy Spirit and to teach his own words.

In the middle of Matthew is a series of quotations that illustrate Matthew's word and deed theme. In Matt 11:4–5, Jesus instructs some would-be disciples: "Go and tell John what you hear and see: the blind receive their sight, the lame walk, the lepers are cleansed, the deaf hear, the dead are raised, and the poor have good news brought to them." Next is Jesus's teaching in Matt 12:49b–50, which I also mentioned above regarding *mimesis*. The verses state, "Here are ... my brothers! For whoever does the will of my Father in heaven is my brother." Jesus's realignment of family here follows his teaching concerning tree/fruit in relation to the tongue (Matt 12:30–37) and the sign of Jonah and Solomon (Matt 12:38–42). Jesus instructs his disciple that words proceed from the heart and must be carefully tendered. After this teaching, the Pharisees request a sign. Jesus explains that signs alone are profitable if the hearer listens. Nineveh was given a sign, and the Queen of the South came to hear Solomon's

---

[44] These verses serve both as part of Matthew's macro-level word/deed combination and his micro-level word/deed combination.

[45] France states, "This transitional paragraph (9:35–38) serves both as a summary of the ministry in word and deed which has been depicted in chs. 5–9 and as an introduction to the theme of mission which follows. Its first verse closely echoes the language of 4:23 which introduced the Galilean ministry, thus forming a framework around the anthology of words and deeds which Matthew has put together. Its closing verses provide the basis for the sending out of the Twelve as 'workers in the harvest.'" *Gospel of Matthew*, 371. Cf. also, Luz, *Theology of the Gospel of Matthew*, 62–8.

[46] France notes that the one will lead to the other, the ones praying will be the ones who respond to the prayer. *Gospel of Matthew*, 374.

wisdom. In both cases, the word/sign was important, and now, more importantly, Jesus is the sign that must be heeded. From these passages, we can deduce a couple of things. Matthew 23:1–3 begins a long condemnation of the Pharisees. In this, Jesus criticizes a variety of Pharisaical practices but chooses to begin by noting that their teachings and lifestyle do not align. Verses 2–3 state: "The scribes and the Pharisees sit on Moses' seat; therefore, do whatever they teach you and follow it; but do not do as they do, for they do not practice what they teach." The rebuke and reciprocal prohibition are clear. The Pharisees claim an authority that is not validated by their actions, and Jesus calls out their blatant hypocrisy.

Third, Matthew records specific prayers alongside prescribed deeds. For the sake of space, I will only examine those passages that are distinctive to Matthew's Gospel.[47] Having previously mentioned Matt 9:37–38, here I will note three additional examples: Matt 18:19–20, 19:13–15, and 26:36–46. To begin, Matt 18:19–20 states, "Again, truly I tell you, if two of you agree on earth about anything you ask, it will be done for you by my Father in heaven. For where two or three are gathered in my name, I am there among them." In the previous verses (Matt 18:15–18), Jesus teaches on church discipline. The focus of Jesus's teaching in Matt 18:15–18 is the proper reproving of one who is in sin. After detailing the steps of confrontation (18:15–17), Jesus issues a final word in v. 18 on the power of his disciples to "bind and loose" on earth (cf. also 16:19). Verses 19–20 do not seem to have a connection with the context in which they are found, but the addition of "again" (Πάλιν) signals continuance with v. 18.[48] Additionally, both sets of verses share an emphasis on "heaven and earth," the repetition of "two or three," and Matthew's phrase the "Father in heaven." These parallels between vv. 15–18 and 19–20 enjoin prayer and the reproving of one's sin. France notes, "The authority exercised in dealing with the offending brother or sister is grounded in the privileged access of the agreeing community to God in prayer."[49] It is during times of repairing the community that disciples ask of the Father in heaven for strength and forgiveness (cf. Matt 18:21–35).

In Matt 19:13–15, Jesus blesses children with the laying on of hands and prayer.[50] Jesus's teaching here addresses specific children but draws comparisons to those who are of a childlike state (cf. 18:1–5). The comparison is signaled in the Greek with the use of τοιοῦτος without a noun. The NRSV correctly translates the adjective as "such as these." The lack of specificity in the adjective highlights Jesus's development of sonship.

---

[47] In this context, "distinctive" refers to those nuances and verses that are found in only Matthew's Gospel.

[48] So, France, 695. France suggests that a better translation for πάλιν is "moreover" to avoid the suggestion that v. 19 is a repetition of v. 18. We would argue that the repetition is precisely Matthew's intention as he is furthering his heaven and earth theme. This creates parallels between the two verses and strengthens the concern of prayers to heaven and living on earth. Cf. 6:10.

[49] France, 696.

[50] Matthew 19:13–15 state,

> Then little children were being brought to him in order that he might lay his hands on them and pray. The disciples spoke sternly to those who brought them; but Jesus said, "Let the little children come to me, and do not stop them; for it is to such as these that the kingdom of heaven belongs." And he laid his hands on them and went on his way.

Sonship is fundamental to Matthew's understanding of discipleship. As Matthew focuses attention on Jesus's depiction of God as the "Father who is in heaven," so he develops the theme of discipleship for his "children."[51] Those of a childlike state are given the "kingdom of heaven." Jesus has already mentioned those who are recipients of the "kingdom of heaven" in the Sermon's introduction (5:3–12). The poor in spirit and persecuted therefore parallel the status of children mentioned here. Interestingly, Matthew is the only Synoptic writer to include the instruction to pray in this narrative. While the specific prayer is not mentioned, it is through the laying on of hands and the blessing of children that Jesus incorporates the prayer. Prayer then becomes part of the discipleship that leads to the kingdom.

Matthew 26:36–46 recounts the anguish of Jesus in the Garden of Gethsemane. Jesus enters the garden with three of his disciples to pray about his forthcoming death. During this time, the disciples, with their refusal to stay awake, serve as a foil to Jesus's instruction. While in the garden, Jesus utters three prayers. The first two prayers are recorded, while the third is the "same words" as the second. The prayers are as follows:

> 1st prayer—"My Father, if it is possible, let this cup pass from me; yet not what I want but what you want."
> 2nd prayer—"My Father, if this cannot pass unless I drink it, your will be done."

Jesus's prayers concerning the will of the Father precipitate his actions of performing the will of the Father. As Nygaard notes, "The Gethsemane scene shows how the Scriptures are enacted in his life through prayer. The result is that prayer is presented as a performance of tradition."[52] Jesus goes to the cross as the means of embodying the prayers uttered in Gethsemane. Jesus's deeds combine with the praying affirmation of "your will be done."

These previous examples are consistent with the teaching in the Sermon on the Mount and Lord's Prayer. Concluding and summarizing the contents of the Sermon is a parable concerning foundations (Matt 7:24–27). The parable contrasts two ways of living. One group will act as fools and build their house on shifting sand that falls, the other will be wise and build upon solid foundations to weather the storms of life. The parable, which is the Sermon's conclusion, ends with: "Everyone then who *hears these words of mine and acts on them* will be like a wise man who built his house on rock" (Matt 7:24). Jesus is equating those who follow his teachings to those who are choosing the way of wisdom, and at the heart of this teaching is hearing and doing.

In addition to this reference to hearing and doing, the Sermon has structural markers that combine words and deeds. Matthew 5:17 and 7:12 form an *inclusio* around the body of the Sermon on the Mount, united by their shared references to the "law and the prophets." Specifically, in 5:17, Jesus explains that "he has come" to fulfill the "law and prophets." The significance of Jesus's "coming" and his relationship to the words of the "law and prophets" is too often underemphasized. In this passage, Jesus pairs his

---

[51] "As the Father, so his children/disciples" is a consistent theme throughout the Sermon on the Mount.
[52] Mathias Nygaard, *Prayer in the Gospels: A Theological Exegesis of the Ideal Pray-er*, BIS 114 (Leiden: Brill, 2012), 62.

life and actions to the teachings in the Hebrew Scriptures. France provides a helpful translation, "Far from wanting to set aside the law and the prophets, it is my role to bring into being that to which they have pointed forward, to carry them into a new era of fulfillment."[53] Jesus commands that his disciples display "surpassing righteousness." The righteousness commanded refers to the performance of God's will, which Jesus outlines in his teaching on the Law that follows (Matt 5:21–48). Jesus's point is that his life and teaching are the means through which the words of the Hebrew Scriptures find new and practical fulfillment. This emphasis on deeds as a means through which one fulfills the "law and prophets" is reemphasized in Matt 7:12. Here, Matthew enjoins the "law and prophets" to the Golden Rule. As it states, "So in everything, do to others what you would have them do to you."[54] Therefore, the emphasis on Jesus's "coming" as a means of fulfilling the words of the law and prophets is reinforced with the summation of the law and prophets as an ethical command in 7:12.

Ulrich Luz notes an interesting progression in the Sermon's structure and the role of the Lord's Prayer as its centerpiece. He writes, "Thus the Sermon on the Mount takes its readers along a way that leads them from God's radical demands into the 'interior' of faith where they experience the Father's nearness in prayer. Then it leads them back into the praxis of renouncing possessions and of love."[55] Luz's comments are insightful in that he notes the dynamics between the "interior" posture of the prayer and its relationship to the outside world.[56] The material before the prayer gives Jesus's fulfilling work as an exemplar (as Roland Dienes calls it, "Jesus-righteousness")[57] on how to live the *Torah* and the material after the prayer details how to treat others (as summarized in the Golden Rule). As the centerpiece, the Lord's Prayer gives words to pray so that one can carry out the will of God.

7.7 Conclusion and Implications

In conclusion, one might question if anything is truly novel (pun intended) in what has preceded. In many ways, the information above (except for reading the Lord's Prayer in/through Matthew's Gospel) is typical of treatments of the Lord's Prayer. What is truly novel is the arrangement of the information. The *Bildungsroman* genre provides a framework for tying the various strands of information concerning the Lord's Prayer into a cohesive whole—one that is concerned with the prayer's context and *telos*. This

---

[53] France, *Gospel of Matthew*, 183.
[54] In parallel literature, notably the teachings of Hillel and the *Didache*, the Golden Rule has a negative connotation. One must avoid doing to others the things which they hate. Jesus' articulation of the principle gives an affirmative aspect in which a disciple is called to show neighbor love without recourse to their negative reactions (cf. also Matt 22:40).
[55] Luz, *Matthew*, 172.
[56] Luz's comment also highlights an inherent cohesion to the Sermon. This observation is important because it notes the holistic nature of the Sermon and the importance of seeing the Sermon as unified instruction.
[57] Roland Deines, "Not the Law but the Messiah: Law and Righteousness in the Gospel of Matthew—An Ongoing Debate," in *Built Upon the Rock: Studies in the Gospel of Matthew*, ed. Daniel M. Gurtner and John Nolland (Grand Rapids, MI: Eerdmans, 2008), 53–84.

sort of holistic picture is precisely what Tertullian imagined in his own understanding of the prayer. He states, "In the Prayer is comprised an epitome of the whole Gospel." Tertullian's reference extends to much more but certainly not less than Matthew's Gospel. Like the *Bildungsroman* genre, the Lord's Prayer within its Matthean context extends an invitation to a "common" human to be formed into his or her ideal self.

8

Discipled to Be a Scribe for the Kingdom of Heaven

John Nolland

8.1 Introduction

The aim here is to clarify the metaphorical use of scribe language in Matt 13:52.[1] Here we outline the stages of the journey. First, we explore the language of Matt 13:52 to clarify how γραμματεύς functions in the syntax of the sentence. What exactly is the statement that we are seeking to understand? Second, comes a survey of Matthew's uses of scribe language. Though all the other uses are literal, except 23:34, they provide the larger literary context for the metaphorical use in 13:52—more analytical attention later. Third, we offer reflections on how meaning might operate with the kind of word "scribe" is: fixedness or fluidity; meaning and referent; meaning and role-in-context. Fourth, we look back to the scribes of Second Temple period for possible relevance to Matthew's use. Fifth and correspondingly, we look forward to the early Rabbinic period. In neither direction will we see any close kinship, but various threads resonate to a degree with Matthew's uses and provide helpful background. The mix of fixedness and fluidity can help sensitize us to something of the range of Matthew's use. Sixth, we proceed to an analysis of Matthew's uses of "scribe." Four conceptual areas guide the analysis: (1) status, (2) influence, (3) power as a set; and then (4) evaluation language treated separately. Seventh, we turn finally to the aspects of the place of the disciples in Matthew's story that might have a bearing on disciples becoming "scribes." Here we will be especially concerned with the relationship between the disciples and blocks of teaching and reference to teaching in the Gospel. Are there clues here about how the evangelist sees this scribal role being prepared for and working out for the disciples? Eighth and with the journey completed, we briefly overview.

---

[1] To the best of my knowledge, this has not received significant scholarly attention since David E. Orton, *The Understanding Scribe. Matthew and the Apocalyptic Ideal*, JSNT Supplement Series 25 (Sheffield: Sheffield Academic Press, 1989). See also Ched Spellman, "The Scribe Who Has Become a Disciple: Identifying and Becoming the Ideal Reader of the Biblical Canon," *Themelios* 41.1 (2016): 37–51. A more popular study is Brightstar Jones Syiemlieh, "Portrait of a Christian Scribe (Matthew 13:52)," *AJT* 20.1 (2006): 57–66. Of little relevance to the present study is William E. Arnal, *Jesus and the Village Scribes: Galilean Conflicts and the Setting of Q* (Minneapolis, MN: Fortress, 2001).

8.2 Syntax of Matt 13:52

After a long block of public teaching in parables, during which the disciples have benefited from additional private explanation, Jesus asks the disciples, "Have you understood all these things?" "Yes, Lord" is their response, which in turn elicits from Jesus the comment in v. 52.

διὰ τοῦτο πᾶς γραμματεὺς μαθητευθεὶς τῇ βασιλείᾳ τῶν οὐρανῶν ὅμοιός ἐστιν ἀνθρώπῳ οἰκοδεσπότῃ, ὅστις ἐκβάλλει ἐκ τοῦ θησαυροῦ αὐτοῦ καινὰ καὶ παλαιά.

πᾶς and γραμματεύς are regularly read together as "every scribe." The words come in immediate sequence, agreeing in gender, number, and case. πᾶς γραμματεύς could be seen as having a quasi-parallel in ἀνθρώπῳ οἰκοδεσπότῃ ("a person who is master of a household/landowner"). Matthew has quite a number of uses of πᾶς with a following noun where the two words are to be read together: 3:10 ("every tree"); 4:4 ("every word"); 4:23 ("every disease"; "every sickness"); 5:11 ("all kinds of evil"); 7:17 ("every tree"); 7:19 ("every tree"); 10:1 ("every disease"; "every sickness"); 12:25 ("every kingdom"; "every city"); 12:31 ("every sin"); 12:36 ("every word"); 18:16 ("every word").

But there are difficulties. In the narrative no scribe is in sight, as there is no scribe among the disciples. Despite the regular translation, every interpreter goes on to apply the language to the disciples.[2] Occasionally this involves imagining that some early Christian leaders were converted scribes. This is possible – but it requires not just imagining here later Christian leaders – but requires a fracturing of the narrative which is otherwise about educating the disciples.[3] Perhaps that is the best we can do but maybe not. Is it significant that none of the cases where Matthew uses πᾶς with a following noun where the two words are to be read together involve reference to people? In the Synoptic Gospels the closest to this is πᾶν ἄρσεν ("every male") in Luke 2:23, but the text applies to animals as well as people; it is not male people, but male entities more generally. What would appear to be an obvious idiom is not necessarily such a natural idiom for the Gospel writers. And the possible quasi-parallel in ἀνθρώπῳ οἰκοδεσπότῃ has no evidential value.

Is there another way of construing the text? I think there is. Could we be dealing with making scribes rather than discipling scribes?[4] The process of being discipled is

---

[2] Richard T. France, *The Gospel of Matthew*, NICNT (Grand Rapids, MI: Eerdmans, 2007), 544–5, is aware of the difficulties and is not entirely happy with either of the alternatives that he sees as available: "neither seems to me to account entirely satisfactorily for the way this saying is worded." But he feels he must opt for one: "Jesus uses the term to designate his chosen disciples as a new 'alternative' scribal school, trained not in the rabbinic schools but by his own instruction to bring his new and radical understanding of the law to Israel." His own way of articulating the application to the disciples is to suggest: "the saying envisages disciples in their 'scribal' function, that is as authorized teachers for the kingdom of heaven." Since on this understanding the scribal training consists of the being discipled, the translation proposed as part of this article would serve France's view much better than his own translation.

[3] Matthew 8:19 may be retrospectively described as reporting an attempt on the part of Jesus to disciple a scribe for the kingdom of heaven, but that doesn't help us here.

[4] Suggested in John Nolland, *The Gospel of Matthew: A Commentary on the Greek Text*, NIGTC (Grand Rapids, MI: Eerdmans, 2005), 570–1.

so closely linked conceptually with the notion of the scribe as the one who has been educated and is therefore knowledgeable that it may be better to take πᾶς separately ("everyone") and to link γραμματεύς via the verb ("discipled [to be] a scribe"). Matthew certainly wants his readers to see that it is the disciples who are being discipled in this chapter. μαθητεύειν ("to disciple") is quite a rare verb, not found in the LXX and used just four times in the New Testament (NT) (elsewhere Matt 27:57; 28:19; Acts 14:21), and only here and 27:57 in the passive, but "discipled to be a scribe for the kingdom of heaven" seems a natural enough translation of γραμματεὺς μαθητευθεὶς τῇ βασιλείᾳ τῶν οὐρανῶν.[5] "Scribe" would then serve as a mediating term to take us from the becoming-disciples of the main Gospel narrative, especially their education as in Matt 13, to the making-of-disciples role (not the further training as scribes, reserved for the twelve) that comes their way in 28:16–20, where a strong educating role is again evident (see 8.6).[6]

8.3 Survey of the Matthean Texts

First an overview of the Matthew data. An individual scribe only has a narrative role in Matthew in 8:19 (as a would-be disciple). Scribes have a collective narrative role in 2:4; 16:21; 20:18; 21:15; 26:57; 27:41. In this second set of texts they form a duo with the chief priests in 2:4; 20:18; 21:15 and a duo with the elders in 26:57; 27:41 (in the latter the scribes and elders form a pair, but this pair is, as well, associated with the chief priests). For these texts, the action is in each case in Jerusalem, in the one case they are called upon to identify for Herod the place of the messiah's birth and in the other cases they express indignation with Jesus and then play a role in his condemnation. Matthew 16:21 announces ahead of time a narrative role for the elders, the chief priests, and the scribes in the coming passion; in 20:18 this is trimmed to the chief priests and the scribes.

"Some of the scribes" have a narrative role in 9:3, where they accuse Jesus of blasphemy for speaking words of forgiveness. "Some of the scribes" are linked with Pharisees in 12:38, as requesting a validating sign from Jesus, presumably in relation to his implicit claim to be speaking for God, and in 15:1 "Pharisees and scribes" (reverse order) ask Jesus a question that is critical of the eating habits of his disciples. The action here is not in Jerusalem, but the Matt 15 scribes (and Pharisees) come from Jerusalem.

Other texts involve, without a narrative role, characterizations and evaluations of scribes in company with Pharisees: 5:20 attributes to scribes an inadequate righteousness; and using the much-repeated phrase "Woe to you scribes and Pharisees,

---

[5] The construction is only possible with verbs of identification, coming to be or transformation. Cf. 4 Macc 16:9 μάμμη κληθεῖσα ("called [to be a] grandmother"); Ps 121:3 Ιερουσαλημ οἰκοδομουμένη ὡς πόλις (Jerusalem built as a city"); 2 Pet 1:16 ἐπόπται γενηθέντες ("became eyewitnesses"); Matt 2:2 τεχθεὶς βασιλεύς (Matt 2:2 BGM) ("born [to be] king").

[6] Joseph of Arimathea shares with the disciples the experience of being discipled by Jesus (Matt 27:57) but probably with no thought that he would participate in the coming "scribal" role of the disciples.

hypocrites" (23:13, 14, 15, 23, 25, 27, 29), the scribes' failure to live up to the standards of the Mosaic heritage is insisted upon in ch. 23.[7] The focus is both on the exposing of false assumptions of exemplary piety and on the leading of others onto a path of religious disaster. For this final set the action is once again in Jerusalem, but it is not narrowly Jerusalem scribes who are being addressed.

Scribes are a source of knowledge of the religious traditions already in 2:4 (with the chief priests) and implicitly in 15:1 (with Pharisees). Their limitations in this role are marked by contrast with Jesus in 7:29 and in some of the specifics of ch. 23. But the importance of this role, shared with Pharisees, is marked in 23:2–3, with the focus on the Mosaic legacy. The disciples assume a significant role for the scribes in promulgating religious teaching in 17:10.

That leaves only the use of "scribe" in 13:52, which is the special focus of this study and the future-oriented Matt 23:34, where Matthew envisages scribes who are very different to the scribes that otherwise populate his narrative.

8.4 What Kind of Term Is "Scribe"?

Like many others I tended in earlier days to work with an unexamined and therefore out-of-focus assumption that "scribe" in the Gospels denotes, at least in broad terms, a single social and cultural role and that the role of the use of the word was to point to a person who occupied this role.[8] In writing on Luke I reflected the onetime consensus that scribes of the NT period were the antecedents to the later Jewish rabbis.[9] As we will see, we were retrojecting back into the NT period something of the situation that pertained in the rabbinic period. Since then we have become much more cautious of this procedure. But we were also thinking of meaning in a somewhat wooden manner. Attention to referent tended to dominate the horizon. And we thought too much about meaning and not enough about "job of work."

"Scribe" has a certain kinship with the English term, "secretary." A brief exploration of "secretary" might help to tune our perceptions for digging further into the use of "scribe" language.

For "secretary" Google's English dictionary (supplied by Oxford languages) offers the following definitions:

> A person employed by an individual or in an office to assist with correspondence, make appointments, and carry out administrative tasks; an official of a society or other organization who conducts its correspondence and keeps its records; the

---

[7] In the immediately preceding pericope (Matt 22:41–46), Mathew has the interaction with Pharisees, where in the Markan parallel the view Jesus interacts with is said to be a view of the scribes (Mark 12:35). This is unlikely to have any particular significance for Matthew, who in ch. 23 has a tight solidarity between scribes and Pharisees.
[8] Nolland, *Matthew*, 112n120.
[9] John Nolland, *Luke*, WBC 35A-C (Dallas, TX: Word, 1989–93), 1:233–34, commenting on Luke 5:17. Jacob Neusner, *The Mishnah, a New Translation* (New Haven, CT: Yale University Press, 1991), xxxii, sees this development as taking place in the period beyond the Mishnah.

principal assistant of a UK government minister or ambassador; an official in charge of a US government department.

To these we may add for the UK the use in "secretary of state" for one area of responsibility or another. These are the most senior government ministers, other than the prime minister.

The approach of Google's English dictionary is typical: it does not provide any clear distinction between meaning and referent. We note that "secretary" is used for roles from the quite modest through to the very powerful. There is, however, a common thread of meaning that ties these together—all secretaries actually or symbolically serve a person or organization above them and serve them in ways that are somewhat analogous. The meaning of the word "secretary" is held in what is common across the different uses, along with some sense that context or associated words may trigger recognition that a secretary of a certain level and kind is in mind. When we get to uses like "secretary of state," however, this phrase has a meaning in which the meaning of "secretary" recedes in favor of the sense of the whole phrase taken as a single unit.

All these secretaries have a shared role only at the most general of levels. When it comes to specifics the activity, status, and power to influence are about as different as they could be and can only be discerned from context or associated terms. Quite often the more important question is not what the word means but why it has been chosen in the particular context.

Finally for this section we remind ourselves that the use of "scribe" in Matt 13:52 is metaphorical and not literal. Our final goal is to discern the thrust and scope of the metaphor.

8.5 Scribes in the Second Temple Period

It will be primarily the documents of the NT we will look to for clarifying the significance of scribes in Matthew, but we can be aided in our inquiry to some degree by looking back from the first century and looking on from the first century.

We first look back to the Second Temple period that comes to an end in the first century. This term was applied to quite a range of persons and roles. In her careful study Christine Schams engages solely with the texts in which a technical term for a scribe (לבלר, סופר, ספרא, γραμματεύς, λιβλάριος) is to be found or ones in which reference is made to professional writing expertise.[10] Schams hopes that with this approach the perception of the ancient Jews themselves will come through, rather than the concepts of modern readers of the evidence. In this way she has avoided the theory-laden dimensions of some other studies.[11] She is critical of the tendency of earlier

---

[10] Christine Schams, *Jewish Scribes in the Second Temple Period*, JSGTSup 291 (Sheffield: Sheffield Academic Press, 1998).

[11] We can deduce the necessity of various ancient roles that are in some sense scribal, but it is we who label the occupants of these rolls as scribes. Perhaps they were termed such in their own day, but in the absence of evidence it is well to be cautious.

studies to shape the understanding of the scribal category from texts where no word for scribe is found, which has led to unfortunate conflation. Her conclusion is that there seem to be at least eight different kinds of functionary who might be identified as scribes. There is the military official, the political official, the levitical scribe, the wise man (Enoch), legal officials associated with judges, some who are partially identified with οἱ Ἀσιδαῖοι (1 Macc 7:12–13), village scribes of low status, and sacred scribes who may also have had interpretative functions.[12]

This is not to say that across these documents the term "scribe" should be thought to have different meanings. The choice of the shared term has to do with the fact that in each case the person is one who provides literacy services of one kind or another, whether this be in mundane record keeping, in copying documents, recording the details of meetings, advising superiors in the formulation of treaties or bringing forward from a repository of documents what is appropriate in each situation (whether the relevant information is legal or religious or is of political significance). Being a "lettered" person identifies the scribe as an educated person at some level or other, able to advise others in some sphere of competence. Being "lettered" in a predominantly illiterate culture made for the capacity to have influence on others. Even illiterate people needed a range of legal documents written for them to protect their rights or to press their claims; on some occasions they might need scribal help to write a letter or to read a letter. Inasmuch as the Torah was central to Jewish life, scribes focused there would have significant religious status. A reputation for wisdom was also a possibility from extensive acquaintance with the written word, and the like; literary context and cultural awareness determine what might be evoked by a particular use of the language, but the diversity of evocation is built upon a shared basic meaning, having to do with providing literacy services. It is worth noting, however, that how sharply in focus literary skills were could vary a great deal. In most cases consulting written text and/or producing something written is quite sharply in focus. What varies characteristically is kinds of documents consulted and kinds of writing undertaken. But at times the focus moves away from literacy services to rest more upon the capacity of the person, signaled by their education; the knowledge, wisdom, and relevant experience of the person in the appropriate area come to the fore, in conjunction with their status, rather than any literal connection with reading and writing.

8.6 Scribes in the Mishnaic Period

We now turn our gaze in the opposite direction. What follows is said of the scribes who are mentioned in the Mishnah.[13] They are, collectively, the repository of a body of religious lore that sets out to regulate Jewish life (Orlah 3:9 M; Yebamot 2:4 A; Sanhedrin

---

[12] Contrast this recognition of the application of the term "scribe" to very different roles and levels with the tendency of Orton, *The Understanding Scribe*, to amalgamate into a single core concept for Matthew features he identifies for scribes from different kinds of sources.

[13] We focus on the Mishnah as its traditions were well formed by the end of the second century. For comparison, we have noted extra material from the somewhat later Tosefta, the later Jerusalem Talmud, and the rather later again Babylonian Talmud.

11:3 A, C; Kelim 13:7 C; Parah 11:5 A, 6 A; Tohorot 4:7 L, 11 C, 11 I; Tebul-Yom 4:6 C; Yadayim 3:2 E). The boundaries of this lore are not always certain, so we must allow for doubtful rulings (Kelim 13:7 C; Tohorot 4:7 L, 11 C; Tebul-Yom 4:6 C). Scribal rulings are not to be confused or merged with those of Torah;[14] indeed, the scribal rulings are to be considered one by one, not treated as parts of an integrated system (Yadayim 3:2 E). There is a curious claim that "a more strict rule applies to the teachings of scribes than to the teachings of Torah" (Sanhedrin 11:3 A), but what this is likely to boil down to is that the Torah rule operates at a more general level and depends on interpretation of the Torah while the scribal rule is precise and narrowly focused (see discussion of phylacteries in Sanhedrin 11:3 A–3 C).[15] The only named scribe in the Mishnah is Nahum the scribe (Peah 2:6 C).[16] He functions as a transmission point of a tradition traced back through generations of rabbis to the prophets and thence rooted in Moses. Presumably, the claim for the collective repository is that its individual elements come from many such transmissions.

Most often we see scribes functioning in local communities, providing legal services for a fee.[17] The tools of their trade include pen and scribe's paste (Shabbat 3:1 C; Pesahim 1:3 C). They produce divorce papers (Gittin 3:1N; 7:2B; 8:8D; 9:8D) and contract documents (Baba Mesia 5:11 C; Baba Batra 10:3 C, 3 G, 3 J, 4 B, 4 D, 4 F).[18]

We glimpse scribes educating trainee scribes in a scene with a practice session in scribing from dictation (Gittin 3:1 C). We get a further tiny glimpse into the education of scribes in Qiddushin 4:13 A, 13 B, 13 C, where there is a purity requirement that there be no teaching from women or unmarried men.[19] However, becoming a scribe seems not always to have been a predicable outcome of an educational track: becoming a scribe was sufficiently unpredictable as to provide justification for voiding certain vows (Nedarim 9:2 D, 2 F).

These last texts also point to significant scribal status. Rabbi Eliezer the Great imagines a decline that sets in from the destruction of the temple in which "sages

---

[14] For a different view in practice, see t. *Tebul-Yom* 1:10.
[15] Some texts in the Jerusalem Talmud make more than this of the significance of scribal teaching. See, e.g., Berakhot 1:3, 1:3.D, where the words of the scribes are considered to be of similar importance to the words of Torah and more dear than the words of Torah. But other texts there assert the priority of Torah. See, e.g. y. *Ketubot* 10:2, I.1.C.
[16] Named scribes become much more frequent in the Jerusalem Talmud. The relationship between rabbis and scribes is not well specified, but, unlike scribes, rabbis are nearly always named and emerge with individual significance as well as being part of a web of relationships. In b. *Baba Mesia* 10:6, II.3.A we read of a "rabbi Ephraim, the scribe." Perhaps his scribal role has to do with making copies of scrolls of Scripture.
[17] The Jerusalem Talmud contemplates a more salaried possibility (alongside salaried teachers). See y. *Peah* 8:6, III 8.G. b. Baba Batra 2:3e, I.13 may imply that scribes sometimes functioned as elementary teachers.
[18] There is no reference to scribes as copying scrolls of Scripture in the Mishnah. It is only "the scribes of the nations" who make copies of Scripture in the Jerusalem Talmud (y. *Sotah* 7:5, I.1.C), and in the Tosefta this is actually a translation task in the first instance (t. *Sotah* 8:6 M). The possibility of a scribe making a copy of a Scripture scroll emerges in t. Bikkurim 15 B, but only in the Babylonian Talmud is making copies of Scripture rolls spoken of as an established part of the task of scribes. See, e.g., b. *Megillah* 2:1, VI.3.A; b. *Gittin* 2:3, II.17.B; b. *Baba Batra* 1:6, IV.2.B.
[19] The cost of being educated as a scribe is first alluded to in the Jerusalem Talmud. See y. *Baba Batra* 9:3, I.4.C.

began to be like scribes, and scribes like ministers, and ministers like ordinary folk" (Sotah 9:15 S; and cf. 9:15 EE). This would seem to be to glamorize the earlier period rather than to belittle the later time.[20]

By comparison with the Second Temple period the scribes of these documents constitute a much more uniform group, largely thanks to their collective role as a repository of religious lore. Here the use of the language of scribe functions significantly differently from the earlier use. No longer is there a sense that quite a range of people performing quite different roles might be called scribes, with just a basic core meaning of one who provides literacy service. Now the language points exclusively to a single identifiable societal group. The meaning of the term has become much more precise and limited. However varied the status and function of individual scribes might have been,[21] to be a scribe here is to be a member of the scribal guild with its collective identity. At least to a degree we should answer the questions: What kind of term is "scribe" and is it used differently for the Second Temple period than for the Mishnaic period?

8.7 What Is Matthew Seeking to Get Across in How He Makes Use of the Scribe Category?

Our difficulty is that Matthew assumes his readers will be already informed about who scribes were and what they did. In any case that is not his concern; it is rather in giving an evaluative account of the scribes whose activity intersected with the ministry of Jesus.

Three conceptual areas we might work with in seeking to clarify the identity of the Matthean scribes are status, influence, and power, which are all typically interrelated. A fourth will be how scribes are evaluated—unrelated directly to the other three but prominent in Matthew's account. Armed with these four conceptual foci we will work our way through Matthew's references to scribes.

If we start from the ministry of Jesus in Galilee, it would be low-level village scribes that we would mostly encounter, but Matthew offers no report of normal scribal activity at this level. We are probably to imagine the scribes of Matt 9:3 as local Capernaum scribes and those of 12:38, where they act in concert with Pharisees, as local scribes. These encounter Jesus out and about in public. In the former they make a negative religious evaluation of Jesus's behavior, and in the latter they make a demand upon him to justify his claims and actions. Theirs are not power roles, but their activity does reflect some recognized claim to status, which in turn suggests the capacity to influence others.[22] The link with Pharisees in the latter is a link with people of strong

---

[20] Judge's scribes make an appearance first in the Jerusalem Talmud (y. *Qiddushin* 4:5, I.1; y. *Sanhedrin* 1:4, III.1.B; y. *Sanhedrin* 5:4, I.1.I).

[21] With its "Find us a man to interpret Scripture, serve as a judge and a scribe and to do all that we need done," y. *Shebiit* 6:1, III.15.A suggests that the scribal function by necessity needed to fall to any person who had some capacity to interpret Scripture, who could be a jack of all trades in this realm.

[22] Matthew 8:19 offers nothing about the role of the scribes, but it has a twofold importance for Matthew. First, it allows Matthew to showcase a particular piece of Jesus's teaching about

religious conviction who, while only part of a minority movement, are presented as having a significant effect on public sentiment.[23]

It is likely that we should make distinction between scribes throughout the land and scribes in Jerusalem. By ascribing the activity of scribes in 15:1 to scribes who come from Jerusalem Matthew suggests this. However, that they act in concert with Pharisees who also come from Jerusalem means we should not make too much of this. These are not totally different kinds of scribes but rather scribes who have come from the power center of Jewish life. They bring with them the status and influence that comes of being in some sense part of the central elite. They want to bring their influence to bear on a situation in which a newly emergent popular teacher is allowing the behavior of his closest followers to fall below what they consider to be vital standards for the pious life.

There is also an association with Jerusalem in the case of many of the other references to scribes in Matthew, where their activity takes place in Jerusalem. They are paired with chief priests in 20:18, 21:15, and 27:41. They are linked with the elders in 26:57, but this fresh term does not immediately clarify the standing of the scribes here. When, however, we see that chief priests and elders are paired in 21:23; 26:3, 47; 27:1, 3, 12, 20 and form a trio with chief priests and scribes in 16:21 and almost so in 27:41, it becomes clear that the elders involved are more Jerusalem city fathers than village elders. These scribes constitute a powerful force in national affairs. They deal with the Roman governor; they have a significant say in whether Jesus should be labeled a heinous criminal whose judicial death should be promoted (Jesus is to suffer at their hands, be betrayed by them, be condemned by them; they participate in his Jewish trial; they mock him on the cross). Power, influence, and status all play a role here.

Early on Jerusalem scribes are associated with the chief priests as providing authoritative religious teaching to Herod (Matt 2:4). The role of scribes in providing and promoting religious teaching is, however, pervasive and not limited to Jerusalem scribes. Jerusalem scribes are implicitly a source of knowledge of the religious traditions in 15:1 (with Pharisees), but the particular tradition they seek to enforce here is resisted resolutely by Jesus, who further points to aspects of their tradition that stand in defiance of the standards of Scripture. By means of a contrast with Jesus in 7:29, whose charismatic authority is seen as self-evident, scribes are said not to teach with authority. Certainly, if they functioned to teach and champion a shared central tradition anything like as in the Mishnah, the contrast with the personal authority of Jesus is marked.[24] The disciples assume a significant role for the scribes in promulgating religious teaching in 17:10, which Jesus does nothing to dislodge.

In ch. 23 an authoritative teaching role for scribes is both commended and criticized. The importance of this role, shared with Pharisees, is marked in 23:2–3, with the focus on the Mosaic legacy. The social reality of this teaching role is

---

discipleship. But as well, it makes the important point that there was not solid opposition to Jesus among all the scribes.

[23] For a brief overview of the Pharisaic movement, see Nolland, *Matthew*, 224–5.

[24] The traditions affirmed by Matthean scribes in Matt 15 are not yet thought of as held collectively by a guild of scribes. They are something collectively held, but the traditions are called "traditions of the elders" in Matt 15:2, not scribal teaching, and they are held up to Jesus by specifically Jerusalem based scribes and Pharisees.

recognized in v. 4 but criticized as the action of those who make demands but fail to provide support. In v. 13 the destructive impact of misguided scribal religious influence is marked, with much the same in v. 15. Verses 17–22 take up for criticism one particular piece of scribal teaching: the graded significance for the weightiness of oaths of that by which one swears. In v. 24 they are called "blind guides." Here they are imaged as teaching by example, because in their own lives "they strain out a gnat and swallow a camel." What is being commented on is attention to minutiae coupled with neglect of the more significant core matters of the law: "justice, mercy and faith."

In an overall sense Matt 23 functions to knock the scribes and Pharisees off their pedestal. They preach but do not practice (v. 3). They are self-important and conduct themselves in a manner that is all about public image (vv. 5–7, 25–26, 27–28). Their religion is a cloak for rapacity (v. 14).

A scribal role as religious teachers is given qualified approval in Matthew.[25] But structured and regular instruction is not what we, with our culture of formal education, should imagine for the teaching role of the first-century scribe. The scribe was the one considered to know. Therefore, he would be consulted from time to time and would use such opportunities as came his way to put people right. Preaching in the synagogue would be a very likely opportunity for promulgating scribal teaching. Scribes probably had no more of a *formal* teaching role than Pharisees. In both cases we are dealing with recognized founts of knowledge.

In a largely illiterate society scribes are important repositories of religious knowledge, but especially of knowledge of the Mosaic law.[26] Their authority is not beyond question and criticism, but with safeguards in place it has a valid place in the Matthean scheme of things.

Elements of evaluation of scribal teaching and living are scattered through the discussion above, but Matt 5:20 is all about evaluation. Again in company with the Pharisees, 5:20 attributes to scribes an inadequate righteousness. This can only mean that the background assumption is that the scribes and Pharisees offer what in the culture of the narrative is an exemplary level of righteousness. There is a deliberate shock value to this assertion. The assumed status of the people of these paired categories is undercut.

Except in 8:19, Matthew's interest in scribes is always related to their status, influence, and power.[27] We meet the scribes as people of significant influence, with the Jerusalem scribes having a more powerful influence than scribes in other locations. The Matthean Jesus affirms their role as custodians of the Mosaic Law but is fiercely critical of their behavior and sees some of their traditions as in conflict with the very law of which they are custodians.

---

[25] It is sometimes claimed that the scribes of Jesus's day acted as teachers to the village children. I have not been able to find any evidence for this assertion for any period before the Babylonian Talmud.

[26] Luke uses νομικός as an alternative to γραμματεύς (7:30; 10:25; 11:45, 46, 52; 14:13). He switches terms between 11:52 and 53. Once he uses νομοδιδάσκαλος (5:17).

[27] And even in Matt 8:19 the scribe is identified as a scribe because as such he is a "somebody" and not a "nobody."

8.8 The Disciples as (Trainee) Scribes in Matthew's Story

From Matt 13:52 it has seemed likely that Matthew wants to present the disciples as being discipled to become scribes of the kingdom of heaven. What is in mind? Here finally we examine the text of Matthew more broadly for clues about how the evangelist might see this scribal role working out for the disciples. There has been a considerable scholarly investment in the place of disciples in Matthew,[28] but most of it is not relevant to our concerns here. Our focus can be restricted to those aspects of the place of the disciples in Matthew's story that might have a bearing on disciples becoming "scribes."

However, before we turn our attention to the disciples in Matthew, we gather up the relevant threads from our attention to scribes in the Second Temple period, the Mishnaic period, and in the text of the Gospel.

In the Mishnaic period there is a sharp focus on the literacy services provided by the scribes. *Literacy* services as such do not seem to be in view in Matthew. But for the Mishnaic period, being custodians of a sacred tradition was also prominent, and this does feature strongly in Matthew's treatment of scribes and seems pertinent to Matt 13. In the Second Temple period various kinds of scribes emerge, but not so in Matthew (unless we count the higher status of Jerusalem scribes). In this respect Matthew is much closer to what we find in the Mishnaic period.

Significant status, along with an attendant capacity to influence, is a common quality of the varied kinds of scribes in the Second Temple period, perhaps not so much the (indirect) power that we saw to be linked with these qualities in Matthew's treatment of the scribes. The Mishnaic scribes are perhaps not at the status level of various of the Second Temple scribes, but they are people of status and influence, but again power as such does not seem to come into focus. Matthew's interest in the power of the scribes is mostly linked with the Jerusalem scribes as part of the elite. And the exercise of power

---

[28] On disciples in Matthew, see Celia M. Deutsch, "Torah, Jesus and Discipleship in the Gospel of Matthew," *SIDIC* 24 (1991): 43–52; B. Rod Doyle, "Disciples, Sages and Scribes in Matthew's Gospel," *Word in Life* 32.4 (1984): 6–7; Richard A. Edwards, "Characterization of the Disciples as a Feature of Matthew's Narrative," in *The Four Gospels, 1992*, FS Frans Neirynck, ed. Frans van Segbroeck, BETL 100 (Leuven: Leuven University Press/Peeters, 1992), 1305–24; Richard A. Edwards, "Uncertain Faith: Matthew's Portrait of the Disciple," in *Discipleship in the New Testament*, ed. Fernando F. Segovia (Philadelphia, PA: Fortress, 1985), 47–61; Richard A. Edwards, *Matthew's Narrative Portrait of Disciples: How the Text Connoted Reader is Informed* (Harrisburg, PA: Trinity Press International, 1997); Robert H. Gundry, *Peter: False Disciple and Apostate According to Saint Matthew* (Grand Rapids, MI: Eerdmans, 2015); Patrick J. Hartin, "Disciples as Authorities within Matthew's Christian-Jewish Community," *NeoT* 32 (1998): 389–404; Bertram L. Melbourne, *Slow to Understand: The Disciples in Synoptic Perspective* (Lanham, MD: University Press of America, 1988), esp. 58–72. Leon Morris, "Disciples of Jesus," in *Jesus of Nazareth, Lord and Christ: Essays on the Historical Jesus and New Testament Christology*, ed. Joel B. Green and Max Turner (Grand Rapids, MI: Eerdmans, 1994), 112–27; Matthew Palachuvattil, *"The One Who Does the Will of the Father": Distinguishing Character of Disciples according to Matthew. An Exegetical Theological Study*, TG 154 (Rome: EPUG, 2007); Patrick Schreiner, *Matthew, Disciple and Scribe: The First Gospel and Its Portrait of Jesus* (Grand Rapids, MI: Baker Academic, 2019); Michael Trainor, "The Begetting of Wisdom: The Teacher and the Disciples in Matthew's Community," *Pacifica* 4 (1991): 148–64; Michael J. Wilkins, *The Concept of Disciple in Matthew's Gospel as Reflected in the Use of the Term Μαθητής*, NovTSup 59 (Leiden: Brill, 1988); Michael J. Wilkins, "Named and Unnamed Disciples in Matthew: A Literary-Theological Study," *SBLSP* 30 (1991): 418–39.

that interests Matthew is in the context of the power conflict between Jesus and those who oppose his claim upon the people. At this point it is an open question whether power comes into view for the disciples as scribes.

In connection with the Matthean disciples we turn first to Matt 13. Notable here is the privileged access to knowledge that they are given by Jesus.[29] At the end of the discourse Jesus asks, "Have you understood all this?" And their affirmative answer leads into Jesus's comment in v. 52. The use of μαθητεύειν ("to disciple") here fits well seeing Matt 13 as discipleship training for the twelve, while the next use of the verb in 27:57 might suggest that not all who are discipled are discipled to be "scribes." Once 28:19 is reached with its next and final use of this verb, we have the twelve now doing the discipling, but it is very unlikely that they are to be seen as training the next round of scribes. Rather what they do is more akin to what Jesus has done (off stage) in relation to Joseph of Arimathea. We can suggest now that the disciples are not seen as made scribes to make scribes but that rather the receiving of knowledge and the capacity to dispense knowledge of a scribe is being used as an image to highlight the receiving-and-having-for-passing-on knowledge dimensions of disciple-making. But more and more precision might be involved.

τῇ βασιλείᾳ τῶν οὐρανῶν ("in relation to the kingdom of heaven") in Matt 13:52 reinforces the connection between the education about the kingdom of heaven provided in Matt 13—with this same phrase already used six times in the chapter—and kingdom language also in four other verses there.[30] That the scribe role is articulated in v. 52b with a mini-parable introduced with the same "is like" (ὅμοιός/ ὁμοία ἐστιν) as found in five earlier verses in the chapter further ties the scribe role to the outcome of the education provided in the chapter.[31]

It is a householder not a scribe who brings out of his treasure things new, but this is what our scribe, under this second image, does. The new and the old link clearly to the message of Jesus and indirectly identifies the resource from which these new scribes will operate.[32]

Since central to the role of the scribe as reflected in Matthew is custodianship of a sacred tradition, it follows that their education into this tradition is self-evidently important, despite not otherwise coming into focus in Matthew's own material on scribes. Taking our cue from the place of Matt 13:52 at the end of a block in which the disciples are taught, here we will now be specifically concerned with the relationship between the disciples of the narrative and blocks of teaching and reference to teaching in the Gospel.

We meet the word disciple first in Matt 5:1, where disciples are the primary audience for the Sermon on the Mount. Four fishermen are earlier called by Jesus to follow

---

[29] See Matt 13:11, "To you it has been given to know the mysteries of the kingdom of heaven"; v. 16, "Blessed are your … ears, for they hear," followed by the explanation of the Sower to the disciples in vv. 18–23; v. 36, "Explain to us the parable of the weeds in the field," and Jesus does so in vv. 37–43.

[30] For the full phrase, Matt 13:11, 24, 31, 33, 44, 45, 47, with further kingdom language in vv. 19, 38, 41, 43.

[31] Matt 13:31, 33, 44, 45, 47.

[32] The new is pervasive, but the term comes in 9:17 where the old is also found. The old is the burden of 5:17–19.

him in 4:18–22. These are later included in the named list in 10:2–4. They are called "his twelve disciples" in v. 1 and are in turn equated with "the twelve apostles" in v. 2. From 10:5 the block of teaching that it prefaces seems to be identified as "marching orders," including instruction in v. 7 to "proclaim the good news that that the kingdom of heaven has come near you." But 11:1 leaves no room for an actual mission of the disciples: Matthew prefers to keep any mission offstage, probably because the scope of Jesus's teaching that he gathers into the block is, in the end, much too wide for mission instructions and where he wants to ultimately function is on the education of the disciples. (The role of the disciples will become sharply focused on mission when we come to 28:16–20.) Embedded in the ch. 10 teaching block at v. 24 is a reminder of the etymological link of μαθητής to being instructed by a teacher: "a disciple is not above the teacher." The next major teaching block comes in Matt 18. It is provoked by a question of the disciples related to the kingdom of heaven—providing a link with Matt 13. The resultant teaching is directed solely at the disciples. The extended critique of Pharisees and scribes in Matt 23 is directed to the crowds and to the disciples. The final extended block of teaching, Matt 24–25, is directed solely at the disciples. A remark about the temple buildings sets off the discourse. This block engages the future, including the proclaiming of the good news of the kingdom throughout the world—with echo of Matt 10:7. Overall, Jesus teaches on a wide front,[33] but the primary recipients of his teaching are the disciples.

Being a disciple is, for the Gospel disciples, much more than learning from Jesus's own teaching. There is clearly important learning from the life they shared with Jesus as he engaged both with them and with a wider public. But preparing to be a scribe is unlikely to be generally in focus on this journey. At two points, however, the foundational role of *understanding* for being successfully discipled to be a scribe reappears. In 16:12 the disciples learn to distance themselves from the teaching of the Pharisees and Sadducees (not here the scribes). In 17:13 they learn that Jesus had been speaking obliquely of John the Baptist—intending the suffering of John the Baptist to point them toward the coming suffering of the Son of Man. In both cases they transition to understanding via additional explanation from Jesus, as in Matt 13.

Unaddressed yet is the eschatological judgment role assigned to the twelve disciples in Matt 19:28. Authority based on divinely given insight is assigned to Peter in 16:19 and set in 18:18 within a wider framework of authority in and of the church.

While it is obvious that the place of the disciples in the Gospel narrative is fraught with implications for the life of the church, Matthew does little to disambiguate them. The twelve (eleven) disciples play a complex role in Matthew, where they are in part intended to be paradigmatic and in part intended to be sui generis. The challenge of the more general call to be a disciple of Jesus is surely intended to be felt by the Gospel reader in the call and response of the twelve. In part Matthew uses "follow" language to establish the bridge.[34] The central and even unique role of Peter in 16:19 is extended and generalized into the binding role for the church in 18:18. Despite the important teaching role assigned to the disciples in 28:19, the title "teacher" is jealously restricted

---

[33] See further Matt 4:23; 9:35; 11:1; 13;54; 21:23; 26:55.
[34] See Matt 4:19; 8:19, 22; 9:9; 10:38; 16:24; 19:21.

to Jesus, something made explicit in 23:8: "But do not be called Rabbi; for One is your Teacher, and you are all brothers."

Where does being a scribe for the kingdom fit? It would seem to be a unique role for the Gospel disciples. Nothing in our further exploration has given us reason to expand upon our preliminary conclusion that the metaphor is about a scribe's receiving of knowledge and having it to pass on.

One detail of Matt 28:20 may, however, focus this further. From our exploration of scribal functions, we have failed to find a strong connection between scribe and teacher, and we can add to this that the disciples are distanced from being called teachers. In Matt 28:20 what the disciples are called upon to teach is not exactly all that Jesus has taught them. The emphasis is, rather, on faithful observance. The disciples are to teach the need for faithful observance of all that Jesus had directed the disciples to observe.[35] People will know what this is from those discipled to be scribes for the kingdom of heaven. There is instruction, as called for, here, but not a full-scale need to embed in the would-be disciples this newly transformed sacred tradition. These new "scribes" are the fount to be returned to again and again, not those in the formal role of teachers who cause their full body of knowledge to now be embedded once and for all in those taught. In this respect their role is like that of the scribes of Matthew's Gospel. To partly repeat myself, now in relation to these disciple-scribes, they would be considered the correct people to be consulted in relation to the demands of Jesus's teaching and would use such opportunities as came their way to put people right. Preaching in the church would give major opportunity for promulgating the sacred teaching. To become a scribe is to have become a recognized fount of knowledge.

8.9 Conclusion

In Matt 13:52 it is implied that the disciples are being prepared to be scribes for the kingdom of heaven. Though this will involve elements of teaching, they are not to be established as teachers—Jesus is the unique teacher. The metaphor of "scribe" does not link with a leadership or judging role; rather, it is not a power role but a servant role. The sacred tradition out of which the Christian church will live has been embedded into the twelve (eleven) disciples. The church can resource from there the new and the old that characterized Jesus's vision and will undergird its own engagement with the kingdom of heaven.

---

[35] Elsewhere (Nolland, *Matthew*, 1270), commenting on Matt 28:20, I have said, "Matthew shares the general Jewish impulse to view true religion as involving a way of life and not simply a pattern of beliefs," but more is involved here.

9

Jesus as a Teacher of Forgiveness

Jon Coutts

9.1 Go and Learn What This Means: A Manifesto

In Matthew, Jesus is nothing if not a teacher of forgiveness. In each of the synoptic gospels Jesus defends his practice of dining with "tax collectors" by saying he came "to call not the righteous but sinners" (Matt 9:13, cf., Mark 2:17; Luke 5:32). Only in Matthew does Jesus explains this with reference to Hos 6:6, where the Lord says, "I desire mercy, not sacrifice" (Matt 9:13 NRSV). Since tax collectors were notoriously unjust, their presence makes readers less likely to miss the point: Everyone at the table needs mercy. The inference is that one could be devoted to the sacrificial system but still miss its primary function, which was to foster perpetual reliance upon the mercy of God. But what is most remarkable about the exchange, for our purposes, is that Jesus prefaced this with the instruction to "go and learn what this means" (9:13). For those with the ears to hear, this was more than self-defense; it was a commissioning. To this end, Matthew would have us notice that Hos 6:6 is not primarily about the mercy God *gives*, but the mercy God *desires*. Their dining together discloses this. Through it Jesus teaches them that self-righteousness is an obstacle to receiving God's mercy, and as such is an obstacle to sharing it.

There is an important setup to this in the preceding story, where Jesus forgives a man's sins and the Pharisees consider it *blasphemy* (9:3). Perceiving this, Jesus heals the man's paralysis in order to assure them of his "authority on earth to forgive sins" (9:6). The Pharisees' resistance is presented not as a matter of self-righteousness but of authority.[1] By asking them "which is easier"—to call a sin forgiven or to say "stand up and walk"—Jesus may be playing on the idea that one would be easier to pretend than the other (v. 5). But given that Jesus also called their thinking "evil" (v. 4), there seems to be more going on. Could it be that Jesus gives forgiveness too *easily* because he does so apart from sacrifice?[2] Sacrifice is not mentioned until v. 13, but it is important to note that Jesus said "take heart son, your sins are forgiven" when he "saw the faith" of the people carrying the man (9:2). Might Jesus be joining them in helping the man, by

---

[1] Simply put, they do not recognize Jesus as fulfiller and master-teacher of the law. See Patrick Schreiner, *Matthew, Disciple and Scribe: The First Gospel and its Portrait of Jesus* (Grand Rapids, MI: Baker Academic, 2019), 244.
[2] See Hyam Maccoby, *Early Rabbinic Writings* (Cambridge: Cambridge University Press, 1988), 91.

treating his relative inaccessibility to, among other places, the temple?[3] Perhaps Jesus is considered blasphemous not because forgiveness is for "God alone" (an objection that is absent from Matt 9:3 but present in Mark 2:7 and Luke 5:21) but because Jesus overrides divinely mandated sacrificial requirements in order to forgive and heal this man on the spot. Matthew's readers are about to read about God's desire for mercy rather than sacrifice—and the reason the crowd is "filled with awe" is because God "had given such authority to human beings" (9:8). Is this the mercy the disciples are meant to "go and learn" (9:13)?

In Matthew, Jesus is nothing if not the gatherer of a merciful community and, as such, a teacher of forgiveness and reconciliation. By ch. 9 Jesus has already said "blessed are the merciful, for they will be shown mercy" (5:7), taught the disciples to pray "forgive us our debts as we also have forgiven our debtors" (6:12), and explained that "if you forgive others their trespasses, your heavenly Father will also forgive you" (6:14). Readers of ch. 9 who are familiar with Hosea might recall that Ephraim and Judah were confronted for a love that disappears like morning dew rather than remaining "steadfast" (Hos 6:4–6). In this light, forgiving one another appears to be part of the mercy God desires—not as an end in itself but as a gateway to lasting love. In the Sermon on the Mount Jesus was explicit: "If you remember that your brother or sister has something against you, leave your gift there before the altar and go; first be reconciled to your brother or sister, and then come and offer your gift" (Matt 5:23–24). It was not a matter of mercy *or* sacrifice, but mercy *and* sacrifice, as long as one did not bring the latter without seeking the former. One cannot presume to be made right with God without seeking to be made right with the other children of God that one has harmed.[4]

Does this mean that salvation comes by works to those who match the almighty God for mercy? Or is this simply what it means for God's kingdom to come "on earth as it is in heaven" (6:10)? Matthew's Gospel is an invitation to "go and learn what this means" from Jesus, which means learning to practice forgiveness and reconciliation in order to truly pray "our Father" (6:9). To show how this is so, this chapter will proceed in three parts, with an emphasis on Matt 18. First it will consider how the "binding and loosing" statements of Jesus shape the community to carry on with Jesus as their teacher (16:19 and 18:18). After entangling this with forgiveness, the second section will interpret the parable of the unmerciful servant in light of Jesus's call to forgive "seventy-seven times" (18:21–35). Finally, having established the mercy-sharing ethos of the Christ-taught community, the third section will outline Jesus's instructions for reconciliation (18:15–20), showing the life Jesus was teaching his disciples to go and learn.

---

[3] Though it offers a slightly different reading, this suggestion stems from insights in Amos Yong, *The Bible, Disability, and the Church: A New Vision of the People of God* (Grand Rapids, MI: Eerdmans, 2011), 60–3.

[4] The early church applied this instruction to the Lord's Supper, as seen in *Did* 14:2 and in 1 Cor 11:17–34, where Paul says to "wait for one another" in order to truly "come together" when they eat (11:33). See David P. Scaer, *Discourses in Matthew: Jesus Teaches the Church* (Saint Louis, MO: Concordia, 2004), 220–1.

9.2 Binding and Loosing: The Forgiving Teacher

In Matthew 16, after confessing Jesus as "the Christ, the Son of the living God," Simon Son of Jonah is called Peter, the "rock" on which Jesus will build his church, against which "the gates of Hades will not prevail" (vv. 16–18). As if to keep those gates from shutting, Peter is given the "keys to the kingdom," which Jesus explains in terms of "binding" and "loosing" (19). The implication is that Peter is meant to *open* rather than "lock people out of the kingdom of heaven," as Jesus later depicts the "scribes and Pharisees" doing (23:13).[5] What is the meaning of all this?

Despite the word-play with Peter's name, it is unlikely that Peter is being given an infallible teaching authority of his own, as signaled by the fact that he is rebuked in the very next scene (16:23). What is most noteworthy for Jesus about Peter's confession, in fact, is that "flesh and blood has not revealed this to you, but my Father in heaven" (16:17). It is a misreading to interpret the keys and the rock as a fixed capacity, when the thing that singles Peter out is his responsiveness to divine instruction. After the rebuke (not to mention Peter's later denials) it should be clear to Matthew's audience that the church is built *by Jesus*, on the rock of that renewable confession of Christ which Peter served to exemplify. *That* is the key to the kingdom (perhaps an echo of the earlier teaching on the two foundations in the Sermon; 7:24–27). But how does it work?

Jesus explains to Peter what he would later repeat to all the disciples: "whatever you bind on earth will be bound in heaven, and whatever you loose on earth will be loosed in heaven" (16:19, cf., 18:18).[6] As many have noted, this resonates with the language of later rabbinic literature, wherein the language of binding and loosing denoted the "permitting" or "not permitting" of a given action.[7] Although these writings call upon an oral tradition that reached back to Jesus's time, it is difficult to ascertain exactly what the original audience would have heard the phrase to mean.[8] Jesus certainly engages

---

[5] Matthias Konradt, *The Gospel According to Matthew: A Commentary*, trans. M. Eugene Boring (Waco, TX: Baylor University Press, 2020), 254. See also Robert T. Fortna, *The Gospel of Matthew* (Santa Rosa, CA: Polebridge Books, 2005), 145.

[6] The could say "shall have been" bound and loosed (NASB), but we will proceed without a translation debate.

[7] Maccoby, *Early Rabbinic Writings*, 18–20. Josephus used the expression to speak of "administrators" who were "at liberty to banish and to recall, to loose and to bind." Josephus, *The Jewish War* 1.111, trans. H. St. J. Thackeray (Cambridge, MA: Harvard University Press, 1927), 54–5, cf., W. D. Davies and Dale C. Allison Jr., *A Critical and Exegetical Commentary on the Gospel According to Saint Matthew, volume II: Commentary on Matthew VIII-XVIII* (Edinburgh: T&T Clark, 1991), 635. See Mark Allen Powell, "Binding and Loosing: Asserting the Moral Authority of Scripture in Light of a Matthean Paradigm," *Ex Auditu* 19 (2004): 82–3; Raymond F. Collins, "Binding and Loosing," *Anchor Bible Dictionary* 1, ed. David Noel Freedman (New York: Doubleday, 1992), 744.

[8] The rabbinical writings where this phrase is found were written between AD 70 and 200. Maccoby, *Early Rabbinic Writings*, 30, cf., 40–1. See also Jacob Neusner, *Introduction to Rabbinic Literature* (New York: Doubleday, 1994), xxii, Jacob Neusner, "Rabbinic Literature: Mishnah and Tosefta," *Dictionary of New Testament Background*, ed. Craig A. Evans and Stanley E. Porter (Downers Grove, IL: InterVarsity Press, 2000), 896, and P. Enns, "Biblical Interpretation: Jewish," *Dictionary of New Testament Background*, ed. Craig A. Evans and Stanley E. Porter (Downers Grove, IL: InterVarsity Press, 2000), 161. Davies and Allison survey thirteen scholarly interpretations of binding and loosing, including ability to distinguish church from kingdom or "determine who goes to heaven," general conferral of power or "magical practices," authority for upholding or absolving vows or

and identifies with known rabbinical activity, but since Matthew presents him as the fulfiller and interpreter of the law it is best to *define* binding and loosing by its *internal* rather than its extra-canonical use. In that respect, it simply cannot be ignored that Jesus reuses the binding and loosing statement in Matthew 18:18. There it comes after a process of ecclesial reflection about who is at fault (vv. 15–17) and is followed by an assurance of the Father's help (v. 19), of Jesus's presence (v. 20), and of relentless forgiveness (vv. 21–22). Expanding wider, all of this is bookended by parables about restoring lost sheep (vv. 10–14) and forgiving "your brother or sister from your heart" (vv. 22–35).[9] This puts the binding and loosing statement in the context of moral and theological deliberation processes wherein it is decided whether something needs to be forgiven or not. This resonates with the echo of binding and loosing in John 20:23—where the risen Jesus says "if you forgive the sins of any, they are forgiven them; if you retain the sins of any, they are retained"—but it does raise the question why the disciples would ever be given the option *not* to forgive.[10]

It might seem odd for the early church to be given the option *not* to forgive, but there are at least two reasons why they might not: Either the accused could be found resistant or innocent. In other words, the person in question could *show no interest in being forgiven*, or an investigation could *find no need for it*. It must be remembered that forgiveness *is* an ethical judgment. This is why Karl Barth described the cross of Christ as an act of judgment and forgiveness at once, and it seems to be why he read Matthew 18:18 in light of John 20:23, taking the view that *binding* and *loosing* meant *not forgiving* or *forgiving*, and concluded that the church should always be loosing from sin.[11] Forgiveness is always on offer, but it will not be exchanged if either party believes

---

community bans, authority for exorcism, "authority to forgive or not forgive," and five variations of "teaching authority" (rooted in everything from *pre-set* knowledge to *interpretive* knowledge to *individual* authorization to authorization of an *office* to a combination of the above). Davies and Allison reject the notion of combining interpretations and side with the Epistle of Clement to James (ch. 2), where Peter "communicates" to Clement the Christ-given "power of binding and loosing"; of "knowing the rule of the Church." This is despite the fact that they "find no insuperable objection" to the forgiveness interpretation, and that Matt 18:17–18 extends binding and loosing not only to all of the disciples but to the "ecclesia" that follows Jesus's reconciliation instructions. Davies and Allison, *Critical and Exegetical Commentary*, 635–41.

[9] See J. Duncan and M. Derrett, "Binding and Loosing (Matt 16:19; 18:18; John 29:23 [sic])," *Journal of Biblical Literature* 102.1 (1983): 113, and Craig S. Keener, *A Commentary on the Gospel of Matthew* (Grand Rapids, MI: Eerdmans, 1999), 430. Even if one concludes (as Robert Fortna does) that binding and loosing refers strictly to the forbidding or permitting of behaviors, it is a false dilemma to hold this apart from Jesus's teaching on forgiveness, as if it is not integrally informed by it. See Fortna, *Gospel of Matthew*, 157.

[10] Mark Allen Powell, "Binding and Loosing," 82–3. Davies and Allison note that portions of Matt 16:13–20 are scattered through John, suggesting shared material. Davies and Allison, *Critical and Exegetical Commentary*, 608.

[11] Karl Barth, *Church Dogmatics*, IV/3.2 (London: T&T Clark, 2004), 861, cf., "The Judge who was Judged in our Place," CD IV/1, 211–82. On this see Jon Coutts, *A Shared Mercy: Karl Barth on Forgiveness and the Church* (Downers Grove, IL: IVP Academic, 2016), which incorporates material from "Binding or Loosing: Forgiveness and Truth-Seeking in Karl Barth's *Doctrine of Reconciliation*," a paper presented to the Scottish Postgraduates in Divinity Conference, Aberdeen, UK, June, 2010. See also the discussion of forgiveness as a "judgment of grace" in L. Gregory Jones, *Embodying Forgiveness: A Theological Analysis* (Grand Rapids, MI: Eerdmans, 1995), 135–62.

there is no sin to forgive. Thus, the need for teaching and deliberation. If something is *loosed* or *forgiven*, then it follows a determination that it was sin, at which point it is up to the sinner to receive the forgiveness or not. If something is *bound* or *not forgiven* then it either follows a determination that it was not a sin or follows a refusal to accept the forgiveness.

In Matthew 18 Jesus taught the disciples how to extend God's forgiveness to one another—just as he had taught them to pray (6:12–15)—and when Jesus ascended, it reverberated forward in a significant way. As Jeannine Brown and Kyle Roberts observe, binding and loosing appears to undergo "a fascinating transformation" after Jesus' resurrection (in 28:16–20), at which point "ultimate authority is not delegated to [Jesus's] followers" but "goes with them only as his presence accompanies them."[12] Going forward, it would behove readers of Matthew's Gospel to return to ch. 18 and take note of the *manner* of Jesus's presence, which is "wherever two or three are gathered" for the purpose of reconciliation.[13] This is what Peter seems to have realized when he asked how many times to forgive, and to this, we now turn.

9.3 Seventy-Seven Times: The Forgiveness Community

What does it mean to pray "forgive us our debts, as we also have forgiven our debtors" (12)? Matthew immediately has Jesus explain: "For if you forgive others their trespasses, your heavenly Father will also forgive you; but if you do not forgive others, neither will your Father forgive your trespasses" (14–15). Such a notion was not unprecedented in the ancient world, as seen in the intertestamental teaching of Jesus ben Sira in Sir 28:1–4:

> The vengeful man will face the vengeance of the Lord, who keeps strict account of his sins. Forgive your neighbour his wrongdoing; then, when you pray, your sins will be forgiven. If a man harbours a grudge against another is he to expect healing from the Lord? If he has no mercy on his fellow-man, is he still to ask forgiveness for his own sins?[14]

It is nonetheless striking that Jesus appears to make divine forgiveness conditional upon interpersonal forgiveness. The portrait Matthew paints, however, is not so much that God is a scrupulous forgiver, refusing to forgive until humans make the first move, but that God sets the conditions whereby forgiveness is properly received. As Isaac Mbabazi argues, the Matthean passages do not necessitate "the interpretation that

---

[12] Jeannine K. Brown and Kyle Roberts, *Matthew* (Grand Rapids, MI: Eerdmans, 2018), 481.
[13] As Myers and Enns note, this oft-quoted promise of presence applies *specifically* to gatherings for the "difficult church practice of confronting and healing incidents." Ched Myers and Elaine Enns, *Ambassadors of Reconciliation, Volume I: New Testament Reflections on Restorative Justice and Peacemaking* (Maryknoll, NY: Orbis, 2009), 50.
[14] *Ecclesiasticus, or The Wisdom of Jesus Son of Sirach* (Cambridge: Cambridge University Press, 1974), 139. See also Hyam Maccoby, *Early Rabbinic Writings* (Cambridge: Cambridge University Press, 1988), 89.

forgiving *earns* God's forgiveness" but do give shape to the covenantal life wherein "reciprocity" is part and parcel of the divine gift of forgiveness.¹⁵ This is underlined by Jesus's instruction to forgive "seventy-seven times" (18:22). In Matthew, the human failure to forgive is portrayed as a *disassociation* with the plenitude of divine mercy rather than an *impediment* to it.

Despite the break between Matthew 18:20 and 21 in many English Bibles, it is unhelpful to interpret Jesus's forgiveness teaching (22–35) apart from his preceding instructions about confrontation and reconciliation (15–21, cf., 5–14). As indicated by the "then" of v. 21, when Peter asks "how often should I forgive?" he is pulling Jesus aside for a further explanation and gets one. Matthew ensures that Jesus's answer reaches the rest of the disciples along with the subsequent parable, thereby sandwiching Jesus's promises of presence and binding and loosing between his confrontation instructions and his parable of the unmerciful servant. These should therefore be interpreted together.

Peter's immediate suggestion of sevenfold forgiveness is likely an embellishment of existing Jewish tradition, wherein "rabbis had considered three times sufficient for the forgiveness of the same sin."¹⁶ In that tradition it appears repentance was assumed before forgiveness was (re)given, as is explicit in Luke 17:4, where Jesus says a person who repents "seven times a day" must be forgiven seven times. The presence of repentance is not explicit in Matthew 18 but is implied by the preceding instructions wherein the person who "listens" is "regained" and the person who does not is no longer considered a sibling (vv. 15–17). It is the person who wishes to be regained to the community that Peter seems primarily to be asking about. That said, if Jesus's practice of dining with tax collectors is any indication, Matthew's lack of explicit reference to repentance could imply that there is a form of forgiveness to offer the unrepentant as well. This may be indicated by the answer Peter received in v. 22, where "Jesus said to him, 'Not seven times, but, I tell you, seventy-seven times.'"

The phrase Jesus uses is the same one found in the ancient Greek translation of Gen 4:24, where Lamech referred to Cain's sevenfold divine protection and promised to avenge himself not seven but "seventy-seven times" [ἑβδομηκοντάκις ἑπτά].¹⁷ In that context, God had provided Cain with a graciously protective measure that Lamech later usurped for self-protective purposes in the furthering of a city (Gen 4:13–24). In the context of Matthew, then, it is significant that Jesus not only exaggerates Peter's suggestion but also flips Lamech's preemptive threat on its head. In concert with the parable that follows, Jesus is taking back the divine initiative and replacing the social script of vengeful self-protection with one where mercy is extended instead. It could be argued that this is a total *reversal* of the *lex talionis* (eye for eye) in Exodus 21:23–24,

---

[15] Isaac Kahwa Mbabazi, *The Significance of Interpersonal Forgiveness in the Gospel of Matthew* (Eugene, OR: Pickwick, 2013), 139, 142.

[16] Donald A. Hagner, *Word Biblical Commentary, volume 33B: Matthew 14–28* (Dallas, TX: Word Books, 1995), 537, 540, c.f., b. Yoma 86b-87a and m. Yoma 8:9. See also Maccoby, *Early Rabbinic Writings*, 89, 91.

[17] Compare "ὅτι ἑπτάκις ἐκδεδίκηται ἐκ Καιν, ἐκ δὲ Λαμεχ ἑβδομηκοντάκις ἑπτά" (Gen 4:24 LXX) and "οὐ λέγω σοι ἕως ἑπτάκις ἀλλὰ ἕως ἑβδομηκοντάκις ἑπτά" (Matt 18:22). See Brown and Roberts, *Matthew*, 173.

Leviticus 24:19–20, and Deuteronomy 19:21, except that the *lex talionis* itself counteracted Lamech's motto and laid a trajectory that aligns with Jesus's teaching.

Illustrating the continuity between Jesus's teaching and the Hebrew scriptures, Ched Myers and Elaine Enns observe that "the mark of Cain represents a warning to any would-be vigilantes that any act of retribution will reignite the logic of vengeance, which will inevitably spiral out of control until they are all consumed by it."[18] As Brown and Roberts explain, if "the *lex talionis* functioned to limit retribution (thereby curbing revenge), then Jesus's teaching intensifies the command by limiting further retribution and revenge."[19] In this "echo" and "reversal" of Lamech, then, "Matthew juxtaposes two portraits: the first is of human sin and revenge spiralling out of control" and "the second is the effusiveness of forgiveness within the human community as the kingdom is manifested."[20] In other words, by extending the limiting factor of the law into the realm of interpersonal forgiveness and reconciliation, Jesus comes "not to abolish [the law] but to fulfill" it (Matt 5:17). The interplay between Peter and Jesus is a Matthean allusion to the mark of Cain, which Jesus turns *against* the mark of Lamech in order to portray the *ecclesia* as a sanctuary for reconciliation.[21]

All of the above is underlined by the parable of the unforgiving servant. It is "for this reason" that Matthew relays Jesus's story. In it a servant asks a "king" (βασιλεῖ) for patience to pay off an impossibly-sized debt, which moves his "lord" (κύριος) to grant a gift of "pity" (σπλαγχνισθεὶς) that forgives (ἀφῆκεν) the debt (18:23–27). Seemingly unchanged by this, the parable's servant turns around to seek repayment from a fellow servant for a much smaller debt, and despite a nearly identical request for patience he has the servant thrown in prison (28–30). In response to this the fellow servants report the disparity to their lord, who rebukes the servant for "not [having] mercy on your fellow slave, as I had mercy on you" (31–33). With that the lord angrily hands the servant over to torturers "until he would pay his entire debt," at which point Jesus explains: "So my heavenly Father will also do to every one of you, if you do not forgive your brother or sister from your heart" (34–35). While it is unclear who is the king and who is the lord in this parable, it is clear that the parable is positioned to root the requirement of interpersonal forgiveness in the abundant forgiveness of God.

Is this to say that the heavenly Father is not, at the end of the day, very forgiving? In our interpretation of the parable it may be worth distinguishing between a "condition" and a "precondition." Strictly speaking, the *precondition* for forgiveness is *the debtor's request for patience*, which is in turn *conditioned* by the lord's compassion (26–27). As such the first part of the parable illustrates exactly what has been said in the dialogue before it; namely, that the Father in heaven offers forgiveness to all who will receive it in repentance, which Jesus describes in exponential terms (15–22). It is only in the second part of the parable, where the debtor refuses to pass this forgiveness on, that the forgiveness of the debt is revoked and another form of punishment is paid (28–34). This might seem like a reversal of the prior decision, on the basis of a new precondition

---

[18] Myers and Enns, *Ambassadors of Reconciliation I*, 64.
[19] Brown and Roberts, *Matthew*, 65.
[20] Brown and Roberts, *Matthew*, 173.
[21] See Myers and Enns, *Ambassadors of Reconciliation I*, 63.

of shared forgiveness, but it could just as well refer us back to the prior precondition, which was the debtor's request for patience. Understood in this way, the failure to pass on forgiveness is an exposure of the "heart" of the debtor in the first place, which it turns out was only bluffing all along (as might have been suspected based on the promise to pay back the entirety of the impossibly sized debt).

This distinction may not make much difference until one tries to apply the parable to the question of eschatological forgiveness. If the parable is meant to indicate that those who consider themselves forgiven might discover themselves unsaved on account of their unwillingness to forgive, it might be in good company with the parable of the sheep and goats that is to come (in Matt 25). However, in Matthew 18 it is not explicitly stated that the debt is *eternally* unpayable. Verse 34 has the unmerciful servant "handed ... over to the torturers until he would repay" (NASB), but there is no internal reason to extend this into infinity, as if the mercy of the Father could never again be known.[22] The debt may be large, but it is nevertheless finite. For this reason, it is better to interpret the parable of the unmerciful servant as a warning about the conditions of historical life that are created by divine forgiveness, leaving open the question what ramifications there might be in the eschaton.[23]

Ched Myers and Elaine Enns have done well to point out the difficulty in squaring the outlandish mercy of vv. 22–27 with the apparent ultimatum in v. 35. Is God offering a seventy-sevenfold forgiveness of ten-thousand-talent debts, only to condemn anyone who fails to forgive a debt that is just a fraction of that size? Rather than take Matthew 18 as a revelation that "the cosmos is ultimately retributive," Myers and Enns interpret it as "historical ultimatum"; namely, that "God will not save us from the consequences of *not* interrupting the spiral of vengeance."[24] By the end of Matthew 18, readers should recognize that unmerciful servants have millstones around their necks and need to repent of not sharing the divine gift of forgiveness to the extent that it is given. It is a warning to be heeded immediately. If the outlandish debt could be forgiven once, Matthew has given

---

[22] See Brown and Roberts, *Matthew*, 174–5. "Handing over" [παρέδωκεν] is what Jesus subjects himself to in order to be "poured out for many for the forgiveness of sins" (26:28, c.f., 17:22–23; 20:17–19; 26:2, 15–16; 27:2).

[23] The warning at the end of the parable is stark, but it is not a threat of eternal punishment with no recourse to forgiveness. To be sure, the subsequent chapter doubles down on the difficulty of entering eternal life—leading the disciples to cry "who can be saved?"—but in that context the outlandishness of God's mercy still echoes forward in the statement that "for mortals it is impossible, but for God all things are possible" (19:26). Lest readers be too sure of their eschatological judgments, Matt 25 will leave open the possibility of an eschatological revealing wherein the presumed sheep turn out to be goats, and vice versa. This does not diminish the ethical teaching in Matthew 18, since the basis for that later eschatological judgment is how the individuals treat the "least of these" (25:40, 45), but it does unsettle any overconfidence that renders "binding and loosing" an eschatological determination. If binding and loosing is on earth as it is in heaven it should be understood in the spirit of the prayer in 6:10 rather than the conferral of powers of eschatological judgment, which Jesus explicitly did not give the disciples (12:33).

[24] Myers and Enns, *Ambassadors of Reconciliation I*, 80. Myers and Enns suggest that "if we allegorize this parable as a teaching about God's ultimate justice, the entirety of Matthew 18 becomes incoherent." Read in conversation with the preceding verses "the parable forces us to examine how we ourselves are deeply mired in the logic of retributive justice, unwilling, like the [parable's] king, to forgive more than once." Rather than assume the parable's king is representative of God's character, the parable puts the onus on the parable's servants to either be bound or loosed by their response to God's mercy. "The alternative to Jesus' alternative is ... Lamech's cold world" (71, 80).

reason to believe that this could be done seventy-six times more. In the parable the debt was forgiven not because it was paid—and thus certainly not because it was extracted from others—but was forgiven precisely because of the pity of the lord that was aroused by the servant's request for patience (26–27). The specific warning, then, is to do as Jesus instructed, which means heeding the church's rebuke when one is the offender (15–17) and forgiving "from the heart" when one is the offended (21–22, 35). The Father's Kingdom will not be participated in *on earth* unless the Father's mercy is shared rather than hoarded. As Donald Hagner expresses it: "Failure in this respect creates an intolerable inconsistency at the very point where the kingdom is to manifest itself."[25]

Chrysostom said it should be unsettling to hear Jesus end the parable of the unmerciful servant with reference to "*my* heavenly Father" rather than "our[s]" (18:35; 6:9). For him this meant that the unmerciful servant was resorting to someone else's politic: If "thou art not become better by the kindness shown thee, it remains that by vengeance thou be corrected."[26] A politic other than Lamech's is on offer, and it is absurd to try to have it both ways, reserving kindness for oneself and offering vengeance to others. The gift that is given is to be given in turn. When it comes to the confrontation of wrongdoing, then, what does this alternate politic entail?

In the twentieth century, Hannah Arendt brought renewed attention to the politics of forgiveness and in this regard referred to Jesus as "the Discoverer of the role of forgiveness in the realm of human affairs."[27] Arendt was aware that "Jesus made 'this discovery in a religious context and articulated it in religious language,'" explains Richard Gibson, so the point was not that Jesus invented this but that Jesus applied a preexisting concept in an arguably new way.[28] Jesus did not invent the pivot from divine to interpersonal forgiveness, but intensified and expanded its applicability. As Gibson puts it, Arendt thought Jesus brought interpersonal forgiveness into "the rhythm of a thriving public sphere," just as John Robert Seeley thought Jesus's "innovation" was to take a practice normally reserved for the "charmed circle of friends and family" and to "extend" it "to strangers and enemies."[29] This is also the view of Desmond Tutu, who

---

[25] Hagner, *Matthew 14–28*, 541. Calvin wondered whether God could remove a previously given forgiveness and concluded that the primary point was that those who do not extend the divinely given forgiveness to others are thereby "unworthy of enjoying it." John Calvin, *Commentary on a Harmony of the Evangelists* II (Edinburgh: Calvin Translation Society, Edinburgh Printing, 1845), 368. In Matt 12 Jesus warns that a house emptied of unclean spirits will be revisited by seven more, so it is not enough for it simply to be "swept" and "put in order" (12:43–45). Contrast this with his statement that "whoever does the will of my Father in heaven is my brother and sister and mother" (12:50). It seems Jesus would rather have sevenfold cycles of binding and loosing than people who order their own affairs.

[26] Chrysostom, "The Gospel of St. Matthew, Homily LXI," from "The Homilies of Chrysostom," in *Nicene and Post-Nicene Fathers*, volume X, ed. Philip Schaff (Grand Rapids, MI: Eerdmans, 1975), 379–80.

[27] Hannah Arendt, *The Human Condition*, 2nd ed. (Chicago: University of Chicago Press, 2013), 238.

[28] Richard Hughes Gibson, *Forgiveness in Victorian Literature: Grammar, Narrative, and Community* (New York: Bloomsbury, 2015), 29, quoting Arendt, *Human Condition*, 238, cf., 272. Isaac Mbabazi compares Matthew with the interpersonal forgiveness in first-century Greek and Jewish literature and finds Jesus made it more "central" to reception of divine forgiveness. See Mbabazi, *Interpersonal Forgiveness*, 1, 4, cf., 30–61, 86–7, 115–16.

[29] Gibson, *Forgiveness in Victorian Literature*, 29, referring to John Robert Seeley, *Ecce Homo: A Survey of the Life and Work of Jesus Christ*, 19th ed. (London: Macmillan, 1886).

traced forgiveness into the sociopolitical realm by associating it with the Xhosa concept of *ubuntu*, or common humanity. Tutu argued that forgiveness is "the best form of self-interest since anger, resentment, and revenge are corrosive of that *summum bonum*, that greatest good, communal harmony that enhances the humanity and personhood of all in the community."[30] Whatever the therapeutic or political benefits may be, in the context of Matthew it was Jesus's first concern to teach the politics of forgiveness to the *ecclesia*, from which a further understanding of its mission could be formed. It is to this that our final section turns.

9.4 Go and Point Out the Fault: Forgiveness as Reconciliation

It is a mistake to imagine seventy-sevenfold forgiveness in terms of a nonconfrontational false peace that privileges the status quo. Churches that reduce forgiveness to a personal coping mechanism in service of conflict avoidance have not only taken it out of context but turned it into a stumbling block that harms the vulnerable (Matt 18:6–7). Forgiveness can be problematic if it enables further offence rather than confronting it. As the objection in William Shakespeare's *Measure for Measure* goes: "Mercy is not itself that oft looks so; Pardon is the nurse of second woe."[31] At first glance, Matthew 18:21–22 does appear to be less concerned with accountability than its parallel in Luke 17:4. In Luke, Jesus says "if the same person sins against you seven times a day, and turns back to you seven times and says, 'I repent,' you must forgive," whereas Matthew 18:22 omits explicit mention of repentance and multiplies the forgiveness to "seventy-seven times." However, it is important to note that Matthew places this on the immediate heels of Jesus's instructions for confrontation (vv. 15–20), which is itself the follow up to his warning about allowing "stumbling blocks" to lead "little ones" astray (6–14). Luke's Jesus is more explicit, but Matthew's Jesus is no less concerned about seeking repentance.

As Roberts and Brown observe, "stumbling blocks" can include things that bring harm "to both the other (18:6–7) and to the self (18:8–9)."[32] Reminiscent of the "eye for an eye" logic that Jesus previously amended (5:38–39), in Matthew 18 Jesus says the eye that causes stumbling is better off removed (18:6–10). It is not specified whether the "eye" is a literal reference to the sense organ that is prone to sin or is symbolic of a person in the social body who must be removed for the sake of the whole. In any case it is a rhetorical hyperbole positioned to highlight the importance of what Matthew

---

[30] Desmond Tutu, *No Future Without Forgiveness* (New York: Random House, 2009), 34–5. Lewis Smedes traced the personal therapeutic benefits of forgiveness in Lewis B. Smedes, *Forgive and Forget: Healing the Hurts We Don't Deserve* (New York: Harper and Row, 1984). For a critique of this, see L. Gregory Jones, *Embodying Forgiveness: A Theological Analysis* (Grand Rapids, MI: Eerdmans, 1995), 48–53.

[31] This is in Act 2, scene 1, lines 261–2, where Escalus explains why Lord Angelo's severity is "needful." William Shakespeare, *Measure for Measure*, ed. Cedric Watts (Ware, Hertfordshire: Wordsworth Classics, 2005), 51, cf., 55.

[32] Brown and Roberts, *Matthew*, 167.

relays next. Removal of the eye is the very last resort, and a loving confrontation of sin and harm is the process that precedes and hopefully avoids it. The "little one" harmed by sin (either from self or another) is a sheep who has gone astray, and the flock is to concern itself with recovery (18:10–18). This, then, is how it is done:

> If another member of the church sins against you, go and point out the fault when the two of you are alone. If the member listens to you, you have regained that one. But if you are not listened to, take one or two others along with you, so that every word may be confirmed by the evidence of two or three witnesses. If the member refuses to listen to them, tell it to the church; and if the offender refuses to listen even to the church, let such a one be to you as a Gentile and a tax collector. (15–17)

In v. 22, Jesus affirms the relentlessness of forgiveness, but context does not allow this to be interpreted in terms of blanket pardons that take place apart from confrontation, discernment, and care. What should not be overlooked is the fact that the following parable not only rebukes the unmerciful servant but also affirms those who were "distressed" by his treatment of lesser servants and "reported to their lord all that had taken place" (18:31). Thus it is clear that the forgiveness of the lord does not create a confrontation-free zone but fosters a context of accountability wherein the beneficiaries of mercy still look out for the vulnerable.

As Myers and Enns explain, "*if* and *when* victims feel able to press their case for justice and accountability, Jesus says, the support and accompaniment of the whole community should be marshalled."³³ By giving agency to the victims of wrongdoing Jesus's instructions might be said to be overburdening them, except the process involves the help of witnesses and is the responsibility of the whole church. A community that lives by this pattern will be one where victims feel more confident to speak and be heard. In Matthew 5:23–24 Jesus notably reversed the roles and put the onus on offenders to seek reconciliation with those who have "something against" them. On that occasion Jesus instructed the offended party not to foster vengeful outbursts of anger (5:21–22)–which foreshadowed Jesus's teaching of forgiveness and embedded it in a primary concern for reconciliation–but the teaching still privileges the offended party by ensuring that their feelings are prioritized over personal access to the altar. This is also implied when Matthew 18:15 instructs the victim to approach the offender but does *not* say they must refrain from worship until the situation is resolved. Whether or not Jesus foresaw all possibilities, it is providential that this precludes a situation wherein the victim could be held hostage from worship due to the insensitivity of their offender. Instead, the victim is empowered to pursue a manifestation of the mercy that is preferred to sacrifice. The presence of witnesses (and the fellow servants in the parable) should guard against the prevailing of false accusation but should also provide an environment that makes reconciliation processes feel accessible to "little ones."³⁴ Put together, Jesus's teachings in 5:23–24 and 18:15–18 ensure that Jesus has

---

[33] Myers and Enns, *Ambassadors of Reconciliation I*, 66, cf., 71–81.
[34] See Myers and Enns, *Ambassadors of Reconciliation I*, 66–7. In Deut 19:15–21 the requirement of witnesses protects confronted parties from false accusation, but it can also ensure that false pity is not afforded to those who might have the power or persuasiveness to wiggle out of an accusation.

told both sides of any given problem to "go" and "be reconciled." This is not prevented but fuelled by the unrelenting forgiveness of God that is shared in Christ.

Things do not always work out, of course. Where there is an outstanding disagreement about the nature of the fault, a sheep may be lost from the flock, or a member may be lost from the body (18:6–14). For Jesus this is neither the goal nor the end of the matter, but there is also to be no pretending about a lack of consensus (v. 17). Until forgiveness is accepted as such the offender who "refuses to listen" is in an inherently new relation to the community. To say the unreconciled offender is no longer a sibling [ἀδελφός] but a foreigner [ἐθνικὸς] or a "tax collector" (18:17) may sound like a slur or an act of shaming, but against this reading it should be remembered that Matthew previously depicted Jesus taking criticism precisely for spending time with "tax collectors and sinners" (9:11) as one would with a "friend" (11:19). Earlier in Matthew, Jesus defended his mission (9:12–13) to tax collectors and sinners with the saying that "wisdom is vindicated by her deeds" (11:19). Put together with Matthew 18:17, this seems to mean that *time will tell*, but when there is a prevailing disagreement about the fault (and therefore a lack of repentance), there needs to be a distinction between siblings and neighbors.[35] The distinction does not rule out love or friendship but has to do with the nature of the social bond, which has shifted from ecclesial "sibling" to extra-ecclesial "friend" or "neighbour" or "enemy" (18:17; 11:19; 5:43). The call is still to love the person, but there is to be no denying that the particularity and reciprocity of the relation has changed. This is more than a change of relationship status; the larger point is that the politics within *ecclesia* are decidedly different.

Jesus previously used the tax collector to teach the difference between self-interested love and the self-giving love for which he was calling: "If you love those who love you, what reward will you get? Are not even the tax collectors doing that? And if you greet only your own people, what are you doing more than others? Do not even pagans [ἐθνικοὶ] do that?" (5:46–47). The point of Matthew 18:17, then, is that a breakdown between the community and the unrepentant offender does not lead to an unloving posture but to a form of love that is no longer reciprocated within a shared confession of Christ. Love toward this person is not *determined* by this shift, but the form love takes is certainly *informed* by the new strain in the social relationship.

If one imagines this in terms of shunning and shaming and violence (ostensibly in the name of "tough love"), one forgets the care taken to resolve the matter and the posture Jesus took toward sinners. That said, it is important not to forget Jesus's concern in this passage for the protection of vulnerable members from further harm

---

[35] In any case, as Brown and Roberts observe, Jesus's provision for witnesses serves to "complicat[e] a simple binary between a 'sinner' and a 'sinned against,'" by which "the reader is invited to pause after each 'step' to see if something has changed." Brown and Roberts, *Matthew*, 480. If anyone proves to be falsely accused, they may return to Jesus's instruction at v. 15.
Such a person is no longer a sibling, no longer a member of the church, but must now be viewed as someone who still needs to be made a disciple (by being taught to obey Christ's commandments). Notably, the offense that excludes the person from membership in God's eschatological community is not the offense for which he or she was rebuked but the more serious matter of refusing to listen to the church. Powell, "Binding and Loosing," 89–90.

by unrepentant offenders. Seventy-sevenfold forgiveness is not a free pass to disregard harm to self and others. According to the parable of the lost sheep, the community's rejoicing remains relative to the prospect of return (18:13), but the care for the flock remains.[36] Community relations cannot be dishonestly or unsafely maintained in the face of a breakdown. The fact that the alleged offender is approached personally and discreetly before the worst-case scenario of involving the wider church shows that this concern for vulnerability extends also to the offender.[37] A breakdown of relationship is a grievous matter, and the parable of the unmerciful servant makes clear that the community had better be careful not to exact demands from the offender that are anything less than an offer of merciful restoration. The parable focuses on non-forgiveness, but it does not negate the concern for justice and care.

Jesus's parable of the unmerciful servant rebukes those who would accept debt-release without extending it to others but does not renounce concern for the prevailing conditions of the kingdom wherein debts are owed.[38] Matthew does not include the story of Zacchaeus or of Jesus's announcement of Jubilee, as Luke does (in 19:1–10 and 4:16–21), but it is illuminating to think of Zacchaeus as a Jubilary counterexample to Matthew's unmerciful servant. What Zacchaeus and the unmerciful servant have in common is the (eventual) repayment of debts, but the difference is that when Zacchaeus is forgiven his sins he repays his wrongful earnings and lowers himself to the social class he exploited, whereas the unmerciful servant uses his debt-forgiveness *not* to make common cause with the other servants but to further "distress" them. In Luke 19:10, Jesus was sent to "seek out and save the lost," and in Zacchaeus's case restoration meant debt-repayment. In Matthew 18:14, Jesus called the disciples to seek the lost, and in the unmerciful servant's case restoration should have meant debt-forgiveness. The circumstances are different and must be discerned, but what is common about both is that forgiveness leads to reconciliation. Zacchaeus is the model tax collector of Matthew 18:17, because instead of refusing to listen and persisting in sin he is chastened and responds to Jesus's offer of friendship with repentance and reparation (Luke 19:7–9). In contrast to this, the unmerciful servant is the "tax collector" of Matthew 18:17, who has refused to learn his fault, has carried on extracting debts, and has been removed from the community. Matthew provides a negative rather than a positive example, but in both gospels it is clear that forgiveness is not without social ramifications.[39] Forgiveness issues forward in a concern for reparation and reconciliation.

This raises the question whether it might be possible for a church community to bind and loose incorrectly and, if so, whether it might be possible for a church's decision to be appealed. If a church makes a questionable decision that alienates a member of

---

[36] These Matthean intratextualities are also observed in a similar way by Brown and Roberts, *Matthew*, 166–70.
[37] See Konradt, *Gospel According to Matthew*, 279.
[38] The parable shows that Peter's question about forgiveness "cannot be adequately discussed in the framework that considers only an isolated incident between the two persons involved." Konradt, *Gospel According to Matthew*, 284.
[39] In this way forgiving carries notions of reciprocity similar to what John Barclay finds in ancient gift-giving. See John M. G. Barclay, *Paul and the Gift* (Grand Rapids, MI: Eerdmans, 2015). I am grateful to Rev. Chris Gercke for tracing this connection in his 2017 master's thesis at Trinity College Bristol (UK).

the community, perhaps to the advantage of the powers that be, need that be the end of the matter? Jesus's instructions are very compact, but they do leave room for prolonged and careful processes of discernment that lead to the decisions made. Similarly, they do not rule out the possibility of deliberations being entered into again. Despite the connotations of the English translation "binding," ancient rabbinical decisions were not fixed universals but temporal rulings to be revisited on a case-by-case basis "in a continuous process of legislation."[40] With his binding and loosing promise, Jesus surely indicates a divine commitment to whatever the disciples decide, but that does not mean decisions are unalterably binding. This is suggested not only by Peter's rebuke in Matthew 16:22–23 but also by Jesus's openness to amendment in Matthew 15:21–28. There, when a Canaanite woman asks for "mercy" and "help," Jesus first reiterates his mission "only to the lost sheep of the house of Israel" (15:22–24, cf., 10:5–6). When the woman kneels and persists in her request, Jesus relents, saying, "Woman, great is your faith! Let it be done for you as you wish" (15:28). In Mark Allan Powell's view this is "presented as 'loosing' a commandment that Jesus himself had given earlier," which Jesus does not consider embarrassing but praiseworthy.[41] In other words, if a decision is made it is binding, but that is not to say it is forever off limits from revisitation. As Konradt observes, Matthew 18:18 "presupposes a congregational consensus on ethical norms" but as such implies that an absence of consensus may require persistence in discernment.[42]

Those who care for the integrity of the church will want to be cautious about fickleness and flippancy, but there is nothing to suggest that churches should never return to a matter for further deliberation. In fact, the possibility of seventy-sevenfold forgiveness implies the alternate possibility that on one or more of those occasions the church might find deeper layers to the problem. Perhaps the offender remains guilty but is embedded in systemic dynamics that also need to be addressed. Or perhaps the church that once found an offender guilty has since found new ways to address the issue. Binders and loosers are always praying for further harmony with heaven. Once a person has been absented from the church for "refusing to listen" it may become harder for them to access the re-discernment processes, but a church that looks out for little ones (vv. 6–9), lost sheep (vv. 10–14), and vulnerable servants (vv. 23–35) will aim not to misunderstand and exclude where it ought to have listened and learned. Where there is doubt there might be solace in releasing an unreconciled member to another congregation, but this leads to a second question; namely, whether local church decisions must be binding on the ecumenical church as a whole.

This ecumenical question may fall out of the scope of Jesus's instructions in Matthew 18, but in an expanding church it is increasingly the case that the findings of one congregation might be considered suspect by another. As the universal church has become divided in its designation of sins, it raises the question whether a person estranged from one congregation might remain with Christ in another. On a case-by-case basis there would have to be a conversation about whether ecumenical accountability is required, but it is at least conceivable that a separation might take the

---

[40] Maccoby, *Early Rabbinic Writings*, 21.
[41] Powell, "Binding and Loosing," 90.
[42] Konradt, *Gospel According to Matthew*, 281.

form of a blessing to join another church body, perhaps with a caveat about unresolved ethical or doctrinal concerns. Rather than deepening church division this could involve a recommitment to the ecumenical discernment processes and learning opportunities entailed.[43] In Matthew 18, Jesus imagines a person rather than a church being shown its fault, but his instructions can and do translate to inter-ecclesial deliberations as well.

As Powell notes, the promise of Matthew 18:15-20 is not necessarily unanimity or accuracy (though these are the implied ideal); rather, the promise is that Jesus will be present "where two or three are gathered" in his name for reconciliation, and the Father will honor the proceedings (18:18-20).[44] On the terms of Matthew's Gospel, then, any prolonged disagreement of the Church should be worked on until such a time as there is agreement in Jesus's name. Meanwhile, the gates of Hades will not prevail against a church that gathers for this, and the presence of Jesus will be known not only at the end but *in the process* (16:18; 18:20).

9.5 Conclusion: Go and Teach Them to Obey

By the end of Matthew's Gospel it is not as if the disciples have ceased to be learners. Having taught the disciples to "go and learn" what it means for God to "desire mercy" (9:13), Jesus commissions them to "go" and "make disciples of all nations, baptizing ... and teaching them to obey everything that I have commanded you" (28:19-20). Rather than finish with the addition of a twelfth disciple, Matthew expands the disciple-making process to the four corners of earth.[45] In this Jesus is ascending but not leaving them alone. Retaining "authority in heaven and earth" (18), Jesus does not delegate teaching authority *in absentia* but promises to be with them to "the end of the age" (20).[46] So it is that Jesus's disciples are to persist in a shared pursuit of obedience that is embedded in processes of discernment that are propelled by a mutual commitment to forgiveness and reconciliation in Jesus's name. To expand on a phrase from Miroslav Volf, if careful listening is the "epistemological side of faith in the crucified," then gathering for reconciliation is the epistemological side of faith in the risen Lord.[47] Given that they are to follow and understand Jesus *as a community*, their interpersonal forgiveness is necessary. So it is that Jesus teaches them not only *about* forgiveness but *through* it.

---

[43] Powell observes that "Matthew's Gospel never addresses the question, 'What if the church is wrong?'" and suggests that local churches ought to be careful about making "definitive judgment" on behalf of the whole Church. This leads to the realization that if churches err then individuals may find solace elsewhere, and/or have to bear it and look to raise the issue in a manner consistent with Jesus's teaching. See Powell, "Binding and Loosing," 91-3.

[44] Powell, "Binding and Loosing," 94. See also Myers and Enns, *Ambassadors of Reconciliation I*, 50.

[45] See Schreiner, *Matthew, Disciple and Scribe*, 185.

[46] See Samuel Byrskog, *Jesus the Only Teacher: Didactic Authority and Transmission in Ancient Israel, Ancient Judaism and the Matthaean Community*, Coniectanea Biblica NT 24 (Stockholm: Almqvist & Wiksell International, 1994), 261.

[47] Miroslav Volf, *Exclusion and Embrace: A Theological Exploration of Identity, Otherness, and Reconciliation* (Nashville, TN: Abingdon, 1996), 214.

Part 3

Jesus's Students

10

Jesus and Matthew: Matthew as a Discipled Scribe

Patrick Schreiner

10.1 Introduction

Both early and modern interpreters have argued that Matt 13:52 is an autobiographical statement from the author of the First Gospel.[1]

> Therefore, every scribe who has been discipled for the kingdom of heaven is like a master of a house, who brings out of his treasure what is new and old.[2]

> διὰ τοῦτο πᾶς γραμματεὺς μαθητευθεὶς τῇ βασιλείᾳ τῶν οὐρανῶν ὅμοιός ἐστιν ἀνθρώπῳ οἰκοδεσπότῃ, ὅστις ἐκβάλλει ἐκ τοῦ θησαυροῦ αὐτοῦ καινὰ καὶ παλαιά.

In this chapter, I will argue that Matthew was a student, scribe, and transmitter of his teacher, Jesus.[3] I will first show that Matthew was an apostle of Jesus and most likely the author of what is commonly called the Gospel according to Matthew. Second, I will turn to Matt 13:52 as a possible window into how Jesus trained Matthew as a "discipled scribe."

As one unknown author said, "teaching is the one profession that creates all other professions." By being a teacher, Jesus created a chain reaction. Many of his students would turn into future teachers who would pass on his deeds and words onto future generations. Matthew is one of these students. The purpose of training is the formation of a certain type of person. Pupils would help form new communities in the tradition of their teacher. Matthew stands as an intermediary who transmits the words and life of Jesus to the world.

---

[1] While most believe in Markan priority, I will refer to the Gospel of Matthew as the "First Gospel" since it is the first book in the English ordering of the NT. This is a canonical statement, not a historical statement.
[2] Author's translation.
[3] This chapter is a reworking, summary, and sometimes expansion of my argument in *Matthew, Disciple and Scribe: The First Gospel and Its Portrait of Jesus* (Grand Rapids, MI: Baker Academic, 2019). Used with permission from Baker Academic.

10.2 Matthew as an Apostle and Author

All three of the Synoptic Gospels claim a certain Matthew was a disciple of Jesus, and even one of the twelve apostles. Mark and Luke, as they catalog the twelve disciples of Jesus, lists Matthew as the seventh of the twelve apostles (Mark 3:18; Luke 6:15). The Gospel of Matthew also includes Matthew, but he is the only one to append Matthew's name with his vocation: he was Matthew, *the tax collector* (10:3).

All three Synoptics also include the story of the call of Matthew. In the midst of a larger section on Jesus's healings, Matthew's Gospel tells of how Jesus saw Matthew sitting at the tax booth and called him to follow Jesus (Matt 9:9). After this Jesus has fellowship in a house with many tax collectors and sinners, which causes the Pharisees to ask questions (Matt 9:10–11). Luke and Mark give a few more details on this scene. They call this tax collector Levi and identify that it is in Levi's house that this meal takes place (Luke 5:27–32; Mark 2:14–17). The sinners and tax collectors must have been Matthew's friends.

Some interpreters find it confusing that a person would have two Semitic personal names (Matthew and Levi). Palestinian Jews sometimes had a Semitic name (Simon) and a Greek or Latin name (Peter), but there are no clear examples of a Palestinian Jew having two Semitic personal names. Levi could refer to Matthew's tribe, but this is unlikely, as a tribal name was not typically attributed as a personal name.

More likely, "Matthew" is the Aramaic nickname given to Levi by Jesus. Matthew means "gift of God" and could have some connection to Matthew's vocation as a tax collector. In addition, it was quite common for YAHWEH to give people names based on their new status in God's covenant family (Abram to Abraham; Sarai to Sarah; Jacob to Israel).

10.2.1 External Evidence for Matthean Authorship

Matthew was an apostle, but this does not necessarily mean he was the author of the Gospel that bears his name. The Gospels, like other ancient biographies, are officially anonymous. The Gospel of Matthew doesn't explicitly identify the author. Later, I will argue Matt 13:52 gives us a pointer in that direction, but first we will look at the external evidence.[4] Only the external evidence allows readers to dig more deeply into Matt 13:52.

The earliest surviving manuscript containing the title of Matthew (or any Gospel title) is a fragment from the flyleaf found with $\mathfrak{P}^4$ (a fragment of Luke). The flyleaf probably dates to the late second or early third century and reads "Gospel according to Matthew" (εὐαγγέλιον κατὰ Μαθθαῖον). Outside of manuscript evidence,

---

[4] Some point to other internal evidence for Matthean authorship including the following: First, Matthew's expertise in taxation. Matthew 22:15–22 uses the more precise phrase for the poll tax. Second, the author is familiar with Jewish customs (1:18–19), Jewish history, and had a concern for Jewish law (5:17–20). Third, there are Semitic indications in Matthew's work. He uses τότε 89x, asyndeton, and the indefinite plural. Yet, only the first one points to Matthean authorship; the rest merely indicate Jewish authorship.

the earliest affirmation of Matthew's authorship appears in the *Expositions of the Lord's Logia* by Papias (early second century) where he states, "Therefore, Matthew arranged in order the *logia* in the Hebrew language; but each translated these to the best of his ability."

The evidence for Matthean authorship continues. The Gospel of Thomas, Saying 13, portrays Thomas as having superior insight into Jesus's true identity than either Peter or Matthew. Irenaeus of Lyons asserts: "Matthew published a Gospel book for the Hebrews in their own language while Peter and Paul were preaching the gospel in Rome and establishing the church."[5] Clement of Alexandria (*Strom*. I) identified Matthew as the author of this Gospel around AD 198. In the middle of the third century, Origen wrote:

> As I learned in the tradition about the four Gospels which alone are incontrovertible in the church of God under heaven, the first written was that according to Matthew, the one-time tax-collector, but later apostle of Jesus Christ. He published it for the Jews who believed, since it was composed in the Hebrew language.[6]

In the early fourth century, Eusebius of Caesarea said:

> After Matthew previously preached to the Hebrews, as he was about to go to other nations, he published the Gospel according to Matthew in written form in his native language so that he could compensate for his absence from those he was leaving behind.[7]

Jerome compares the four canonical Gospels to the four rivers that flowed from Paradise. He then says, "The first of all is Matthew, the tax collector, who is also named Levi, who published a Gospel in Judea in the Hebrew language, chiefly for the sake of those from the Jews who had believed in Jesus."[8]

10.2.2 Considering the Evidence

It is possible that all these early witnesses to the authorship of the First Gospel are wrong. However, more likely they speak of a commonly held tradition based in reliable, historical testimony. Additionally, Richard Bauckham has argued that eyewitness testimony was highly valued in first-century history writing. The Prologue to Luke's Gospel indicates eyewitnesses "delivered" or "traditioned" (παραδίδωμι) what was fulfilled among those who followed Jesus (Luke 1:1–2). Other New Testament (NT) authors speak of the importance of eyewitness testimony, including Paul (1 Cor 9:1; 15:5–8; Gal 1:16), Luke (Luke 1:1–4; Acts 1:21–22; 10:39–41), John (John 19:35; 21:24;

---

[5] Irenaeus, *Haer.* 3.1. Quoted in Eusebius, *Hist. eccl.* 5.8.2.
[6] Origen, *Comm. Matt.* 1 (Heine, *Origen on the Gospel of St. Matthew*, 1:320). This portion is quoted in Eusebius, *Hist. eccl.* 6.25.3–6.
[7] Eusebius, *Hist. eccl.* 3.24.6. In *Hist. eccl.* 5.10.3.
[8] Jerome, *Comm. Matt.* Prol. 2 (FC). Cf. Jerome, *Vir. Ill.* 3; *Comm. Os.* 11.2.

1 John 1:1–4), and Peter (1 Pet 1:8; 2 Pet 1:16–21). Eyewitnesses likely functioned to "police" the developing oral and written traditions about a figure, and the eyewitnesses to Jesus did the same for their teacher.

Objections to Matthean authorship arise, however. One of the main protests is that it is unlikely Matthew could have composed so sophisticated a literary work, as he was likely not trained in Greek literacy to the extent that the First Gospel displays.[9] Bauckham himself argues that this work was related to Matthew or a Matthean school but was not likely written by Matthew himself. However, this literacy objection can also be countered.

First, while it is true that literacy rates were very low, that does not preclude Matthean authorship. It simply makes it less of a possibility. Second, if Matthew was a tax collector it is likely that he did have training in using notebooks and taking notes.[10] This assumes at least some level of literacy. It is hard to imagine a tax collector that is not trained to check balances and collect records. While some of the Jesus tradition certainly was passed down orally, we need to be careful to not construct too strict of a binary between orality and textuality. The lines between these two modes are likely more fluid than not. There is a good possibility that there were notebooks being used to aid in remembrance and transmission of the Jesus teachings.[11] It was common in the Greco-Roman world, among the elites, to take notes to aid in learning. Jews would also use notebooks to aid a pupil's memorization of their rabbi's words. The Qumran scrolls provide first-century evidence of *testimonia* collections (11QMelch) used in the community. We also find reference to a "book" and "parchments" in 2 Tim 4:13, which might be Paul's notebook.

While we don't know for certain who wrote the Gospel of Matthew, the early external evidence does point toward the apostle and former tax collector being the author. With this argument in place, we can now turn to Matt 13:52 that provides a hint that Matthew is the model student of Jesus who has been "trained" or "discipled" to pass the Jesus tradition onto new generations.

10.3 Matthew as a Disciple and Scribe

Matthew 13:52 indicates the type of students Jesus formed.[12] Two sections will be examined here. First, I will show that many view Matt 13:52 as the author's signature. Second, I will look at key terms in Matt 13:52 to describe what type of student Matthew was to his teacher Jesus.

---

[9] For a detailed study on literacy, see Chris Keith, *Jesus' Literacy: Scribal Culture and the Teacher from Galilee*, LNTS 413 (New York, NY: T&T Clark, 2011).

[10] See the arguments for Matthew having some literate skills from E. J. Goodspeed, *Matthew, Apostle and Evangelist* (Philadelphia, PA: J. C. Winston, 1959) and R. H. Gundry, *The Use of the Old Testament in St. Matthew's Gospel* (Leiden: Brill, 1967), 182–5.

[11] Michael F. Bird, *The Gospel of the Lord: How the Early Church Wrote the Story of Jesus* (Grand Rapids, MI: Eerdmans, 2014), 45n69.

[12] Even if one does not agree this verse describes Matthew, it can still function as a verse through which we understand Jesus's students.

10.3.1 Matthew 13:52 as Matthew's Signature

Though there is no explicit claim to authorship in Matthew's Gospel, some think Matthew left his fingerprints in Matt 13:52.[13] Both early and modern interpreters have argued that this verse depicts Jesus's students; some even go further and say it is about Matthew more specifically.

Origen, one of the earliest commentators on Matthew, viewed this verse as representing the disciples as scribes of the kingdom.[14] Jerome, likewise, states, "the apostles, as the scribes and secretaries of the Savior impressed his words and commands on the fleshly tablets of their heart."[15] In the Reformation period, Erasmus Sarcerius says this verse applies to preachers who should be "learned scribes." He continues, "These should teach others after the example of the disciples. They have need of being thoroughly instructed in the doctrine of both the Old and New Testaments."[16] While these authors don't tie the statement directly to Matthew, they do indicate the disciples are the scribes, and therefore Matthew would be among them.

As we turn to the modern period, Krister Stendahl asserted Matt 13:52 may be a veiled reference to the author.[17] C. F. D. Moule asserts Matt 13:52 points to Matthew's secretarial role. He claims:

> The writer of the Gospel was himself a well-educated, literate scribe in this sense. But so much also have been that tax-collector who was called by Jesus to be a disciple. Is it not conceivable that the Lord really did say to that tax-collector Matthew: you have been a "writer" (as the Navy would put it); you have had plenty to do with the commercial side of just the topics alluded to in the parables—farmer's stock, fields, treasure-trove, fishing revenues; now that you have become a disciple, you can bring all this out again—but with a difference.[18]

Moule says this "scribe" (Matthew) collected the Aramaic traditions to form the present Gospel of Matthew, but later Greek scribes wrote this Gospel and collected the traditions from Matthew. While Moule does not argue for apostolic authorship, Moule does give Matthew a prominent role.

---

[13] Just like Mark might have left his fingerprints with the anonymous young man who followed Jesus after his arrest (Mark 14:51–52).
[14] Origen questions how the disciples can be scribes when Acts 4:13 says that they are unlearned and ignorant. His solution is that one becomes a scribe when one receives the teaching of Christ, but on a deeper level when one, having received elementary knowledge through the letter of the Scriptures, ascends to things spiritual. *Commentary on Matthew* 10.15 (*ANF* 10:423); GCS 10:9–10.
[15] Jerome, *Commentary on Matthew*, trans. Thomas P. Scheck (Washington, DC: Catholic University of America Press, 2008), 165.
[16] Erasmus Sarcerius, *In Matthaeum evangelistam* (1538), 193v–94r (see James K. Lee and William M. Marsh, eds., *Matthew*, Reformation Commentary on Scripture, NT vol. 1 (Downers Grove, IL: IVP Academic, 2021), 180.)
[17] Krister Stendahl, *The School of St. Matthew: And Its Use of the Old Testament* (Ramsey: Sigler Press, 1991), 30.
[18] C. F. D. Moule, 'St. Matthew's Gospel: Some Neglected Features', *Studia Evangelica*, vol. 2, TU 87 (Berlin: Akademies-Verlag, 1964), 90–9; reprinted in Moule's *Essays in New Testament Interpretation* (Cambridge: Cambridge University Press, 1982), 67–74.

M. D. Goulder also considers that in this verse "Matthew appends his own signature," while D. E. Orton thinks that the term scribe refers more generally to disciples but also finds a Matthean self-reference in 13:52.[19] D. A. Carson says, "since Jesus' disciples have now understood his parables, they can legitimately be called 'scribe' themselves, as can all of his disciples with a similar understanding."[20] Daniel J. Harrington comments that this "self-portrait of the evangelist" is a very widespread view, one might say almost the universal view.[21]

A larger contextual hint also gives further evidence that Matthew views himself as Jesus's scribe: the first word of his Gospel, βίβλος. Matthew begins his description of the life of Jesus by speaking about his scroll. The scroll was a primary tool of the scribe. If anything defined what the scribe did, it was the surface on which the scribe wrote (βίβλος), the tool they employed (σχοῖνος), and the action of writing itself (γράφω). Therefore, Matthew begins his narrative by speaking of his work as a scroll. He lets his readers know he is the scribe penning the life of Jesus.

All this amounts to the possibility that Matt 13:52 is Matthew's signature on his work. If this is the case, the verse becomes a window through which we can view how Jesus formed his students, maybe even Matthew himself. We now turn to some key terms in this verse that describe what sort of student Matthew was. He was a (1) disciple and (2) scribe who (3) brought forth treasures new and old.

10.3.2 Disciple

The word usually translated as *trained* (μαθητευθείς) is the cognate Greek term for disciple. Matthew's verse could therefore be translated: "Therefore every *discipled scribe* for the kingdom of heaven is like a master of a house, who brings out his treasures new and old."[22] Matthew and other followers of Jesus are disciples.[23]

---

[19] Goulder, *Midrash*, 375; D. E. Orton, *The Understanding Scribe: Matthew and the Apocalyptic Ideal* (London: T&T Clark, 2004), 165–74.

[20] D. A. Carson, "Matthew," in *Matthew and Mark*, EBC 9 (Grand Rapids, MI: Zondervan, 2010), 380.

[21] Daniel J. Harrington, *The Gospel of Matthew*, Sacra Pagina (Collegeville, MN: Liturgical Press, 2007), 208.

[22] The dative phrase τῇ βασιλείᾳ τῶν οὐρανῶν could be taken as sphere (in the kingdom of heaven), respect (concerning the kingdom of heaven), or dative of advantage (for the sake of the kingdom). I lean toward taking it as a dative of advantage or interest. Carson, Orton, and Luz agree. D. A. Carson, "Matthew," in *Matthew & Mark*, vol. 9 of *The Expositor's Bible Commentary* (Grand Rapids, MI: Zondervan, 2010), 380; Ulrich Luz, *Matthew 8–20*, trans. Wilhelm C. Linss, Hermeneia (Minneapolis, MN: Fortress, 2001), 286.

[23] Discipleship in Matthew has been viewed usually under two lenses: redaction criticism or narrative criticism. See Günther Bornkamm, Gerhard Barth, and Heinz Joachim Held, *Tradition and Interpretation in Matthew* (Philadelphia, PA: Westminster Press, 1963); Ulrich Luz, "The Disciples in the Gospel According to Matthew," in *The Interpretation of Matthew*, ed. Graham Stanton, 2nd ed. (Edinburgh: T&T Clark, 1995), 98–128; Mark Sheridan, "Disciples and Discipleship in Matthew and Luke," *BTB* (1973): 235–55; Jeannine K. Brown, *The Disciples in Narrative Perspective: The Portrayal and Function of the Matthean Disciples* (Leiden: Brill, 2002); Michael J. Wilkins, *Discipleship in the Ancient World and Matthew's Gospel*, 2nd ed. (Eugene: Wipf and Stock, 2015); Jack Dean Kingsbury, *Matthew as Story*, 2nd ed. (Philadelphia, PA: Fortress Press, 1988); Richard A. Edwards, "Uncertain Faith: Matthew's Portrait of the Disciples," in *Discipleship in the New Testament*, ed. F. F. Segovia (Philadelphia, PA: Fortress, 1985), 47–61; Edwards, *Matthew's Narrative Portrait of Disciples: How the Text-Connoted Reader is Informed* (Harrisburg: Trinity Press International, 1997). Many of them note that the disciples' understanding functions to highlight Jesus as an effective teacher.

The term μαθητής (disciple) occurs only in the first five books of the NT and appears the most in Matthew and John. Seventy-eight times it appears in Matthew's work. The term means that someone is an adherent, pupil, apprentice, or follower.[24] More specifically, a "disciple" is regularly defined in the realm of knowledge and learning. Jesus even said, "it is enough for the disciple (μαθητῇ) to be like his teacher (διδάσκαλος)" (10:25). According to BDAG (609), μαθητής is "one who engages in *learning* through *instruction* from another" or "one who is rather constantly associated with someone who has a *pedagogical* reputation." A disciple is thus someone who learns, who understands, and who gains wisdom.

This lines up with Matthew's presentation of the disciples as a whole, for as Gerhard Barth (and many others after him) has noted, Matthew omitted or interpreted differently all of the passages in Mark's Gospel that speak of the lack of understanding on the part of the disciples.[25] Barth even claims that the "faith" (πίστις) concept in Paul, John, and Mark is transferred to "understanding" (συνίημι) in Matthew.[26] Whether or not the entirety of Barth's claim is true, the characterization of the Matthean disciples does uniquely highlight their *understanding* of Jesus's teaching.[27] Wilkins claims that Matthew has a special interest in the disciples as literary figures.

Matthew's Gospel is at least in part a manual on discipleship. While all the major discourses directed at least in part to the μαθηταί, and with the disciples called and trained and commissioned to carry out the climactic mandate to "make disciples" in the conclusion of the gospel, Matthew has constructed a gospel that will equip the disciples in the making of disciples.[28]

Matthew is, therefore, a disciple of his teacher.[29] Jesus's statement in Matt 23:8, "You have one teacher," carries with it significance that goes far beyond the immediate context.

---

[24] Wilkins explicitly ties discipleship into the notion of scribes and wise men. Wilkins, *Discipleship in the Ancient World*, 43–91.

[25] Gerhard Barth, "Matthew's Understanding of the Law," in *Tradition and Interpretation in Matthew*, 106. My claim is not that the disciples in Matthew are portrayed only in a positive light—they certainly have conflicting traits. As Donald J. Verseput notes, even at the end of the Gospel, Matthew speaks of their hesitation (28:17) (Verseput, "The Faith of the Reader and the Narrative of Matthew 13.53–16.20," *JSNT* 46 (1992): 3–24).

[26] Though I am not convinced that this transfer can be substantiated, multiple scholars (Conzelmann, Byrskog) note the particular interest of Matthew in "understanding." Nine times Matthew employs συνίημι, but none of them occur before ch. 13, and six of the nine occur in ch. 13 itself (13:13, 14, 15, 19, 23, 51; 15:10; 16:12; 17:13).

[27] See Samuel Byrskog, *Jesus the Only Teacher: Didactic Authority and Translation in Ancient Israel, Ancient Judaism, and the Matthean Community*, Coniectanea Biblica, New Testament Series 24 (Stockholm: Almqvist & Wiksell International, 1994), 221 for a similar suggestion. Sirach claims, "Every *understanding* person knows wisdom ... Those who are *understanding* in words become wise themselves, and pour forth precise parables" (Sir 18:28–29 AT).

[28] Wilkins, *Discipleship in the Ancient World*, 172.

[29] About referring to Jesus as a teacher, R. Riesner claims, "It seems not too risky to assume that this was quite the way in which many contemporaries could have looked at Jesus" ("Jesus as Preacher and Teacher," in *Jesus and the Oral Gospel Tradition*, ed. H. Wansbrough, JSNTSup 64 (Sheffield: JSOT Press, 1991), 185). All four times when Jesus uses "teacher," he speaks to his disciples (10:24, 25; 23:8; 26:17–18). Jesus never speaks of himself directly as a teacher except to the disciples. However, outsiders also identify Jesus as a teacher twice to his disciples (9:10–11; 17:24).

10.3.3 Scribe

Matthew is not only a disciple of Jesus, the teacher of wisdom, but also a discipled *scribe*. Labeling Matthew as a scribe should inform us both of his task and how he will accomplish it. Although the word "scribe" (γραμματεύς) in 13:52 might carry a nontechnical meaning, this does not necessarily mean historical scribal background can't help inform Matthew's usage.[30]

Though it can be tempting to think of scribes merely as those who wrote, most scribes in both Matthew's time and before Matthew's time engaged in at least four activities that mirror and illuminate Matthew's composition: (1) learning (2) writing/interpreting, (3) distributing, (4) teaching.[31]

The first activity of a scribe can be described as learning.[32] All of the rest of these roles and capacities depend on scribes being learned or educated.[33] A scribe is literally "one who knows things." They learned these things from their sages, kings, or public rulers. The OT evidence indicates that scribes were valued for the wisdom and understanding they possessed (1 Chron 27:32), and they were known as "wise" (Isa 33:18; 1 Cor 1:20). Horsley confirms this, saying that the increasing information about scribes in the ancient Near East confirms that the cultivation of wisdom was integrally related to their function.[34]

Ezra, one of the most well-known scribes, is introduced as "a scribe skilled in the Law of Moses that the LORD, the God of Israel, had given" (Ezra 7:6), and "learned in matters of the commandments of the LORD and his statutes for Israel" (7:11). Ezra was responsible not only for reading the Torah to the people (Neh 8:1–8) but also for its study (8:13). Ezra's fundamental commission sounds similar to Matthew's, especially with the emphasis on the "secrets of the kingdom" (Matt 13:11). Ezra was to "write all these things that you have seen in a book; ... and you shall teach them to the wise

---

[30] R. T. France, *The Gospel of Matthew*, NICNT (Grand Rapids, MI: Eerdmans, 2007), 544 asserts, "All that we are told about the background from which the Twelve have come gives us no ground to believe that any of them was a 'scribe' in the normal NT sense." My analysis in this chapter suggests otherwise. Γραμματεύς in BDAG is defined as one who has special functions in connection with documents, but it also includes as a subcategory "an expert in matters relating to divine revelation." BDAG, 206.

[31] David E. Orton, *The Understanding Scribe: Matthew and the Apocalyptic Ideal* (New York: T&T Clark International, 2004), 161-2, comes to a similar conclusion when he says the ideal scribe includes the following elements: (1) the exercise of wisdom and the gift of special understanding; (2) the notion of authority; (3) the notion of righteous teaching, including the right interpretation of the law and the prophets; (4) a close association with true prophecy; and (5) a sense of inspiration. Later in the Christian tradition, scribes were known more only for their copying, but this is not the picture the OT nor one that Matthew presents.

[32] Richard A. Horsley says, "Asking for advice about upcoming events or plans, the scribes searched their repertoire for earlier predictions that might bear on the future events. By interpreting ominous things, wise scribes predicted the future for the king" (Horsley, *Scribes Visionaries, and the Politics of Second Temple Judea* (Louisville, KY: Westminster John Knox Press, 2007), 72).

[33] See Karel van der Toorn, *Scribal Culture and the Making of the Hebrew Bible* (Cambridge, MA: Harvard University Press, 2007), 51–108 on the education of scribes. See Cribiore for Greek education from the time of Alexander the Great to the end of the Roman period. Raffaella Cribiore, *Gymnastics of the Mind: Greek Education in Hellenistic and Roman Egypt* (Princeton, NJ: Princeton University Press, 2005). See Winsbury for Roman book publishing. Rex Winsbury, *The Roman Book: Books, Publishing and Performance in Classical Rome* (London: Duckworth, 2009).

[34] Horsley, *Scribes, Visionaries, and the Politics of Second Temple Judea*, 71.

among your people, whose hearts you know are able to comprehend and keep these secrets" (2 Esd 12:37).

This emphasis on understanding fits perfectly with how Matthew employs the term in 13:51–52. After Jesus has recounted the kingdom parables, he asks them, "'Have you *understood* all these things?' They said to him, 'Yes.'" Then Jesus continues to speak about the scribe. Matthew's Jesus uses the term "scribe" in relation to the disciples precisely because they have understood the parables.[35] A discipled scribe is one who understands the mysteries of the kingdom of heaven.

The second activity of a scribe is *writing*. Having learned, Matthew also transmits his learning to future generations. In Jubilees, Enoch is identified as the first one who learned writing and knowledge and wisdom ... and wrote in a book the signs of heaven (Jub 4:16–18). But scribes in this period were more than just recorders; they were also interpreters. Matthew did not just copy Mark's material, nor did he merely sit down and tell a step-by-step story of Jesus. He adapted his narrative for his own purposes and therefore was a unique type of scribe. There is evidence that Ben Sira similarly adapted wisdom traditions for his own purposes.

This is important to recognize for Matthew's narrative, because he is not just copying down the life of Jesus but also crafting it. As Orton says, Matthew is a "charismatic, creative interpretation of the scriptures in light of ... the eschatological events going on around him."[36] More specifically, he crafts it under the shadow of Jewish history. Thus, we must recognize both faithfulness and flexibility in the role of a scribe. Matthew is the discipled, careful, and creative scribe, bringing out treasures new and old through his writing.[37]

Third, scribes were not only learners and writers, but their writings were also *distributed*. The evidence for this third task comes directly from Matthew. While we might think of scribes as writing notes in a dark room, Matthew gives evidence that scribes were "sent out." In Matt 23:34, Jesus says, "Therefore I send you prophets and wise men and scribes." While the statement from Jesus should probably be interpreted as a "divine sending," this is not opposed to distributing but coheres with it.

Scribes needed their work to be transmitted to have its effect. They wrote, copied, and interpreted so that they could have a public hearing. If they themselves were "sent out," then they would be the natural ones to "read aloud" the copies and interpret them

---

[35] In 13:52 διὰ τοῦτο, then, isn't merely a literary device introducing a saying. Rather, Matthew is using it in a position of climax, linking the two verses together.

[36] Orton, *Understanding Scribe*, 168. Some may be nervous about this language of creativity, assuming that it contradicts the "correct" sense of the OT text. But by using the term "creative," I am simply asserting something similar to Moo and Naselli. "NT authors do not always use OT language as authoritative proof ... So when they appear to deduce a meaning from the OT or when they apply it to a new situation, they are not necessarily misusing the text or treating it as errant" ("Use of the Old Testament," 706). Later (709) they say, "It is unfair to apply a rigid concept of meaning to ... an OT law and then charge him with misinterpreting the OT for going beyond what the OT specifically intends."

[37] See Stephen Westerholm, *Jesus and Scribal Authority*, Coniectanea Biblica, New Testament Series 10 (Lund: CWK Gleerup, 1978). In Matt 2:4 Herod asks "the chief priests and the *scribes* of the people where the Christ was to be born" (emphasis added). "They told him, 'In Bethlehem of Judea, for so it is written by the prophet'" (2:5). They not only copied texts but also answered questions about the texts and therefore interpreted them

for people. The scribe portrayed by Ben Sira "appears before rulers" and "travels in foreign lands" (Sir 39:4). Scribes therefore, it seems, interpreted texts for others and were distributing them as needed. Readers get some sense of this reality when Jesus castigates the scribes and Pharisees in Matt 23 implying they must have been involved in the distribution.

Finally, scribes are also viewed as *teachers* and therefore wise.[38] As Matthew walks with Jesus, he becomes wise. Proverbs 13:20 says, "Whoever walks with the wise becomes wise." Matthew 23:2 also establishes the authority of scribes, with Jesus saying, "The scribes and Pharisees sit on Moses' seat." While Jesus will go onto critique them for how they are using their authority, the assumption is that they should be good teachers. Matthew sets himself up as the authoritative teacher in the same tradition as his rabbi. He presents his Gospel as a learned and trustworthy transmission of Jesus's life and teaching. Readers are therefore not only to learn from Jesus but also to learn from Matthew's presentation of Jesus. Matthew is the discipled, careful, and creative scribe who learns, interprets, distributes, and teaches readers about the Messiah.

10.3.4 Treasures New and Old

We have seen how Matthew was a discipled-scribe, but the task is more clearly defined. A discipled-scribe brings forth treasures both new and old. The word "treasures" (θησαυρός) here is a metaphor for goods in the domain of knowledge. The use of treasures probably reflects the OT wisdom tradition.[39] Proverbs 2:1–8 parallels treasures with wisdom, understanding, and knowledge, while having other conceptual parallels to Matthew's language as emphasized below.

> My son, if you accept my words and store up *my commands* within you, turning your ear to *wisdom* and applying your heart to *understanding*—indeed, if you call out for *insight* and cry aloud for *understanding*, and if you look for it as for silver and search for it as for *hidden treasure*, then you will understand the fear of the Lord and find *knowledge* of God. For the Lord gives *wisdom*; from his mouth comes *knowledge* and *understanding*. He holds success in store for the upright, he is the shield to those whose walk is blameless, for he guards the course of the just and protects the way of his faithful ones. (Prov 2:1–8 NIV, emphasis added)

Colossians 2:3 develops our understanding of these Proverbs by arguing that in Christ are hidden "all the treasures of wisdom and knowledge." The treasure that the discipled scribe is to bring forth is therefore the secrets of the kingdom with Christ himself at

---

[38] This teaching was oral in nature. I don't want to give the false impression that the first-century culture was a reading culture, for it was mainly an oral culture. Thus Isa 29:18 predicts a time when "the deaf shall hear the words of a book." See the first chapter of van der Toorn, *Scribal Culture*. Phillips even argues the verb ἐκβάλλω could have the sense of "speaking" or "expelling" words in Matt 13:52. Peter M. Phillips, "Casting Out the Treasure: A New Reading of Matthew 13.52," *JSNT* 31.1 (2008): 12–13.

[39] Sirach parallels wisdom and treasure in Sir 1:25; 20:30; 41:14 (see also Isa 33:6). Baruch does as well (2 Bar 44:14; 54:13).

the center (Ps 51:6). On at least three occasions, Matthew claims that the disciples "understand" Jesus's teaching (13:51; 16:12; 17:13). The parallel passages in Mark indicate that the disciples do not understand (Mark 6:52; 8:21; 9:10, 32). True disciples of Jesus will understand his teaching in the sense of gaining wisdom.[40]

Matthew further defines what this treasure is, labeling it as both "new and old" (καινὰ καὶ παλαιά; see also 9:17). Many church fathers understood the new and old with reference to the new and old covenants.[41] Jesus is the new, while the old is the Jewish tradition before the time of Jesus. Jesus himself brings out the old, as confirmed in his teaching in Matt 5:17-19, where he says that he has come to fulfill the Law and Prophets.[42]

As a student of Jesus, Matthew, and the other disciples, will also teach in a way that shows the relationship between the new and old. They will confirm the continuation of the old, when rightly understood, while also uncovering how the new clarifies the old. The relevant point for Matthew's Gospel is the new and old come in tandem. Discontinuity and continuity ultimately belong together.[43] However, the word order is important. As Barton observes, "the new has priority over the old."[44] And as Morris says,

> If the word order is significant, the new matters more than the old and Jesus is saying that the new teachings his followers are embracing do not do away the old teachings (those in the Old Testament), but are the key to understanding them. The new age has dawned, and it is only in recognition of that fact that the old can be understood in its essential function of preparing the way for the new.[45]

Matthew is now this discipled scribe who interweaves the new-old paradigm as the key for describing the life of Jesus. As many have pointed out, Matthew is more explicit when engaging the Hebrew Scriptures.[46] He uses the word "fulfillment" far more than the other Gospels. On some estimations, Matthew uses some sixty-one

---

[40] In Exod 35:31, 35 and 36:1 Bezalel and Oholiab are filled with wisdom (σοφίας) and understanding (συνέσεως) to perform a task of understanding (συνίημι). See also Ps 107:43; Prov 21:11; Hos 14:9; Dan 1:4, 17; 2:21; 2 Chr 1:10-12; 2:12-13 where wisdom and understanding are linked.

[41] Irenaeus, *Haer.* 4.9.1. Craig L. Blomberg says it refers to the teaching and meaning of the Hebrew Scriptures while showing how they are fulfilled in the kingdom age (*Matthew*, NAC 22 (Nashville: Holman Reference, 1992), 225).

[42] Sirach parallels the law and prophets with instruction and wisdom (Sir 0.1, 0.5, 0.10)

[43] Donald Hagner, *How New Is the New Testament? First Century Judaism and the Emergence of Christianity* (Grand Rapids, MI: Baker, 2018), 12. Hagner continues by asserting, "While there is a plenty of continuity here, at the same time the extent of newness in the Gospels—and indeed the whole of the NT—is such that an unavoidable discontinuity with Judaism is created. Fulfillment includes forward movement and thus inevitably involves discontinuity" (Hagner, 20).

[44] Stephen C. Barton, "The Gospel of Matthew," in *The Cambridge Companion to the Gospels*, ed. Stephen C. Barton (Cambridge: Cambridge University Press, 2006), 122.

[45] Morris, *Gospel according to Matthew*, 363. Phillips notes the old does precede the new and outside of ecclesiastical commentary, the new before the old only appears three times in the whole of Greek literature. Peter M. Phillips, "Casting Out the Treasure: A New Reading of Matthew 13.52," *JSNT* 31.1 (2008): 19.

[46] Richard B. Hays, *Reading Backwards: Figural Christology and the Fourfold Gospel* (Waco, TX: Baylor University Press, 2016), 106-9.

quotes from the Hebrew Scriptures. According to the NA²⁸, forty of these are explicit citations, and twenty-one are quotations without explicit citation. When allusions (which are harder to quantify) are taken into account, the number soars to about three hundred.⁴⁷ Therefore, the biblical tradition is the lifeblood of Matthew's presentation.

10.4 The Alternate Scribal School

One other argument gives further evidence that Matthew and the other disciples are Jesus's new scribal school. In Matthew's Gospel, Jesus often critiques the scribes of his day. Matthew contains the most references to scribes among the other Gospels and appears to have a special interest in the scribes.

Chris Keith has argued that Jesus, as a teacher, clashes with the scribal authorities.⁴⁸ The conflict between Jesus and the scribal authorities strengthens the idea that Matthew was a part of Jesus's new scribal tradition. Part of the way Jesus combats the scribal elite is through constructing his own scribal school.⁴⁹

The clash of the schools is often centered on Scripture and authority.⁵⁰ In most of the controversy narratives, the debate revolves around the interpretation of the Jewish Scriptures. Matthew says Jesus teaches the people as one with authority, not as their scribes (7:29). The scribes say Jesus is a blasphemer (9:3). They ask for a sign (12:38). The scribal authorities challenge Jesus's disciples for not washing their hands before eating (Matt 15:2). Jesus says he will suffer at the hands of the scribes (16:21; 20:18). The scribes are indignant that the people praise Jesus (21:15). Jesus says the scribes and authorities sit on Moses's seat, but he goes on to critique them (23:2). Most notable is Matt 23, where Jesus goes on a tirade against the scribes and Pharisees.

> Woe to you, scribes and Pharisees, hypocrites! For you lock people out of the kingdom of heaven! (23:13 NRSV)
>
> Woe to you, scribes and Pharisees, hypocrites! For you cross sea and land to make a single convert, and you make the new convert twice as much a child of hell as yourselves. (23:15 NRSV)

---

⁴⁷ Richard B. Hays, *Echoes of Scripture in the Gospels* (Waco, TX: Baylor University Press, 2016), 109.

⁴⁸ Chris Keith, *Jesus against the Scribal Elite: The Origins of the Conflict* (Grand Rapids, MI: Baker Academic, 2014), 6. Keith more specifically argues that Jesus's reputation as an authoritative teacher of the law was itself debated because Jesus was part of the manual-labor populace, a carpenter. The elite class did not like that Jesus claimed authority as an interpreter of the Torah.

⁴⁹ The new scribal school does not need to be understood in the technical sense, but Jesus's disciples are the ones who will transmit the teachings of Jesus to future generations. Most scholars would say that the first clear evidence of scribal schools comes from Ben Sira (Sir 51:23), but it is likely that by around 700 BCE there was an informal class of sages. Proverbs 25:1 speaks of a group of people who produced a body of oral and written wisdom material. Ben Witherington III, *Jesus the Sage: The Pilgrimage of Wisdom* (Minneapolis, MN: Fortress Press, 2000), 4. Later Israelite kings had sage counselors (2 Sam 16:23; 1 King 4:1–19; 10:1). This data is supported by the fact of early scribal schools in Egypt.

⁵⁰ Keith, *Jesus against the Scribal Elite*, 112.

> Woe to you, scribes and Pharisees, hypocrites! For you are like whitewashed tombs, which on the outside look beautiful, but inside they are full of the bones of the dead and of all kinds of filth. (23:27 NRSV)

Jesus continues to pronounce "woes" upon them (23:16, 23, 25, 29). Those linked to the scribes (Pharisees and Sadducees) often ask questions about interpretation. They ask about the Mosaic exceptions to divorce (19:7). The Sadducees attempt to trap Jesus concerning the resurrection (22:23–33). When Jesus goes into the temple (21:12–13), the religious leaders ask him, "By what authority are you doing these things?" (21:23). In summary, they differ on how the new relates to the old—or maybe more precisely, if there is such a thing as "the new."

It is only natural, therefore, that Jesus not only combats hostility but also forms a new community.[51] From the start of his ministry, Jesus gathers a group of disciples to follow him. Jesus may thus be using this term "scribe" in 13:52 to identify his disciples as authorized teachers *for* the kingdom of heaven in contrast with the Pharisaic scribes, who have failed to grasp the message.[52] Jesus urges his disciples to be trained in the ways of the kingdom, so they too can bring out riches new and old and teach and instruct with the authority that has been given to Jesus.

This view is supported by other texts in Matthew, where he subtly associates scribes and disciples. In Matt 8:19, it says, "And *a scribe* came up and said to him, 'Teacher, I will follow you wherever you go'" (emphasis added). Notice this scribe comes to his "teacher" (διδάσκαλος) and says, "I will follow [ἀκολουθέω] you." The Greek word for "follow" is the dominant term Matthew uses for the disciples. This is confirmed when the text says in 8:21, "Another of *his disciples* said, 'Lord, …'" The sequence implies that there is some overlap between the idea of scribe and disciple.[53] This is confirmed as Matthew elsewhere explicitly connects scribes/disciples to the title of teacher throughout his Gospel (9:11; 10:24–25; 12:38; 17:24; 22:16).

One final example correlates scribes and disciples. After Jesus castigates the scribes and Pharisees, he says this:

> Therefore I send you prophets, sages, and scribes, some of whom you will kill and crucify, and some you will flog in your synagogues and pursue from town to town. (23:34, NRSV)

Jesus speaks in the present tense. Interestingly, Jesus does not say that he sends them evangelists, apostles, or disciples; he uses this alternative triad now in a positive sense. The implication is clear. He does so in contrast to the "scribes" whom he has just condemned. He censures one group and forms another. But the religious leaders will only kill, crucify, flog, and persecute these new messengers.

---

[51] John Yueh-Han Yieh, *One Teacher: Jesus' Teaching Role in Matthew's Gospel Report*, BZNW 124 (Berlin: Walter de Gruyter, 2004). Matthew also emphasizes the small size of the group of disciples and contrasts the disciples with two other groups in his Gospel: the crowd and the religious leaders.

[52] I am thus taking the dative as indicating advantage or interest.

[53] Robert H. Gundry, "Short Studies on True and False Disciples in Matthew 8.18–22," NTS 40 (1994): 433–41.

In the narrative, readers have already heard about Jesus sending out his disciples, but nothing more has been made of their mission since then. Here that mission picks up again, and Jesus describes his "sent ones" positively as scribes. These scribes will find themselves in opposition to the "scribes" of the day, and therefore they represent an alternative school that Jesus is forming.

Thus, in at least three places (8:19; 13:52; 23:34) Matthew correlates scribes and disciples. Although scribes are regularly perceived as the group of characters who oppose Jesus, Matthew speaks of the scribe in a positive sense and probably in contrast to those who oppose him, the trained scribe of the kingdom of heaven who wisely brings out treasures new and old.

10.5 Conclusion

In this chapter, I have argued that Matthew is a disciple of Jesus, but I argued even more than that. Matthew is not only a disciple, but an apostle; he is not only an apostle, but the very author of this work. He is therefore a faithful student, scribe, and transmitter of the Jesus tradition. External evidence points in this direction, and while not much internal evidence allows us to make this conclusion, Matt 13:52 may stand as an authorial signature.

Through Matt 13:52 we can see that Matthew (or Jesus's students more generally) was trained by his teacher to become a scribe who would bring forth treasures both new and old. Matthew serves as his teacher's envoy or representative as he delivers this message to new generations. This is precisely what Jesus called his followers to do on the mountain in Galilee: *make disciples* of all nations *by teaching* them to observe all that Jesus said (Matt 28:19–20). Matthew took this command literally. He wrote about Jesus for future generations.

11

The Influence of Matthew's Gospel on the Petrine Letters

Dennis R. Edwards

11.1 Introduction

Both NT letters that bear Peter's name appear to rely—at least to some degree—on the tradition behind Matthew's Gospel. Several places within 1 Peter coincide with Matthew's Gospel, particularly the Sermon on the Mount. A few verses in 2 Peter reverberate with Matthew, especially 1:16–18, which recalls Jesus's Transfiguration in Matt 17:1–13. This chapter discusses various connections between Matthew and the Petrine letters but focuses primarily on one passage in each letter to spotlight how Matthew's Gospel helps to frame the mission of the readers of both Petrine letters. Some might narrowly define Christian mission as referring primarily to evangelistic preaching and other activities designed to convert non-Christians, but others allow for *mission* to have a broader focus. As Christopher J. H. Wright insists, "Mission is what the Bible is all about."[1] A robust notion of *mission*, such as Wright's, includes the paraenetical sections of NT letter-writers, which offer instruction intended to guide Christian communities in all areas, not merely in communicating a formal *kerygma* to outsiders. Part of mission, for example, is the way that Christians deal with opposition, which is the central message in both 1 and 2 Peter. The Christian recipients of 1 Peter, predominately converted gentiles, are ostracized, blasphemed, and otherwise alienated, which seems to be the reason why Peter refers to them as *parepidēmos* ("resident alien" in 1:1 and 2:11) and *paroikos* ("sojourner," "exile" in 2:11). In 2 Peter, opposition emerges from *pseudodidaskaloi* ("false teachers" in 2:1), so the author urges faithfulness to Christ and to apostolic teaching. Scholars have long been aware of various sayings of Jesus as recorded in Matthew's Gospel that resonate with aspects of 1 Peter, but this chapter explores a connection between 1 Pet 1:1–2 and

---

[1] Christopher J. H. Wright, *The Mission of God: Unlocking the Bible's Grand Narrative* (Downers Grove, IL: IVP Academic, 2006), 29. Wright defines Christian mission as "our committed participation as God's people, at God's invitation and command, in God's own mission within the history of God's world for the redemption of God's creation" (23). Wright goes on to develop a missional hermeneutic as a framework for reading Scripture with a view to participating in God's redemptive work. Michael J. Gorman, ed., *Scripture and Its Interpretation: A Global, Ecumenical Introduction to the Bible*, Annotated edition (Grand Rapids, MI: Baker Academic, 2017), 416, defines missional hermeneutics as "an interpretative approach that emphasizes engaging Scripture to discern and participate in the *missio Dei*."

Matt 28:18–20 that is not often considered. Furthermore, I highlight how Matthew's account of Jesus's Transfiguration, recounted in 2 Pet 1:16–18, serves to strengthen the author's message. Both passages, 1 Pet 1:1–2 and 2 Pet 2:16–18, prepare readers for their mission of engaging social, ethical, and ideological adversaries. In the two Petrine epistles, Matthew's Gospel provides material that shaped how the authors equipped their readers for Christian witness in their contexts. After discussing authorship and the literary influences on both letters, this chapter delves into ways that Matthew's Gospel rests behind 1 Pet 1:1–2 and 2 Pet 1:16–18.

11.2 Authorship

The argument of this chapter does not depend upon resolving the question of authorship of either epistle, but it is important to note that some scholars allege both letters to be pseudonymous. For those who consider Peter to be the author of either—or both—letters, echoes of Jesus's sayings and stories of his actions might serve as evidence of the historical Peter's association with Jesus. Some have indeed argued that Gospel echoes (including but not limited to Matthew) demonstrate Petrine authorship.[2] However, some scholars consider the same evidence and surmise that the letters, in reflecting a direct dependence on the Synoptic Gospels—written after Peter's martyrdom—mean that Peter could not have written the letters that bear his name.[3] This chapter does not make a case for Petrine authorship but does suggest that Jesus, according to Matthew's Gospel, provides language and imagery that undergirds the letters' messages.

11.3 First Peter's Literary Influences

Beyond the obvious influence of Greco-Roman letters, there are at least a few other literary works that likely influenced 1 Peter. The LXX is a significant factor in 1 Peter, as the letter relies upon quotations (e.g., use of Lev 19:2 in 1:16), as well as numerous allusions (e.g., 2:9 drawing on Exod 19:6).[4] While 1 Peter depends upon the LXX, as well as other Jewish literature, such as *1 Enoch*, scholarly debate surrounds the letter's use of Pauline material.[5] A reading of 1 Peter reveals several phrases and notions that resonate with Pauline ideas.[6]

---

[2] Note upcoming discussion of Robert H. Gundry, "'Verba Christi' in 1 Peter: Their Implications Concerning the Authorship of 1 Peter and the Authenticity of the Gospel Tradition," *NTS* 13.4 (1967): 336–50 and "Further Verba on Verba Christi in First Peter," *Bib* 55 (1974): 211–32.

[3] Also see Ernest Best, "1 Peter and the Gospel Tradition," *NTS* 16.2 (1970): 95–113. Best (95) points out, "It should be remembered that knowledge of the gospel tradition on the part of any author in the N. T. does not logically imply that he was present when that part of the gospel tradition was spoken by Jesus, otherwise we should have to argue that Paul was present when certain sayings of Jesus were spoken."

[4] Paul J. Achtemeier, *1 Peter*, Hermeneia (Minneapolis, MN: Fortress, 1996), 6–7.

[5] See my summary of the arguments in Dennis R. Edwards, "Participation in Christ in 1 Peter," in *Cruciform Scripture: Cross, Participation, and Mission*, ed. Nijay K. Gupta, Andy Johnson, Christopher W. Skinner, Drew J. Strait (Grand Rapids, MI: Eerdmans, 2021), 146–8.

[6] Two examples are 2:21 and 3:18a where Christ's vicarious suffering serves as both example and motivation for the beleaguered Christians in Anatolia.

Perhaps there is common Christian tradition that explains the similarities between 1 Peter and Pauline writings.[7]

The Gospels are another influence on 1 Peter, and relevant for this chapter. First Peter's use of the Gospels suggests that the sayings of Jesus and possibly the historical Peter's personal recollections are contained in the letter. Several decades ago (late 1960s into the early 1970s), Robert Gundry wrote two essays exploring the *verba Christi* in 1 Peter with a view to establish Petrine authorship.[8] Between the publication of Gundry's essays, Ernst Best evaluated 1 Peter's alleged dependence upon the Gospel tradition and concluded the opposite of Gundry that, "There is no reason to conclude that the Apostle Peter wrote 1 Peter."[9] About a decade after the Gundry and Best essays, German scholar Gerhard Maier investigated 1 Peter's possible dependence upon the Jesus tradition in the Gospels.[10] Maier starts his analysis by delving into the passages that Gundry and Best discussed, observing that both authors assume some association between 1 Peter and the Gospel tradition, even if they draw opposite conclusions regarding authorship of the epistle.[11] Maier notes echoes of the words of Christ in 1 Peter, especially in what he considered to be brief catechetical material (*Kurzcatechismen*) and acknowledges that the author of 1 Peter had some Jesus tradition available, orally or in some early written state.[12] Maier, however, draws attention away from the words of Jesus and places it more broadly on what 1 Peter and the Gospels have in common concerning Jesus's life and ministry, concluding, "*Jedenfalls sind für den 1. Petr die Berichte vom Geschick Jesu ebenso wichtig die verba Christi* ("At any rate, for 1 Peter the reports of the fate

---

[7] After surveying several passages, David G. Horrell, *1 Peter*, NTG (New York: T&T Clark, 2008), 38, offers an assessment that respects the similarities and differences between 1 Peter and Pauline epistles:

> What these various examples show is that there are indeed close points of contact between 1 Peter and the Pauline tradition. The parallels do not suggest that there is a literary relationship between the texts, such as we see between the three Synoptic Gospels since the overlaps in wording are generally few and imprecise. But they do suggest that the author of 1 Peter knows and uses in his letter some forms and turns of phrase that reflect some knowledge of Paul's letters. However, this does not mean that we should regard 1 Peter as essentially "Pauline" in character ... 1 Peter has its own distinctive character, its own particular use of tradition.

[8] Gundry, "'Verba Christi' in 1 Peter: Their Implications Concerning the Authorship of 1 Peter and the Authenticity of the Gospel Tradition," *NTS* 13.4 (1967): 336–50 and "Further Verba on Verba Christi in First Peter," *Bib* 55 (1974): 211–32.

[9] Ernest Best, "1 Peter and the Gospel Tradition," in *NTS* 16.2 (1970): 95–113 (here, 112).

[10] Gerhard Maier, "Jesustradition im 1. Petrusbrief?" in *The Jesus Tradition Outside the Gospels*, ed. David Wenham, GP 5 (Sheffield: JSOT Press, 1984), 85–128.

[11] Maier, "Jesustradition," 86, "Dennoch sollten wir nicht übersehen, daß es zumindest eine Gemeinsamkeit zwischen Gundry und Best gibt: Beide nehmen tatsächliche Kontakte zwischen 1. Petr und der Evangelientradition an. Offen bleibt die Frage, wieweit sie reichen" ("However, we should not overlook that there is at least one commonality between Gundry and Best: both assume actual "contacts" between 1 Pet and the Gospel tradition. The question remains as to how far they go." My translation).

[12] Maier, "Jesustradition," 118, "dann neigt sich die Waage bezüglich aller Jesuslogien zugunsten der Annahme, daß Petrus unabhängig von den kanonischen Evangelien Jesustradition—mündlich oder in vorläufigen Notizen—zur Verfügung hatte." ("Then, with regard to all Jesus sayings, the scale tips in favor of the assumption that Peter had Jesus tradition available—orally or in preliminary notes—independently of the canonical gospels." My translation).

of Jesus are just as important as the words of Christ").[13] Questions linger concerning the extent to which 1 Peter directly depends upon the Gospels, but commonalities between the documents are evident.

With respect to Matthew's Gospel, which is the primary focus of this chapter, there are several resonances with 1 Peter—linguistic or conceptual—especially from the Sermon on the Mount, as Table 11.1 illustrates (see below).[14]

In most cases, similar or duplicate vocabulary is what connects Matthew and 1 Peter, but as in the case of 1 Pet 2:13-15 and Matt 17:24-27, which both address responsibility to the government, some parallels are conceptual. Ulrich Luz urges that "we must seriously consider the likelihood that 1 Peter presupposes the Gospel of Matthew."[15] Luz cites Rainer Metzner, who argues for a direct literary connection between Matthew's Gospel and 1 Peter.[16]

Metzner devotes most of his analysis to 1 Peter's relationship to sections contained within Matt 4-6.[17] John H. Elliott finds several shortcomings with Metzner's work, such as his reliance upon a few common terms to prove literary dependence (e.g., *doxa* ("glory") and *kala erga* ("good works") in 1 Pet 2:12 and Matt 5:16), and also that Metzner's suggestion that 1 Peter's readers' situation mirrors that of Matthew's readers is insufficient to explain why the letter depends upon the Gospel.[18] Proving literary dependence is a high bar to vault over, and the various analyses do not yield definitive results. Horrell points out that while there may be some value in exploring the Jesus tradition to discern the *verba Christi* in writings such as 1 Peter, a different (and perhaps better) question is "What kind of image of Jesus is presented in 1 Peter?"[19] Horrell proceeds to explain the role of Isa 53 in shaping the image of Jesus in 1 Peter. This chapter respects the admonition of Horrell and does not seek to make a direct linguistic connection between Matthew's Gospel and 1 Peter, but neither does it focus solely on the image of Jesus, per se. The emphasis of this chapter is 1 Peter's apparent

---

[13] Maier, "Jesustradition," 118 (My translation).
[14] See Gundry, "Verba Christi," 337-50; Horrell, *1 Peter*, 35-6; Maier, "Jesustradition," 87-105.
[15] Ulrich Luz *Matthew 1-7: A Commentary*, trans. Helmut Koester, Hermeneia (Minneapolis, MN: Fortress, 2007), 59.
[16] Rainer Metzner, *Die Rezeption Des Matthäusevangeliums im 1. Petrusbrief: Studien zum traditionsgeschichtlichen und theologischen Einfluss des 1. Evangeliums auf den 1. Petrusbrief*, WUNT 74 (Tübingen: J.C.B. Mohr, 1995). Metzner concludes, "Die vorliegende Arbeit hat gezeigt, daß das Matthäusevangelium in vielfältiger Weise den 1. Petrusbrief beeinflußt hat. Traditionen, Motive und Gedanken, die für das 1. Evangelium charakteristisch sind, werden im Brief entsprechend den Erfordenissen und Bedingungen der Adressatengemeinden aufgenommen, variert, interpretiert un aktualisiert." "This work has shown that the Gospel of Matthew influenced 1 Peter in many ways. Traditions, motifs and thoughts characteristic of the first gospel are taken up, varied, interpreted and updated in the epistle according to the addressees' needs and conditions" (my translation).
[17] Metzner compares Matt 5:10 and 1 Pet 3:14; Matt 5:11 and 1 Pet 4:13; Matt 5:16 and 1 Pet 2:12; Matt 5:38-48 and 1 Pet 3:9 and 1:15; Matt 4:1-11 and 6:25-34 with 1 Pet 5:6-9. He also compares the ecclesiology, Christology, and eschatology that he finds in Matthew and 1 Peter.
[18] John H. Elliott, "Review of Rainer Metzner, *Die Reception des Matthäusevangelium im 1. Petrusbrief*," *JBL* 116 (1997): 379-82.
[19] David G. Horrell, "Jesus Remembered in 1 Peter? Early Jesus Traditions, Isaiah 53, and 1 Peter 2.21-25," in *James, 1 & 2 Peter, and Early Jesus Traditions*, LNTS 478, ed. Alicia J. Batten and John S. Kloppenborg (New York: Bloomsbury, 2014), 123-50.

Table 11.1 First Peter and the Sermon on the Mount

1 Peter	Matthew
For it is written, "You shall be holy, for I am holy" (1:15).	"Be perfect, therefore, as your heavenly Father is perfect" (5:48).
Conduct yourselves honorably among the Gentiles, so that, though they malign you as evildoers, they may see your honorable deeds (*kalōn ergōn*) and glorify (*doxasōsin*) God when he comes to judge (2:12).	In the same way, let your light shine before others, so that they may see your good works (*kala erga*) and give glory (*doxasōsin*) to your Father in heaven (5:16).
For the Lord's sake accept the authority of every human institution, whether of the emperor as supreme, or of governors, as sent by him to punish those who do wrong and to praise those who do right. For it is God's will that by doing right you should silence the ignorance of the foolish (2:13–15).	When they reached Capernaum, the collectors of the temple tax came to Peter and said, "Does your teacher not pay the temple tax?" He said, "Yes, he does." And when he came home, Jesus spoke of it first, asking, "What do you think, Simon? From whom do kings of the earth take toll or tribute? From their children or from others?" When Peter said, "From others," Jesus said to him, "Then the children are free. However, so that we do not give offense to them, go to the sea and cast a hook; take the first fish that comes up; and when you open its mouth, you will find a coin; take that and give it to them for you and me" (17:24–27).
Do not repay evil for evil or abuse for abuse; but, on the contrary, repay with a blessing. It is for this that you were called—that you might inherit a blessing (3:9).	You have heard that it was said, "An eye for an eye and a tooth for a tooth." But I say to you, Do not resist an evildoer. But if anyone strikes you on the right cheek, turn the other also ... You have heard that it was said, "You shall love your neighbor and hate your enemy." But I say to you, Love your enemies and pray for those who persecute you (5:38–39, 43–44).
But even if you do suffer for doing what is right, you are blessed (*makarioi*) (3:14a).	Blessed (*makarioi*) are those who are persecuted for righteousness' sake, for theirs is the kingdom of heaven (5:10).
But rejoice insofar as you are sharing Christ's sufferings, so that you may also be glad and shout for joy when his glory is revealed. If you are reviled for the name of Christ, you are blessed, because the spirit of glory, which is the Spirit of God, is resting on you (4:13–14).	Blessed are you when people revile you and persecute you and utter all kinds of evil against you falsely on my account. Rejoice and be glad, for your reward is great in heaven, for in the same way they persecuted the prophets who were before you (5:11–12).

use of elements of a Matthean presentation of apostolic mission, particularly the one found in the so-called Great Commission of Matt 28:18–20.

11.4 Matthew's Gospel and 1 Peter's Mission

First Peter 1:1–2 addresses the recipients as if to prepare them for their mission of engaging an unsympathetic society, which Peter elaborates upon throughout the letter.

The mission is not explicitly preaching, although oral defense may at times be required (cf. 3:15), but the main task of the recipients is faithful endurance within a hostile environment. The idiosyncratic greeting, where Peter establishes his authority and addresses the readers with a trinitarian formulation possessing baptismal undertones, is reminiscent of Matt 28:18–20, a passage not found in the other Gospels.[20] Peter's vocabulary is distinct from Matthew's, but the overall tenor of the letter's opening is evocative of the end of Matthew's Gospel. Peter's prescript identifies him as *apostle of Jesus Christ*, thereby noting his authority to represent the risen Lord.[21] While there is nothing surprising about Peter's use of *apostle*, he does so here to establish his receipt of divine authorization to address vulnerable Christians similarly to the way the risen Christ spoke to his remaining eleven disciples in Matt 28:16–20. Peter's authority to guide his readers in their mission among "the nations" suggests—but does not establish—his familiarity with Jesus's commission at the end of Matthew's Gospel.[22] In 1 Pet 5:1, the author connects himself explicitly to Jesus Christ's earthly ministry, claiming to be an eyewitness of Christ's sufferings, but here in the letter's opening salutation Peter primarily establishes his authoritative voice as he admonishes the Christians of Pontus, Galatia, Cappadocia, Asia, and Bithynia.[23] Peter's first words are reminiscent of the Lord's final words, at least as they appear in Matthew's Gospel. The commonality between the passages is not primarily linguistic, but instead establishes or reinforces the nature of Christian witness, particularly to "the nations." After his resurrection from the dead, the Lord Jesus Christ could assert that he possessed divine authority to commission his disciples for mission, which involved baptism and catechesis. The apostles are to initiate new converts into the church by baptizing in water and teaching obedience to Jesus's instructions. Peter acts similarly to Jesus, by first noting his authority, then addressing the Anatolian Christians, specifically with regard to their witness among the various *ethne*. Elliott's discussion of 1 Pet 1:1 cites Matt 28:16–20 (along with Pauline passages 1 Cor 15:3–11; Rom 1:1; Gal 1:1), observing that "the Christian concept of *apostle* is linked essentially and theologically with a personal encounter with, and commissioning by, Jesus the resurrected Christ."[24] Edward Gordon Selwyn points out that the Pauline usage of *apostle* is typically accompanied by "some conditioning phrase or adjective."[25] A closer look at Elliott's references bear out Selwyn's point:

---

[20] Strictly speaking, "trinitarian" is anachronistic since 1 Peter predates any formal creedal declarations of the Trinity. Yet, subsequent declarations emerged from passages such as 1 Pet 1:2 and Matt 28:19.
[21] E.g., Achtemeier, *1 Peter*, 80; Craig S. Keener, *1 Peter: A Commentary* (Grand Rapids, MI: Baker Academic, 2021), 43.
[22] Matt 16:13–20 describes the unique apostolic role that Jesus gives to Peter. First Peter does not directly refer to that Matthean episode, but Gundry finds the epistle's use of the stone motif in 2:4–8 to be an allusion to the Gospel (see Gundry, "'Verba Christi' in 1 Peter," 346).
[23] The need to establish authority might have been especially necessary if the author is indeed the Peter we meet in the Gospels, since he may not have been an evangelist in Asia Minor. See, e.g., Keener, *1 Peter*, 44. Achtemeier, who does not think Peter wrote 1 Peter, understands the apostolic designation as providing the letter a hearing "despite the fact that Peter had not been a missionary to the areas addressed" (*1 Peter*, 80–1).
[24] Elliott, *1 Peter*, 310.
[25] Edward Gordon Selwyn, *The First Epistle of St. Peter* (London: Macmillan, 1946), 117.

Paul, a servant of Jesus Christ, called to be an apostle, set apart for the gospel of God. (Rom 1:1)

Paul an apostle—sent neither by human commission nor from human authorities, but through Jesus Christ and God the Father, who raised him from the dead. (Gal 1:1)

One could cite additional examples of Pauline usage, but the point is that Peter does not qualify his use of *apostle* and consequently places emphasis on the sender rather than the one being sent.[26] The "fullest articulation of the developing concept of *apostle*," according to Elliott, is found in the Pauline and Deutero-Pauline writings, "often when Paul feels called upon to defend his apostolic credentials."[27] On the contrary, Peter does not use *apostle* as a defense, in the way that Paul often did, but simply to point out the divine authority he has to direct the Christians in their mission—that is, how they are to live with each other and also how to demonstrate the teachings of Jesus to unbelieving onlookers. Furthermore, Paul relays the tradition that Peter was the first of the Twelve to see the risen Lord Jesus (1 Cor 15:3–8).[28]

Scholars continue to explore the significance of Peter's terms for the addressees, the details of which are beyond this chapter.[29] Yet, the effect of the terms *eklektos* ("chosen"), *parepidēmos* ("resident alien"), and *diaspora* ("dispersion") is to conjure an image of a community near to God but ethically and socially far away from the broader society. Matthew's readers, although predominately Jewish while 1 Peter's readers were mostly gentile, likely found themselves similarly at odds with their neighbors (e.g., Matt 5:11), yet encouraged to see God as close—like a parent (e.g., Matt 6:9; cf. 1 Pet 1:3).[30] Despite the intriguing descriptions Peter uses, the way he conceptualizes the recipients' initiation into God's family is of greater relevance than the appellations. Verse 2 refers to the readers in ways that suggest the baptism and catechesis of converts, reminiscent of the way Matt 28:19–20 presents baptism and the teaching of Jesus's commands.

First Peter 1:2 contains three prepositional phrases, referring to God the Father, the Spirit, and Jesus Christ, a construction unique among letter openings in the NT.[31] These four passages are similar to 1 Pet 1:2 in that they refer to the Father, Son, and Spirit in relatively close proximity:

- "The grace of the Lord Jesus Christ, the love of God, and the communion of the Holy Spirit be with all of you" (2 Cor 13:13), a closing doxology.

---

[26] Achtemeier, *1 Peter*, 80.
[27] Elliott, *1 Peter*, 310.
[28] Ibid.
[29] All the exegetical commentaries examine the terms "elect," "exile," and "diaspora" and how Peter's readers may have understood those notions. Recent examples include Keener, *1 Peter*, 42–8, and Dennis R. Edwards, *1 Peter*, SGBC (Grand Rapids, MI: Zondervan, 2017), 20–1; 29–31.
[30] Peter seems to be incorporating his gentile readers into Israel's story so as to create for them a new family that possess a long history of relating to God. See Shively T. J. Smith, *Strangers to Family: Diaspora and 1 Peter's Invention of God's Household* (Waco, TX: Baylor University Press, 2016), 17–43.
[31] See Achtemeier, *1 Peter*, 86.

- "There is one body and one Spirit, just as you were called to the one hope of your calling, one Lord, one faith, one baptism, one God and Father of all, who is above all and through all and in all" (Eph 4:4–6), part of an appeal to unity but also with a reference to baptism.
- "But we must always give thanks to God for you, brothers and sisters beloved by the Lord, because God chose you as the first fruits for salvation through sanctification by the Spirit and through belief in the truth" (2 Thess 2:13), part of an ethical appeal, yet similar to 1 Pet 1:2 in stating that God chooses and the Spirit sanctifies.
- "But you, beloved, build yourselves up on your most holy faith; pray in the Holy Spirit; keep yourselves in the love of God; look forward to the mercy of our Lord Jesus Christ that leads to eternal life" (Jude 20–21), as part of a closing appeal for fidelity.

Yet Peter's proto-trinitarian formulation has Father, Spirit, and Son closer together than in the other occurrences.[32] In 1 Pet 1:1–2, God's foreknowledge assures the readers of their divine status—their election—despite the ominous circumstances in which they find themselves. It is the Spirit who consecrates, or sanctifies, or sets apart these Christians. The sprinkling of Jesus's blood refers to the Lord's sacrificial death and also recalls OT acts designed to signify purity (e.g., Exod 29:16, 20–21). For the early Christian readers, the sprinkling of blood may have also reminded them of their baptism.[33] The joining of obedience with the sprinkling of Jesus's blood—an act of ritual cleansing—connects to the baptism and teaching of Matt 28:19–20.[34] While Achtemeier ultimately finds only the Exodus imagery to be behind the "sprinkling of Jesus Christ's blood," he does note how the combination of sprinkling, obedience, and the "triadic reference to God used in the baptism ceremony" leads some commentators to take 1:2 as referring to baptism.[35] Baptism in water is not a foreign topic for Peter, as he refers to it in 3:21. Perhaps it is not far-fetched to consider the combination of the elements (sprinkling, obedience, and proto-trinitarian reference) in 1:2 to be at least an allusion to baptism. And such allusion points to the uniquely Matthean commission and its baptismal formula rather than Luke's depiction of Peter in Acts 2:38 calling for baptism with a non-trinitarian formula: "in the name of Jesus Christ." Of course, we cannot prove that 1 Pet 1:1–2 is evidence of the historic Peter's recollection of the

---

[32] Keener, *1 Peter*, 59.
[33] Note the association of sprinkling and water in Heb 9:19; 10:22. More recent commentators seem less inclined to see any allusion to baptism, but note older works, such as Selwyn, *First Epistle of St. Peter*, 119–20; J. N. D. Kelly, *A Commentary on the Epistles of Peter and of Jude*, BNTC (London: A. & C. Black, 1969), 43–4. Also, Elliott, *1 Peter*, 320, notes that earlier commentator Leonhard Goppelt may have a point in seeing an allusion to baptism in 1:2 but suggests that "it is the theme of election rather than the process of baptism that is the focus here, as Goppelt also acknowledges." Ceslas Spicq, *Les Épîtres de Saint Pierre*, Sources Bibliques (Paris: Librairie Lecoffre. J. Gabalda & Cie, 1966), 14–15, discusses how some commentators considered 1 Peter to be a baptism homily.
[34] The syntax is notoriously difficult. The phrase is literally, "*eis hypakoēn kai rhantismon haimatos Iēsou Christou*" and could be rendered "for obedience and sprinkling of Jesus Christ's blood." Most commentators take obedience to refer to the readers, but Joel B. Green, *1 Peter*, THNTC (Grand Rapids, MI: Eerdmans, 2007), 19–20, relates obedience to Jesus's life of faithfulness.
[35] Achtemeier, *1 Peter*, 88–9.

Lord's commission in Matthew, but the parallel is distinct, intriguing, and not usually treated in detail.

First Peter 1:1–2 might contain an echo of Matt 28:18-20 in that both passages establish the divine authority of the commissioner, both offer a triadic, or proto-trinitarian formulation, both refer to ritual cleansing, and both admonish obedience. Furthermore, both commissions prepare followers of Jesus to be witnesses among *ethne* ("nations"): Matt 28:19; cf., 1 Pet 2:12. Both the Great Commission and 1 Peter's opening address serve a preparatory missional function. Matthew 28:18-20 prepares the disciples to represent Jesus in the work of making more disciples and 1 Pet 1:1–2— through Peter's peculiar terms of identification, which likely invigorates the faith of his readers—prepares Christians in Anatolia to represent Jesus among unbelieving and hostile neighbors. Likewise, 2 Pet 1:16-19 serves a preparatory role in that the author establishes their authority to address the readers in a way to bolster faith as the community engages false teaching concerning Jesus. Matthew's Gospel rests behind the author's testimony and is one of several probable influences on 2 Peter.

11.5 Second Peter's Literary Influences

The list of possible influences on 2 Peter includes not only the LXX and other Hellenistic Jewish Literature—as with 1 Peter—but also Petrine Pseudepigrapha and the writings of the Apostolic Fathers.[36] There are few LXX quotations (e.g., Ps 89:4 at 2 Pet 3:8), but several mentions of OT people and events (e.g., fallen angels, the flood, Noah, Sodom and Gomorrah, Lot, and Balaam in 2 Pet 2). Also, most scholars, noting the similarities between Jude and 2 Peter, conclude that 2 Peter depends upon Jude and not vice versa. Interestingly, even though 2 Peter proports to be the second letter from Peter (2 Pet 3:1), there is no clear dependence upon 1 Peter.[37] Pauline writings, however, are a factor in 2 Pet 3:15-16, where the author refers to Paul's letters as scripture. Yet, there seems to be no direct connection to Paul's letters beyond that mention in 3:15-16.[38] More pertinent for this chapter is 2 Peter's dependence upon the canonical Gospels, especially Matthew.

Bauckham identifies "four certain allusions to gospel traditions" in 2 Peter: John 21:18 in 2 Pet 1:14; Matt 17:1-13 (and Synoptic parallels of the Transfiguration) in 1:16-18; Matt 12:45 (// Luke 11:26) in 2:20; Matt 24:43 (// Luke 12:39) in 3:10.[39]

---

[36] See Richard J. Bauckham, *Jude, 2 Peter*, WBC 50 (Waco, TX: Word, 1983), 148-9; Jörg Frey, *Letter of Jude and the Second Letter of Peter: A Theological Commentary*, tran. Kathleen Ess (Waco, TX: Baylor University Press, 2018), 179-82. There are, of course, many commentaries on Jude and 2 Peter, but Frey and Bauckham not only provide depth, they also diverge at points, making them helpful conversation partners for my analysis.

[37] See Frey, *Jude and Second Peter*, 192-4; Bauckham, *Jude, 2 Peter*, 143-7.

[38] Frey, *Jude and Second Peter*, 194-6; Bauckham, *Jude, 2 Peter*, 147-8.

[39] Bauckham, *Jude, 2 Peter*, 148. Bauckham also includes possible allusions: Mark 9:1 (// Matt 16:28) in 1:16 Matt 6:13 in 2:9; Mark 9:42; 14:21 in 2:21; Mark 9:1 in 3:4. See also Terrance Callan, "The Gospels of Matthew and John in the Second Letter of Peter," in *James, 1 & 2 Peter, and Early Jesus Traditions*, LNTS 478, ed. Alicia J. Batten and John S. Kloppenborg (New York: Bloomsbury, 2014), 166-80.

Matthew's Gospel is responsible for most of the Gospel allusions in 2 Peter, and his account of Jesus's Transfiguration may be behind 1:16–18, a passage that prepares the readers to take on their mission of representing Christ in their context.[40] One of the clearest points of connection are the following phrases (Table 11.2).

Table 11.2 Second Peter and the Sermon on the Mount

Matt 7:5	2 Pet 1:17
houtos estin ho hyios mou ho agapētos en hō eudokēsa "this is my beloved son, in whom I am well pleased" (my translation)	*ho hyios mou ho agapētos mou estin eis hon ego eudokēsa* "this is my son—my beloved—in whom I am well pleased" (my translation)

While there are different emphases in the two passages, it is significant that the other Synoptic accounts of the Transfiguration do not have *en hō eudokēsa*.[41] Even so, Matthew's Transfiguration episode reflected in 2 Pet 1:16–18 is not as much about linguistic similarities as it is about its apologetic function in developing the mission described in the letter.

11.6 Matthew's Gospel and 2 Peter's Mission

The mission of 2 Peter is to guide Jesus-followers to ultimate salvation and as with 1 Peter, salvation is in the future (cf. 1 Pet 1:5). Second Peter's readers are to remain steadfast in their faith and knowledge of Jesus Christ while arresting theological opposition (e.g., 1:20–21; 2:9–11; 3:17–18). The opponents apparently accused the author of "myths" concerning Christ—and especially his *parousia* (1:16). But the author makes an *apologia* defending his apostolicity and affirming his teaching before proceeding to denounce the heretical teachers. In 2:17, the author refers to the "glory" that the beloved Son received at the Transfiguration from God, the "Majestic Glory," indicating Jesus's messianic role (cf. Ps 2:7).[42] As Bauckham asserts, "He [author of 2 Peter] is presenting Jesus as eschatological divine viceregent, not as eschatological prophet."[43] Jesus, the divine viceregent, will return to earth and subdue the rebellious (cf. Ps 2:8–9), which includes those the author of 2 Peter denounces, especially in 2:1–22. Verse 18 reinforces the author's apostolic authority, mentioning how he witnessed divine revelation.

---

[40] Bauckham considers 2 Pet 1:16–18 to rely on a Transfiguration account independent of the Synoptic Gospels, but see Frey, *Jude and Second Peter*, 197–9; 294–6. In both places, Frey refutes Bauckham's assessment regarding the influence of a non-canonical Transfiguration account. The differences in the Matthean and Petrine accounts are due to the fact that they serve different theological agendas.
[41] Frey, *Jude and Second Peter*, 198, argues that when it comes to 2 Pet 1:16–18's reliance on the Synoptics, "Overall, the evidence shows the greatest proximity to the version found in Matt."
[42] Bauckham, *Jude, 2 Peter*, 217, comments that "glory" (*doxa*) is used throughout the Synoptic Gospels to refer to the *parousia* (except at Luke 2:9; 9:32).
[43] Bauckham, *Jude, 2 Peter*, 219.

Jerome H. Neyrey explores the apologetic function of the Transfiguration in 2 Peter, concluding that the letter's author relies on it not only for apostolic credibility but to prophesy of Christ's *parousia*.[44] Gene L. Green also finds an apologetic function of 2 Pet 1:16–18's reliance upon the Transfiguration but emphasizes the role of "eye- and earwitness in shaping a testimony."[45] Green points out what might be 2 Pet 1:16–18's missional focus in that "the testimony presented in its various forms makes faith possible while simultaneously undercutting the testimony and scepticism [*sic*] of the false teachers."[46] Emboldening the community for opposition is part of 2 Peter's mission. Frey aptly summarizes the argument of 1:16–20,

> If the Scriptures are reliable as prophecy and this reliability is now once again particularly confirmed by the revelation of Christ's divine glory, then it is necessary to constantly keep one's attention directed toward that prophecy (προσέχειν) and to orient one's life around it. The author urgently admonishes his addressees about this: καλῶς ποιεῖτε introduces not just a recommendation or plea but, in view of Peter's apostolic authority, a clear warning, which continues in v. 20 with an instruction, connected participially, that is especially emphasized.[47]

Frey's assessment communicates how 1:16–18 contributes to the author's admonition for vigilance against false prophets and acceptance of apostolic teaching. The recounting of the Transfiguration assists the readers for their mission, a portion of which is touched upon in 1:19 ("So we have the prophetic message more fully confirmed. You will do well to be attentive to this as to a lamp shining in a dark place, until the day dawns and the morning star rises in your hearts"). Peter's presence at the Transfiguration serves to bolster the message and also to engender faith in a sovereign Lord who will return and to mete out judgment.

11.7 Conclusion

In both 1 and 2 Peter, the letter recipients are urged to stand firm in their faith despite hostility and antagonism. In 1 Peter, the opposition is social alienation from non-Christians, which includes some measure of physical suffering. In 2 Peter the antagonists are those familiar with the story of Jesus but are "false teachers" (2:1) who scoff and doubt Christ's promised *parousia* (3:3–4). In both letters that bear Peter's name, the authors appeal to Matthew's Gospel to prepare their readers for their mission. The

---

[44] Jerome H. Neyrey, "The Apologetic Use of the Transfiguration in 2 Peter 1:16–21," *CBQ* 42 (1980): 504–19. Neyrey writes, "The 'transfiguration' is functioning in the apologetic argument as a prophecy of the parousia" (519), and a few sentences later, "Thus 1:16–21 represents a coherent formal apology for the prophecy of the parousia, establishing the author's credentials for leaving an accurate remembrance of it" (519).

[45] Gene L. Green, "The Testimony of Peter: 2 Peter and the Gospel Traditions," in *James, 1 & 2 Peter, and Early Jesus Traditions*, LNTS 478, ed. Alicia J. Batten and John S. Kloppenborg (New York: Bloomsbury, 2014), 181–98 (here 197).

[46] Ibid., 198.

[47] Frey, *Jude and Second Peter*, 304.

unique greeting in 1 Pet 1:1–2 resonates with Matthew's Great Commission (28:18–20), a passage found only in that Gospel. Regarding 2 Pet 1:16–18, the connection to Matthew's Gospel is an appeal to the apostle Peter's experience with Jesus on the Mount of Transfiguration. Whether or not the historic Peter wrote 1 or 2 Peter, his personal connection with Jesus according to the Gospel tradition—especially Matthew—is intended to confirm his authority in both letters and to motivate both audiences in their mission to represent Jesus while holding their ground against opposing forces.

12

The Matthean Jesus Teaches John

Bruce Henning

12.1 Introduction

Does Matthew's depiction of Jesus as teacher affect the Gospel of John? This essay answers in the affirmative by considering the overlap of some significant Matthean concepts with their Johannine counterparts. Though we can find traces of these motifs in Mark and Luke, they are especially significant for Matthew and reoccur in John to play a strategic role, suggesting that Matthew's vision of Jesus has impacted John's telling of the gospel story. After some introductory remarks to situate our research and explain our aims, we will see a few examples of this thematic overlap as it pertains to their shared intertextual presentation of Jesus, namely their motifs of the new Moses, Ezekiel's shepherd, and the eschatological temple builder.

To clarify, our question is not so much if John knew and used the document we call the "Gospel of Matthew" but lies at the conceptual level regarding the influence evidenced in the Gospel of Matthew and whether that same influence has also impacted John. Whether the material comes from the Gospel of Matthew proper, "M," or oral traditions will not affect us here, and so lack of lexical correspondence or literary dependence is not our concern. Others have argued for literary dependence based on lexical and chronological similarities.[1] Our purpose is to focus on a few exemplary, significant, concepts, aiming to show that Matthew's vision of Jesus as teacher resurfaces in John, thus pointing to a wide circle of influence of "The Teacher" considered in this

---

[1] Esp. James Barker, *John's Use of Matthew* (Minneapolis, MN: Fortress, 2015). Cf. Gerhard Maier, "Johannes und Matthäus – Zwiespalt oder Viergestalt des Evangeliums?" in *Gospel Perspectives: Studies on History and Tradition in the Four Gospels*, ed. R. T. France and David Wenham (Sheffield: JSOT, 1981), 2:267–91, who argues John used Mark from the similarities between their structure, as well as theological themes like "I am" statements, "son" language, the role of John the Baptist, and the use of signs. My essay is most similar to Maier's in that it considers major conceptual parallels. See also Gilbert Van Belle and David R. M. Godecharle, "C. H. Dodd and John 13:16 (and 15:20): St John's Knowledge of Matthew Revisited" in *Engaging with C. H. Dodd on the Gospel of John: Sixty Years of Tradition and Interpretation* (Cambridge: Cambridge University Press, 2013), 86–106. Hedley Sparks, "St. John's Knowledge of Matthew: The Evidence of John 13:16 and 15:20" *JTS* 3.1 (1952): 58–61 (which Van Belle and Godecharle compare with Dodd's perspective and to which Percival Gardner-Smith responded in "St. John's Knowledge of Matthew" *JTS* 4.1 (1953): 31–5) and John Muddiman, "John's Use of Matthew: A British Exponent of the Theory," *Ephemerides Theologicae Lovanienses* 59.4 (1984): 333–7.

current volume. At the least, we will see that there are *topoi* in Matthew's depiction of Jesus as a teacher that find their way into the student John's writings, regardless of what this means for the nature of John's composition.

We also leave room for the likelihood that John differs from Matthew in significant ways, even when he has picked up a Matthean motif. We are thus interested in times when Matthew and John intersect rather than diverge. Traditionally, Matthew is the last gospel "admitted" into the circle of John's influences, and typically the arguments rest on contrasts between the gospels.[2] However, the premise that divergences indicate independence is problematic at a fundamental level. Keith shows that the reasoning "if John knew a gospel then he would not have diverged" does not account for how "even individuals appropriate the past in their present on the basis of their social context" and that later users need not completely accept or reject a source, but can adapt it for their own purposes.[3] Thus, any number of factors may have influenced the author of the Fourth Gospel to exclude or nuance the teaching of the Matthean Jesus. These areas of non-overlap are worth exploring—and we will note some in this research—but addressing the question of influence requires focusing on the areas of overlap.

Keith's observations particularly respond to Gardner-Smith's influential work, whose argument relies on the problematic premise above and which turned the tides in favor of Johannine independence over eighty years ago.[4] Keith is part of a growing number of scholars who see John adapting Mark in his Gospel, in contrast to an earlier position of Johannine independence. Given the renewed interest in Markan influence, it seems especially apropos to turn our attention to Matthew and explore how several features of the Matthean Jesus's teaching have affected John.

Thus, while Matthew and John use Scripture differently at points, we would do a disservice to our subject to overlook their significant amount of agreement. Each of the canonical Gospels describe Jesus as guided by the Scriptures that have an abiding authority over him and his teaching, and Matthew is no exception.[5] Matthew 5:17–20 is

---

[2] Over a century ago, B. H. Streeter still well represents this tendency, *The Four Gospels: A Study of Origins, Treating of the Manuscript Tradition, Sources, Authorship, & Dates* (London: Macmillan, 1924), esp. 394, 408–9, 416).

[3] Chris Keith, "'If John Knew Mark': Critical Inheritance and Johannine Disagreements with Mark," in *John's Transformation of Mark*, ed. Eve-Marie Becker, Helen Bond, and Catrin Williams (London: T&T Clark, 2021), 31–40; This shows affinity with what Jean Zumstein calls "hypertextuality" (*Das Johannesevangelium*, KEK (Göttingen: Vandenhoeck & Ruprecht, 2016), 44–7).

[4] Keith, "If John Knew Mark," 37–50. Percival Gardner-Smith, *Saint John and the Synoptic Gospels* (Cambridge: Cambridge University Press, 1938). See discussion in Stanley Porter, *John, His Gospel, and Jesus; in Pursuit of the Johannine Voice* (Grand Rapids, MI: Eerdmans, 2015), 65–7, who points to earlier proponents of this view. Still, Gardner-Smith's work changed the trajectory of scholarship historically. Porter also observes that Gardner-Smith allows for a "a number of sources, as do all of the Synoptic Gospels, and that John shares a stream of tradition with the author of Luke's Gospel" (66). For an overview of the history of John's sources, see the helpful essay by Harold Attridge, "John and Mark in the History of Research," in *John's Transformation of Mark*, ed. Eve-Marie Becker, Helen Bond, and Catrin Williams (London: T&T Clark, 2021), 9–22. That the volume of collected essays, taken from a 2018 conference in which Markan and Johannine scholars were simply asked to compare the two Gospels, consists of independent pieces that all fit under this provocative title demonstrates how widespread the view of Markan influence has become.

[5] See Chapter 2 in this volume, "Jesus's Teachings and Hebrew Bible Influences."

one of the strongest statements in the New Testament regarding Scripture's permanent authority and is without parallel in the other Gospels. Moreover, Matthew uses these Scriptures in a variety of ways with "fulfillment" being his prominent hermeneutic. In light of the clustering of "fulfillment quotations" in his infancy narratives, France goes so far as to say it is his "preoccupation" and "central focus of his theology."[6] That Matthew's first record of Jesus's words are Ἄφες ἄρτι, οὕτως γὰρ πρέπον ἐστὶν ἡμῖν πληρῶσαι πᾶσαν δικαιοσύνην reinforces the centrality of Scriptural fulfillment in this Gospel.[7] Of the uses of πληρόω in connection to the Scriptures, Matthew leads the NT in number of uses (14x).[8] France writes concerning Matthew, "The introductory formula itself, for all the minor variations in wording, is clearly distinctive. Similar formulae are surprisingly absent from other Jewish and Christian literature of the period, the only significant parallel being John's use of the formula 'that the Scripture might be fulfilled' or the like."[9]

In fact, the Gospel of John stands second in this line with six (perhaps eight) uses.[10] Of course, this number excludes synonyms, like τελέω, strikingly used in 19:30, clear references like 3:14, or more subtle references such as 1:14 (see discussion below). Clearly, John views Scripture in such a way as finding its "end" and "fulfillment" in Jesus. Carson well summarizes,

> When we ask more narrowly what kind of hermeneutical axioms and appropriation techniques ... John adopts when he cites the OT, the answers prove complex and the literature on each quotation legion. At the risk of oversimplification, the dominant approach is that of various forms of typology ... which is itself based on a perception of patterns of continuity across the sweep of salvation history.[11]

---

[6] R. T. France, *Matthew: Evangelist and Teacher* (Grand Rapids, MI: Zondervan, 1989), 166–205. For an overview of scholarship's treatment of this theme in Matthew in the last quarter of the twentieth century, see Donald Senior, "The Lure of the Formula Quotations: Re-assessing Matthew's Use of the Old Testament with the Passion Narrative as a Test Case," in *The Scriptures in the Gospels*, ed. C. M. Tuckett, BETL (Leuven: Leuven University, 1997), 89–115 and more recently, J. R. Daniel Kirk, "Conceptualizing Fulfillment in Matthew" *TynBul* 59.1 (2008): 77–98.

[7] John Nolland, *The Gospel of Matthew: A Commentary on the Greek Text*, NIGTC (Grand Rapids, MI: Eerdmans, 2005), 154 rightly connects this to the uses of πληρόω in the infancy narratives and the use in 5:17. At least part of what Jesus means by "fulfilling all righteousness" has to do with the Scriptural program of the kingdom.

[8] Matt 1:22; 2:15, 17, 23; 3:15 (see above footnote); 4:14; 5:17; 8:17; 12:17; 13:35; 21:32; 26:54, 56; 27:9. Only in 13:48 and 23:32 is the verb used in a different context. Πληρόω also occurs 16x in Acts but only refers to Scriptural fulfillment 3x (1:16, 3:18, and 13:27).

[9] France, *Matthew: Evangelist and Teacher*, 172.

[10] John 12:38; 13:18; 15:25; 17:12; 18:9, 32 (these two are in reference to Jesus's own words); 19:24, 36. It is used in other contexts in 3:29; 7:8; 12:3; 15:11; 16:6, 24; 17:13. Πληρόω occurs 2x in Mark (both Scriptural) and 9x in Luke (only 2 clear uses in connection to Scripture—Luke 4:21 and 24:44).

[11] D. A. Carson, "John and the Johannine Epistles," in *It is Written: Scripture Citing Scripture: Essays in Honour of Barnabas Lindars*, ed. D. A. Carson and H. G. M. Williamson (Cambridge: Cambridge University Press, 1988), 249.

Space does not allow an exploration of scholarship's examination of either Matthew's[12] or John's[13] use of Scriptural fulfillment, but the following examples of Christology showcase similarities between their approaches. That both Matthew and John so strongly utilize the same images from a variety of Scriptural backgrounds support the Matthean Jesus being a source of Johannine thought.

12.2 The New Moses

Both Mark and Luke use Moses typology, but Matthew adds large blocks of material that develop the comparison in a way that pushes Moses forward far more than the other Synoptics. Though Moses is absent in the genealogy (1:1–17) for obvious reasons, connections between Jesus and Moses occur within the uniquely Matthean narrative accounts (1:18–2:23), presenting a "New Moses" theme from early on. These are the same accounts that foreground the "fulfillment" quotations, intertwining the themes of Moses and fulfillment. Allison's volume remains the most thorough exploration of Moses typology in Matthew,[14] and scholarship mostly agrees on seeing a significant connection between the two. Allison summarizes the connections under the following headings: "infancy narrative," "crossing the water," "wilderness temptation," "Mountain of lawgiving," "reciprocal knowledge of God," "Transfiguration," "Last Supper/Passover," and "Commissioning of successor."[15] Matthew uses such similarities to advance several Christological ideas. Thus, for example, when Matthew introduces Jesus going up onto the mountain to give his sermon (chs 5–7), we should see a connection to Moses ascending Mt. Sinai to give the law.[16] By making these kinds of comparisons, Matthew likely taps into hopes that the "second Moses" would be the messianic redeemer (e.g. *Qoh. Rab.* 1:9). His portrayal of salvation as restoration from exile (e.g. Matt 1:11, 17) and entrance into the land also meshes nicely with this motif.[17] Moses's rule as "king" would find resonance as well.[18] Thus, to say Jesus is a new Moses is to make a significant claim about him being king and savior, as well as teacher.

---

[12] I have explored Matthew's fulfillment hermeneutic, particularly the difficulties of an exclusively messianic approach in *Matthew's Non-Messianic Mapping of Messianic Texts: Evidences of a Broadly Eschatological Hermeneutic*, BINS (Leiden: Brill, 2020).

[13] For a recent discussion of John's use of Scripture, see *Biblical Interpretation in Early Christian Gospels: Volume 4: The Gospel of John*, LNTS (London: Bloomsbury, 2020).

[14] Dale C. Allison Jr., *The New Moses: A Matthean Typology* (Minneapolis, MN: Fortress Press, 1993).

[15] Allison, *New Moses*, 289. Charles L. Quarles, *A Theology of Matthew: Jesus Revealed as Deliverer, King, and Incarnate Creator*, ed. Robert A. Peterson, Explorations in Biblical Theology (Phillipsburg: P&R Publishing, 2013), 33–44 summarizes them under the headings: infancy, teaching, fasting, miracles, and transfiguration. Cf. Patrick Schreiner, *Matthew, Disciple and Scribe: The First Gospel and Its Portrait of Jesus* (Grand Rapids, MI: Baker, 2019), 133–4.

[16] Quarles, *A Theology of Matthew*, 37–8. And his article "The Blessings of the New Moses: An Examination of the Theological Purpose of the Matthean Beatitudes," *JSHJ* 13 (2015): 307–27.

[17] This has been well established. See Schreiner, *Matthew, Disciple and Scribe*, 131–67 for a recent overview.

[18] Wayne Meeks, *The Prophet King: Moses Traditions and the Johannine Christology* (Leiden: Brill, 1967); John Lierman, *The New Testament Moses: Christian Perceptions of Moses and Israel in the Setting of Jewish Religion*, WUNT 2.173 (Tübingen: Mohr Siebeck, 2004).

Yet, Matthew's piling up of an impressive amount of similarities between Jesus and Moses does not exclude contrasts. This is most clearly seen in the parallel sections of Peter's declaration at Caesarea Philippi (Matt 16:13–28) and the Mount of Transfiguration (17:1–8). Each of the Synoptics reports the people's inadequate perception of Jesus as John the Baptist, Elijah, or the prophets (Matt 16:14, Mark 8:28, Luke 9:19), which corresponds to the actual appearance of Elijah and Moses in the next scene (Matt 17:3, Mark 9:4, Luke 9:30). Though there are certainly similarities made here between Jesus and Moses,[19] in both Caesarea Philippi and the Mount of Transfiguration, Jesus stands in a category sui generis, qualitatively superior to Moses and Elijah.[20] Each of the Synoptics records the voice from heaven declaring Jesus's superiority as "son" (Matt 17:5, Mark 9:7, Luke 9:35),[21] but Matthew uniquely adds the descriptor ἐν ᾧ εὐδόκησα[22] as well as ὁ υἱὸς τοῦ θεοῦ τοῦ ζῶντος to Peter's confession (Matt 16:16; cf. Mark 8:29,[23] Luke 9:20[24]), an expression that links the statement with the worshipped Son of God in Matt 14:33 (again, uniquely Matthean).[25] Thus, in scenes where Matthew compares Jesus to Moses, not only does he provide several elements of similarity but especially portrays Jesus as the unique and divine Son of God in a way that goes beyond Moses typology.

Similarly, the Gospel of John strongly utilizes the figure of Moses, connecting him to Jesus in a way best described as "fulfillment." As with Moses in Matthew, a number of scholars have turned their attention to this figure's presence in John.[26] Moses is

---

[19] E.g., the echoes of Moses shining on the mountain have been well explored. (W. D. Davies and Dale C. Allison Jr, *A Critical and Exegetical Commentary on the Gospel according to Saint Matthew*, ICC (London: T&T Clark, 1988–91), 2:685).

[20] Davies and Allison, *Gospel of Matthew*, 2:641; Nolland, *Gospel of Matthew*, 701.

[21] Luke 9:35 most likely has Οὗτός ἐστιν ὁ υἱός μου ὁ ἐκλελεγμένος, though several manuscripts (i.e., Alexandrinus, Ephraemi Rescriptus, Bezae, Washintonianus) have ἀγαπητός instead of ἐκλελεγμένος.

[22] Luke 9:35 has this expression too in Bezae and the third corrector of Ephraemi Rescriptus.

[23] Some manuscripts differ. E.g., Sinaiticus adds ο υιος του θεου, and Washintonianus adds ο υιος του θεου του ζωντος to Mark 8:29.

[24] Some manuscripts differ. Bezae adds υιον to Luke 9:20.

[25] Robert H. Gundry (*Matthew: A Commentary on His Handbook for a Mixed Church Under Persecution*, 2nd ed. (Grand Rapids, MI: Eerdmans, 1994), 330) notes this link and argues the expression communicates "the stronger connotation of essential deity." For a fuller study of the divine connotations present here, see Ray M. Lozano, *The Proskynesis of Jesus in the New Testament: A Study on the Significance of Jesus as an Object of "Proskuneo" in the New Testament Writings*, LNTS 609 (London: T&T Clark, 2020), 51–82, pace J. R. Daniel Kirk, *A Man Attested by God: The Human Jesus of the Synoptic Gospels* (Grand Rapids, MI: Eerdmans, 2016), 246–53. Unfortunately, Kirk brackets out the Gospel of John in his discussion, taking its ascriptions of deity to Jesus as unique to the Fourth Gospel. However, studies like the one here demonstrate strong similarity between it and the Synoptics.

[26] E.g., Thomas Francis Glasson, *Moses in the Fourth Gospel* (London: SCM Press, 1963); Marie-Emile Boismard, *Moses or Jesus; An Essay in Johannine Christology*, trans. Benedict Thomas Viviano, BETL (Leuven: Peters, 1993); Stan Harstine, *Moses as a Character in the Fourth Gospel: A Study of Ancient Reading Techniques*, JSNTSup, vol. 229 (Sheffield: Sheffield Academic Press, 2002); Stefan Schapdick, "Religious Authority Re-Evaluated: The Character of Moses in the Fourth Gospel," in *Moses in Biblical and Extra-Biblical Traditions*, ed. Azel Graupner and Michael Wolter, BZAW 372 (Berlin: De Gruyter, 2007), 181–209; Carsten Claussen, "Die Gestsalt des Mose im Johannesevengelium," in *Mosebilder: Gedanken Zur Rezeption einer Literarischen Figur Im Fruhjudentum Fruhen Christintum und Der Romisch-hellenistischen Literatur*, ed. Erik Eynikel et al., WUNT 3 (Tübingen: Mohr Siebeck, 2017), 189–210; Jan Roskovec, "Jesus and Moses in John," in

explicitly referenced 12x—John 1:17, 45; 3:14; 5:45, 46; 6:32; 7:19, 22 (twice), 23; 9:28, 29,[27] though only the first six of these are positive correlations. Yet, as with Matthew, the number of correspondences far exceeds the figure's lexical appearances (the word Μωϋσῆς only occurs 7x in Matthew). Glasson's classic study illustrates the kind of connections, exploring similarities like the prophet (Deut 18:15–18; John 6:14), the serpent in the wilderness (Num 21:9; John 3:14), those "on either side" (Exod 17:12; John 19:18), the manna (Exod 16:15; John 6:1–65), the living water from the rock (Exod 17:6; John 7:38), beholding glory (Exod 34:29–35; John 1:14) and a common farewell discourse (Deuteronomy; John 13–16).[28] Space does not allow even a brief exploration into these, let alone the many other parallels scholars have investigated, but the headings at least illustrate how prominent Moses is in the Fourth Gospel. Such strong Moses themes lead Ruzer to go so far as to say, "For the sake of contriving Jesus' messianic biography, John's narrative shows explicit interest in one and only biblical figure as its core point of reference—the foundational prototype of Moses."[29] Both Matthew and John similarly focus their attention on Moses repeatedly throughout their narrative to explain who Jesus is.

Moreover, not only is Moses prominent in both Gospels, but he is a typological figure as well. In the first occurrence of Μωϋσῆς in John (1:17), he is not so much presented as a foil for Jesus but as a type.[30] In light of the larger theology of John, the Mosaic law points forward to Jesus (e.g., John 5:38). We do not have a Pauline contrast between "law" and "grace" here, but one of type and antitype, so that ἡ χάρις καὶ ἡ ἀλήθεια (1:14, 17) forms a hendiadys–"true grace," in which ἀλήθεια refers to fulfillment (e.g., 1:9, 6:32, 55, 15:1).[31] Some scholars resist the language of "typology" to describe John's use of Moses, but it seems like this is due to an artificially imposed definition of what counts as a "type" or because a correspondence besides typology is also at play.[32] At times, John does go beyond typology to what has been called "prosopological exegesis," in which Jesus corresponds not to an object, human figure,

---

Biblical Interpretation in Early Christian Gospels: Vol. 4: The Gospel of John, LNTS (London: T&T Clark, 2020).

[27] John 8:5 also refers to Moses but is likely not original.
[28] Glasson, *Moses in the Fourth Gospel*.
[29] Serge Ruzer, *Early Jewish Messianism in the New Testament: Reflections in the Dim Mirror*, JCPS 36 (Leiden: Brill, 2020), 132.
[30] *Pace* Schapdick, "The Character of Moses," 207.
[31] Andreas Köstenberger, *John*, BECNT (Grand Rapids, MI: Baker, 2004), 47. See longer discussion in Raymond Brown, *The Gospel According to John I–XII*, AB 29 (New York: Doubleday, 1966), 499–501.
[32] E.g., G. Reim, *Studien zum altentestamenlichen Hintergrund des Johannesevangelium* (Cambridge: Cambridge University Press, 1974), 262–7; Leonhard Goppelt, *Typos: The Typological Interpretation of the Old Testament in the New*, trans. Donald H. Madvig (Grand Rapids, MI: Eerdmans, 1982), 194; Roskovec, "Jesus and Moses in John," 173 ("The way the scriptural text [Num 21] is used and interpreted here is clearly typological. But the typological relationship is not asserted between Moses and Jesus. The 'protype' of Jesus is not Moses but the serpent. For John, Jesus is *not* a 'New Moses' as is probably the case in Matthew ... Moses is just a provider or a mediator. In John's typology, Jesus is related to the saving image as the effective means of salvation, not to its assistant.") Such is the case in this instance, but it neglects other features like the importance of Deut 18:15–18 (cf. John 6:14) and Jesus as the worker of "signs" to effect the Exodus (cf. Ruzer, *early Jewish Messiasm*, 132–9). Roskovec seems to allow for this point later (177–9).

or event in the OT, but to YAHWEH himself.³³ These differences are worthy of examination, but our query about the Matthean Jesus's impact on John requires allowing for "critical inheritance" by not letting differences distract from the similarities. To continue using 1:17 as an example, ἡ χάρις καὶ ἡ ἀλήθεια also alludes to Exod 34. In that context, Moses sees YAHWEH's glory (33:18, הראני נא את כבדך) as the one who is "great of mercy and truth" (34:6, ורב חסד ואמת).³⁴ Since Jesus is the λογός who "exegetes" God (John 1:18), John's purpose is to draw a line between YAHWEH in Exod 34 to Jesus.³⁵ In cases like these, we have Moses tradition being evoked, but the net effect is to portray Jesus as far beyond Moses, as divine. Though this is not quite the same approach used by Matthew, the similarities should not be missed since, as we have seen, Matthew also alludes to Moses tradition with the purpose of showing Jesus's superiority to his prophetic precursors as the Son of God. Thus, when it comes to using the figure of Moses, both Matthew and John are similar in their allusions in that they both use the image prominently, typologically, and to show Jesus's superiority.

12.3 Ezekiel's Shepherd

Matthew alludes to the shepherd of Ezek 34 and 37 in three primary locations—Matt 9:36, 15:24, and 25:31–46.³⁶ The latter two are uniquely Matthean, and the volume of the echo in 9:36 is greatly increased by the nearby 10:6 compared to Mark who only has the former (Mark 6:34), so here again we are looking at a particularly Matthean emphasis. For the purposes of this essay, we can consider three reasons Matthew uses this figure, each of which will find resonance in John. First, Matthew alludes to Ezekiel's shepherd to indict the Pharisees. Ezekiel 34 begins with a description of "shepherds" who only "shepherd" themselves and not the flock (v. 2). The result is that the sheep are slaughtered and unfed (v. 3) and that those who need help do not receive it (v. 5).

---

[33] E.g., I examine a surprising shift from typological to prosopological exegesis of Isa 6 in John 12 in "Jesus as the Rejected Prophet and Exalted Lord: The Rhetorical Effect of Type Shifting John 12:38–41," *JETS* 62.2 (June 2019): 329–40. For an exploration of prosopological exegesis, see Matthew Bates, *The Birth of the Trinity: Jesus, God, and Spirit in New Testament and Early Christian Interpretations of the Old Testament* (Oxford: Oxford University Press, 2015).

[34] All biblical translations are mine from NA28, BHS, or Rahlfs' edition of the LXX.

[35] Harstine, *Moses as Character*, 45–6; Roskovec, "Jesus and Moses in John," 174; D. A. Carson, *The Gospel according to John*, PNTC (Grand Rapids, MI: Eerdmans, 1991), 129–30. George R. Beasley-Murray, *John*, WBC 36 (Nashville, TN: Nelson, 1999), 14–15; Brown, *John I–XII*, 14.

[36] Scholarly discussion include Robert H. Gundry, *Use of the Old Testament in Saint Matthew's Gospel: With Special Reference to the Messianic Hope* (Leiden: Brill, 1975), 32–3; Young Chae, *Jesus as the Eschatological Davidic Shepherd: Studies in the Old Testament, Second Temple Judaism, and in the Gospel of Matthew*, WUNT 2.216 (Tübingen: Mohr Siebeck, 2006); Joel Willitts, *Matthew's Messianic Shepherd King: In Search of the Lost Sheep of the House of Israel*, BZVW 147 (Berlin: De Gruyter, 2007); Wayne Baxter, *Israel's Only Shepherd: Matthew's Shepherd Motif and His Social Setting*, LNTS 457 (London: T&T Clark, 2012); H. Daniel Zacharias, *Matthew's Presentation of the Son of David: Davidic Tradition and Typology in the Gospel of Matthew* (London: Bloomsbury, 2016); J. P. Heil, "Ezekiel 34 and the Narrative Strategy of the Shepherd and Sheep Metaphor in Matthew," *CBQ* 55 (1993): 700–2; Henning, *Matthew's Non-Messianic Mapping*, 45–67. Schreiner, *Matthew, Disciple and Scribe*, 65–130, summarizes the theme of Jesus as Shepherd as the "royal shepherd," "the ministering shepherd," "the merciful shepherd," "the shepherd judge," and the "sacrificial shepherd" (113).

This represents the callous attitudes of the leaders in Ezekiel's time, leading to their dispersion (i.e., the exile) and sets the background for why the intervening work of God in shepherding (vv. 11–34) is necessary. The text thus fits hand in glove with the scene in Matt 9, where the people are described as "sheep without a shepherd" and as ἐσκυλμένοι καὶ ἐρριμμένοι (Matt 9:36), best understood as something like "flayed and abandoned."[37] The passive voice of these participles emphasizes their condition and not agency, but overall Matthean thought immediately suggests the religious leaders (e.g., the Pharisees) as the perpetrators. Matthew's statement that the people did not have shepherds is a biting condemnation of the current leadership. In fact, the immediately previous pericope, the same callous and selfish attitude seen in Ezek 34 manifests itself in the Pharisees who see unprecedented exorcism (vv. 32–33) but can only conclude, "By the ruler of demons he casts out demons" (v. 34).

Second, Matthew's portrayals of Jesus as Ezekiel's shepherd depict his healings as messianic. Young Chae's monograph focuses particularly on this issue, arguing that the belief that the Son of David is characterized by miraculous healings stems from texts like Ezek 34.[38] There are several reasons to see the shepherd David of Ezek 34:23–24 as a messianic figure as well as evidences of such an understanding in the later use of the text (whether the text in consideration is specifically vv. 23–24 or the unit of ch. 34 more broadly).[39] The statement in 9:35, that Jesus was θεραπεύων πᾶσαν νόσον καὶ πᾶσαν μαλακίαν, in such close proximity to the allusion to Ezek 34 in Matt 9:36, maps actions like seeking the lost, returning the scattered, binding the injured, and strengthening the weak (Ezek 34:16) to Jesus. Similarly, Jesus's exorcism of the Canaanite woman's daughter not only echoes Ezekiel's vision of searching for the lost sheep of Israel (Matt 15:24), but the connection to eating at a banquet colors the whole scene eschatologically.[40]

Third, Matthew's references to Ezekiel's shepherd supports the mission to Israel and the Gentiles. The original context of Ezek 34 describes the lost sheep, who are the "house of Israel" (v. 30), as "scattered over all the face of the earth" (v. 6) so that YAHWEH says "I will bring them from the peoples/gentiles" (והוצאתים מן־העמים; καὶ ἐξάξω αὐτοὺς ἐκ τῶν ἐθνῶν [v.13]) back to the land that will experience blessing (vv. 26–29). The allusion in Matt 9:36 coheres well with Ezekiel's vision since Jesus directs his ministry toward the crowds as he went through "all the cities and villages, teaching in their synagogues" (9:35). This is then made more prominent in 10:5–6 as the

---

[37] For a defense, see Henning, *Matthew's Non-Messianic Mapping*, 64.
[38] Chae, *Jesus as the Eschatological Davidic Shepherd*, as opposed to, say, explanations that Solomon was an exorcist (e.g., John P. Meier, *A Marginal Jew: Rethinking the Historical Jesus: Volume Two: Mentor, Message, and Miracles*, AB (New York: Doubleday, 1994), 689–90).
[39] Daniel I. Block, "Bringing Back David: Ezekiel's Messianic Hope," in *The Lord's Anointed: Interpretation of Old Testament Messianic Texts*, ed. Philip E. Satterthwaite, Richard S. Hess, and Gordon J. Wenham (Grand Rapids, MI: Baker, 1995), 167–88; Henning, *Matthew's Non-Messianic Mapping*, 49–63.
[40] Scholars often connect this to messianic banquet imagery (e.g., Donald A. Hagner, *Matthew*, WBC 33A/B (Dallas, TX: Word, 1993–5), 2:442; Joachim Jeremias, *The Eucharistic Words of Jesus* (London: SCM Press, 1966), 255–61; Douglas O'Donnell, "O Woman, Great Is Your Faith!": Faith in the Gospel of Matthew (Eugene, OR: Wipf and Stock, 2021), 101). Davies and Allison, *Matthew*, 2:553, strangely resist the option, a choice that seems odd in light of the connection to 8:13 and the nearby uses of that imagery (15:29) that they do see as messianic (e.g., 2:566).

disciples engage in this mission, specifically and only to "the lost sheep of the house of Israel" and not the Gentiles or Samaritans. Yet, Matthew's continued use of Ezek 34 in Matt 15:24, which strongly echoes 10:6, demonstrates this mission does go beyond Israel. Matthew 25:31–46 similarly mentions πάντα τὰ ἔθνη (v. 32), some of which receive his shepherding work in receiving eternal life (vv. 34–40) and some for eternal judgment (vv. 41–46).

Each of these features of the use of Ezekiel's shepherd in Matthew reoccur in John, suggesting that Matthew's Jesus has influenced the composition of John's Gospel. First, John uses this scriptural background to condemn his opponents as he too echoes Ezek 34 in John 10.[41] The famous "Good Shepherd" discourse of John 10 comes in response to the Pharisees' actions toward the once-blind man (9:13–41). Their callous excommunication of the man shows they "care nothing for the sheep" (10:14). Carter accurately assesses their role vis-à-vis Ezek 34 thus,

> In John 9:40, these shepherds allied with Rome; these members of this elite governing alliance are identified as "blind" and unable to "see" themselves accurately as sinners. Wherein lies their sin? Jesus's statement that the thieves, robbers/brigands, and hirelings do not care for and destroy the sheep—represented by the man born blind now healed by Jesus—are strong criticisms of these leaders and the sinful imperial society that they oversee and from which they benefit (10:8, 10, 12–13).[42]

This is strikingly similar to what we saw in Matthew. Both evangelists use Ezek 34 to say that Jesus's work is necessary because of the negligence and even harassment of the people by those who were assigned responsibility for their care.

Second, like Matthew, John uses Ezekiel's shepherd to highlight the messianic element to Jesus's actions. It is the case that John emphasizes the shepherd's sacrificial death (e.g., 10:11) as his quintessential messianic action to provide for the sheep's well-being, whereas Matthew does not go in this direction. However, this emphasis is not to the neglect of other actions as messianic. As the good shepherd, Jesus ensures that his sheep ζωὴν ἔχωσιν καὶ περισσὸν ἔχωσιν, in contrast to the thief who only brings death (10:10). Carter notes that John's Gospel is "peopled with disabled bodies" because the current structures did not provide for their well-being.[43] The blind man is thus one

---

[41] Gary T. Manning Jr., *Echoes of a Prophet: The Use of Ezekiel in the Gospel of John and in Literature of the Second Temple Period*, LNTS (London: T&T Clark, 2004), 112–13, observes they "share three phrases, eleven key words, five close synonyms, and four weaker synonyms. The amount of verbal parallelism demonstrates that John is not merely drawing on everyday shepherd life." So also M. Deeley, "Ezekiel's Shepherd and John's Jesus: A Case Study in the Appropriation of Biblical Texts," in *Early Christian Interpretation of the Scriptures of Israel: Investigations and Proposals*, ed. Craig A. Evans and James A. Sanders, JSNTSup 148 (Sheffield: Sheffield Academic, 1997), 264; Craig R. Koester, *Symbolism in the Fourth Gospel: Meaning, Mystery, Community* (Minneapolis, MN: Fortress Press, 1995), 27–8.

[42] Warren Carter, "Jesus the Good Shepherd: An Intertextual Approach to Ezekiel 34 and John 10," in *Biblical Interpretation in Early Christian Gospels: Volume 4: The Gospel of John*, LNTS 613 (London: T&T Clark, 2020), 54. So also Carson, *John*, 381; Andrew T. Lincoln, *The Gospel According to Saint John*, BNTC (London: Continuum, 2005), 296.

[43] Carter, "Jesus the Good Shepherd," 51.

among many characters in John who experiences "death," the antithesis of the "life" Jesus came to bring. John frames this action of restoring sight, in addition to other actions like healing the lame, feeding the hungry, and raising the dead as messianic "signs" (20:31).

Third, John also compares similarly to Matthew in using Ezekiel's shepherd to communicate Gentile inclusion. Though, like Matthew, John initially uses the image to discuss Jesus taking over the shepherding role from the current leaders to bring in eschatological salvation for Israel, the shepherd eventually provides salvation for Gentiles as well in 10:16. This is the most likely referent to the "other sheep which are not of this fold"[44] as confirmed by parallel texts like John 11:51–52, 12:20, and 32. Köstenberger helpfully observes that the flock is essentially based on the Jews whom Jesus calls, so that "the Gentiles are not presented as a separate, second flock that needs to be merged with the Jewish flock. Rather, individual believing Gentiles ('other sheep') will be added to the flock."[45] Thus, though Jesus's sheep leave the old "fold," (10:1–4) the imagery does not require Jewish believers abandoning their ethnic identity. The reference is more likely to leaving the temple system associated with the Pharisees. Though Porter's rejection of Gentile mission in John 10 goes too far, his point is well taken that the discourse falls between that of the Synagogue (9:1–41) and the temple (10:22–42) so that the issue is not Jewish ethnicity as such, but concerns the question of a "'temple-removed' context,"[46] resulting in the different folds now being united in following the shepherd Jesus. Since Ezek 34 only goes so far as to say that the coming shepherd will rescue "the house of Israel" from the Gentiles and bring them back into their own land, that both Matthew and John map this text to Jesus in such a way that he ends up rescuing Gentiles themselves as his sheep is remarkable and suggests some level of influence.

12.4 The Temple Building and Temple Builder

Matthew has a strong interest in the temple and temple-related imagery. Though scholars vary as to how often temple concepts occur in Matthew,[47] *that* they occur

---

[44] This is the majority of scholarly opinion. Carson, *John*, 390 interacts with a few detractors (e.g., J. L. Martyn, *The Gospel of John in Christian History: Essays for Interpreters* (New York: Paulist, 1978), 15; J. A. T. Robinson, *Twelve New Testament Studies* (London: SCM, 1962), 114–15; L. van Hartingsveld, *Die Eschatologie des Johannesevangeliums* (Assen: van Gorcum, 1962) 94–98). Christopher Porter ("Of Sheep, Shepherds, and Temples: A Social Identity Reading of the Good Shepherd *Paroemia* on the Way to a Destroyed Temple," *Conspectus* 32 (Oct. 2021): 158–71) also recently argues that the "other fold" of John 10:16 refers to the Jews of the Diaspora. However, one of his primary arguments for an exclusively Jewish mission in John 10 is that the intertexts only refer to restoration of Jewish individuals (167). However, we have already seen Matthew make this sort of extension in Matt 15:24–28 and 25:31–46.

[45] Andreas Köstenberger, "Jesus the Good Shepherd Who Will Also Bring Other Sheep (John 10:16): The Old Testament Background of a Familiar Metaphor," *BBR* 12.1 (2002): 71n.17.

[46] "Of Sheep, Shepherds, Porter, and Temples," 165.

[47] E.g., John W. Welch, *The Sermon on the Mount in Light of the Temple* (Burlington: Ashgate, 2009), explores temple themes in the Sermon on the Mount and finds 119 parallels (esp. 122). This is on the extreme end of the spectrum but illustrates how far some see the motif extending.

in some significant moments is clear. The scope of this burgeoning interest among scholars is so large that we can do little more than build on the findings of others at this point.[48] But for those already convinced of temple imagery, John's overlap with Matthew is striking. Both the ideas of a temple builder and the building itself had messianic import by the first century, so, paradoxically, the messiah was both the one who built the edifice, as well as the edifice itself (or at least a significant part of it).[49] Matthew 21:42 follows Mark 12:10-11 in exemplifying the latter approach. Not only does it contain a direct reference to Ps 118:27, which was frequently understood as messianic,[50] but it also occurs in a context thick with temple imagery[51] to support the overall argument that Jesus is the son of God (= son of the vineyard owner, 21:37).

Furthermore, Matthew uses this imagery to indict the religious leaders for actively opposing the function of the temple, leading to its destruction. They are the wicked tenant farmers who seek to keep the fruit and the inheritance for themselves (21:38, 41). Yet, ironically, their desire for the things related to the temple leads to their malpractice, which, in its larger literary context, is the reason for the temple's destruction. The current temple structure had turned it into a den of thieves (Matt 21:13, echoing Jer 7:11 and the fate described there), which, like the barren fig tree can only be cursed (21:18-19) and so the temple is left desolate (23:38—after the seven woes to the Pharisees in 23:1-36) without one stone on another (24:2). As with Ezekiel's shepherd, the significance of this imagery is twofold: to vindicate Jesus's messianic identity and to condemn the current leadership.[52] But with the temple imagery, there is

---

[48] For a fuller defense, see my discussion in *Matthew's Non-Messianic Mapping*, 139-79 and "The Church's One Foundation? Peter as the Messianic Temple Stone in Matt 16:18," in *Practicing Intertextuality: Ancient Jewish and Greco-Roman Exegetical Techniques in the New Testament*, ed. Max J. Lee and B. J. Oropeza (Eugene: Cascade, 2021), 77-90.

[49] Donald Juel, *Messiah and Temple: The Trial of Jesus in the Gospel of Mark*, SBLDS 31 (Missoula, MT: Scholars Press, 1977), 189-98; N. T. Wright, *Jesus and the Victory of God* (London: SPCK, 1996), 411; J. Adna, *Jesu Stellung zum Tempel: Die Tempelaktion und das Tempelwort als Ausdruck seiner messianischen Sendung*, WUNT 2.119 (Tübingen: Mohr Siebeck, 2000), 50-3; Andrew J. Chester, *Messiah and Exaltation: Jewish Messianic and Visionary Traditions and New Testament Christology*, WUNT 207 (Tübingen: Mohr Siebeck, 2007), 471-96; Joseph A. Fitzmyer, *The One Who Is To Come* (Grand Rapids, MI: Eerdmans, 2008), 172; Nicholas Perrin, *Jesus and the Temple* (Grand Rapids, MI: Baker, 2010), 80-113; Grant Macaskil, *Union with Christ in the New Testament* (Oxford: Oxford University Press, 2013), 100-27, 147-71; Henning, *Non-Messianic Mapping*, 144-9, 155-60, 169-72.

[50] Andrew C. Brunson, *Psalm 118 in the Gospel of John: An Intertextual Study on the New Exodus*, WUNT 2.158 (Tübingen: Mohr Siebeck, 2003), 34-7; Jeremias, *Eucharistic Words*, 169-74; J. Ross Wagner, "Psalm 118 in Luke-Acts: Tracing a Narrative Thread," in *Early Christian Interpretation of the Scriptures of Israel: Investigations and Proposals*, ed. Craig A. Evans and James A. Sanders, JSNTSup 148 (Sheffield: Sheffield Academic, 1997), 158.

[51] Scholarship is almost unanimous that the wicked tenant parable points back to Isa 5, which was later interpreted in light of the temple. See esp. George J. Brooke "4Q500 1 and the Use of Scripture in the Parable of the Vineyard," *DSD* 2.3 (1995): 287-8.

[52] Many (if not most) Matthean scholars currently see the new farmers as replacement leaders over Israel (e.g., J. Andrew Overman, *Church and Community in Crisis: The Gospel According to Matthew* (Valley Forge, PA: Trinity press, 1996), 299-304; David Sim, *The Gospel of Matthew and Christian Judaism* (Edinburgh: T&T Clark, 1998), 148-9; Warren Carter, *Matthew and the Margins: A Socio-Political and Religious Reading* (Sheffield: Sheffield Academic, 2000), 429-30; Charles H. Talbert, *Matthew*, Paideia Commentary on the New Testament (Grand Rapids, MI: Baker Academic, 2010), 252; David Turner, *Israel's Last Prophet* (Minneapolis, MN: Fortress Press, 2015), 225-51.

an additional layer of the leaders' eagerness to grasp control over the temple so tightly that leads to its demise since their eagerness compels them to reject Jesus. Though this ironic tragedy surfaces in Mark, the theme is nonetheless significant for Matthew.

Beyond using the imagery of the building of a temple, Matthew also picks up the concept of the builder of a temple to portray Jesus as the messiah. Whereas he follows Mark in portraying Jesus as part of the temple building, Matthew contains unique material that depicts him as temple builder in Matt 16:18. Granted, the object of οἰκοδομήσω is μου τὴν ἐκκλησίαν. Yet there are several reasons to see a temple reference here.[53] By depicting Jesus as the builder of this new temple, he underscores his messianic identity, the main topic of the pericope (cf. 16:13). Furthermore, since Jesus as messiah builds this temple, it is sure to endure despite the conflict with "the gates of hades" (16:19). To intertwine the two threads of temple imagery, the Pharisees have been negligent builders and because they miss the "cornerstone," the temple will ultimately be destroyed. In contrast, Jesus's work in temple building cannot be destroyed but lasts forever.

Like Matthew, John also makes much of temple imagery.[54] John 2:13–22 is particularly significant for our purposes inasmuch as it evidences both of the Matthean features discussed above. John mirrors Matthew's description of the irony of Jewish "zeal" for the temple as the reason for its replacement with Jesus's work. Steven M. Bryan has convincingly argued that the quotation in 2:17 of Ps 69:9 (Ὁ ζῆλος τοῦ οἴκου σου καταφάγεταί με) refers to Jesus's opponents' emotion since it fits more naturally in the context of Ps 69, it coheres with statements about the "Jews" fearing the well-being of the nation because of Rome (11:48–50; cf. 18:13–14), and John does not elsewhere depict Jesus's death as stemming from his own concern for Herod's temple.[55] Verses 17 and 19 (Λύσατε τὸν ναὸν τοῦτον καὶ ἐν τρισὶν ἡμέραις ἐγερῶ αὐτόν) thus go hand in hand to form a riddle which the disciples can only discern after Jesus's resurrection (2:17, 22). Jesus's opponents are zealous for the temple (v. 17), so much so that they destroy the temple of Jesus's body (vv. 17, 19), but this results in the erection of a new

---

[53] Henning, "The Church's One Foundation?" 78–83; Michael P. Barber, "Jesus as the Davidic Temple Builder and Peter's Priestly Role in Matthew 16:16–19," *JBL* 132.4 (2013): 935–53; G. K. Beale, *The Temple and the Church's Mission: A Biblical Theology of the Dwelling Place of God*, NSBT (Downers Grove, IL: IVP Academic, 2004), 187; Peter Shäfer, "Tempel und Schopfung: Zur Interpretation einiger Heiligtumstraditionen in der rabbischen Literatur," in *Studien zur geschichte und Theologie des rabbinischen Judentums*, AGJU (Leiden: Brill, 1978), 126.

[54] Several monographs on this theme have been written in the past two decades, e.g., Margaret Barker, *King of the Jews: Temple Theology in John's Gospel* (London: SPCK, 2014); Stephen T. Urn, *The Theme of Temple Christology in John's Gospel*, LNTS vol (London: T&T Clark, 2006); Paul M. Hoskins, *Jesus as the Fulfillment of the Temple in the Gospel of John*, Paternoster Biblical Monographs (Carlisle: Paternoster, 2006); Alan R. Kerr, *The Temple of Jesus' Body: The Temple Theme in the Gospel of John*, JSNTSup 220 (Sheffield: Sheffield Academic Press, 2002); Mary L. Coloe, *God Dwells with Us: Temple Symbolism in the Fourth Gospel* (Collegeville, MN: Liturgical Press, 2001).

[55] Steven M. Bryan, "Consumed by Zeal: John's Use of Psalm 69:9 and the Action in the Temple," *BBR* 21.4 (2011): 479–94. So also Benjamin L. Lappenga, "Whose Zeal Is It Anyway? The Citation of Psam 69:9 in John 2:17 as a Double Entendre," in *Abiding Words: The Use of Scripture in the Gospel of John*, ed. Alicia D. Myers and Bruce G. Schuchard, RBS (Atlanta, GA: SBL Press, 2015), 141–59 and Rafael Rodríguez, "Zeal That Consumed: Memory of Jerusalem's Temple and Jesus's Body in the Gospel of John," in *Biblical Interpretation in Early Christian Gospels: Volume 4: The Gospel of John*, LNTS (London: T&T Clark, 2020), 214–15.

temple built three days later (v. 19). John may also expect us to think of the destruction of Herod's temple in the wake of Jesus's action since the coming of the "new temple" renders the old obsolete. Bryan suggests, "Jesus' action symbolically enacts the inability of Herod's temple to function as the new temple. If Jesus' action declares the necessity of a new temple and the riddle anticipates the nature of that new temple, the citation of Ps 69 anticipates the role of Jewish zeal for the old temple in bringing about the new."[56]

Furthermore, John similarly follows Matthew's lead by combining the conflicting imagery of messiah as temple and temple builder. In their zeal (v. 17), Jesus's opponents would destroy him (v. 19), but even after being destroyed, Jesus would rebuild a new temple. That these events are a "sign" (v. 18) means they are meant to foster belief in Jesus as messiah and Son of God (20:30–31). It thus seems highly likely that John participates in the same thought world mentioned earlier in which the messiah is a temple builder. And yet, simultaneously, John presents Jesus as the messiah by also being the temple itself. Though Matthew follows Mark in portraying Jesus as part of the temple (κεφαλὴν γωνίας, Matt 21:42//Mark 11:10), whereas John 2:21 speaks of τοῦ ναοῦ τοῦ σώματος αὐτοῦ, this should not distract from the similarities.[57] Though Mark makes use of temple building imagery, we saw that Matthew uniquely combines the seemingly contradictory imagery of messiah as temple builder (Matt 16:18) and building (Matt 21:42). John does likewise, but all in the span of one verse (2:19).

12.5 Conclusion

Certainly Matthew and John differ. Even in regard to the concepts selected here to showcase their overlap, areas of divergence clearly emerge. Yet, allowing for "critical inheritance" means these do not add up so as to outweigh the similarities. Instead, whether or not the Matthean Jesus has influenced John is determined by the explanatory power of their similarities. We have seen a few examples that point in this direction. Matthew and John both have a prominent new Moses motif and use that imagery to show Jesus is the messianic fulfillment of this type, yet in a way that emphasizes his divine transcendence. Matthew and John both portray Jesus as the fulfillment of Ezekiel's shepherd prophecy to indict the Pharisees, to bring out the messianic nature of Jesus's healings, and to extend Jesus's mission to the Gentiles. Both Matthew and John address expectations of an eschatological temple, combining imagery of a temple and temple builder to ironically blame the Pharisees' "zeal" and to establish the permanence of Jesus's new temple. Though John takes these images in his own directions at times, these areas of consideration show such affinity to one another that they point to John having learned from Matthew's depiction of his master teacher.

---

[56] Bryan, "Consumed by Zeal," 481–2.
[57] However, that John describes the whole discipleship community as being indwelled by the Spirit (e.g., John 14:17) and united in the Father and the Son (17:23) means the imagery is flexible enough to not require *only* Jesus as the temple but allows that "in a derivatory sense the community of faith, his disciples, are also the temple" (Kerr, *The Temple of Jesus' Body*, 66).

13

The Teaching of Jesus in Matthew, Galatians, and Paul's Letters

David Wenham

13.1 Introduction

Matthew's Gospel famously contains some of the most striking and well-known sayings of Jesus, like the Sermon on the Mount in chs 5–7 and the Great Commission in 28:16–20. This chapter argues that there is evidence in Paul's letters indicating that he and his readers, in AD 40s and 50s, were familiar with some if not many of the sayings that are uniquely preserved by Matthew.[1]

That Paul knew some traditions of Jesus at a very early date is hard to dispute. In his first letter to the Corinthians written around AD 55 he explicitly speaks of having "received" and then "passed on" traditions of the Last Supper and of the Resurrection, and also of Jesus's teaching on divorce (1 Cor 11:23; 15:3; 7:10, 11). He does not explicitly refer to many other dominical traditions, but there are loads of possible echoes and likely allusions to Jesus's traditions.[2] Some of the most important evidence for Paul being familiar with distinctive Matthean traditions comes, intriguingly, in the two letters that have a claim to being the first written, namely 1 Thessalonians, which can confidently be dated to around AD 50, and Galatians, which could have been written even earlier.

First Thessalonians addresses some of the Thessalonian Christians who were worried because Christian friends or relatives had died before the Lord's expected and promised return—would they miss out on the coming kingdom? Paul's comment has striking parallels to the teaching of Jesus in Matthew, Mark, and Luke, for example, with the reference to Jesus's future coming being unexpected like the coming of a thief in the night—a probable allusion to Jesus's parable of the thief found in both Matthew and Luke (1 Thess 5:2, Matt 24:43, Luke 17:24). But there

---

[1] Scholars often see such "M" material as Matthean redaction, reflecting Matthew's church context (identified by many as the late first century in a context of church-synagogue conflict) and without a strong claim to originating with Jesus himself.

[2] I have written extensively on the Paul and Jesus question, including on how to identify likely allusions; most fully see my *Paul, Follower of Jesus or Founder of Christianity* (Grand Rapids, MI: Eerdmans, 1985), also Michael Thompson *Clothed with Christ* (Sheffield: JSOT, 1991) and Detlev Häusser, *Christus Bekenntnis und Jesusüberlieferung bei Paulus* (Tübingen, Mohr Siebeck, 2006).

is also a likely allusion to a parable found only in Matthew. Paul refers to a "word of the Lord," which is probably Jesus's parable of the wise and foolish girls (1 Thess 4:13–18, Matt 25:1–13). This parable is explicitly about the Lord's return, picturing a bridegroom who came late to the wedding feast so that the group of girls waiting for him "fell asleep" (an expression often used of death), but when he finally arrives the wise girls were ready, "rose up" "to meet" the bridegroom, and went in with him to the banquet. Paul uses precisely this phraseology in reassuring the Thessalonians that their friends who have fallen asleep will rise to meet Jesus when he returns and will go to be with him in his heavenly kingdom. It was an ideal word of the Lord for the anxious Thessalonians. It looks as though Paul was familiar with a version of Jesus's teaching/discourse about the end-times that all the gospel writers drew on, but more likely Matthew who is the only evangelist to record the parable of the wise and foolish girls.

More important for this article is Paul's letter to the Galatians. Scholars differ as to the date of Galatians, with some arguing rather persuasively for it being Paul's earliest letter written as early as AD 48, but even if a later date in the 50s is preferred, it includes a rather lengthy description of a fierce dispute that seems to have happened in late AD 40's. The conflict was all to do with the early Christian mission to the Gentiles. The book of Acts credibly suggests that it was in the important city of Syrian Antioch that Gentiles began to be converted to Christian faith in some numbers. These conversions raised acute questions for the almost entirely Jewish-Christian church in Jerusalem. Should the Gentile converts be expected to be circumcised and to live by the Jewish law, for example, its dietary rules? It was a tricky and divisive question. According to Acts, the answer given by Barnabas, who was sent from Jerusalem to check out the situation was, No, they did not need to "Judaize," and he was joined in his leadership of the mixed Jew-Gentile Antioch church by the ex-Pharisee Saul/Paul of Tarsus. After some time, Barnabas and Paul were sent from Antioch on a Mediterranean mission, which among other places took them to Galatia. They planted churches, and eventually returned to Antioch (Acts 11 and 13).

It was after this that the situation exploded into a major conflict, as reflected in Paul's letter to the Galatians. Two things contributed to this. First, reports came to Antioch from Galatia of pressure being put on newly established converts to Judaize and (in the case of the men) to get circumcised, contrary to what Paul and Barnabas had taught. Second, in the Antioch church itself the related issue of table fellowship between Jewish and Gentile Christians blew up. Simon Peter, the apostle of Jesus and the first leader of the church in Jerusalem, had come to the vibrant majority-Gentile church in Antioch and at first mixed and ate with Gentile Christians not worrying about Jewish food laws.[3] But then, he was pressured by "men who came from James" into withdrawing from table fellowship with the Gentiles. James, the brother of Jesus, had succeeded Peter as leader of the church in Jerusalem, and he (or others claiming his authority) evidently put pressure on Peter not to go native and not to defile himself by eating unclean food (they probably argued that this seriously compromised the

---

[3] Acts says that he had had a vision from God telling him not to call some foods or by inference some people unclean (Acts 10).

witness of the church in Jerusalem among Jews). Paul was flabbergasted at Peter's volte-face, as he explains in his letter to the Galatians, and confronted Peter face-to-face accusing him of effectively betraying the gospel of Christ. To make matters worse, Barnabas, Paul's mentor and colleague, sides with Peter's view and practice (Gal 2:11–14)!

It was a crisis moment, and the outcome of the dispute is debated by scholars. Some say that Paul's failure to tell us in Galatians what happened next is because Paul lost the argument and even had to sever his long-standing links with the Antioch church. Others argue that the debate went on and resulted in the so-called Council of Jerusalem as described in Acts 15. The discussions involved Peter, Paul, Barnabas, and James, and Acts suggests that something like a compromise was reached with Paul's insistence that Gentile converts need not be circumcised and Judaized being accepted. Additionally, Gentile converts were asked to respect Jewish scruples about food for the sake of fellowship within the church.

It is not necessary to resolve all the questions that scholars have debated about the events described in Galatians and Acts, but there is no doubt that, as Acts 15 puts it, there was "no small dissension and debate" in and beyond Antioch. Galatians also makes that clear, as it is surely the most distressed and vitriolic book in the New Testament (NT). The division of opinion was over Gentiles, the Jewish law, circumcision, and Jewish food laws, with the ex-Pharisee Paul on the one side and with Jewish Christians from Jerusalem on the other, and with Barnabas and Peter wavering between the two.

What can also hardly be doubted is that a key debating point will have been, what did Jesus do and teach in relation to these questions, if anything? It was only around twenty years since his death and resurrection, and some of the key parties in the discussions were Peter, Jesus's close friend and disciple, and James, Jesus's brother. So far as the circumcision question was concerned, there was nothing to report about Jesus, except probably that he himself was a circumcised Jew[4]; the question of Gentile circumcision was just not an issue in Jesus's ministry in Palestine. But all the gospels agree that Jesus did have positive contact with Gentile individuals and that he had plenty to say about the Old Testament (OT) law positively and about Jewish traditions critically, particularly as interpreted by the Pharisees. They were vocal in criticizing what they saw as his liberal behaviour in mixing and eating with lawless sinners and in his relaxed Sabbath observance. All of this evidence regarding Jesus (and much more!) is likely to have been grist for the mill in the discussions in Antioch.

There is good evidence for Paul presupposing Jesus-traditions in Galatians. So, for example, the way that he can speak of God "sending the Spirit of his Son into our hearts, crying 'Abba! Father'" (Gal 4:6) is striking, given that the Galatians did not mostly speak Aramaic. It seems that addressing God using the intimate "Abba" was something memorably distinctive of Jesus and so it was recalled not just among the

---

[4] So, Luke 2:21. The reference in Gal 4:4 to Jesus being born "under the law," i.e., the Jewish law, clearly reflects Paul's familiarity with this undisputed fact; and the phraseology that he uses "when the fullness of time had come, God sent forth his Son, born of woman … etc." is intriguingly reminiscent of the Lukan account of Jesus's birth.

first Aramaic-speaking Christians, whom Paul will have known, but even passed on and explained to Gentile converts in places like Galatia.[5]

The Galatians may have known the story of Jesus in Gethsemane which is where Mark describes Jesus crying "Abba" (14:36), maybe indeed much of the passion story, with Paul in chapter 3 chiding them "you foolish Galatians ... it was before your eyes that Jesus Christ was publicly displayed as crucified" (3:1). The unusual phrase "publicly displayed" may suggest that the vivid but gruesome story of the crucifixion was narrated to the Galatians (see chapter 6). Certainly the crucifixion of Jesus was a major given for Paul, as a saving event and as something that believers came to share in—being crucified with Christ. And the two references in 1 Corinthians to traditions being "received and passed on" are specifically related to the passion and resurrection of the Lord.

This suggestion is not particularly revolutionary; scholars have often seen the passion narrative as one of the earliest parts of the gospel traditions to have been brought together, with Mark drawing on that narrative. But the more unusual suggestion of this article is that Paul in Galatians shows knowledge of stories or sayings of Jesus that are unique to Matthew and were an important ingredient to the heated discussion between Paul and Peter and others.

We will examine the evidence under three headings: (1) Apostles and the Church, (2) Mission to Jews and Gentiles, and (3) Law and Freedom.

13.2 Apostles and the Church

A significant part of the discussion in Galatians is Paul asserting his independence and equality with the "pillars" of the church in Jerusalem, that is, Peter, James, and John, and also the authenticity of the gospel as he preached it.[6] The pillars were recognized as the apostolic leaders of the church, and their authority was based on their first-hand relationship with, and call from, Jesus, which is why Paul has to work hard to assert his claim to a comparable first-hand relationship.[7] He opens Galatians with a very emphatic "Paul an apostle not from men not through man but through Jesus Christ and God the Father ... (1:1)."[8]

---

[5] The importance of the Aramaic word to Paul and the first Christians is clear given Paul's use of it also in Rom 8:15. Another example of an Aramaism that passed into the Greek-speaking church is Maranatha, "Our Lord come," see 1 Cor 16:21.

[6] The title "pillars" probably reflects the idea of the church as the new temple—an idea with roots in Jesus's own teaching. Paul's words to Peter in Gal 2:18 that "if I build up again those things that I destroyed" have been connected to Jesus's words about the temple, e.g., in Matt 26:17. The pillars in this Jesus-community-temple notably Peter and James are evidently the key players in relation to Paul—not just at the time of the Antioch incident, but earlier on Paul's first visit to Jerusalem after his conversion. See my *Paul Follower*, 205–9.

[7] See *Paul, Follower*, chapter 5, for more detail and references relating to the following argument.

[8] In chapter 2 he speaks of the Jerusalem church leaders recognizing God's working through Peter "for apostleship to the circumcision" and through me "for the Gentiles" (v.8); what is not explicit is that the Jerusalem pillars recognized him as having apostleship.

We see some of the same thoughts expressed in Paul's question in 1 Cor 9:1: "Am I not an apostle? Have I not seen the Lord," to which the implied answer is "Yes, I am." What follows in that chapter is Paul speaking of having the same "rights" as the other apostles—rights among other things to "our food and drink" and to being supported in his ministry. His argument includes one of the most widely recognized quotes from the Jesus tradition, since he comments: "In the same way, *the Lord commanded* that those who proclaim the gospel should get their living by the gospel" (9:14). This is a probable allusion to the saying found in the mission discourses of Matt 10 and Luke 10, where Jesus says, "the labourer is worthy of his food/hire" (Matt 10:10/Luke 10:7). It is likely that Paul knew not just that saying on its own, but in the context of a version of the mission discourse, which specifically referred to Jesus "sending out" disciples (the verb *apostello* related to the word *apostolos*) and to them accepting food and drink (as in Luke 10).[9]

Paul's assertion of his own apostleship also recurs in 1 Cor 15, where in speaking of Jesus's resurrection appearances, he refers to Jesus appearing to "Cephas," then to the twelve, then to a group of more than 500 people, then to James and to all the apostles, and then "last of all, as to one untimely born, he appeared also to me. For I am the least of the apostles, unfit to be called an apostle, because I persecuted the church of God."[10] Paul here admits his oddity and even his unfitness to be an apostle, and yet he is making a point by including himself in what is a highly selective list of top resurrection witnesses, which starts with Peter, and James and the twelve and the apostles, but concludes with Paul.

In Galatians Paul does not emphasize his least-ness among the apostles, indeed he can be seen as doing almost the opposite, bringing out his missionary equality even to Cephas.[11] His emphasis on this is understandable, given the Antioch confrontation and other people's questioning of his ministry.

What is obvious both in Galatians and elsewhere is that Paul knew not just of Jesus's sending out of the apostles in general but of Peter's priority and commissioning by the Lord (hence Paul's own emphasis on his own commissioning). What specifically did he know? Even before his fifteen-day stay with Peter after his conversion (Gal 1:18), it is likely that he knew a lot about Peter's experiences with Jesus. Peter's priority among Jesus's first disciples is clear in all the Gospels. Matthew, Mark, and Luke all describe Jesus's journeying with Peter, James, and John to Caesarea Philippi in the North of Palestine and reviewing the effects of his ministry with them. When he asks the threesome "Who do you think that I am?," it is Peter who responds: "You are the Christ" (Mark 8:29), "the Christ of God" (Luke 9:20), "the Christ the Son of living God" (Matt 16:16). It is clear that for all the Gospel writers this is the right and an important answer; but Mark and Luke don't say so, simply recording that Jesus told them not to

---

[9] Matthew and Luke are widely seen as having both Mark and also another version, hence the two mission discourses in Luke 9 and 10. The non-Markan version, often ascribed to the source "Q" postulated by scholars, has the saying about the laborer, which Paul knew, and about accepting gifts of food and drink. Compare Gal 6:6 for a similar sentiment.

[10] Paul's list of appearances is clearly selective, overlapping at points with the resurrection accounts in the gospels.

[11] Mind you, in Jewish terms an apostleship to the uncircumcised might be seen as an inferior role by comparison with going to Israel!

broadcast the fact, then going on to speak of his coming sufferings. Matthew, on the other hand, has Jesus say: "Blessed are you, Simon Barjona, flesh and blood has not revealed this to you, but my father in heaven. And I tell you that you are Peter, and on this rock, I will build my church, and the gates of hades will not prevail against it. I will give you the keys of the kingdom of heaven" (vv.17–20).

This unique "M" tradition is one of only two references to the "church" in the Gospels and is often assumed to derive from Matthew rather than from Jesus. But there are several strong reasons for questioning that opinion. First, the language used is strongly Semitic, for example, the phrase "flesh and blood." Second, it is impossible to imagine Jesus not responding to Peter's confession, but it is quite possible to imagine Mark or Mark's source (traditionally thought to be Peter) omitting a saying honoring Peter and getting on with Jesus's priority teaching about his own coming suffering. Third, it has been argued that Paul probably knew the tradition, with Galatians being the crucial evidence.

The evidence is primarily in terms of possible Pauline echoes of the Matthean story, with Paul describing his own call in Gal 1:15, 16 in phraseology reminiscent of Matt 16:16–20. Paul speaks of having a "revelation" of "God's Son" and of not conferring with "flesh and blood," all in the context of his calling to "mission" and in a context where his relationship with Peter is a pressing and a key issue.[12]

Some of these possible connections are more speculative than others, but the case for Paul and his readers knowing that "Matthean" story of Peter as the rock on which Jesus's community will be built is plausible. Interestingly the same may be said of the other Matthean passage where Jesus refers to "the church" (cf., Matt 18). This is part of a discourse about relationships in the church. Paul's writing has parallels in Matthew, Mark, and Luke, but the central discussion of what to do about a church member who "sins against you" is only in Matthew, with the instruction being that you should speak personally to the person, then, if that fails, take one or two others with you to address the offender, and then, if that fails, tell it to "the church." If the offender still refuses to listen, then "let such a one be to you as a Gentile and a tax-collector." A promise follows that what "you bind on earth will be bound in heaven" and that "if two of you agree on earth ... it will be done for you by my Father in heaven. For where two of three are gathered in my name, I am there among (*en meso*) them" (Matt 18:15–20).

The reference to "a Gentile and a tax-collector" is an example of the almost anti-Gentile flavour of some of Jesus's teaching in Matthew, but this teaching of the Lord may well have been known to Paul. So, in 1 Cor 5 when he is dealing with a case of sexual immorality in the church, he comments that the offender should have been removed from among (*ek mesou*) you. He goes on to say that, although he is

> "absent in body, I am present in spirit; and, as if present have already pronounced judgment on the one who has done this, that when you together with my spirit are gathered in the name of the Lord Jesus with the power of the Lord Jesus. You are to hand the man over to Satan for the destruction of the flesh, so that his spirit may be saved" (5:1–5).

---

[12] This might a clue as to why unusually Paul in Gal 2:7–8 uses the Greek name *Petros* rather than the Aramaic *Cephas*.

Paul's Greek here is not easy to construe, but the language and thought are interestingly similar to the Matthean passage. It is at least possible that Paul is again drawing on the instructions of Jesus for church life.[13]

We conclude: it is certain that Paul knew about the apostles, the twelve and Peter's "primacy"; it is likely that he knew the Matthean account of Jesus congratulating Peter for his understanding; it is possible that he knew the Lord's teachings about "the church."

13.3 Mission to Jews and to Gentiles

It is relatively uncontroversial to say that Paul knew Jesus's saying: "the labourer is worth of his food/hire" (Matt 10:10/Luke 10:7), quite probably in the context of a non-Markan version of the mission discourse known to Matthew and Luke, and often identified by scholars as "Q" material. But it is arguable that the version of the discourse known to Paul was not "Q" but "Q+M"!

Using such labels in connection with Paul's oral traditions is anachronistic and potentially confusing, but there is reason to believe that Paul's version of the mission discourse probably included traditions that are unique to Matthew. Notably, he refers very specifically to Peter's apostleship as "for the circumcision" (Gal 2:7–8). This is intriguing and importantly similar to Matthew's version of the mission discourse in which he says to those he is sending out, "Go nowhere among the Gentiles and enter no town of the Samaritans, but go rather to the lost sheep of the house of Israel" (10:5). This Jewish priority is also expressed by Jesus in relation to his own ministry, when he is approached by a Syro-Phoenician (Matthew has "Canaanite") woman asking for him to heal her daughter. Jesus responds with an apparent negativity: "I was sent only to the lost sheep of the house of Israel," before going on to heal the sick girl (15:21–28).

Neither of these Jew-focused sayings of Jesus are paralleled in Mark or Luke, but Paul knows the tradition, as evidenced also in his letter to the Romans; there, when discussing Jewish and Gentile Christians coexisting in the church, the apostle to the Gentiles several times refers to "the Jew *first* and also to Greek," and in speaking of Jesus he refers to him as a "servant of the circumcised … in order that he might confirm the promises given to the patriarchs, and in order that the Gentiles might glorify God for his mercy" (15:8,9, 1:16, 3:29, etc.).

Scholars have sometimes seen the references in Matt 10 and 15 to specifically Jewish mission as Matthean additions to the Markan form of the tradition, reflecting the strongly Jewish point of view of the author of the gospel. That is possible, but implausible. First, Matthew as we have it now is by no means exclusively Jewish. Gentile mission comes into great prominence in the climactic end of the gospel and the sending of the disciples to "all nations" (28:16–20). Second, as we have just seen, Paul knows of Jesus's prioritizing of the Jews during his ministry. Third, it is entirely probable that Mark writing for Gentiles (as is evident at the start of the chapter where

---

[13] Gal 6:1 expresses a similar sentiment: "Brothers, if a man is in some transgression, you who are spiritual correct such a one in a spirit of humility."

he refers to the Syro-Phoenician woman, 7:3–4) is the one who has edited the relevant traditions and who omitted or watered down the apparently anti-Gentile tone of Jesus's words.

Mark's editorial tendency is made clear in the passage preceding the incident with the Syro-Phoenician woman, where Jesus responds to Pharisees who have questioned his disciples' eating with "defiled hands" by explaining that real uncleanness has to do not with externals but with what comes out of the heart. Mark comments that by saying this, Jesus was "cleansing all foods" (7:19). He is clearly applying the teaching of Jesus to an issue that was not important in Jesus's own ministry but was very important and controversial in Pauline churches, as is evident in Galatians and also in Romans. In Romans, Paul is arguably making exactly the same point as Mark and probably referring to exactly the same teaching when he says "I know and am persuaded in the Lord Jesus that nothing is unclean in itself" (14:14).[14]

The idea that Matthew has reversed the Markan interpretation is a much more complicated hypothesis. With Mark turning the Jewish Jesus into a more Gentile-friendly Jesus and Matthew then turning Mark's Gentile-friendly Jesus back into a more Jewish figure, it is historically probable that Jesus started his ministry seeing his ministry as fulfilling the Jews' hopes and longings for the redemption of Israel. Even Mark's less explicit version of the story of the Syro-Phoenician woman suggests that, with Jesus commenting that the "children" need to be fed before the "dogs." But Jesus's experience of rejection and hostility led to an increased consciousness that Jerusalem and its leaders were leading the nation into terrible judgment, and that God's plan, as indeed hinted in the Scriptures and suggested by some of his own experiences (e.g., with the Syro-Phoenician woman), was going to be more international.

We conclude it is widely held that Matthew and Luke knew the Markan and "Q" versions of the mission discourse. Paul shows knowledge of knowing that discourse, not of course in Mark and Q, but in the oral tradition. And that oral tradition very likely included the go-not-among-the-Gentiles saying of Jesus attested in Matthew, with Mark and Luke softening its apparent exclusivism.[15] In the story of the Syro-Phoenician woman, Matthew's version was also probably the more original, which Mark edited and Luke omitted altogether, because they were both writing with Gentiles in mind. But, Mark less directly than Matthew indicates that the incident had a controversially Jewish bias, and Paul knows that the "lost sheep of the house of Israel" were the focus of Jesus's ministry.[16] Paul thus turns out to be a witness to the early dating of "M" traditions.[17]

---

[14] Matthew's version of the story reflects Jesus's Jewish context, with Jesus addressing the difference between the Pharisaic traditions focusing on outward rituals such as handwashing and his own prioritizing of God's law and the heart.

[15] It may have included other Matthean elements, e.g., "You received without payment (*dorean* in Greek), give without payment" (10:8). Paul uses the word *dorean* in 2 Cor 11:7 when comparing his gospel with that of "false apostles." Compare also Gal 6:6.

[16] Strikingly, Paul in the ending of his letter, which he is writing with his own hand, comments that neither circumcision nor uncircumcision counts for anything, but new creation, and then blesses those who recognize this and on "the Israel of God" (6:16).

[17] There is further possible evidence of the Pauline churches being familiar with Jesus's teaching about "what goes into a person" not defiling them, but rather what comes out from the heart (as in Mark 7 and Matt 15). It has been suggested that some Corinthian Christians were going to prostitutes

13.4 Law and Freedom

In Galatians, Paul was engaging with discussion about Jesus's teaching, especially on apostleship, Peter, and mission to Jews and Gentiles, including with some of the teaching unique to Matthew. It is a case, as typically with his letters, of the context setting the agenda. But one of the biggest questions in Galatians and in the acrimonious debate it describes was the question of the OT law, and that is a major concern also in Matthew.

The key passage is Matt 5:17-48 in Jesus's so-called Sermon on the Mount. It opens with programmatic statements about Jesus and the law, which are then followed by an exposition of Jesus's higher righteousness when compared to Jewish rabbinic teaching (5:17-48). Most of this material is not paralleled in the Lukan version of the sermon (Luke 6:20-49), and Luke's has often been regarded as the more original account with Jewish Matthew having added to it redactionally. However, there is a good case for suspecting that it is Luke who has edited out some of the Jewishly focused discussion in his gospel designed for Gentiles. Paul is arguably a witness to the Matthean version.

The section is introduced by Jesus's declaration, "Do not think that I have come to destroy the law and the prophets but to fulfil them," (Matt 5:17) which is followed by a strong statement that not an iota or dot will pass from the law until all is accomplished and by a warning that anyone breaking or teaching against "the least of these commandments will called least in the kingdom of heaven" (Matt 5:18-19). Then Jesus says, "Unless your righteousness exceeds that of the scribes and Pharisees, you will never enter the kingdom of heaven" (Matt 5:20), and then follows a series of so-called antitheses where that sort of higher righteousness is illustrated (Matt 5:21-48).

These verses are unquestionably very Matthean with the themes of kingdom of heaven, fulfillment, the law, and righteousness being extremely important in the Gospel and most likely a result of Matthew's own redaction (compare Matt 3:15, 6:33). But this conclusion is not all certain.[18] Yes, Matthew prefers the phrase "kingdom of heaven" to "kingdom of God,"[19] but Jesus fulfilling the OT including the law is a theme that permeates all the Gospels (e.g., Mark 1:15, Luke 4:21, 24:44, John 15:25, etc.). More specifically, there is a partial parallel to Matthew's 5:17-18 on iotas and dots in Luke 16:17.

There is reason to think that Paul was familiar with the dominical emphasis on fulfillment. He specifically refers to Jesus's way of love as the "fulfilling" of the

---

by applying Jesus's teaching on food to sex as something irrelevant for spiritual life (1 Cor 6, hence Paul's reference there to foods). See *Paul Follower*, 90-7, also John Nolland, "'Every Sin That a Person Commits Is Outside the Body' (1 Cor 6:18b): Paul's Likely Dependence on the Jesus Tradition," in *Who Created Christianity?*, ed. Craig Evans and Aaron White (Peabody: Hendrickson, 2020), 381-96.

[18] The saying simply underlines the point of the previous saying about the iota and dot and of the whole paragraph in Matt 5:17-20, which is a rebuttal of the idea that Jesus is a law-destroyer; on the contrary, he is a law-fulfiller, whose righteous standards go beyond the law and the traditions of the scribes and Pharisees.

[19] But the meaning is the same, whether Matthew rephrased for the sake of Jewish sensitivities about the name of God or to clarify that the kingdom of God was a heavenly reality come down to earth rather than an earthly political kingdom.

"whole law" or "every law" (Gal 5:14; Rom 13:8-10). The wording and sentiment are reminiscent of Matt 5:17-18, with the following exposition of Jesus's meaning in Matthew's antitheses being all about love in practice (5:21-48). The passage climaxes and ends with the revolutionary advance on "love your neighbour" in Jesus's "I say to you, love your enemies," an injunction strikingly paralleled in Paul's letters (see further below).

The prevalence of the fulfillment theme throughout the Gospels and the NT means that it would be unwise to claim too confidently that Paul knew Matt 5:17-18; however, the parallels are notable, and if Matt 5:17 and 18 were known traditions of Jesus, it is entirely likely that they would have featured in discussions between Paul and his opponents in Antioch.

But then there is also the saying in Matt 5:20 about no one entering the "kingdom of heaven unless your righteousness exceeds that of the scribes and Pharisees." Like vv. 17-18, this sounds very Matthean, but there are interesting parallels in Paul's letters (e.g., in 1 Cor 6:9, "Do you not know that unrighteous people will not inherit the kingdom of God"; Rom 14:17, "The kingdom of God is not food and drink but righteousness and peace and joy in the Holy Spirit"; and also Gal 5:21, "I told you before that those who do such things will not inherit the kingdom of God").

What is striking about these Pauline verses is that elsewhere Paul uses the expression "kingdom of God" infrequently (contrast Jesus who used it very often). The probability is that "kingdom of God" made sense in Jesus's Jewish context, but less sense in the Gentile world where Paul mainly ministered.[20] The fact that it was not a favorite usage of Paul makes his infrequent uses all the more striking and may suggest that at these points he is echoing and drawing on received and known Jesus-traditions. This may be confirmed by some of the hints that he gives that he is reminding his readers of what they have been taught previously—"do you not know?", "as I warned you before."[21]

Paul's references to the kingdom of God parallel the sayings of Jesus in seeing the kingdom as something present and also future; but of particular interest for our discussion is the way that the kingdom for Paul is very specifically associated with "righteous" living. We may reasonably conclude that Paul knew and passed on the teaching of Jesus associating the kingdom and righteousness such as is expressed in Matthew "unless your righteousness exceeds that of the scribes and Pharisees you will not enter the kingdom of heaven" (5:20).

So, there is a surprisingly good case for Paul having known the "M" traditions of Matt 5:17-20. That case is reinforced if there is reason to think he may also have been acquainted with the antitheses that follow and illustrate the "higher" righteousness of Matt 5:20. Jesus here contrasts what "you have heard" with what "I say to you." These antitheses are not in the Lukan sermon and could have been added to the Q sermon tradition by Matthew. So, we have two questions: (1) do they go back to Matthew or to Jesus? (2) Is there any reason to suppose that Paul knew them?

---

[20] Something similar may be true of John's gospel's preference for "eternal life" rather than "kingdom of God."

[21] 1 Cor 6:9-10; Gal 5:19-21. See my *Paul Follower*, 71-80.

To the first question the answer is that several of the antitheses have a strongly Jewish and Palestinian flavor that would make sense in Jesus's context and also explain Luke's failure to include them (e.g., the first antithesis in Matt 5:21–26 refers to bringing gifts to "the altar" and uses Aramaic terms, *Raca* and *Gehenna*[22]; the fourth antithesis speaks of the Jewish scribes' ideas of valid vs. invalid oaths).

To the second question, the answer is also yes! So, Paul, in warning of sexual sin in 1 Thess 4:1–8, refers to "instructions we gave you through the Lord Jesus," quite probably alluding to Jesus's teaching about sexual immorality in antitheses 2 and 3.[23] He certainly knew of Jesus's teaching on divorce as in antithesis 3, hence explicitly in 1 Cor 7:10–11.[24] He quite possibly echoes antithesis 4 about oaths and truthfulness in 2 Cor 1:17–20.[25]

Most striking of all is the evidence relating to antitheses 5 and 6 concerning revenge and loving even one's enemies. The substance of both of the last two antitheses is paralleled in Luke's version of the sermon (contrast the earlier antitheses, 6:27–36). That is notable, and what is remarkable is the fact that Luke introduces the sayings with Jesus saying: "But I say to you who are hearing." This is unmistakably reminiscent of the phraseology used throughout the antitheses in Matthew: "You have heard that it was said, but I say to you." The phrase does not fit particularly well or logically after what precedes it in Luke, and the probability is that Luke here betrays his familiarity with the form of the antitheses attested by Matthew. It seems likely that Luke, having jumped over the earlier and distinctly Jewish antitheses (understandably), reproduces and conflates the climactic two with their call to revolutionary love of enemies. The radical call to love is something of great importance to Luke[26] and of as much relevance to Gentiles as well as to Jews (though he naturally omits the disparaging reference to the Gentiles of Matt 5:36).

As for Paul, the evidence of his familiarity with the last two antitheses is strong.[27] There are striking echoes of Jesus's teaching on non-retaliation and love of enemies. For example, Jesus's "don't resist evil, but..." has a notable parallel in the very early 1 Thessalonians: "See that you don't pay back evil for evil, but always pursue the good in relation to each other and to everyone" (5:15). The same sentiment is found in Rom 12:17, "do not repay anyone evil for evil, but..." Just before this in Rom 12, Paul has said "bless those who persecute you, bless and do not curse" and just afterward he speaks of feeding hungry "enemies," in a way that is strikingly similar to Matthew's and Luke's words of Jesus "love your enemies" and especially to Luke's "bless those who curse you" (Rom 12:14; Matt 5:43; Luke 6:27). Gospel scholars noting the connections will often

---

[22] There is no clear evidence that Paul was familiar with this antithesis, though his advocacy of brotherly love and decrying of "biting and devouring one another" in Gal 5:13–15 comes in a discussion of the OT law and concludes with the warning "lest you consume one another." The verb "consume" often having connotations of fiery judgment as does the Jewish term *Gehenna*.

[23] In Galatians the same concern is much more briefly expressed in Paul's warning of the "desire/lust of the flesh" in Gal 5:16, 24, again in the context of his discussion of freedom in the Spirit and law.

[24] On the complex relationship of the two different forms of the synoptic divorce, see my discussion in *Gospel Perspectives 5* (Sheffield: JSOT), 7–15.

[25] See Wenham, *Paul Follower*, 271–4.

[26] See the parable of the Good Samaritan in Luke 10:25–37, also 23:34.

[27] See Thompson, *Clothed*, 87–110.

bring in the Q hypothesis, usually seeing Luke as closer to Q than Matthew. Although there are respects in which Luke's version of the sermon is arguably more original, Matthew's version has a claim to being more original in other respects, including in the antithetical form with its specific relating of Jesus's teaching to the OT law.[28]

13.5 Conclusions on Paul's Knowledge of Matthew's Unique Traditions

The cumulative case for Paul knowing and alluding to stories and sayings of Jesus only attested in Matthew is strong. He probably knew the "Matthean" versions of Jesus's teaching about the apostles and Peter, about mission to Jews and Gentiles, and about the OT law. This conclusion has all sorts of ramifications. First, it reinforces the already strong case for Paul's knowledge and use of Jesus's traditions. Second, it adds significantly to our understanding of Matthew's Gospel and in particular to our understanding of his sources. Third, it throws light on the wider questions of Gospel origins showing the importance of the oral tradition and the inadequacy of some simple solutions.

13.6 The Antioch Incident and Controversy

It is stating the obvious to say that the evidence presented also offers insights into what we might call the first great division in the history of the church—that between Pauline Christianity and Jerusalem Christianity, with the Antioch incident being anything but incidental, but rather reflecting a serious theological argument and potential parting of the ways. Galatians describes the incident and was written in response to it, whether very soon after the events, if Galatians was written between AD 48 and 50, or as a still-raw retrospective reflection a few years later.

It is entirely probable that the Jesus traditions to which Paul alludes to will have featured in the debates and divisions between Paul and his critics, with the "circumcision" party from Jerusalem accusing Paul of being unfaithful to Jesus and his teaching, questioning his credentials, and contrasting him with Peter, Jesus's rock,[29] stressing that Jesus was a Jew who defined his mission-priority and that of his community as to the Jews rather than to the uncircumcised Gentiles, unlike Paul, emphasizing Jesus's affirmation of the whole OT law, including, in their view, circumcision and dietary laws, and saying that Paul was effectively destroying the law and morality by his gospel of freedom. They may have pointed to some unrighteous behavior in Paul's "spiritually" excited converts (as was evidenced soon after in the Corinthian and Thessalonian congregations [see 1 Cor 6, 1 Thess 4 and 5]).

---

[28] For a detailed attempt to explain the relationships between Matthew, Luke, and Paul here, see my article in *Gospel Perspectives V*, 15–24.
[29] And, of course, James was the Lord's brother!

In replying, Paul recognizes Peter's special position but affirms his own calling as an apostle comparable to Peter's. He recognizes the priority given to Jewish mission by Jesus and the first apostles, but he insists that the cross of Christ and the coming of the Spirit have brought a new age of freedom and new creation with the old distinctions between Jew and Gentile being abolished. He personally has been commissioned to bring in the Gentiles; and all is in fulfillment of God's promises to Abraham and Israel. Paul agrees entirely about Jesus "fulfilling" the law, with the Spirit of Jesus producing love and practical righteousness from the heart, that is, emphatically non-antinomian "fleshly" living, but very much in keeping with the Sermon on the Mount.

It is easy to see how the same data (i.e., the same teaching of Jesus) could have been divisively used by the different parties, coming from their different contexts and so with different agendas. The "circumcision party" reflected the pressures on the young Christian church in Jerusalem from the often-hostile Jewish authorities who accused them of betrayal of Judaism. The Gentile churches founded by Paul were disturbed by the idea that they should Judaize. The debate between Paul and his critics was acrimonious.

Galatians is explicitly a response to the Antioch incident and the issues it raised, arguing the Pauline case. Might Matthew's Gospel implicitly be a Jewish-Christian response? Matthew has indeed been seen by some scholars as having an anti-Pauline motif running through it, notably in Matt 5:17–20—the denunciation of the person who relaxes even the "least of the commandments" in 5:19 has been seen as directed at Paul in particular. This reading of Matthew has typically been located in a Jewish-Christian church context after AD 70, when church and synagogue were at logger heads.

This could be right. However, two observations are worth making. First, the differences between Paul and Matthew should not be exaggerated. Matthew's Gospel is very Jewish, but also highly critical of Judaism and not anti-Gentile. Matthew is strong on the fulfillment of the OT, but also on the newness of what Jesus has brought (i.e., the kingdom of heaven, and on Jesus as bringing freedom in relation to aspects of Judaism [11:12–13; 12:1–14; 17:24–27], and also on the era-changing impact of Jesus's death [21:43, 27:51–53]).[30]

Matthew may at first appear to be thoroughly legalistic with reference to the iotas and dots of the law, but the thrust of Matt 5 is on Jesus's higher righteousness, on his call to extreme love, and Jesus is specifically critical of the hypocritical legalism of the rabbis, whether on divorce, or oath-taking, or other things. Indeed, for Jesus in Matthew it is the heart that is primary (15:1–18), and it is the teaching of Jesus rather than the OT law (which he "fulfills") that has the final word.[31]

---

[30] Despite the saying about the ongoing validity of "the least of these commandments," the following explanation is entirely on what can be called the "moral" law as opposed to matters of ritual (including the Sabbath). On rituals Jesus in Matthew is consistently critical of rabbinic interpretations, and he is himself accused of culpable liberalism. A significant and curious story is that of the temple tax and the coin in the fish's mouth, with its reference to "the sons" being free in relation to the temple (18:24–27).

[31] In the antitheses it is what "I say to you…" that supersedes and surpasses even the OT commands, and the Gospel concludes with Jesus sending his disciples to evangelize and to teach all that "I have commanded you" (28:20). Compare also 7:21–23.

As for Paul, Galatians is in some ways a very Jewish letter, with much space given to Abraham and the OT, with an allusion to the priority of Jewish mission, and with a concluding greeting addressing the Galatians as the "Israel of God." Yes, Galatians massively emphasizes the freedom that Christ has brought and denounces the imposing of the OT law on Gentiles (notably circumcision and dietary regulations), but Paul also warns of fatal impact of "fleshly" living and contrasts that with the fruit of the Spirit. There are very striking parallels between Paul's description of Spirit-living and both the Matthean beatitudes and the traditions about sins arising from the heart (Mark 7, Matt 15). And Paul specifically identifies Holy-Spirit-inspired-living as love and as fulfilling "the whole law."[32]

One of the most intriguing texts in Galatians is Gal 6:2: "bear one another's burdens and so fulfil '*the law of Christ.*'" What was this "law" of Christ for Paul? Just a few verses earlier he had said "*through love be slaves to one another,*" following that with his comment about the whole law being fulfilled through love (Gal 5:13–14). The probability is that loving and humble serving was the "law of Christ" for Paul. All the Gospels attest Jesus's emphatic and repeated challenge to his disciples to follow him in self-sacrificial service of one another. It was his "new commandment" and was to be the hallmark of their discipleship and their leadership (John 13:34–35; Matt 20:24–28).

If that is the primary reference of the "law of Christ," it is another example of a Jesus-tradition in Galatians, but the interesting wider relevance is that it shows Paul, like Matthew, seeing Jesus and his "law," that is, teaching, both as fulfilling and also taking precedence over the OT.[33] Therefore, the differences between Matthew and Galatians are greatly exaggerated.

Second, scholarly proposals about Matthew being written in the context of church-synagogue tensions toward the end of the first century are distinctly speculative.[34] But there were very serious tensions between Pauline and Jewish Christians that came to a head in the Antioch incident around AD 50, and the idea that a version of Matthew was written in that context deserves a hearing. We have observed how plausibly Matthew, as well as Galatians (with its echoes of M traditions), can be seen as reflecting the two "sides" of the argument—with Paul arguing the freedom case and Matthew presenting what we might call the Peter/James position, bringing out Jesus's positive affirmation of the law and righteousness and also of the role of Peter and the twelve disciples. Matthew very likely knew about the "lawlessness" of some in the new, charismatically endowed Pauline churches and their interpretation of Christian freedom (see Matt

---

[32] One agreement with the Jerusalem "pillars" specifically noted by Paul was over remembering the poor, "which very thing I was eager to do" (Gal 2:10); the priority of care for the poor is in Jesus's teaching in all the gospels, including Matthew, e.g., in the climactic sheep and goats parable (25:31–46).

[33] For other positive references in Paul's letters to the commands of the OT, see 1 Cor 7:19; Gal 6:15; Rom 7:12.

[34] E.g., the once popular view that Matthew reflects the situation following the so-called Council of Jamnia at the end of the first century has been widely questioned. Matthew's polemic against the Pharisees makes perfectly good and less speculative sense in the context of the Peter-Paul incident if Acts is to be believed in suggesting that it was Pharisees who were pressing for Gentile circumcision and law-keeping and arguing against ex-Pharisee Paul (Acts 15:5).

7:21–23), and Matt 5:19 on the person "losing" the OT laws could represent Matthew's warning of the dangers of Pauline freedom.[35]

The idea that Matthew's Gospel reflects the divisions in the early church of AD 40s and 50s is an intriguing possibility, though it raises many questions.[36] The main conclusions of this article, however, about Paul in Galatians, 1 Thessalonians, and other letters drawing on "Matthean" traditions of Jesus are probable and significant. Either way, Matthew is a hugely important source for our understanding of Jesus's teaching.

---

[35] Matt 5:19 might be seen as a Matthean gloss or marginal note, like Mark's "cleansing all foods" (7:19). The fact that the verse speaks of the "liberal" teacher as least in the kingdom rather than as finally excluded could reflect a context of difficult debate within the church community rather than a more final break-up.

[36] For example, about the hypothesis of Markan priority, though a form of the hypothesis is not ruled out by the proposal. See Rainer Reisner's fascinating proposal of how the oral traditions of Jesus could have ended up in our Gospels. "The Orality and Memory Hypothesis," in *The Synoptic Problem*, ed. Stanley E. Porter and Bryan R. Dyer (Grand Rapids, MI: Baker, 2016), 106–7. I also find myself going back to my father's creative and sadly neglected 1991 study *Redating Matthew, Mark and Luke*, where he dates Matthew around AD 40.

14

Reading James to Understand Jesus

Mariam Kovalishyn

Every now and then, something arises in my scholarship that sets off a trajectory for years after. One such was a line I stumbled across some fifteen years ago, from a commentary on Matthew by the Canadian scholar Francis Wright Beare. Beare, holding a view of salvation strictly by grace, is troubled by Jesus's story of the Sheep and the Goats in Matt 25 and concludes, "It is to be noted that in this whole passage there is no trace of a doctrine of the forgiveness of sins, or of the grace of God. The righteous are invited to enter into the Kingdom because they have shown themselves worthy by their kind deeds, not because their sins are forgiven ... There is no trace of saving *faith*—the righteous have done their good deeds without any thought that they were serving Christ (or God)."[1] He concludes by asking unironically whether such a teaching can be considered Christian. But Matthew presents this story as the words of Jesus, so this seems an example where Beare's theology leads him to be unable to hear Jesus well. In contrast, as someone steeped in the epistle of James, the story of the Sheep and the Goats does not seem surprising. To read James is to hear the teaching of Jesus being passed on.

Too often, the epistle of James has simply been judged the book about "works" and thus ignored in preference for a specific interpretation of Pauline theology. This, however, has left us with an unfortunately truncated view of the Christian life, wherein it has been possible to teach that all someone needs to do is have a moment where they prayed a sinner's prayer, and they are saved forever, no matter what. Not only is that a bad misreading of Paul-and in fairness, Luther—but also of what Jesus taught, and James can help readers make sense of this.

Matthew is structured around the five primary blocks of teaching, and it is in these that we see the bulk of the resonances in James. Richard Bauckham most brilliantly maps out for his readers how James is a responsible wisdom teacher resetting the teaching of the greatest teacher of all, Jesus, for a new audience.[2] His work is essential, because James does not *quote* Jesus aside from once in chapter 5, but the influence of Jesus's teaching is in every line of the epistle. Bruce Metzger observed that "Luther was right in applying the criterion 'whatever promotes Christ is apostolic,' but wrong in not

---

[1] Francis Wright Beare, *The Gospel According to Matthew: A Commentary* (Oxford: Basil Blackwell, 1981), 496–7.
[2] Richard Bauckham, *James: Wisdom of James, Disciple of Jesus the Sage* (London: Routledge, 1999).

recognizing that the epistle of James also 'promotes Christ' by its practical application of the Sermon on the Mount."[3] Dean Deppe notes that critical scholars have observed over 175 links with Jesus's teaching,[4] while Sam Grottenberg argues that the links aren't solely to Jesus's didactic teaching but also to his parables.[5] Ultimately, Douglas Moo concludes that "no New Testament document is more influenced by the teaching of Jesus than James."[6] If we take these scholars seriously, then the epistle of James may be one of the earliest and most comprehensive interpretations of the Jesus tradition for the early church, helping us understand both what Jesus taught and how to apply it.

This chapter does not seek to give a comprehensive list of the parallels in James's epistle to the Gospel of Matthew. Deppe listed over 175 possible parallels to the Gospels, many of which are in Matthew. Nor does it seek to make a claim of direct literary dependence.[7] Moreover, the structure of James as wisdom, where themes overlap, develop, and interrelate, makes comparisons complicated.[8] To navigate a comparison, therefore, we will first examine some of the widely agreed theses and themes of James and explore how they echo and illumine Jesus's teaching, then conclude with some final thoughts about the implications of reading Matthew and James together. James closely echoes Jesus's teachings, and by paying attention to the overlaps, we see a vision of the Christian life that calls for transformed speech and generous and merciful lives, initiated by and modeled on the grace of God.

To begin, there are two possible theses for the epistle of James. One suggestion is that 1:4 expresses the goal of the epistle. James 1:4 is at the culmination of an introductory sequence about enduring trials, trusting that God is at work. The reader is called to "let endurance have its full effect, so that you may be mature and complete, lacking in nothing."[9] The language of maturity or perfection, toward which they strive, is *teleios*, a perfection that comes through maturity, through enduring trials with faithfulness and

---

[3] Bruce M. Metzger, *The Canon of the New Testament* (Oxford: Clarendon, 1987), 244.
[4] Dean B. Deppe, *The Sayings of Jesus in the Epistle of James* (Chelsea, MI: Bookcrafters, 1989).
[5] Samuel P. Grottenberg, *Deparabolization in James: A Study of the Theological and Thematic Appropriation of the Synoptic Parables of Jesus in the Epistle of James* (MA Thesis, Regent College, 2018).
[6] Douglas J. Moo, *The Letter of James*, Pillar NTC (Grand Rapids, MI: Eerdmans, 2000), 27.
[7] See Patrick J. Hartin, *James and the Q Sayings of Jesus* (Sheffield: Sheffield Academic Press, 1991). While I do not agree with all of his reconstruction, his conclusion regarding James and Matthew is helpful:

> Not only does James show an awareness of the Q tradition, but he is also conscious of the way it developed within the Matthean community. James shows that he has emerged from a world which holds as sacred traditions that are common to the Gospel of Matthew. This perspective again places James in an intermediary position between Q and the Gospel of Matthew. This does not mean that Matthew utilized the Epistle of James or vice versa. The knowledge that James has of the traditions and sources that go to the Gospel of Matthew is such that the epistle situates itself before the codification of these sources took place within the Gospel of Matthew. (243)

[8] This is also a trait of Matthew. R. T. France, *Matthew: Evangelist and Teacher* (Grand Rapids, MI: Zondervan, 1989), 129, observes, "Matthew seems more like the preacher, whose favourite phrases and illustrations recur without embarrassment, and who regards repetition as a valuable teaching aid, rather than the literary purist who regards repetition as a stylistic *faux pas*."
[9] NRSV throughout.

thus growing in knowledge and relationship with God, fully developed morally.[10] It is not a changeless platonic perfection but an active maturity gained through a lifetime of faithfulness. So, on the one hand, James points in a *direction for growth* if we take 1:4 as a thesis.

Intriguingly, the only two uses of *teleios* in the Gospels are in Matthew. The first is in Matt 5:48, where it summarizes Jesus's recasting of the Mosaic Law: "Be perfect (ἔσεσθε οὖν ὑμεῖς τέλειοι), therefore, as your heavenly Father is perfect," itself an obvious mirror of Lev 19:2: "You shall be holy (Ἅγιοι ἔσεσθε), for I the LORD your God am holy." While the Lucan version of this saying opts for "merciful" (Γίνεσθε οἰκτίρμονες; Luke 6:36), James follows Matthew in choosing *teleios* for the call to the imitation of God's character. Matthew's other use of *teleios* occurs in 19:21, at the conclusion of Jesus's exchange with the rich young man: "If you wish to be perfect, go, sell your possessions, and give the money to the poor, and you will have treasure in heaven; then come, follow me." In this encounter, Jesus expands the young man's definition of perfection and obedience, and James follows this in varied ways, as we will see below. In short, in both Jesus's teaching in Matthew and in the epistle of James, the law is more than the sum of its commands. The links between Matthew and James solely around the term *teleios* are revealing of their common teaching about the follower's calling and identity.

On the other hand, Jas 1:26–27 neatly maps out the *themes* of the book in describing the worship that God desires from his people. Verse 26 sets its statement out in the negative, "If any *think* they are religious, and do not bridle their tongues but deceive their hearts, their religion is worthless." Uncontrolled speech is a sign of an unredeemed life, and the requirement for careful speech threads all through the epistle, although it comes into central focus in chapters 3 and 4. Verse 27, then, breaks into two positive statements describing the worship that God wants from his people. The first half reads thus: "Religion that is pure and undefiled before God, the Father, is this: to care for orphans and widows in their distress." The description of "pure and undefiled" echoes both priestly language as well as prophetic calls to Israel regarding how they are supposed to appear before their God. In Matthew, Jesus promises that the "pure in heart" are blessed "for they will see God" (Matt 5:8) and warns that the Pharisees need not merely to perform righteous deeds but become pure from the inside (Matt 23:26), much as James contrasts the true (pure) religion with a false and self-deceptive one.

Pure and undefiled worship will be shown through controlled speech (Jas 1:26), but the first positive act of Jas 1:27 is to care for those who are marginalized in society. Widows and orphans, lacking a man in a patriarchal society, had no access to the functioning of society. Biblically, they often stand in pairs with other marginalized groups like foreigners and resident aliens, or the poor and oppressed. To be mindful of those who do not have access into society is to engage in societal critique and to practice the ethics of the right-side-up kingdom where God hears the cry of those who

---

[10] Peter H. Davids, *The Epistle of James*, NIGTC (Grand Rapids, MI: Eerdmans, 1982), 70, summarizes it as "a fully rounded uprightness, an approach toward the character of God or an imitation of Christ."

are marginalized and suffering.[11] Finally, the last clause of 1:27 calls for people who "keep oneself unstained by the world." This phrase has at times been mistaken as a call to remove oneself from being *involved* in society, but rather, as Darian Lockett argues, "'to keep oneself unstained from the world' is to resist theological and sociological acculturation and the dividedness that attends those who attempt to live both for God and for 'the world,'" recognizing the "absolute incompatibility of [the] two construals of reality and two modes of behavior following from such diverse understandings."[12] One cannot, as James will say, be both friends of the world and friends of God, because the world's priorities and values are directly opposed to God's. This can be seen in valuing a rich person over a poor person and prioritizing high status over low status, but being stained by the world can also be revealed in whether one endures temptations or prefers selfish indulgence, whether one is generous or possessive, and whether one's loyalty ultimately is given. It is within this last category, perhaps, that we return to that initial thesis of 1:4 and its call to becoming "mature, or perfect, and complete, lacking in nothing." People's moral and spiritual growth reveals itself as they separate from the values of the world and engage the world instead through God's lenses.

While the introductions to both the thesis and the key themes of James show verbal relation to teachings of Jesus in Matthew, it is worth further exploration of how James's three themes of speech and its link with judgment, a practical concern for the marginalized, and moral purity, are all expansions on teaching by Jesus as recorded in Matthew. How James interprets Jesus's teaching can help us listen to Jesus better ourselves.

First, both Jesus and James consistently teach that the one who is wise and faithful will show it through their speech, while careless speech is cause for judgment. This is a persistent theme of Jesus's teaching, and one with deep resonance to the world today in which the pressure to be quotable, to be biting and edgy in sound-bite form, is endless. In contrast, James follows Jesus in arguing that one's speech needs to be careful, for uncontrolled speech leads to judgment. Intriguingly, this is the only topic in which James quotes Jesus directly, commanding speech that is direct and honest (Matt 5:33-37; Jas 5:12). This concern about a person's speech and the danger of judgment is a surprisingly central focus of teaching for both James and Jesus.

The first example explores how Jesus cemented the tie between speech and the potential for judgment. In Matt 5:21-22, he refuses to let speech be considered of less significance than actions. Jesus warns:

---

[11] Douglas J. Moo, *The Letter of James*, Pillar NTC (Grand Rapids, MI: Eerdmans, 2000), 96, cautions: "James is not polemicizing against religious ritual per se but against a ritual that goes no further than outward show and mere words. He is probably somewhat dependent on a widespread pagan and Jewish tradition that emphasized that proper cultic worship must be accompanied by ethical conduct." He continues to give an overview of the OT background for this, summarizing, "One test of pure religion, therefore, is the degree to which we extend aid to the 'helpless' in our world—whether they be widows and orphans, immigrants trying to adjust to a new life, impoverished third-world dwellers, the handicapped, or the homeless" (97). See also Donald J. Verseput, "Reworking the Puzzle of Faith and Deeds in James 2.14-26," *NTS* 43 (1997): 101-4.

[12] Darian Lockett, *Purity and Worldview in the Epistle of James* (London: T&T Clark, 2008), 105, 79.

> You have heard that it was said to those of ancient times, "You shall not murder"; and "whoever murders shall be liable to judgment." But I say to you that if you are angry with a brother or sister, you will be liable to judgment; and if you insult a brother or sister, you will be liable to the council; and if you say, "You fool," you will be liable to the hell of fire.

This first of the "antitheses" of the Sermon on the Mount warns that to slander another person in anger or dismissal is dangerous. France observes,

> The actual committing of murder is only the outward manifestation of an inward attitude which is itself culpable, whether or not it actually issues in the act of murder. Angry thoughts and contemptuous words (which equally derive from "the heart," 12:34) deserve equal judgment; indeed, the "hellfire" with which the saying concludes goes far beyond the human death penalty which the OT law envisaged.[13]

Speaking (wrongful) judgmental words brings out from within, where no one but God can see, the truth of one's attitude toward another person. One might suggest that the words spoken *reveal* the cause for judgment.

Two texts from James that might build on this include Jas 1:19-20 and Jas 5:9. In the former, James warns his hearers to be "quick to listen, slow to speak, slow to anger; for your anger does not produce God's righteousness." This text ties together Jesus's warning about anger and judgment and explains it further—in their interactions with others, their hastiness to anger and to speaking without understanding is dangerous. Instead of a "righteous anger" so many like to claim, anger without understanding is the opposite. Lockett notes, "One cannot accomplish God's righteousness by means of human anger because they are opposed to one another. God's righteousness is incongruent with human anger."[14] Meanwhile Jas 5:9 explicitly warns about the judgment awaiting one who speaks against another, no longer threatening the speaker with hellfire as in Matthew, they are now cautioned that the judge who can make such a decision is "standing at the doors." While the first half of 5:9 may sound like Matt 7:1 ("Do not judge, so that you may not be judged"), and the second part of each verse is exactly parallel (ἵνα μὴ κριθῆτε), the first phrase of Jas 5:9 ("do not grumble against one another") ties together the injunction of Matt 5:21-22 against slander with the later warning in 7:1 against judgment, James thereby makes explicit what is wrong with the type of judgment the people were making in Matt 7:1—slanderous judgment, "grumbling" against one another, leads to judgment by God the Judge (cf. Jas 4:11-12).

---

[13] R. T. France, *The Gospel of Matthew*, NIGNT (Grand Rapids, MI: Eerdmans, 2007), 199. Craig L. Blomberg, *Matthew*, NAC (Nashville, TN: Broadman Press, 1992), adds the important note that there is a strong, if likely later interpretive, textual tradition that "adds the phrase 'without cause' following the word 'brother.' ... both of these prohibitions against the use of insulting names undoubtedly carried the implicit qualification of 'where unjustified,' since Jesus himself uses the term *mōros* in 23:17, 19 (in direct address) and in 7:26 (in indirect address) when the label is accurate." This can help us nuance how we are called to be discerning but not allowed to be insulting.

[14] Darian Lockett, *Purity and Worldview in the Epistle of James* (London: T&T Clark, 2008), 90.

Jesus's teaching that speech leads to judgment in 12:33–37 should be noted at this point:

> Either make the tree good, and its fruit good; or make the tree bad, and its fruit bad; for the tree is known by its fruit. You brood of vipers![15] How can you speak good things, when you are evil? For out of the abundance of the heart the mouth speaks. The good person brings good things out of a good treasure, and the evil person brings evil things out of an evil treasure. I tell you, on the day of judgment you will have to give an account for every careless word you utter; for by your words you will be justified, and by your words you will be condemned.

Bauer notes that "Persons act not from predetermined divine fiat, but from the deep intentions of their own hearts (Matt 7:15–19; 12:33–37; 15:17–20; 23:26); accordingly, God will judge them on the basis of their decisions, which mirror their inner life."[16] While his point stands, Bauer does not make clear the emphasis Jesus is placing on *speech* as an act worthy of judgment—for good or ill. But James takes this condemnation on the Pharisees for their misleading teaching (cf. Matt 23:23–24) and warns, "you know that we who teach will be judged with greater strictness" (Jas 3:1). Such a warning is an easy deduction for James to make from Old Testament (OT) prophetic denunciations on false shepherds leading the people astray, but given that this is his introduction to a section specifically dealing with speech, he seems to develop Jesus's warning to make its implications for teachers explicit.[17] Again, this is not to suggest that James wrote while looking at a copy of Matthew, rather, the epistle of James models the integration and application of Jesus's teaching for his new setting. And while some would argue that all of Jas 3 that follows is directed to teachers, many others would see a similar interplay between the specific and general between these two passages.[18] In Matt 12, Jesus warns the "brood of vipers" that they are in trouble, but the warning then expands to the general principle about the good person and evil person bringing out of their abundance. Likewise, Jas 3 begins with the specific warning to teachers but then cautions that "we all stumble" and cannot control our speech (v. 2).

These passages are also tied, however, through their use of imagery to depict the nature of speech as revealing what is inside. Jesus begins his teaching with the principle that good trees produce good fruit and bad trees likewise bad. He subsequently adds the illustration of people bringing out treasure from where it has been hidden away

---

[15] This text provides a good example of why we need to nuance a "do not judge" stance with an understanding of slander. Presumably when Jesus called the Pharisees this, he did not bring judgment upon himself!

[16] David R. Bauer, *The Gospel of the Son of God: An Introduction to Matthew* (Downers Grove, IL: IVP Academic, 2019), 281.

[17] Scot McKnight, *The Letter of James* (Grand Rapids, MI: Eerdmans, 2011), 271, suggests that Matt 23 might be part of a "traditional [code] of behavior for the teaching office that came with special warnings." He continues that "their knowledge leads to responsibility for both what they teach and how they live. This, after all, is precisely the point Jesus makes in Matthew 23 when he excoriates the scribes and Pharisees for both knowing and not doing" (272).

[18] McKnight, *James*, 266–7, exemplifies the former; Patrick J. Hartin, *James*, Sacra Pagina (Collegeville, PA: Liturgical Press, 2003), 182–3 suggests the latter.

from sight. James uses a number of nature illustrations to show the powerful effect of the tongue but then develops Jesus's nature illustration to emphasize that the tongue brings forth what is in its nature (springs →one type of water, either good or bad; fig trees →figs; grapevines →grapes; Jas 3:6–12). James thus follows Jesus's lead using nature imagery (trees and fruit in particular) to show that it is not merely actions, but words, that reveal the truth of one's nature, and thus words warrant judgment as much as actions.[19]

The second theme is that of riches and poverty and how to correctly think about our social status, particularly as related to our money. This is a highly significant theme and one difficult to read from the West. Liberation theologian Pedrito Maynard-Reid went so far as to argue: "For [James] the rich are outside the sphere of salvation and faith."[20] As Maynard-Reid presents, generally the discussion is phrased in terms of "the Rich and the Poor" and "Can the Rich be Saved?" I do not necessarily agree with him at a base definition of "rich" in James as people who have money, but money is undoubtedly a significant danger. Jesus, of course, taught a substantive amount about how people were to relate to their money, and realizing the resonance between the two texts can help the reader develop a careful response to money shaped by generosity and humility (i.e., the second half of the Sermon on the Mount; 6:19–34). For both Jesus and James, generosity is a key sign of humility and faith in God, reflecting the generosity of God in open-handedness for the good of others.

In Matt 5:43–48, Jesus makes explicit that the character of his followers is to conform to God's character. In Jesus's quote in Matt 5:43 the love command from Lev 19:18 appears to have gained unhelpful further defining ("You shall love your neighbor *and hate your enemy*"), in this antithesis Jesus explains that believers are instead called to the imitation of God ("Be perfect, therefore, as your heavenly Father is perfect," 5:48, cf. Jas 1:4). The rhetorical questions Jesus asks are echoed in Jas 2:14–17: Jesus's "what reward do you have?" (τίνα μισθὸν ἔχετε;) sounds much like James's "what is the good of that?" (τί τὸ ὄφελος), both common rhetorical questions meant to stimulate the hearer to reconsider their presuppositions.[21] The call to generosity beyond what is natural, to be able to "give to everyone who begs from you" (Matt 5:42a, cf. Jas 2:15–16),

---

[19] Bauckham, *James*, 101–2:

> James shares Jesus' special concern with the heart as the source of words and actions. Again this can be seen, for example, in his treatment of speech ethics. The extreme difficulty of bridling the tongue (3:7–8), which James portrays in a way unparalleled in other treatments of the tongue in the Jewish wisdom tradition, shows that perfection cannot be a matter of mere outward obedience, but only of consistent behaviour springing from a heart that is wholly devoted to God. It is the mixed motives and divided loyalties of the 'double-minded' that are exposed by their double-tongued speech, flattering God with their lips while cursing their neighbor from the same mouth (3:9–12).

[20] Pedrito U. Maynard-Reid, *Poverty and Wealth in James,* reprint ed. (Eugene, OR: Wipf & Stock, 2004), 63.

[21] Blomberg, *Matthew*, 115: "Jesus' followers must thus demonstrate a higher moral standard than the average unbeliever. ... 'What reward will you get?' (v. 46) parallels 'What are you doing more than others?' (v. 47), suggesting not the idea of compensation for doing good but the recurrent theme of the believer's distinctiveness. ... Jesus is not frustrating his hearers with an unachievable ideal but challenging them to grow in obedience to God's will—to become more like him."

is what mirrors the character of God, "who gives to all generously and ungrudgingly" (Jas 1:5, cf. the illustrations from nature in Matt 5:45). As France summarizes, "Jesus is demanding a different approach, not via laws read as simply rules of conduct but rather by looking behind those laws to the mind and character of God himself ... the limit is perfection, the perfection of God himself."[22] James follows Jesus's teaching in this, particularly concerned that our generosity mirror God's.

This point can be made even more clearly through the parallels of Matt 7:8–12 and Jas 1:5 and 16–17. While in Matt 5, Jesus in passing uses the illustration of how God gives rain and sun to everyone, now in Matt 7, the generosity of God to those who ask is forefronted. God is a better giver, as it were, than any human ever could be: "*how much more* will your Father in heaven give good things to those who ask him" (7:11). This teaching could well lie behind James's demand that God's people ask "in faith, never doubting" (1:6), since the doubt James refers to is doubt in God's character as good and generous. When Jesus repeats "how much more," he forces his audience to grapple with the reality of God's generous nature. And this good generosity of God is the basis on which James expects his audience to act.[23] God gives even to those who don't deserve it and gives to everyone who asks, and Jesus has already instructed his followers to "give to everyone who asks" (Matt 5:42), and so James concludes that those who do not respond to a need with generosity have not yet come to saving faith (Jas 2:14–16). James follows Jesus in seeing generosity as one of God's key attributes and one that God's followers must emulate.

The failure to deal with wealth well, however, brings danger, revealing that one is, in truth, "stained by the world" (cf. Jas 1:27). In his Sermon, Jesus warns against hoarding wealth "where moth and rust consume and where thieves break in and steal" (Matt 5:19). James picks up that imagery and warns: "Your riches have rotted, and your clothes are moth-eaten. Your gold and silver have rusted, and their rust will be evidence against you, and it will eat your flesh like fire" (Jas 5:2–3). The thieves in James's scenario are the wealthy, who have stolen the wages of their workers, and this is cause for judgment upon them. Wealth, for both Jesus and James, is not meant for hoarding, but for doing good (cf. Jas 4:17).[24]

The problem faced by both teachers is that of people identifying themselves with and by their wealth, and thus doubleminded. This becomes most apparent in Jesus's confrontation with the rich young man, who cannot fathom selling his possessions. His identity was found not just in his righteousness, but in his wealth. Jesus watched the rich young man walk away and observed, "Truly I tell you, it will be hard for a rich person to enter the kingdom of heaven. Again I tell you, it is easier for a camel to go through the eye of a needle than for someone who is rich to enter the kingdom of God" (Matt 19:23–24). James likewise nuances between those who have money (as

---

[22] France, *Matthew*, 228.

[23] Scot McKnight, *Sermon on the Mount*, The Story of God Bible Commentary, (Grand Rapids, MI: Zondervan, 2013), 244, also notes the connection between Matt 7:11 and Jas 1:16–17: "For both Jesus and James God is good and God gives nothing but good things."

[24] See Vincent Hirschi, *Friendship or Enmity? The Christian and the World in the Letter of James* (Eugene, OR: Resource Publications, 2019), 76–7, who links Jas 4:17 and Prov 3:27–28 to conclude, "the rebuke in 4:17 concerns those who could give alms but do not."

seen in the merchants of 4:13-17) and those who identify as "rich" (particularly in the condemnation of 5:1-6).[25] James allows that Christians may well have money, but the question is whether they identify themselves as humble before God or whether they rely on their wealth as their security, thus "a friend of the world." The rich young man could not imagine himself without his money, but that ought not be the primary source of security and identity for followers of Jesus.

The problem with this false identity is that it is, in fact, idolatry. Jesus emphasizes this in Matt 6:24, "No one can serve two masters; for a slave will either hate the one and love the other, or be devoted to the one and despise the other. You cannot serve God and wealth." France argues that this warning is "not specifically against ill-gotten wealth but about possessions as such, which, however neutral their character, can become a focus of concern and greed which competes for the disciples' loyalty with God himself."[26] Blomberg carries Frances's thought forward, agreeing with France and others who would argue that "the greatest danger to Western Christianity is … the all-pervasive materialism of our affluent culture … Jesus proclaims that unless we are willing to serve him wholeheartedly in every area of life, but particularly with our material resources, we cannot claim to be serving him at all."[27] This is the conclusion James draws as well, as he turns to stern prophetic language in Jas 4:4: "Adulterers[28]! Do you not know that friendship with the world is enmity with God? Therefore whoever wishes to be a friend of the world becomes an enemy of God." James intensifies Jesus's love/hate dichotomy to make clear that the reality of doublemindedness, of loving wealth, comfort, status, leaves one opposed to God. Lockett explains, "The notion of friendship (φιλία) in the Greco-Roman world meant above all to share, that is, to have the same mindset, the same outlook, the same views of reality. To be a friend of the world is to live in harmony with the values and logic of the world, [… which] is the entire cultural value system or world order which is hostile toward what James frames as the divine value system."[29] The world's system depends on people valuing what it values: external signs of power and wealth. James makes clear that when people are "friends with the world," they are doubleminded in their loyalty to God and commit covenant adultery. Jesus's question to the rich young man put his loyalties to the test and revealed that, despite all of his lawkeeping, he was in fact doubleminded, stained by the world.

As noted above, it is in what one *does* with their money that loyalties are exposed, and thus the theme of faith and works is so prominent in James: deeds are the other means by which the truth of one's relationship with God is revealed. Faith and works might be described as James's third major theme, but all the themes are intertwined

---

[25] I have developed this argument further elsewhere, see Mariam J. Kamell, "The Economics of Humility: The Rich and the Humble in James," in *Economic Dimensions of Early Christianity*, ed. Bruce W. Longenecker, and Kelly Leibengood (Grand Rapids, MI: Eerdmans, 2009), 157-75.
[26] France, *Matthew*, 263.
[27] Blomberg, *Matthew*, 124.
[28] This would be better translated as "Adulteresses," not for gender reasons, but to make the link to the prophetic denunciations of Israel as the adulteress in her relationship with God—often for reasons of comfort—clear.
[29] Lockett, *Purity and Worldview*, 117.

extensively by both James and Jesus. How we speak is tied to how we act in faithfulness, how we use money and position and power God has given us in humility is an act of faithful transformation of our human nature, revealing our moral purity from the priorities of the world. Matthew has Jesus end both his first and last major sermons with the point that true faith obeys what it has heard and illustrates it with parables in his central teaching. James, of course, weaves this point through his epistle, but it comes to its peak in chapter 2 as he concludes, "You see that a person is justified by works and not by faith alone" (2:24, the only place that Scripture explicitly mentions "faith alone," *sola fide*, and yet the point is the opposite of Luther's). Like words, works reveal the truth of a person's loyalties.

In Matt 7:16–21, Jesus uses "fruit" imagery to show that the way a person lives reveals the truth about their faith. First, he calls his hearers to be discerning: "you will know them by their fruits" (7:20). The hearers themselves should be able to discern a teacher's relationship with God by whether they live according to the Sermon's teaching.[30] This of course closely relates to James's warning not to seek to be a teacher for the danger of judgment (3:1). Shockingly, Jesus warns that even those who claim to know him, who call him "Lord," will not enter the kingdom simply based on their claimed relationship. The ones who enter the kingdom are "those who do the will of my Father" (7:21), namely, by putting the teaching of Jesus into practice. To claim Jesus as Lord without obeying his teaching is empty. He is not Lord where lives are not submitted.[31] James concludes his chapter on faith and works with a similar ultimatum, using the examples of Abraham and Rahab (Jas 2:18–26). It is not merely that Abraham and Rahab obeyed, but in their obedience they showed their single-minded loyalty to God at great cost to themselves.[32] Hirschi summarizes and translates Theissen's arguments helpfully:

> Since family and cities were the two main spheres through which identity was derived in the first century, Theissen proposes that the examples of Abraham and Rahab imply more than putting one's faith into practice: these examples also imply the willingness to let one's faith define one's identity, even when doing so

---

[30] McKnight, *Sermon on the Mount*, 267, reminds us that this passage is in context of prophets speaking on behalf of God: "if the disciples hear someone making a claim to speak for God, they are to observe that person's life to see if that person *is doing God's will*. If so, they may be speaking for God; if not, they are false prophets." See France, *Matthew*, 289–91, for a more extended helpful discussion, who concludes, "The constant refrain of the NT is that bad teaching is reflected in bad living" (291).

[31] Charles L. Quarles, *A Theology of Matthew: Jesus Revealed as Deliverer, King, and Incarnate Creator* (Phillipsburg, NJ: P&R Publishing, 2013), 59, observes that "Through the new exodus and the new covenant, Jesus' disciples receive a righteousness that exceeds that of the scribes and Pharisees … They have an extraordinary righteousness that exhibits God's own holy character (5:43–48). Jesus' disciples are 'healthy trees' that produce the 'good fruit' of righteous words and actions (7:17)." This is a helpful reminder to keep Jesus's teaching in context of the new covenant, something also relevant to readers of James, see Mariam J. Kamell, "Incarnating Jeremiah's Promised New Covenant in the 'Law' of James: A Short Study," *EQ* 83 (2011): 19–28.

[32] Gerd Theissen, "Éthique et communauté dans l'Épître de Jacques: Réflexions sur son Sitz im Leben," *ETR* 77 (2002): 176.

entails separation from one's family or one's *polis*. Single-mindedness, therefore ... implies letting God take precedence over any other consideration.[33]

In choosing God at great cost to themselves, Abraham and Rahab revealed that God truly was "Lord" to them, their works thus bore recognizable fruit.

The end of the Sermon on the Mount repeatedly emphasizes that requirement that the hearers do what they have heard in it. In the conclusion, Jesus tells a parable of the wise and foolish builders, and the two parts of the parable are set up by the parallel statement, "Everyone then who hears these words of mine and acts on them // does not act on them will be like ..." (Matt 7:24, 26). The hearing is only one step of the process, it is the doing that matters. James likewise recognizes that contrast in his introduction. In 1:22–25, he concludes his introduction by calling his hearers to be "doers of the word, and not merely hearers who deceive themselves." Much like the hearers of Jesus's Sermon deceive themselves as to the security of their lives if they do not obey, James also warns of the dangers of self-deception for hearing and not obeying. But in the inverse of the Sermon's structure, James ends his warning with a Beatitude: the "doers who act—they will be blessed in their doing" (1:25, οὗτος μακάριος ἐν τῇ ποιήσει). In obedience itself the blessing comes.

In the parable of the sower in Matt 13, Jesus makes the same point he did in the Sermon on the Mount about the need for obedience, but he also nuances the binary of Matt 7 with four kinds of soils. Jesus explains, in Matt 13:18–23, that while some seed is instantly swept away, others initially spring up but due to persecution (cf. Jas 1:2–3; 5:7–11) and through the allure of wealth (see above) fall away. They may even look enthusiastic for a time, but, for instance, the seed on rocky soil hits what James might call in 1:3 "trouble of any sort," and it does not develop perseverance but instead falls away. Likewise, the seed in thorns reveals the challenge of wealth and friendship with the world, and they also fall away before they bear fruit. Their faith does not endure enough to bear fruit. It is only the last, that falls on prepared soil, that *obeys* and does not fall prey to friendship with the world or giving in to temptation or failing to endure, that then the word of God is effective, bringing a harvest of life. The fruit theme appears again to validate the faith of these hearers, as Blomberg summarizes: "The parable provides a sober reminder that even the most enthusiastic outward response to the gospel offers no guarantee that one is a true disciple."[34] Two further passages in James might be brought into dialogue with this parable. The first is Jas 1:21, with its call to prepare the soil ("rid yourselves of all sordidness and rank growth of wickedness") and "welcome with meekness the implanted word that has the power to save your souls." This is not a call to works salvation, but a recognition that the soil matters for the seed to be able to be effective, and the imagery is strongly reminiscent of Matthew's parable with the overgrowth and sown seed. But James also returns to "fruit" language several

---

[33] Hirschi, *Friendship or Enmity?*, 67.
[34] Blomberg, *Matthew*, 218. He continues, "Only the tests of time, perseverance under difficult circumstances, the avoidance of the idolatries of wealth and anxiety over earthly concerns (recall 6:25–34), and above all the appearance of appropriate fruit (consistent obedience to God's will) can prove a profession genuine."

more times, the most intriguing of which is in 3:17-18: wisdom is both "full of mercy and good fruits" (καρπῶν ἀγαθῶν), and "a harvest (fruit, καρπὸς) of righteousness is sown in peace for those who make peace." There are many interconnected threads that can lead one to draw a line from the "doer" of 1:22-25 as one who has accepted the "implanted word" of 1:21 in good soil who thus shows the fruit of wisdom in their lives (3:17-18).[35] This "harvest of righteousness" thus mirrors the one who "bears fruit and yields, in one case a hundredfold, in another sixty, and in another thirty" (Matt 13:23).

This implication that the seed bears fruit in kind is depicted in Jesus's parable of the unmerciful servant in Matt 18:23-35. There, despite being granted forgiveness of his incredible debt by his master, the servant persists in showing no forgiveness of his fellow servant's debt. Jesus summarizes the parable in the master's words in vv. 32-33: "You wicked slave! I forgave you all that debt because you pleaded with me. Should you not have had mercy on your fellow slave, as I had mercy on you?" The fruit Jesus's followers are to bear is in kind to God's own nature, forgive as they have been forgiven. It is worth noting that the parable provides a counterpoint to the Lord's Prayer in the Sermon, for there it is "if you forgive others their trespasses, your heavenly Father will also forgive you" (Matt 6:14), but here the forgiveness is first and the basis for further acts of forgiveness. The parable, thus, gives the context for the demand for our forgiveness in the Sermon and reminds us that God's forgiveness is the first act, which, if allowed to be implanted in us, will transform us to be people who forgive. This same priority of grace but contingent demand for merciful actions can be seen in James. In 1:18, James makes one of his most theologically loaded statements in recognizing that God gave birth to his people "in fulfillment of his own purpose" (βουληθεὶς ἀπεκύησεν).[36] The problem James has is that they are not bearing fruit in accordance with their identity as the "first fruits of his creatures." But the consequence of God's gracious overture to his people echoes the parable of Matt 18: "So speak and so act as those who are to be judged by the law of liberty. For judgment will be without mercy to anyone who has shown no mercy; mercy triumphs over judgment" (Jas 2:12-13). France observes of the Gospel parable: "The master was willing to forgive a debt the slave could never have paid, but will not forgive his refusal of an act of generosity which was within his power. If he is determined to insist on his just deserts, he shall have them."[37] The law that gives freedom requires that people be transformed toward mercy, acting in accordance with the mercy already given to them. Without this fruit, judgment awaits.

And this leads to that final text with which the chapter opened: the Sheep and the Goats in Matt 25.[38] Beare questioned of this passage: "There is no mercy shown to the

---

[35] Teasing these threads was a large portion of my dissertation work: Mariam J. Kamell, "The Soteriology of James in Light of Earlier Jewish Wisdom Literature and the Gospel of Matthew" (PhD dissertation, University of St. Andrews, 2010).

[36] Mariam J. Kamell, "God Gave Us Birth," in *Christian Reflection: The Letter of James*, ed. Robert B. Kruschwitz (Waco, TX: Baylor University Press, 2012), 11–19.

[37] France, *Matthew*, 708.

[38] Its identity as a parable is contested. W. F. Albright and C. S. Mann, *Matthew*, AB 26 (Garden City, NY: Doubleday, 1982), 306–8, defend the status of this narrative as a parable. On the other hand, Alistair I. Wilson, *When Will These Things Happen? A Study of Jesus as Judge in Matthew 21–25* (Carlisle: Paternoster, 2004), 238–41, argues against reading this as a parable, rather, the pericope provides "direct (if image laden) insight into the judgement scene."

accursed, and the blessed have no need of mercy. There is justice for all, but is justice without mercy Christian?"[39] However, that is exactly what James argued in Jas 2:12–13: if one has not *shown* mercy in alignment with mercy already received, then one *will not* receive mercy. By the time of the judgment, Jesus warns "you will know them by their fruits" (Matt 7:20), and "Not everyone who says to me, 'Lord, Lord,' will enter the kingdom of heaven" (7:21). Faith, in both Jesus's teaching and as James follows, entails not simply theological assent to who Jesus is, but also pragmatic actions of obedience, of mercy, of charity, of humility, of watching one's tongue and of watching one's attitude toward wealth—all of these reveal whether one truly believes in the Lordship of Christ. In contrast to Beare's questions, Ulrich Luz shows his fundamental understanding that the Sheep and the Goats narrative does not entail a works-righteousness by which we save ourselves: "The apex of Matthean theology is rather that an authentic confession of the Lord can only consist of obedience to his commandments. If a person's works are not right, then according to Matthew [and James] nothing is right."[40] This narrative is nothing but the culmination of what Jesus has taught through this whole Gospel.

Finally, we can conclude with some comments on Jesus as a teacher and James as his disciple who reset Jesus's teachings for his own audience. It should be obvious how heavily influential the Sermon on the Mount is on the epistle of James. Chris Morgan, among others, finds the Sermon on the Mount to be the primary background and influence behind the epistle of James, a sermon on the Sermon on the Mount, as it were.[41] Every section of the Sermon is well represented in James. While not discussed, each of the Beatitudes appear through James, variously part of a life well lived. Many parts of the antitheses have been discussed above, including the one direct quotation in James of Matt 5:37: "Let your word be 'Yes, Yes' or 'No, No'; anything more than this comes from the evil one" (ἔστω δὲ ὁ λόγος ὑμῶν ναὶ ναί, οὒ οὔ; Jas 5:12: "let your 'Yes' be yes and your 'No' be no, so that you may not fall under condemnation," ἤτω δὲ ὑμῶν τὸ ναὶ ναὶ καὶ τὸ οὒ οὔ, where the second half of the verse follows conceptually but not verbally). Jesus's teaching on anger, on wealth, on prayer, and on fruit-bearing and judgment all find their counterparts in the epistle of James, culminating in Jesus's demand that his hearers be "doers" of his words.

However, while the Sermon undoubtedly is a prime source of teaching for James, Jesus's teaching across the whole of the Gospel(s) should not be neglected. Matthew teaches similarly to James in that his ideas recur and gain in nuance as they are repeated in different forms, and the variety of teaching methods support each other. James clearly draws from the Sermon, but he also builds from the implications of parables and woes. And while Mark, Luke, and John can and should also be drawn upon to understand James's content, Matthew's structure around the five major teaching blocks centers his varied teaching.[42] James, as a wisdom teacher, thus perhaps "sounds" most like the Jesus in Matthew. Moreover, James can help readers hear Jesus's teaching faithfully.

---

[39] Beare, *Matthew*, 496–7.
[40] Ulrich Luz, *Matthew 21–28*, Hermeneia (Minneapolis, MN: Fortress, 2005), 289.
[41] Christopher W. Morgan, *A Theology of James: Wisdom for Consistent Churches* (Phillipsburg: P&R Publishing, 2010), 32.
[42] France, *Matthew: Evangelist*, 130 (among other places), is right to see Matthew's emphasis on Jesus as a teacher.

By reading James and Matthew together, one cannot fall into the false dichotomy of dividing faith from works, as though faith did not entail faithfulness, nor is it possible to underestimate the dangers of speech and money that thread through Jesus's teaching once they are condensed into James's shorter epistle. James, therefore, does not only teach the reader about following Jesus; James also teaches how to read Jesus's teaching.

Contributors

Jon Coutts is Associate Professor of Christian Theology at Ambrose University. His other works include the *Church Leadership Study Guide* and *A Shared Mercy: Karl Barth on Forgiveness and the Church*.

Katherine Davis is research fellow at Sydney Missionary & Bible College, the Australian College of Theology. She completed her doctoral work at Trinity College Bristol on the rhetorical function of Leviticus. Katherine has several publications in edited volumes and her Exodus commentary in the Zondervan Exegetical Commentary on the Old Testament series is forthcoming.

Dennis R. Edwards is Dean of North Park Theological Seminary after having been Associate Professor of New Testament. He has also served as a pastor in Brooklyn, New York; Washington, DC; and Minneapolis, Minnesota. He is the author of *1 Peter* (Story of God Bible Commentary) and *Might from the Margins: The Gospel's Power to Turn the Tables on Injustice* (2020).

Daniel M. Gurtner is Professor of New Testament at Gateway Seminary. He publishes broadly in the New Testament and Second Temple Judaism, notably the award-winning *T&T Clark Encyclopedia of Second Temple Judaism* edited with Loren T. Stuckenbruck (2 vols., 2020). He is a member of the Evangelical Theological Society, Society for Biblical Literature, and the Studiorum Novi Testamenti Societas, among other organizations, and serves on several editorial boards.

Bruce Henning is Assistant Professor of New Testament at Grand Rapids Theological Seminary. He is the author of *Matthew's Non-Messianic Mapping of Messianic Texts: Evidences of a Broadly Eschatological Hermeneutic* (2020) and has written articles and book reviews for *New Testament Studies*, the *Journal of the Study of the New Testament*, *Bulletin of Biblical Research*, and *Journal of the Evangelical Theological Society*.

Craig Keener is the F. M. and Ada Thompson Professor of Biblical Studies, Asbury Theological Seminary. He is the author of 33 books and 100 academic articles, the most relevant books for this subject being *Historical Jesus of the Gospels*, *Christobiography*, and *A Commentary on the Gospel of Matthew*.

Mariam Kovalishyn is associate professor at Regent College. She is the co-author of the ZECNT *James* volume and co-editor of *Key Approaches to Biblical Ethics*. She has also authored numerous articles on James and James in relation to other New Testament texts. Some of those essays have appeared in *The Oxford Handbook of Wisdom and the Bible*, *The State of New Testament Studies*, *Reading the Epistle of James: A Resource for Students*, and *Galatians and Christian Theology*.

Lena Lütticke recently completed her dissertation on "'Your Father who is in secret and sees in secret...' On God's hidden presence in Matt 6:1-6.16-18" at Regensburg University. She is now holding a postdoc position at Tübingen University. Her publications include work in the *Encyclopedia of the Bible and Its Reception*, *Jahrbuch für Biblische Theologie*, and *Impeccability and Temptation: Understanding Christ's Divine and Human Will*.

John Nolland is an Australian but has also lived and worked in Canada and the UK. Now retired, he was on the faculty of Trinity College, Bristol, for many years, serving in various roles including academic dean and vice-principal. He is author of the three-volume WBC commentary on Luke and the NTGTC commentary on Matthew, as well as many journal articles and contributions to multi-author volumes.

Charles L. Quarles is Research Professor of New Testament and Biblical Theology and Charles Page Chair of Biblical Theology at Southeastern Baptist Theological Seminary in Wake Forest, North Carolina. He is the author or editor of eight books including three on the Gospel of Matthew. He has written numerous articles for journals including *New Testament Studies*, *Novum Testamentum*, *Catholic Biblical Quarterly*, *Bulletin for Biblical Research*, and *Journal for the Study of the Historical Jesus*.

Charles Nathan Ridlehoover teaches New Testament and Greek at Columbia Biblical Seminary in Columbia, South Carolina. He is the author of *The Lord's Prayer and the Sermon on the Mount in Matthew's Gospel* with LNTS and contributor to *Who Created Christianity? Fresh Approaches to the Relationship between Paul and Jesus*. He has written articles and book reviews for *New Testament Studies*, *Catholic Biblical Quarterly*, *Bulletin of Biblical Research*, *Horizons of Biblical Theology*, and the *Journal of the Evangelical Theological Society*.

Patrick Schreiner is Associate Professor of New Testament and Biblical Theology at Midwestern Baptist University. He is the author of *Matthew, Disciple and Scribe: The First Gospel and Its Portrait of Jesus*, *Acts: The Christian Standard Commentary*, *The Visual Word*, and *The Mission of the Triune God*.

David Wenham began his teaching career in Central India before working at Tyndale House Cambridge, Wycliffe Hall Oxford, and finally Trinity College Bristol. Now retired, he lives with his wife Clare in Oxford, serving their church. His most recent books have been *From Good News to Gospels: What Did the First Christians Say about Jesus?* (2018) and *Jesus in Context: Making Sense of the Historical Figure* (2021). He is also co-author with Steve Walton of the widely used textbook *Exploring the New Testament, Volume 1: A Guide to the Gospels and Acts* (2021).

The Rev. John Y. H. Yieh, PhD, is the Molly Laird Downs Professor in New Testament at Virginia Theological Seminary. His research focuses on the Gospel of Matthew and the Johannine Literature from the vantage of sociological and history-of-effects approaches. He is also interested in the history and hermeneutics of Chinese biblical interpretation. He has published in each of these areas with the notable *One Teacher: Jesus' Teaching Role In Matthew Gospel Report*.

Hebrew Bible

Genesis
1–3	37
1:1	24, 25 n.20
1:1–2:4	24–5
1:26–27	96
1:27	25, 25 n.20, 33, 36, 47
2:23	25, 37
2:24	33, 36, 37, 47
4:13–24	128
4:24	128, 128 n.17
5:2	33, 35 n.17, 36
6–9	18 n.2
12:4	20
15:1–20	73
15:6	60
18:1–19:25	18 n.2, 24 n.19
19:1–6	18
49:11	70

Exodus
1	70
3:6	18 n.2, 34
3:15	34
3:19	71
12:43–13:16	38
13:9	38
13:16	38
16:15	172
17:6	172
17:12	172
19–20	67
19:3	66, 74
19:6	156
20	47
20:1	37
20:2	37
20:3	37
20:4–6	37
20:7	37
20:8–17	37
20:12	18 n.2, 23, 33, 38, 47
20:12–16	33
20:13	18, 18 n.2, 33, 39, 47
20:13–14	76
20:14	18 n.2, 19, 33, 40, 47
20:15	40, 47
20:16	47
20:17	76
21:1–23:9	39
21:17	18 n.2, 33, 39
21:23–24	128
21:24	18 n.2, 20, 33, 47
23:20	40
24:1	71
24:8	73
24:12	71
24:15–18	71
24:16	71
24:18	74
29:16	162
29:20–21	162
33:18	173
34	173
34:3	71
34:4	74
34:5	71
34:6	173
34:17–26	37
34:29–30	71
34:29–35	172
34:35	71
35:31	151 n.40
35:35	151 n.40
36:1	151 n.40

Leviticus
1–5	18, 18 n.2
2	18 n.2
4–5	18 n.2, 23
4:1–5:13	23
5:20–26	18–19

214 Hebrew Bible

10:10	23	5:17	33, 39, 42, 47
10:11	76	5:18	33, 40, 42, 47
11	21, 23–4, 24 n.18	6–8	18 n.2
11:29–42	21	6:1	77
11:44–45	21, 24	6:1–3	42
13–14	22 n.14	6:4	79 n.47
13:1–44	22	6:4–25	43
13:46	22	6:5	18 n.2, 34, 41–3, 43 n.54
14	22		
14:1–7	22–3		
14:4–31	22	6:6–8	77
15:1–20	22	6:7	14 n.110
16	23	6:8	38
17	18 n.2	6:13	33, 42–3
19	24	6:14–15	43
19–20	23	6:16	33, 35 n.17
19:1–4	37	6:25	60
19:2	21, 76, 156, 197	7:20	41 n.47
		8:1–20	43
19:11–19	37	8:3	33, 43, 43 n.60
19:12	33, 40, 47	9:9	74
19:18	18 n.2, 20, 33, 34, 41–2, 47, 78	10:12	41
		10:12–11:21	38
19:26–37	37	10:20	35 n.18
20:9	18 n.2, 23	11:18	38
20:13	42	11:19	14 n.110, 77
20:14	42	11:28	76
20:26	21	15:11	18 n.2
21:17–23	23	18	70, 75
21:24	40	18:9	76
24:1–9	18 n.2	18:13	76
24:19–20	129	18:15	71–2
24:20	18 n.2, 20, 33, 35 n.18	18:15–18	172, 172 n.32
		18:15–19	67
		18:18	67
Numbers		18:18–19	68
21:9	172	18:20	76
24:17	68	19:15	33, 35 n.18
27:17	42	19:15–21	133 n.34
27:18	42	19:18	41
30:2	33, 35 n.18	19:21	18 n.2, 20, 33, 35 n.18, 129
		20:16	41 n.47
Deuteronomy		23:4	41 n.47
4:44–5:33	43	24:1	18 n.2, 19, 33, 35 n.18, 36
5	47		
5:1–6:9	38		
5:6–21	37	25:5	34, 43–4, 47
5:16	23, 33, 38, 47	27:15–26	37
5:16–20	18 n.2, 34	30:1–10	69 n.21

30:6	69 n.21, 75	**Nehemiah**	
30:7	41 n.47	8:1–8	148
30:15–20	76 n.40	8:13	148
30:19	76		
31:29	76	**Job**	
32	38	16:19	35 n.17
32:35	20		
33:29	74	**Psalms**	
		1	77 n.40
Joshua		2:7	164
22:5	41	2:8–9	164
		5	20 n.9
Judges		6	20 n.9
13:5	72, 72 n.31	6:9	35 n.17
17	39	8:3	29, 29 n.32, 29 n.33, 34, 35 n.17
1 Samuel		12	20 n.9
3:1	4 n.12	15:2–5	37
16:1–13	53	22	93
19:20–24	4 n.12	22:1	17, 34, 35 n.19
		22:2	35 n.17
2 Samuel		22:19	35 n.17
16:23	152 n.49	24:7–10	44
		26:5	41 n.47
1 Kings		37:11	29 n.32
4:1–19	152 n.49	40	20 n.9
10:1	152 n.49	41:4	91
17:17–24	26	41:11	91
		42:2	29 n.32
2 Kings		42:6	35 n.18
2:1	56	42:12	35 n.18
2:3–18	4 n.12	51:6	151
2:11	56	55:1	29 n.32
5:1–19	26	59	20 n.9
		62:13	35 n.17
1 Chronicles		68	44
27:32	148	69	20 n.9, 178
		69:9	178
2 Chronicles		78	74
1:10–12	151 n.40	78:2	29 n.32, 33, 35 n.17, 74
2:12–13	151 n.40	78:4–8 (LXX 77:4–8)	14 n.110
17:9	77	91:11–12	33, 35 n.18
18:16	42	104:12	35 n.18
		107:43	151 n.40
Ezra		109	20 n.9
7:6	148	110:1	29 n.32, 30–1, 34, 35 n.17
7:10	77		
7:11	148	116:13	89 n.21
7:25	77		

118	30	29:18	35 n.17, 150 n.38
118:20	30	32:15	73
118:22–23	29 n.32, 30, 34, 35 n.18, 35 n.19	32:19	58
		33:6	150 n.39
118:25–26	34, 35 n.18	33:18	148
118:26	29 n.32, 34, 35 n.18	34:3	27
118:27	30 n.37, 176	34:4	25 n.23, 27
121:3	111 n.5	35:5	35 n.18
130:8	72, 72 n.31	35:5–6	25, 25 n.23, 29
137	20 n.9	37:15–28	69 n.21
137:7–9	41 n.47	40:1	44
139:19–22	41 n.47	40:1–11	44
143	20 n.9	40:2	44
148:1	35 n.18	40:3	33, 40, 44 n.67, 48, 50, 52, 56
Proverbs		40:3–5	44
2:1–8	150	42:1–3	33, 46
3:27–28	202 n.24	42:1–4	25 n.23
4:10–27	77 n.40	42:4	33, 35 n.18
8–9	56	42:7	25 n.23
8:20	57	42:18	35 n.18
12:28	57	44:3	73
13:20	150	49:13	44
16:31	57	51:3	44
21:11	151 n.40	52:9	44
25:1	152 n.49	52:13–53:12	70
		53	157
Isaiah		53:4	25 n.23, 33, 35 n.18
1:11–13	27	54:1–10	69 n.21
5	177 n.51	55	75
6	173 n.33	55:1–5	69 n.21
6:1–3	26	56:7	29, 34, 35 n.18
6:5–7	26	59:21	69 n.21
6:9–10	25 n.23, 26, 33, 35 n.18	61	74–5
		61:1	25 n.23, 26, 74
6:9–13	26	61:2	74
7:14	33, 35 n.18, 35 n.19	61:2–3	25 n.23
8:8	33	61:3	75
8:10	33, 35 n.18	61:7	74
9:1–2	25 n.23, 33, 35 n.17	61:8–9	69 n.21
9:2	58	61:11	75
10:33–34	58	62:11	34, 35 n.18
13:1–22	27	66:2	25 n.23
13:6	58		
13:9	27, 58	**Jeremiah**	
13:10	25 n.23, 27, 35 n.18	3:15	42
13:13	58	6:16	35 n.17
29:13	25 n.23, 27, 33, 35 n.17	7:11	29, 35 n.17, 177
		31	73, 81

31:15	33, 73	**Hosea**	
31:31	82	6:1–2	28
31:31–34	69 n.21, 73	6:4	28
31:33	75, 82	6:4–6	124
32:36–41	69 n.21	6:5	28
50:2–5	69 n.21	6:6	28, 33
		10:12	60
Ezekiel		11:1	33, 35 n.17
11:18–21	69 n.21		
16:59–63	69 n.21	**Joel**	
18:5–9	37	2:28–29	73
18:30–32	69 n.21		
34	173–6	**Jonah**	
34:2	173	1:17	33
34:3	173	2:1–11	24 n.19
34:5	173		
34:6	174	**Micah**	
34:11–34	173	5:1	35 n.18
34:13	174	5:2	33
34:16	174	5:3	35 n.18
34:20–31	69 n.21	7:6	33
34:23	42		
34:26–29	174	**Zechariah**	
34:30	174	9:9	34, 46, 48
34:32–33	173	9:16	58
34:34	173	9:11	73
36–37	72, 73	11:12–13	34, 35 n.17
36:21–28	73	11:16–17	42
36:24–32	69 n.21	12:4	58
36:26	72, 75	13:7	34, 46, 48
36:26–27	73		
36:29	72	**Malachi**	
37	173	3:1	26, 33, 35 n.17, 50, 56
37:23	72		
39:29	73	3:2	58
47:24	42	3:23–24	40
		4:1	58
Daniel		4:3	58
1:4	151 n.40	4:5	40, 58
1:17	151 n.40	4:5–6	56
2:21	151 n.40	4:6	45
3:6	35 n.17		
7:10	58	New Testament	
7:11	58		
7:13	34, 47	**Matthew**	
9:25–27	69 n.21	1:1–17	55, 170
9:27	47	1:11	170
11:31	47	1:17	170
12:11	47	1:18–19	142 n.4

1:18–2:23	55, 170	4:6	33
1:21	72	4:7	33, 35 n.17
1:22	169 n.8	4:10	33, 35 n.18, 42, 43, 104
1:23	33, 35 n.18, 35 n.19		
2	70	4:12	52, 54–5
2:2	111 n.5	4:14	169 n.8
2:4	111, 117, 149 n.37	4:14–15	25 n.23
2:5	149 n.37	4:15–16	33, 35 n.17
2:6	33, 35 n.18	4:16	35 n.18, 58
2:8	35 n.18	4:17	58–9, 100, 102
2:15	33, 35 n.17, 169 n.8	4:18–22	121
2:17	169 n.8	4:19	53, 121 n.34
2:17–18	73	4:23	58, 61, 102, 104, 110, 121 n.33
2:18	336		
2:20	71	4:23–25	103
2:21	90 n.23	5	40, 74, 192, 202
2:23	169 n.8	5–7	55, 102, 104, 170, 180
3:1–2	44		
3:1–4	52	5:1	74, 120
3:1–10	52	5:1–2	72
3:1–12	52	5:1–7:29	17, 22
3:1–4:11	55	5:3	25 n.23, 79
3:2	58, 100	5:3–12	100, 106
3:3	56	5:4	25 n.23, 79
3:13–17	52	5:5	29 n.32
3:3	33, 44–5	5:6	29 n.32, 60
3:5	52	5:7	79, 124
3:6	53, 59	5:8	197
3:7–10	52	5:10	60, 79, 158 n.17, 159
3:7	58	5:11	110, 158 n.17, 161
3:8	45, 59	5:11–12	159
3:9	59	5:16	75, 86, 158, 158 n.17, 159
3:10	45, 58–9, 110		
3:11	53, 73	5:17	49, 106, 129, 169 n.8, 189
3:11–12	45, 52		
3:12	58	5:17–18	18, 188, 189
3:13	52–3, 59	5:17–19	120 n.32, 151
3:13–15	54	5:17–20	18, 67, 77, 80, 142 n.4, 168, 188, 188 n.18, 189, 192
3:14	45, 53		
3:15	53, 55, 59, 169 n.8, 188		
		5:17–48	18, 83, 86, 188
3:16–17	54	5:19	192, 194, 194 n.35, 202
3:17	91		
4–6	157	5:20	40, 60, 81, 90 n.23, 111, 118, 189
4:1	54		
4:1–11	17, 54, 158 n.17	5:20–48	40
4:4	33, 43, 110	5:21	18, 18 n.2, 33, 40, 42, 75, 79, 81
4:4–10	18 n.2		
4:9–10	104	5:21–22	18, 133, 198–9

5:21–26	190	6:5–13	91
5:21–30	76	6:5–15	83, 91–2
5:21–48	86, 107, 189	6:6	87, 90 n.23, 91–2
5:22	40, 47, 58, 81	6:7	76
5:23–24	18, 18 n.2, 19, 124, 133	6:7–8	95
		6:9	124, 131
5:27	18 n.2, 19, 33, 42, 81	6:10	89, 91, 105 n.48, 124, 130 n.23
5:27–28	76		
5:27–29	40, 47	6:12	124, 127
5:28	19, 40, 75, 81	6:12–15	127
5:31	18 n.2, 19, 33, 35 n.18	6:13	90 n.23, 91, 162 n.39
		6:14	124, 206
5:32	19	6:16–18	85–7, 86 n.16
5:33	33, 35 n.18, 41, 47, 75, 81	6:18	87
		6:19	79
5:33–37	77–8, 198	6:19–34	201
5:34	41, 47	6:24	203
5:36	190	6:25–34	158 n.17, 205 n.34
5:37	41, 207	6:28–30	79
5:38	18 n.2, 33, 35 n.18, 40, 47	6:31–32	76
		6:33	60, 188
5:38–39	159	7	202
5:38–42	83	7:1	199
5:38–47	20	7:1–5	79
5:38–48	158 n.17	7:5	164
5:39	20, 20 n.8, 40, 83	7:7	79
5:39–42	20	7:8–12	202
5:41	81	7:11	202, 202 n.23
5:42	201–2	7:12	106–7
5:43	18 n.2, 33, 41, 134, 190, 201	7:13–14	76
		7:15–20	76, 200
5:43–44	47, 159	7:16–17	75
5:43–47	21	7:16–21	204
5:43–48	78, 201, 204	7:17	110, 204
5:44	41, 81	7:18	79
5:44–45	101	7:19	58, 110
5:45	87, 92, 202	7:20	204, 207
5:46–47	134, 201 n.21	7:21	67, 79, 90 n.23, 90 n.25, 204, 207
5:47	76		
5:48	21, 76, 79, 87, 159, 197, 201	7:21–22	58
		7:21–23	77, 192 n.31, 193–4
6	87, 87 n.18, 88, 91	7:21–24	59
6:1	60, 84, 92	7:23	35 n.17
6:1–6	85–7, 86 n.16	7:24	67, 106, 205
6:1–18	84–5, 91–2	7:24–27	58, 106, 125
6:1–21	83	7:26	77, 79, 199 n.13, 205
6:4	87	7:28	50
6:5	92	7:29	112, 117, 152
6:5–8	84–5, 102	8–9	55, 103–4

8:1–4	22	10:3	142
8:1–9:26	18	10:5	18 n.2, 61, 121, 136, 186
8:1–9:38	22		
8:2	22	10:5–6	174
8:4	23	10:6	102, 136, 175
8:10	102	10:7	102, 121
8:11	9	10:8	102, 187 n.15
8:16–17	25 n.23	10:10	184, 186
8:17	33, 35 n.18, 169 n.8	10:15	24 n.19
8:19	110 n.3, 111, 116 n.22, 118, 118 n.27, 121 n.34, 153–4	10:17	102
		10:18	102
		10:24	121, 147 n.29
8:20	61	10:24–25	101, 153
8:21	153	10:25	102, 147, 147 n.29
8:22	121 n.34	10:35–36	33
9	124, 174	10:38	102, 121 n.34
9:1–2	18 n.2	11:1	121 n.33
9:1–8	22	11:2	52, 54–5, 121
9:2	23, 102, 123	11:2–6	52, 55
9:3	111, 116, 123–4, 152	11:4–5	104
9:4	123	11:4–6	25, 25 n.23
9:5	123	11:5	35 n.17, 35 n.18, 102
9:6	47	11:7	56
9:8	124	11:7–9	52
9:9	121 n.34, 142	11:7–10	56
9:9–13	28	11:7–15	40, 55
9:10–11	142, 147 n.29	11:7–19	52
9:10–13	62	11:10	26, 33, 35 n.17, 40
9:11	134, 153	11:11–13	56
9:12–13	134	11:11–15	56
9:13	28, 33, 123–4, 137	11:12–13	192
9:14	59	11:14	45, 56
9:14–17	52	11:15	56
9:15	59	11:16–19	45, 50, 56
9:17	120 n.32, 151	11:19	56, 62, 134
9:22	102	11:24	18 n.2, 24 n.19
9:29	102	11:28	49
9:32–33	102	11:29	35 n.17
9:34	102	12	131 n.25, 200
9:35	58, 61, 121 n.33, 174	12:1–2	28
9:35–36	103	12:1–14	192
9:35–38	104 n.45	12:5	18 n.2
9:35–11:1	17	12:7	28, 33
9:36	42, 173–4	12:8	47
9:37–38	104–5	12:16	25 n.23
10	55, 104, 121, 186	12:17	169 n.8
10:1	102, 110, 121	12:18–20	33, 47
10:2	121	12:21	33, 35 n.18
10:2–4	121	12:25	110

12:30–37	104		144–6, 148, 149
12:31	110		n.35, 153–4
12:33	130 n.23	13:54	121 n.33
12:33–37	200	13:54–58	102
12:34	75, 199	14–15	127
12:36	110	14:1–2	54
12:38	111, 116, 152–3	14:1–12	52, 92
12:38–42	104	14:12	54
12:39–41	24 n.19	14:13	88, 92
12:40	33	14:13–21	92
12:43–45	131 n.25	14:23	88, 92
12:45	163	14:33	171
12:49–50	101, 104	15	38, 111, 117, 186,
12:50	90 n.25, 131 n.25		187 n.17, 193
13	111, 119–21, 205	15:1	111–12, 117 n.24
13:1–53	17	15:1–6	27
13:11	120 n.29, 120	15:1–18	192
	n.30, 148	15:1–20	23
13:13	26, 147 n.26	15:2	5 n.20, 38, 117
13:13–15	25 n.23, 26		n.24, 152
13:14	147 n.26	15:3	38
13:14–15	33, 35 n.18	15:4	18 n.2, 33, 38, 47
13:15	25 n.25, 147 n.26	15:7–9	25 n.23, 27
13:16	120 n.29	15:8	75
13:18–23	120 n.29, 205	15:8–9	33, 35 n.17
13:19	120 n.30, 147 n.26	15:10	147 n.26
13:23	147 n.26, 206	15:11	23–4, 24 n.18
13:24	120 n.30	15:17–20	200
13:31	120 n.30, 120 n.31	15:19–20	75
13:32	35 n.18	15:21–28	136, 186
13:33	120 n.30, 120 n.31	15:22–24	136
13:34–35	29 n.32, 74	15:24	102, 173–5
13:35	33, 35 n.17, 169 n.8	15:24–28	176 n.44
13:36	120 n.29	15:28	102, 136
13:37–43	120 n.29	16:12	121, 147 n.26, 151
13:38	120 n.30	16:13	178
13:40	58	16:13–15	52
13:41	120 n.30	16:13–20	126 n.10, 160 n.22
13:42	35 n.17, 58	16:13–28	171
13:43	120 n.30	16:14	54, 171
13:44	120 n.30, 120 n.31	16:16	171, 184
13:45	120 n.30, 120 n.31	16:16–18	125
13:47	120 n.30, 120 n.31	16:16–20	185
13:48	169 n.8	16:17	125
13:50	35 n.17, 58	16:17–20	185
13:51	147 n.26, 151	16:18	137, 178–9
13:51–52	149	16:19	105, 121, 124–5, 126
13:52	109–10, 112–13,		n.9, 178
	119–20, 122, 141–2,	16:21	111, 117, 152

16:22–23	136	18:19	126
16:23	125	18:19–20	105
16:24	53, 121 n.34, 174	18:20	102 n.43, 126, 128, 137
16:27	35 n.17		
16:28	163 n.39	18:21	128
17:1	71	18:21–22	126, 131–2
17:1–3	163	18:21–35	105, 124, 126, 128
17:1–8	171	18:22	128, 128 n.17, 132–3
17:1–9	71	18:22–27	130
17:1–13	155	18:23–35	136, 206
17:2	71	18:23–27	129
17:3	171	18:24–27	192 n.30
17:5	71, 72, 91, 171	18:26–27	129, 131
17:6	71	18:28–30	129
17:9–13	52	18:28–34	129
17:10	112, 117	18:31	133
17:11–13	45	18:31–33	129, 206
17:13	121, 147 n.26, 151	18:34–35	129–30
17:22–23	130 n.22	18:35	130–1
17:24	147 n.29, 153	19:1	36
17:24–27	158–9, 192	19:1–6	24
18	121, 124, 127–8, 130, 130 n.23, 130 n.24, 132, 137, 185, 206	19:2	36
		19:3	36
		19:4	33, 35 n.17, 36, 47
		19:5	33, 36, 47
18:1–4	100	19:6	36, 47
18:1–5	105	19:7	33, 35 n.18, 36, 153
18:1–35	17	19:8	36, 75
18:5–14	128, 132	19:9	36
18:6–7	132	19:13–15	105, 105 n.50
18:6–10	132, 136	19:17	38
18:6–14	134	19:18	39–40, 47
18:8–9	58, 132	19:18–19	33
18:10–14	126, 136	19:19	34, 38, 41, 47
18:10–18	133	19:20	38
18:13	135	19:21	81, 121 n.34, 197
18:14	135	19:23–24	202
18:15	134 n.34	19:26	130 n.23
18:15–17	126, 128, 133	19:28	121
18:15–18	105, 133	19:30	100
18:15–20	124, 128, 132, 137, 185	20:17–19	130 n.22
		20:18	111, 117, 152
18:15–22	129	20:19	102
18:16	33, 35 n.18, 110	20:22	89 n.21
18:17	134–135	20:24–28	193
18:17–18	125 n.8	21–22	29
18:18	121, 124–6, 126 n.9, 136	21:5	34, 35 n.18, 46, 48
		21:9	34, 35 n.17, 35 n.18
18:18–20	137	21:12–13	153

21:12–17	29	23	74, 86 n.16, 112, 112 n.7, 117, 121, 150, 200 n.17
21:13	29, 34, 35 n.17, 125, 177		
21:14	29	23:1–3	105
21:15	111, 117, 152	23:1–36	177
21:15–16	29	23:1–25:46	17
21:16	29, 29 n.32, 34, 35 n.17	23:2	74, 150, 152
		23:2–3	112, 117
21:17–18	29	23:3	118
21:18–19	177	23:4	118
21:22	91	23:5	38 n.31
21:23	29, 50, 117, 121 n.33, 153	23:5–7	118
		23:8	1, 122, 147, 147 n.29
21:23–27	52, 56	23:8–10	49
21:24–27	30	23:10	1, 79 n.47
21:25	56	23:13	112, 118, 152
21:28–43	30	23:13–39	58
21:31–32	58	23:14	112, 118
21:32	57, 60, 102, 169 n.8	23:15	112, 118, 152
21:33–41	30	23:16	153
21:37	177	23:17	199 n.13
21:38	177	23:17–22	118
21:41	177	23:19	199 n.13
21:40–41	30	23:23	112, 153
21:42	29 n.32, 30, 34, 35 n.18, 35 n.19, 177, 179	23:23–24	200
		23:24	118
		23:25	112, 153
21:43	59, 192	23:25–26	118
21:43–44	58	23:26	197, 200
22:15–22	142 n.4	23:27	112, 153
22:16	153	23:27–28	118
22:23	44	23:29	112, 153
22:23–33	153	23:32	169 n.8
22:24	34, 43	23:34	109, 112, 149, 153–4
22:24–28	44	23:38	177
22:24–30	48	23:39	29 n.32, 34, 35 n.18
22:29–31	18 n.2	24	2
22:30–32	44	24–25	99–100, 121
22:32	34	24:2	177
22:34–36	41, 47	24:14	47
22:34–39	43	24:29–30	25 n.23, 27
22:37	18 n.2, 34, 41–3	24:30	34
22:39	18 n.2, 34, 41	24:33	80
22:40	41, 107 n.54	24:36–41	18 n.2
22:41–42	30	24:43	163, 180
22:41–46	112 n.7	25	130, 130 n.23, 195, 206
22:44	30, 34, 35 n.17		
22:44–45	29 n.32, 30–1	25:1–13	181
22:46	50	25:31	100

25:31–46	173, 175, 176 n.44, 193 n.32	27:45	93
25:32	175	27:46	17, 34, 35 n.17, 35 n.19, 93
25:34–40	175	27:48	89 n.21
25:40	130 n.23	27:51–53	93, 192
25:41	58	27:54	93
25:41–46	175	27:55–56	102
25:45	130 n.23	27:57	111, 111 n.6, 120
26	88, 91	27:57–60	102
26:2	130 n.22	28:16–20	111, 121, 127, 160, 180, 186
26:3	117		
26:6–13	102	28:18	137
26:9–11	18 n.2	28:18–20	159–60, 163, 166
26:15–16	130 n.22	28:19	59, 61, 111, 120–1, 163
26:17	183 n.6		
26:17–18	147 n.29	28:19–20	49, 54, 59, 137, 154, 161–2
26:27–28	89 n.21		
26:28	18 n.2, 73, 130 n.22	28:20	101, 103 n.43, 104, 122, 122 n.35, 137, 192 n.31
26:31	34, 46, 48		
26:36	88–9, 91–2		
26:36–46	88, 91–2, 105–6		
26:37	88	**Mark**	
26:37–38	90	1:2–3	40
26:38	35 n.18, 91	1:15	188
26:39	62, 88–9, 89 n.21, 91–2	1:30	7
		1:35	93
26:41	90, 90 n.23	2:7	124
26:42	88–9, 91–2	2:13	4, 123
26:44	88–9, 92	2:14	12
26:45	90	2:14–17	142
26:47	102 n.42, 117	3:9	4
26:54	169 n.8	3:14	4
26:55	121 n.33	3:14–16	4
26:56	169 n.8	3:18	142
26:57	111, 117	4:1	4
26:57–68	83, 102	4:10	4
26:64	34, 35 n.17, 47	6:31	92
26:67	83	6:34	4, 173
27:1	117	6:46	92
27:1–26	102	6:52	151
27:2	130 n.22	7	187 n.17, 193
27:3	117	7:3	5 n.20, 10 n.73
27:9	169 n.8	7:3–4	187
27:9–10	34, 35 n.17	7:5	5 n.20
27:12	117	7:8–9	10 n.73
27:19	102	7:13–14	9
27:20	117	7:19	187, 194 n.35
27:35	35 n.17	8:16	5
27:41	111, 117	8:21	151

8:29	171, 184	6:20–49	188
8:34	4	6:27	190
9:1	163 n.39	6:27–36	190
9:2–10	71	6:29–31	81
9:4	171	6:36	197
9:7	72, 171	7:30	118 n.26
9:10	5, 151	7:31–35	50
9:32	151	9:20	171, 184
9:42	163 n.39	9:28–36	71
10:3	12	9:30	171
11:10	179	9:32	164 n.42
11:18	4	9:35	72, 171
12:10–11	177	9	184 n.9
12:35	112 n.7	10	184, 184 n.9
13:29	80	10:7	184, 186
14:21	163 n.39	10:25	118 n.26
14:32	88–9	10:25–37	190 n.26
14:32–42	88	11:1	88
14:33	88	11:1–11	95
14:34	88	11:26	163
14:35	89 n.21	11:45	118 n.26
14:35–38	89	11:46	118 n.26
14:36	89, 183	11:52	118 n.26
14:38	90 n.23, 90 n.28	11:53	118 n.26
14:39	88–9	12:39	163
14:41	88	13:24	9
14:51–52	145 n.13	13:29	9
		14:13	118 n.26
Luke		16:17	188
1:1–2	143	17:4	128, 132
1:1–4	143	17:24	180
1:2	6 n.21	18:1	83 n.1
1:10	83 n.1, 88	19:1–10	135
1:13	83 n.1, 88	19:2	12
1:46–55	83 n.1	19:7–9	135
1:68–79	83 n.1	22:20	73
2:9	164 n.42	22:39–46	88
2:21	182 n.4	22:43	91
2:23	110	23:24	190 n.26
2:29–32	83 n.1	24:44	169 n.10, 188
2:37	83 n.1, 88		
4:16–21	135	**John**	
4:21	169 n.10, 188	1:9	172
5:17	118 n.26	1:14	169, 172
5:21	124	1:17	172–3
5:27	12	1:18	173
5:27–32	142	1:19–20	56 n.17
5:32	123	1:21	50
6:15	142	1:45	172

2:13–22	178	15:25	169 n.10,
2:17	178–9		188
2:18	179	16:6	169 n.10
2:19	178–9	16:24	169 n.10
2:21	179	17:12	169 n.10
2:22	178	17:13	169 n.10
3:14	169, 172	17:23	179 n.57
3:29	169 n.10	18:9	169 n.10
4:25	69–70	18:13–14	178
5:38	172	18:32	169 n.10
5:45	172	19:18	172
5:46	172	19:24	169 n.10
6:1–65	172	19:30	169
6:14	67, 172, 172 n.32	19:35	143
6:32	172	19:36	169 n.10
6:55	172	20:23	126
7:8	169 n.10	20:30–31	179
7:19	172	20:31	176
7:22	172	21:18	163
7:23	172	21:24	143
7:38	172	29:23	126
7:40	67		
9:1–41	176	**Acts**	
9:13–41	175	1:5	50
9:28	172	1:16	169 n.8
9:29	172	1:21–22	4, 143
9:40	175	2:38	162
10	175, 176 n.44	3:11–26	67
10:1–4	176	3:18	169 n.8
10:8	175	4:13	145 n.14
10:10	175	4:36–37	12 n.95
10:11	175	6:6	4 n.7
10:12–13	175	6:7	12 n.95
10:14	175	6:9–10	12 n.95
10:16	176, 176 n.44	7:37	67
10:22–42	176	10	181 n.3
11:48–50	178	10:39–41	143
11:51–52	176	11	181
12	173 n.33	13	181
12:3	169 n.10	13:27	169 n.8
12:20	176	14:21	111
12:32	176	14:23	4 n.7
12:38	169 n.10	15	182
13–16	172	15:5	193 n.34
13:18	169 n.10	15:22–29	12 n.95
13:34–35	193	16:4	6 n.21
14:17	179 n.57	16:37	12 n.95
15:1	172	18:24	12 n.95
15:11	169 n.10	18:25	50

Romans
1:1	159–60
1:16	186
3:29	186
7:12	193 n.33
8:15	183 n.5
12:14	190
12:17	190
13:8–10	189
13:14	80
14:14	187
14:17	189
15:8	186
15:9	186
16:7	12 n.95
16:22–23	12 n.95

1 Corinthians
1:12	5
1:20	148
3:22	5
5:1–5	185
6	188 n.17, 191
6:9	189
6:9–10	189 n.21
6:18	188 n.17
7:10	180
7:10–11	190
7:11	180
7:19	193 n.33
9:1	143, 184
9:5	5
9:14	184
11:17–34	124 n.4
11:23	5 n.18, 6 n.21, 180
11:33	124 n.4
15	184
15:3	6 n.21, 180
15:3–8	161
15:3–11	160
15:5	4
15:5–7	5
15:5–8	143
15:6	12
15:8	12
16:21	183 n.5

2 Corinthians
1:17–20	190
1:19	12 n.95
10:1	80
11:7	187 n.15
13:13	161

Galatians
1:1	160–1, 183
1:14	5 n.20
1:15	185
1:16	143, 185
1:17–19	5
1:18	184
2:1–2	5
2:7–8	185 n.12, 186
2:7–10	5
2:8	183 n.8
2:10	193 n.32
2:11–14	182
2:18	183 n.6
3:1	183
4:4	182 n.4
4:6	182
5:6	80
5:13–14	193
5:13–15	190 n.22
5:14	80, 189
5:16	190 n.23
5:18	80
5:19–21	189 n.21
5:21	189
5:22	80
5:24	190 n.23
6:1	186 n.13
6:2	65, 80, 80 n.56, 193
6:6	4 n.7, 184 n.9, 187 n.15
6:15	193 n.33
6:16	187 n.16

Ephesians
4:4–6	162

Colossians
2:3	150

1 Thessalonians
1:1	12 n.95
4–5	191

4:1–8	190	2:24	204
4:13–18	181	3:1	200, 204
5:2	180	3:2	200
5:12–13	4 n.7	3:6–12	201
5:15	190	3:7–8	201 n.19
		3:9–12	201 n.19
2 Thessalonians		3:17	79
2:13	162	3:17–18	206
2:15	6 n.21	4:4	79, 203
		4:9–10	79
2 Timothy		4:11	79
2:2	4 n.7	4:11–12	199
		4:12	78, 80 n.48
Titus		4:13–17	203
1:5	4 n.7	4:17	202, 202 n.24
3:13	12 n.95	5:1–6	203
4:13	144	5:2	79, 202
		5:3	79, 202
Hebrews		5:7–11	205
9:19	162 n.33	5:8	79, 80 n.48
10:22	162 n.33	5:9	199
		5:12	77–8, 198, 207
James		5:14	4 n.7
1:2–3	205		
1:4	79, 196–7, 201	**1 Peter**	
1:5	202	1:1	160
1:6	202	1:1–2	155–6, 159,
1:10	79		162–3, 166
1:16–17	202, 202 n.23	1:2	161–2, 162 n.33
1:18	206	1:3	161
1:19–20	79, 199	1:5	164
1:21	205–6	1:8	144
1:22	79	1:15	158 n.17, 159
1:22–25	205–6	1:16	156
1:25	65, 205	2:4–8	160 n.22
1:26	197	2:9	156
1:26–27	197	2:12	158, 158 n.17,
1:27	197–8, 202		159, 163
2:5	79	2:13–15	158–9
2:8	65	2:21	156 n.6
2:10	78	3:9	158 n.17,
2:12	65, 78		159
2:12–13	206–7	3:14	158 n.17, 159
2:13	79	3:15	160
2:14	79	3:18	156 n.6
2:14–16	202	3:21	162
2:14–17	201	4:13	158 n.17
2:15–16	201	4:13–14	159
2:18–26	204	5:1	160

5:5	4 n.7	**2 Esdras**	
5:6–9	158 n.17	12:37	149
5:12	12 n.95		
		Tobit	
2 Peter		4:3	39
1:1	155	8:4–7	36, 47
1:14	163	14:7	43
1:16	111 n.5, 163 n.39, 164	14:9	43
1:16–18	155–6, 164, 164 n.40, 164 n.41, 165–6	**Judith**	
		11:13	42
		11:19	42
1:16–19	163		
1:16–21	144, 165, 165 n.44	**Sirach/Ecclesiasticus (Sir)**	
		0:1	151 n.42
1:17	164	0:5	151 n.42
1:18	164	0:10	151 n.42
1:19	165	1:25	150
1:20	165	3	47
1:20–21	164	3:3–4	39
2:1	155, 165	3:5–16	39
2:1–22	164	4:10	34
2:9	163 n.39	6:23–30	34
2:9–11	164	6:34–38	10 n.77
2:11	155	7:27	39
2:16–18	156	7:30	43
2:17	164	8:8–9	10 n.77
2:20	163	13:15	41, 47
2:21	163 n.39	15:14	36
3:1	163	17:3	36
3:3–4	165	18:18–29	147 n.27
3:4	163 n.39	20:30	150
3:8	163	24:8–12	34
3:10	163	28:1–4	127
3:15–16	163	38:34	8 n.53
3:17–18	164	39:2–3	8 n.53
		39:4	150
1 John		39:9	8 n.53
1:1–4	144	41:14	20:30
		48:10	45
3 John		51:23	10 n.77, 152 n.49
9	4 n.7	51:23–27	34
Jude			
20–21	162	**1 Maccabees**	
		4:43	47
<u>Deuterocanonical Books</u>		7:12–13	114
Baruch		**2 Maccabees**	
3:37	34	2:8	71

2:23	34
2:25	10 n.76
6:5	47

Wisdom of Solomon

2:10–20	34
2:23	36
5:5	34
6:12–11:1	34
9:2	36
7:22–8:21	56
16:26	44

Dead Sea Scrolls

1QS

1.10	41
8.1	45, 48
8.1–9.11	44–5
8.1–16	45 n.70
8.13–14	45
8.15–16	45
8.16–19	45
9.12	45
9.12–25	45
9.18–19	45
9.19–20	45
19.5–8	48

1Q28a

2.11–12	35

1Q33 (1QM)

19.1	46
19.2–4	46
19.4	46
19.5	46
19.5–8	46, 48

1QH

12.25	47

4Q158

Frags. 7–8 1.1	39
Frags. 7–8 1.2	40

4Q176

1–2 i.6–7	44 n.66

4Q258

6.6	45 n.69
13.4	45

4Q259

3.4–5	45 n.69

4Q415

9.8–9	37 n.25

4Q416

Frag 2.3.21-iv 1	36
1.15	37
2.ii.21	37
2.iii.15–19	39
2.iii.20–21	37
2.iv.1	37
2.iv.1–7	37
2.iv.4	37

4Q417

1 i 25	37
2 i 1–7	37
2 i 8	37

4Q418

2.7	37
9–10	39
10.4–5	37
81.17	37

4Q494

1.5	46

4Q504

Frag 8 (recto).4	36
1–2 iv 17.6–7	42

4Q558

Frag. 1 ii.3–4	40

6Q15

1.3	36, 47

Damascus Document

CD 1.6	41
CD 6.20–21	42
CD 12.23–13.1	46 n.75

CD 14.19	46 n.75	**Liber antiquitatum biblicarum**	
CD 15.8–9	41	4	39
		4:5	39
CD-A 4.21	47	11:9	39
CD-A 15.3	41, 47	11:10	40
CD-A 8.5–6	42	11:11	39, 47
		12	71 n.28
CD-B col.19 1.10	46	13:7	39
CD-B col.19 2.10–11	46	21:2	39
		44:6	39, 47
7:18	68	44:7	39
		60:3	39

Pseudepigrapha

Pseudo-Phocylides
3 — 40
8 — 39, 47
16–17 — 41, 47
179–180 — 39

Ahiqar
138 — 38

Aristeas the Exegete
159 — 38 n.31
228 — 39, 47

Psalms of Solomon
13:9 — 34
17:21 — 47
17:40 — 42

2 Baruch (Syriac Apocalypse)
44:14 — 150 n.39
54:13 — 150 n.39

Sibylline Oracles
3.594 — 39

1 Enoch
42 — 34
49:1–4 — 47
37–71 — 35

Testament of Naphtali
8:6 — 36

Testament of Solomon
6:8 — 35 n.19
11:6 — 35 n.19
15:12 — 35 n.19
22:7 — 35 n.19
23:4 — 35 n.19

4 Maccabees
2:21 — 36
16:9 — 111 n.5

Prayer of Manasseh
10 — 47

Apostolic Fathers

Letter of Aristeas
154 — 10 n.76
§228 — 41

1 Clement
7.2 — 6 n.21

Jubilees
4:16–18 — 149
4:31 — 40, 47
7:20 — 39, 41, 47
35:12–13 — 39, 47

Didache
8 — 87 n.18, 95
8:1–3 — 87
14:2 — 124 n.4

Ancient Jewish Writers

Josephus
Against Apion
1.8 §39	69 n.20	4.254	44, 48
1.60	10 n.74, 14 n.110	6.5.6 §93	69
2.15 §145	68–9	6.7.3 §133	69
2.171–73	10 n.74	7.13.1 § 318	69
2.173	10 n.75	7.14.2 §338	69
2.174	10 n.75	7.15.1 §384	69
2.178	14 n.110	8.3.7 §90	69
2.204	10 n.74, 14 n.110	8.3.8 §94	69
		8.4.1 §104	69
		8.4.4 §120	69
		8.7.5 §191	69 n.20

Bellum Judaicum
1.111	125 n.7	8.13.7 §349	69
2.8.1 §139–42	77 n.43	8.15.2 §395	69 n.20
2.8.9 §145	69	8.45–9	34
6.300–9	34	9.1.1 §2	69
6.353–5	34	9.7.4 §153	69 n.20
6.363–4	34	9.9.1 §187	69 n.20
6.406–8	34	10.4.2 §59	69 n.20
7.218	34	10.4.3 §63	69 n.20
		10.4.5 §72	69 n.20
		11.1.3 §17	69 n.20

Jewish Antiquities
1.3.6 §95	68–9	11.4.1 §76	69 n.20
1.13.4 §240	68–9	11.4.7 §108	69 n.20
2.205ff	34	11.5.1 §121	69 n.20
2.9.3 §210–16	70 n.25	11.5.5 §154	69 n.20
3.5.4 §90	69	12.5.4 §253	47
3.8.10 §222	69	13.3.4 §79	69 n.20
3.11.4 §266	69	13.10.6 § 297	69 n.20
3.11.5 §269	69	13.297	5 n.20, 10 n.73
3.12.1 §274	69	13.408	5 n.20, 10 n.73
3.12.3 §280	69	17.6.3 §159	69 n.20
3.15.3 §317	69	18.3.5 §81	69 n.20
3.15.3 §319	69 n.20	18.118–19	54
4.6.10 §141	69 n.20	20.2.4 §44	69 n.20
4.8.22 §242	69 n.20	20.5.4 §44	69 n.20
4.8.44 §302	69	20.264–65	10 n.75
4.8.44 §308	69		
4.211	10 n.74, 14 n.110	*Vita*	
4.213	38 n.31	8	10 n.74
4.253	36	9–12	10 n.74
		10	6 n.30

Philo

De Abrahamo
5	68 n.19
28	68 n.19
31	68 n.19

De agricultura
1.51	40
22	68 n.19
27	68 n.19
84	68 n.19
86	68 n.19
144	68 n.19

De cherubim
53	68 n.19

De confusion linguarum
5	68 n.19
23	68 n.19
107	68 n.19
135	68 n.19
142	68 n.19
191	68 n.19

On the Decalogue
1.36	39–40, 47
84	77

Quod deterius potiori insidari soleat
62	68 n.19
115	68 n.19
135	68 n.19
171	68 n.19

Quod Deus sit immutabilis
21	68 n.19
23	68 n.19
52	68 n.19
67	68 n.19
125	68 n.19

De ebrietate
1	68 n.19
2	68 n.19
13	68 n.19
47	68 n.19
109	68 n.19

De fuga et invention
120	68 n.19
173	68 n.19
175	68 n.19
188	68 n.19
194	68 n.19

De gigantibus
32	68 n.19
58	68 n.19
65	68 n.19
66	68 n.19

Quis rerum divinarum heres sit?
48 §231	36
163	68 n.19
292	68 n.19

Hypothetica
7.12–13	10 n.75

Allegorical Interpretation
2.14	68 n.19
3.145	68 n.19
3.174–5	44

On the Embassy to Gaius
210	9 n.70

De migratione Abrahami
1.1	68 n.19
1.128	68 n.19
1.162	68 n.19
1.174	40
1.334	68 n.19
2:3	68 n.19
2:5	68 n.19
2:6	68 n.19
2:8	68 n.19
2:9	68 n.19
2:14	68 n.19
2:45	68 n.19
2:66	68 n.19
2:187	68 n.19
2:188	68 n.19
2:190	68 n.19
2:292	68 n.19
23	68 n.19
113	68 n.19

De vita Moses
2:70	71 n.27

De mutatione nominum
126	68 n.19

De plantation
66	68 n.19
141	68 n.19

De posteritate Caini
47	68 n.19
57	68 n.19
78	68 n.19
128	68 n.19
133	68 n.19
166	68 n.19

De sacrificiis Abelis et Caini
1.45	42
136	68 n.19
138	68 n.19

De sobrietate
1	68 n.19
46	68 n.19

De somniis
1:39	68 n.19
1:93	68 n.19
1:112	68 n.19
1:121	68 n.19
2:4	68 n.19
2:71	68 n.19
2:192	68 n.19

De specialibus legibus
2.235	39
2.248	39
2.261	39
3.30	36
4.1	39–40
4.107	10 n.76
26.137–139	38 n.31

RABBINIC WORKS

Abot
1:1	5 n.18

Abot de Rabbi Nathan
1A	6 n.29
25A	6 n.29

m. Abot
1:1	69
2:8	10 n.79
5:21	6 n.30, 10 n.74, 10 n.75
6:6	10 n.74

Baba Batra
10:3 C	115
10:3 G	115
10:3 J	115
10:4 B	115
10:4 D	115
10:4 F	115

b. Baba Batra
1:6 IV.2.B	115 n.18
2:3e, I.13	115 n.17
75a	71 n.28

y. Baba Batra
9:3, I.4.C	115 n.19

Baba Mesia
5:11 C	115

b. Baba Mesia
10:6, II.3	115 n.16

Berakhot
1:3	115 n.15
1:3 D	115 n.15

t. Bikkurim
15B	115 n.18

Eduyyot
1:3	10 n.79

m. Eduyyot
8:7	5 n.18, 69

Gittim
3:1C	115
3:1N	115

7:2B	115	m. Peah	
8:8D	115	2:6	69
9:8D	115		
		y. Peah	
b. Gittim		8:6	115 n.17
2:3, II.17.b	115 n.18	III.8.G	115 n.17
90a-b	36		
		Pesahim	
m. Gittim		1:3 C	115
9:10	36		
		Pesiqta Rabbati	
Kelim		15:10	68 n.16
13:7 C	115		
		Pesiqta de Rab Kahana	
Ketubbot		24:18	4 n.12
7:6	69		
		Qiddushin	
y. Ketubbot		4:13 A	115
10:2	115 n.15	4:13 B	115
I.1.C	115 n.15	4:13 C	115
		y. Qiddushin	
b. Megillah		4:5 I.1	116 n.20
2:1 VI.3.A	115 n.18		
		Rabbah Genesis	
Mekilta Pisha		88:5	89 n.21
1.135–36	9 n.71	98:9	70
1.150–53	9 n.71		
		Rabbah Leviticus	
Midrash Ecclesiastes		13:3	70 n.23
2:1	70 n.23		
11:8	70, 80	**Rabbah Deuteronomy**	
		11 (207c)	71 n.28
Nedarim			
9:2 D	115	**Rabbah Ruth**	
9:2 F	115	2:14	68 n.16
Nega'im		**Rabbah Ecclesiastes**	
9:3	10 n.79	1:9	68 n.16, 169
Orlah		**Sanhedrin**	
3:9 M	114	11:3 A	114–115
		11:3 C	115
Parah			
11:5 A	115	**y. Sanhedrin**	
11:6 A	115	1:4 III.1.B	116 n.20
		5:4 I.1.I	116 n.20
Peah			
2:6 C	115		

Shabbat
3:1 C	115

Sebiit
6:1 III.15.A	116 n.21

Sipra Behuq
2.264.1.1	12 n.99
8.269.2.14	12 n.99

Sipra Shemini Mekhilta deMiluim
99.5.6	6 n.29

Sipre Numbers
140	71 n.28

Sipre Deuteronomy
24.1	36
48.1.1–4	10 n.79
48.2.6	9 n.71, 10 n.79
115.1.1–2	12 n.99
161.1.3	12 n.99
306.25.1	12 n.99
351.1.2–3	12 n.99

Sotah
9:15 S	116
9:15 EE	116

t. Sotah
8:6M	115 n.18

y. Sotah
7:5 I.1.C	115 n.18

Tg Onqelos Gen
49:11	70

Tg Onqelos Deut
24:1	36

Tg of the Writings
On Songs
5:10	70 n.23

Tg Isaiah
12:3	70 n.23
53:5	70

Palestinian Tg Deut
24:1	36

y. Ta'anit
3.8, §2	4 n.12

Tebul-Yom
1:10	115 n.14
4:6 C	115

Tohorot
4:7 L	115
4:11 C	115
4:11 I	115

Yadayim
3:2 E	115
4:3	10 n.79

m. Yadayim
4:3	69

Yalqut on Isaiah
26:2	70 n.23

Yebamot
2:4 A	114

t. Yebamot
3:1	9 n.71
3:4	10 n.79

b. Yoma
86b–87a	128 n.16

m. Yoma
3:8	69
4:2	69
6:2	69
8:9	128 n.16

EARLY CHRISTIAN WRITINGS and GRECO-ROMAN LITERATURE

Alciphron
Letters of Farmers
11.3.14	12 n.96
38.3.40	12 n.96

Aphthonius
Progymnasmata
3   9 n.59

Arius Didymus
2.7.11k, pg 80.36–82.1   12 n.89

Aulus Gellius
Noctes atticae
7.10.1   6 n.24
8.3   8 n.47

Cicero
Epistulae ad Atticum
14.21   6 n.27, 13 n.101

De oratore
2.351–54   7 n.37

Dio Chrysostom
De dicendi exercitatione (Or. 18)
18   6 n.27
19   8 n.46
36.9   14 n.107

Diodorus Siculus
10.5.1   10 n.78

Diogenes Laertius
Vitae Philosophorum
2.72   8 n.58
6.2.31   8 n.43
6.2.51   8 n.58
10.1.12   6 n.25

Epictetus
Diatribai
Pref. 2   12 n.89
1.pref   12 n.91

Epistle to Diognetus
11.1   6 n.21
11.6   6 n.21

Eunapius
481   8 n.43
493   6 n.31

Eusebius
Historia ecclesiastica
3.24.6   143 n.7
5.8.2   143 n.5
5.10.3   143 n.7
6.25.3–6   143 n.6

Fragments of Papias
3.7   6 n.21
3.8   6 n.21
3.11   6 n.21
3.14   6 n.21
20.1   6 n.21
21.1   6 n.21

Fronto
Ad Verum Imp
2.3   6 n.29

Galen
De indolentia
83   6 n.27

Hermogenes
Inv.
2.7.120–21   8 n.48

Progymnasmata
3   8 n.48, 9 n.59
4   8 n.49

Hesiod
Opera et dies
342–3   41 n.47

Iamblichus
De vita pythagorica
20.94   10 n.78
28.148   5 n.18
28.148–49   5 n.17
28.149   5 n.19
29.164–65   10 n.78
31.188   10 n.78
32.226   5 n.17
35.356   10 n.78

Irenaeus
Against Heresies
3.1   143 n.5

4.9.1	151 n.41	*Somnium (Vita Luciani)*	
4.12.3	81	1	5 n.31
4.13.1	81		
4.34.4	81	**Musonius Rufus**	
		1, 36.6–7	6 n.29
Jerome		51, pg 144.3–7	8 n.43, 8 n.49

Commentariorum in Matthaeum libri IV

2 (FC)	143 n.8	

Nicolaus Sophista
Progymnasmata

4	9 n.59

Commentariorum in Osee libri III

11.1	143 n.8

On Chreia

5	9 n.59

De viris illustribus

3	143 n.8	

6–7	9 n.59
7	8 n.48
23S	9 n.59

John Chrysostom
Homiliae Matthaeum

16.2	81	
16.4	82	
16.8	82	
17.2	82	

4R	9 n.59
19–20	9 n.59

Origen
Contra Celsum

1.63, 65	5 n.15

Justin
Dialogus cum Tryphone

11	65
12	81
12.2	81
14.3	81
18	81
18.3	81
24.1	81
113.6	81
114	81

Commentarium in evangelium Matthaei

1	143 n.6
10:15	145 n.14

Quintilian
Institutio Oratoria

1.pref. 7–8	12 n.91
1.1.35–36	8 n.51
1.1.36	8 n.45
1.3.1	8 n.45
2.2.3	6 n.31
2.4.15	8 n.43
11.2.1–51	8 n.46
11.2.2	12 n.89
11.2.25	12 n.89
11.2.27	6 n.37, 10 n.78
11.2.33–35	6 n.37

Longinus
De sublimitate

11.1	8 n.48

Lucian
Alexander (Pseudomantis)

61	5 n.18

Fugitivi

12	12 n.97
14	12 n.97

Pausonius
Graeciae description

1.23.2	14 n.108

Philostratus
Vita Apollonii

Hermotimus (De sectis)

1	10 n.78
2	12 n.89

1.7	6 n.31
1.14	10 n.78

2.30	10 n.78	**Seneca the Elder**	
3.16	10 n.78	*Controversiae*	
7.22	6 n.29	1.pref.2, 19	7 n.36

Vita sophistarum
Seneca the Younger
Ad Lucilium

1.11.495	7 n.36	94.27–28	8 n.57
1.22.524	5 n.13	108.6	12 n.89
2.8.578	8 n.47	108.17	6 n.29
2.9.621	5 n.17	108.20	6 n.29
2.29.621	6 n.29	108.22	6 n.29
		110.14	6 n.29
Plato		110.20	6 n.29

Meno

71e	41 n.47	**Socratics**	
		Epistle 20	5 n.17, 6 n.24

Republic
Suetonius
De Poetis (Vergil)

375c	41 n.47	22	6 n.27

Timaeus
De Grammaticis

17d–18a	41 n.47	23	7 n.36

Pliny the Younger
Tacitus
Epistulae
Historiae

2.3.5–6	4 n.12	5.5–6	41 n.47

Polybius
Aelius Theon
The Histories
Progymnasmata

18.37.7	41 n.47	1.93–171	3, 13 n.103
		2.115–23	8 n.48
Plutarch		3.224–40	8 n.48
Agesilaus		4.37–42	8 n.48
21.4–5	8 n.58	4.73–79	8 n.56
		4.80–82	8 n.48
De Liberis Educandis		5.388–441	8 n.56
13	8 n.43		

Valerius Maximus

Moralia

9E	8 n.43	8.15.ext.1	6 n.29

Xenophon
Themistocles
Symposium

11.2	9 n.60	3.5–6	7 n.41
		3.6	13 n.106

Rhetorica ad Herennium

3.16.28–40	7 n.37
3.22.35	7 n.37

Name Index

Achtemeier, Paul J. 156, 160–2
Adeyemi, Femi 80–1
Adinolfi, Frederico 51
Adna, J. 177
Albright, W. F. 206
Alexander, Loveday C. A. 5–6, 9–10
Allison, Dale C. 3, 10, 28, 35–6, 41, 44–5, 49, 57, 65, 70–2, 78–80, 86, 101, 125–6, 170–1, 174
Aquinas, Thomas 81
Arendt, Hannah 131
Arnal, William E. 109
Assmann, Jan 10
Averbeck, Richard E. 23

Baasland, Ernst 85
Bacon, Benjamin W. 65, 80, 82
Bagnall, Roger S. 12
Bakker, Arjen 45
Barber, Michael P. 178
Barclay, John M. G. 135
Barker, James 167
Barker, Margaret 178
Barth, Gerhard 146–7
Barth, Karl 86, 126
Barton, Stephen C. 151
Bates, Matthew 173
Bauckham, Richard J. 3–4, 7, 10, 99–100, 143–4, 163–4, 195, 201
Bauer, David R. 200
Baxter, Wayne 42, 173
Beale, G. K. 178
Beare, Francis Wright 195, 206–7
Beasley-Murray, George R. 173
Becker, Jürgen 50
Bennett, Kelsey L. 96–7
Bernier, Jonathan 4, 12
Best, Ernest 156–7
Betz, Hans Dieter 77, 84–5, 87
Beyschlag, Willibald 78, 80
Bird, Michael F. 144

Black, Clifton 94
Black, Matthew 9
Bledsoe, Seth A. 38
Block, Daniel I. 174
Blomberg, Craig L. 19–20, 26–8, 30, 78, 151, 199, 201, 203, 205
Blum, Herwig 7
Boismard, Marie-Emile 171
Bornkamm, Günther 146
Boxall, Ian 49
Boyd, Gregory A. 13–14
Boyles, C. G. 68
Brooke, George J. 177
Brown, Jeannine K. 19–20, 22, 25, 102, 127–30, 132, 134–5, 146
Brown, Raymond 172
Bruce, F. F. 80
Brunson, Andrew C. 177
Bryan, Steven M. 178–9
Burchard, C. 80
Burney, C. F. 9
Burridge, Richard A. 55, 100–1
Byrskog, Samuel 1, 5–6, 10–13, 49, 137, 147

Callan, Terrance 163
Calvin, John 131
Carson, D. A. 20, 25, 28, 66, 73, 146, 169, 173, 175–6
Carter, Warren 86, 102, 175, 177
Chae, Young 173–4
Chester, Andrew J. 177
Chilton, Bruce 58
Christiansen, Duane L. 42–3
Christianson, Sven-Åke 7
Clark, David 95
Claussen, Carsten 171
Collins, J. J. 68
Collins, Raymond F. 125
Coloe, Mary L. 178
Conzelmann, Hans 147 n.26

Coutts, Jon 2, chap. 9, 126
Craigie, Peter C. 44
Cribiore, Raffaella 7–8, 11, 148
Cross, F. M. 44
Crossan, John 56
Crossley, James 58
Cullman, Oscar 83, 87, 91
Culpepper, R. Alan 6, 9, 12
Cuvigny, Hélène 12

Dapaah, Daniel 57
Davids, Peter H. 78, 80, 197
Davies, Philip R. 46
Davies, W. D. 28, 36, 41, 44–5, 53, 65, 72, 80, 86, 98, 125–6, 171
Davis, Katy 2, chap. 2
Deeley, M. 175
Deines, Roland 107
Deppe, Dean B. 78, 196
Derrenbacker Jr., R. A. 13
Derrett, M. 126
Deutsch, Celia M. 49, 119
Dilthey, Wilhelm 97
Dodd, C. H. 80
Douglas, Mary 21
Doyle, B. Rod 119
Duncan, J. 126
Dunn, James D. G. 4, 8–9, 13
Durham, John I. 37

Eddy, Paul Rhodes 13–14
Edwards, Dennis R. chap. 11, 156, 161
Edwards, Richard A. 119, 146
Elliott, John H. 158, 160–2
Enns, Elaine 127, 129–30, 133, 137
Enns, Peter 125
Ernst, Josef 50
Eubank, Nathan 84
Evans, Craig 66
Eve, Eric 5, 10–11

Fiedler, Peter 86
Firth, David G. 20
Fitzgerald, Joseph M. 7
Fitzmyer, Joseph A. 68, 177
Fortna, Robert T. 125–6
Foster, Paul 50

France, R. T. 1, 29, 32–5, 49, 72–3, 98–9, 104–7, 110, 148, 167, 169, 196, 199, 202–7
Frankemölle, H. 78
Frey, Jörg 163–5
Frickenschmidt, Dirk 55
Frye, Roland Mushat 8

Gajsar, Hannah 10
Gardner-Smith, Percival 167–8
Gentry, Peter 69, 73
Gercke, Chris 135
Gibson, Jeffrey B. 90, 94
Gibson, Richard Hughes 131
Gillihan, Yonder Moynihan 41
Glasson, Thomas Francis 171, 172
Gnilka, Joachim 72
Godecharle, David R. M. 167
Goff, Matthew J. 37
Golban, Petru 97, 103
Goldingay, John 44
González, Justo L. 96
Goodspeed, E. J. 144
Goppelt, Leonhard 162, 172
Gorman, Michael J. 155
Goulder, M. D. 146
Grant, Jamie A. 30
Green, Gene L. 165
Grottenberg, Samuel P. 196
Gundry, Robert H. 32, 43, 65, 99, 119, 144, 153, 156–8, 160, 171
Güntürkün, Onur 10
Gurtner, Daniel M. 2, chap. 3, 35, 39–40, 98

Hagner, Donald A. 19–20, 22, 30, 83, 98, 128, 131, 151, 174
Hare, D. R. A. 98
Harrington, Daniel J. 37, 146
Harstine, Stan 171, 173
Hartin, Patrick J. 78, 119, 196, 200
Hartley, John E. 40
Häusser, Detlev 180
Hays, Richard B. 17, 21, 23–4, 26–7, 72
Heil, J. P. 173
Held, Heinz Joachim 146
Hempel, Charlotte 45–6
Hengel, Martin 53, 61
Henning, Bruce chap. 12, 173–4, 177–8
Hirschi, Vincent 202, 204–5

Høgenhaven, Jesper 44
Horrell, David G. 157–8
Horsley, Richard A. 148
Hoskins, Paul M. 178

Jackson-McCabe, M. A. 80
Jeremias, Joachim 9, 69, 95–6, 174, 177
Jones, L. Gregory 126, 132
Joyal, Mark 8
Judge, Edwin A. 10
Juel, Donald 177

Kammel (*See also* Kovalishyn),
    Mariam J. 78
Kaster, Robert A. 6
Keck, Leander 60
Keener, Craig 2, chap. 1, 6, 11–12, 19, 22,
    28, 55, 66, 84, 89–90, 100–1, 126, 160–2
Keith, Chris 50, 144, 152, 168
Kelber, Werner H. 10
Kelly, J. N. D. 162
Kennedy, George A. 6–7, 12
Kerr, Alan R. 178–9
Kingsbury, Jack Dean 146
Kirk, Alan 4, 10, 14
Kirk, J. R. Daniel 169, 171
Kloppenborg, John S. 13
Knibb, M. A. 46
Koester, Craig R. 175
Konradt, Matthias 88–90, 125, 135–6
Köstenberger, Andreas 172, 176
Kottsieper, I. 38
Kovalishyn (*See also* Kammel), Mariam
    chap. 14
Kraus, Hans-Joachim 30
Kruger, Michael J. 95

Lappenga, Benjamin L. 178
Laws, S. 80
Lewis, Naphtalt 12
Lichtenberger, H. 44
Licona, Michael R. 13
Lierman, John 170
Lincoln, Andrew T. 175
Lindenberger, J. M. 38
Lockett, Darian 198–9, 203
Longenecker, Richard 80
Lozano, Ray M. 171
Lundbom, Jack 73

Luther, Martin 81, 96–7, 195, 204
Lütticke, Lena 2, chap. 6, 90
Luz, Ulrich 40, 42, 53–4, 57, 76–7, 85–6,
    104, 107, 146, 158, 207

Macaskil, Grant 177
Maccoby, Hyam 123, 125, 127–8, 136
Maier, Gerhard 157–8, 167
Mann, C. S. 206
Manning Jr., Gary T. 175
Manson, T. W. 9
Marcus, Joel 51
Martens, J.-A. 41
Marty, J. 80
Martyn, J. L. 176
Maynard-Reid, Pedrito U. 201
Mayor, Joseph 78
Mbabazi, Isaac Kahwa 127–8, 131
McDougall, Iain 8
McIver, Robert K. 5, 7–11, 14
McKnight, Scot 66, 80, 200, 202, 204
McManigal, Daniel 73
Meeks, Wayne 170
Meier, John P. 4, 49–51, 54, 57, 174
Melbourne, Bertram L. 119
Merz, Annette 57
Metso, Sarianna 45
Metzger, Bruce M. 195–6
Metzner, Rainer 158
Milton, Helen 72
Moeser, Marion C. 8–9
Moo, Douglas J. 78, 80, 149, 196, 198
Moore, Carey A. 42
Morgan, Christopher W. 207
Morgan, Teresa 8
Morris, Leon 119, 151
Moule, C. F. D. 145
Muddiman, John 167
Murphy, Frederick J. 39
Myers, Ched 127, 129–30, 133, 137

Naselli, Andrew David 149 n. 36
Neusner, Jacob 112, 125
Neyrey, Jerome H. 86, 165
Noll, Mark A. 7
Nolland, John 2, 18–20, 22, 25, 67, 72–3,
    chap. 8, 110, 112, 117, 122, 169, 171, 188
Nygaard, Mathias 106
Nystrom, Carolyn 7

Name Index

O'Donnell, Douglas 174
Orton, David E. 109, 114, 146, 148–9
Osiek, Carolyn 86
Oswalt, John N. 27
Overman, J. Andrew 98, 177

Palachuvattil, Matthew 119
Payne, David 44
Penner, Todd C. 76, 78
Pennington, Jonathan T. 66, 72, 74–5, 99–100
Perkins, Pheme 50
Perrin, Nicholas 177
Phillips, Peter M. 150
Piotrowski, Nicholas 72
Porter, Christopher 176
Porter, Stanley 168
Powell, Mark Allen 125–6, 134, 136–7
Propp, William H. C. 39
Przybylski, Benno 60, 83

Quarles, Charles 1, 2, chap. 5, 66, 68, 70, 74, 75, 170, 204

Reed, Stephen Alan 38
Reim, G. 172
Resseguie, James L. 95
Reumann, John 50
Rey, Jean-Sébastien 37
Richards, E. Randolph 6, 13
Ridlehoover, Charles Nathan 2, chap. 7
Riesner, Rainer 1, 6–7, 9–10, 49, 147
Roberts, Kyle 19–20, 22, 25, 102, 127–30, 132, 134–5
Robinson, J. A. T. 176
Rodriguez, Rafael 178
Roskovec, Jan 171–3
Rubin, David C. 4, 7, 10
Runesson, Anders 98
Ruzer, Serge 172

Safer, Martin A. 7
Safrai, S. 6
Saggs, M. Jack 49
Saldarini, Anthony J. 98
Sanders, E. P. 4
Sarcerius, Erasmus 145
Scaer, David P. 124
Schams, Christine 113

Schapdick, Stefan 171–2
Schmidthals, Walter 90
Schreiner, Patrick 119, 123, 137, chap. 10, 170, 171
Schwartz, Barry 4, 7, 10
Sedley, David 6
Seeley, John Robert 131
Selwyn, Edward Gordon 160, 162
Senior, Donald 98–9, 169
Shäfer, Peter 178
Shakespeare, William 132
Sheridan, Mark 146
Sim, David C. 98, 177
Small, Jocelyn Penny 7, 10, 13
Smedes, Lewis B. 132
Smith, Shively T. J. 161
Sparks, Hedley 167
Spellman, Ched 109
Spicq, Ceslas 162
Stanley, C. D. 44
Stanton, Graham N. 80, 98–9
Stendahl, Krister 145
Stock, Ann-Kathrin 10
Stowers, Stanley K. 10
Strecker, Georg 60
Streeter, B. H. 168
Strugnell, John 37
Syiemlieh, Brightstar Jones 109
Syreeni, Kari 87

Talbert, Charles H. 177
Taylor, Joan 51
Theissen, Gerd 57, 204
Thompson, Michael 180, 190
Tidwell, N. L. 44
Tigay, Jeffrey H. 43
Tigchelaar, E. J. C. 37
Tov, Emanuel 38
Trainor, Michael 119
Trevaskis, Leigh M. 21
Trilling, Wolfgang 51
Tucker, W. Dennis 30
Turner, David 66, 177
Tutu, Desmond 131–2
Twelftree, Graham 54

Urn, Stephen T. 178
Uusimäki, Elisa 37

Van Belle, Gilbert 167
van der Toorn, Karel 148, 150
van Hartingsveld, L. 176
VanderKam, James C. 39–40, 45
Vermes, Geza 8, 59
Verseput, Donald J. 147, 198
Viljoen, F. P. 52
Volf, Miroslav 137

Wagner, J. Ross 177
Webb, Robert 50
Weidemann, H.-U. 90
Welch, John W. 176
Wellum, Stephen 69, 73
Wenham, David 75, 98, chap. 13
Wenham, Gordon J. 21
Westerholm, Stephen 149
Wick, Peter 90

Wilken, Robert 10
Wilkins, Michael J. 5, 67, 83, 119, 146-7
Willitts, Joel 173
Wilson, Alistair I. 206
Wink, Walter 51
Winsbury, Rex 148
Witherington III, Ben 78, 152
Witmer, Stephen E. 70
Wright, Christopher J. H. 155
Wright, N. T. 177

Yardley, J. C. 8
Yieh, John Y. H. 1-2, chap. 4, 49, 55, 67, 153
Yong, Amos 124

Zacharias, H. Daniel 173
Zimmermann, Alfred F. 9
Zumstein, Jean 168

www.ingramcontent.com/pod-product-compliance
Lightning Source LLC
Chambersburg PA
CBHW051519230426
43668CB00012B/1671